Global
Easts

Asia Perspectives
Weatherhead East Asian Institute, Columbia University

Asia Perspectives: History, Society, and Culture

A SERIES OF THE WEATHERHEAD EAST ASIAN INSTITUTE,
COLUMBIA UNIVERSITY

CAROL GLUCK, EDITOR

Comfort Women: Sexual Slavery in the Japanese Military During World War II,
    by Yoshimi Yoshiaki, trans. Suzanne O'Brien

The World Turned Upside Down: Medieval Japanese Society,
    by Pierre François Souyri, trans. Käthe Roth

Yoshimasa and the Silver Pavilion: The Creation of the Soul of Japan,
    by Donald Keene

*Geisha, Harlot, Strangler, Star: A Woman, Sex, and Moral Values in
    Modern Japan*, by William Johnston

Lhasa: Streets with Memories, by Robert Barnett

Frog in the Well: Portraits of Japan by Watanabe Kazan, 1793–1841,
    by Donald Keene

The Modern Murasaki: Writing by Women of Meiji Japan, ed. and trans.
    Rebecca L. Copeland and Melek Ortabasi

So Lovely a Country Will Never Perish: Wartime Diaries of Japanese Writers,
    by Donald Keene

Sayonara Amerika, Sayonara Nippon: A Geopolitical Prehistory of J-Pop,
    by Michael K. Bourdaghs

The Winter Sun Shines In: A Life of Masaoka Shiki, by Donald Keene

*Manchu Princess, Japanese Spy: The Story of Kawashima Yoshiko,
    the Cross-Dressing Spy Who Commanded Her Own Army*,
    by Phyllis Birnbaum

*Imitation and Creativity in Japanese Arts: From Kishida Ryūsei to Miyazaki
    Hayao*, by Michael Lucken, trans. Francesca Simkin

The First Modern Japanese: The Life of Ishikawa Takuboku, by Donald
    Keene

*The Japanese and the War: Expectation, Perception, and the Shaping of
    Memory*, by Michael Lucken, trans. Karen Grimwade

The Merchant's Tale: Yokohama and the Transformation of Japan,
    by Simon Partner

Sōseki: Modern Japan's Greatest Novelist, by John Nathan

Uneven Moments: Reflections on Japan's Modern History,
    by Harry Harootunian

Global Easts

Remembering,
Imagining,
Mobilizing

JIE-HYUN LIM

Columbia

University

Press

New York

Columbia University Press
Publishers Since 1893
New York   Chichester, West Sussex
cup.columbia.edu

Library of Congress Cataloging-in-Publication Data
Names: Lim, Jie-Hyun, author.
Title: Global Easts : remembering, imagining, mobilizing / Jie-Hyun Lim.
Description: New York : Columbia University Press, [2022] | Series: Asia
    perspectives : history, society, and culture | Includes bibliographical
    references and index.
Identifiers: LCCN 2021049220 (print) | LCCN 2021049221 (ebook) |
    ISBN 9780231206761 (hardback) | ISBN 9780231206778 (trade paperback) |
    ISBN 9780231556644 (ebook)
Subjects: LCSH: History, Modern—1945–1989. | Nationalism and collective
    memory. | Socialism—History—20th century. | Cold War. | East and West. |
    Europe, Eastern—History—1945- —Historiography. | East Asia—History—
    1945- —Historiography.
Classification: LCC D842 .L56 2022 (print) | LCC D842 (ebook) |
    DDC 909.08—dc23/eng/20211106
LC record available at https://lccn.loc.gov/2021049220
LC ebook record available at https://lccn.loc.gov/2021049221

Cover design: Elliott S. Cairns
Cover image: Japanese postcard showing caricatures of Russian military
leaders from Russo-Japanese War, February 8, 1904 to May 27, 1906.
Courtesy of the East Asia Image Collection, Lafayette Digital Repository.

Chapter 1 was originally published as "Victimhood Nationalism-Mourning Nations and Global Accountability," in *Memory in a Global Age: Discourses, Practices and Trajectories*, ed. Aleida Assmann and Sebastian Conrad (2010), reproduced with permission of Palgrave Macmillan.

Chapter 2 was originally published in *The Cambridge History of the Second World War*, vol. III, ed. Michael Geyer and Adam Tooze (Cambridge, UK: Cambridge University Press, 2015).

Chapter 3 is derived in part from an article titled "Triple Victimhood: On the Mnemonic Confluence of the Holocaust, Stalinist Crime, and Colonial Genocide," published in the *Journal of Genocide Research*, April 13, 2020, copyright Taylor & Francis, available online: http://www.tandfonline.com/. DOI:10.1080/14623528.2020.1750822. Reproduced with permission.

Chapter 4 was originally published as "A Postcolonial Reading of the *Sonderweg*: Marxist Historicism Revisited" in the *Journal of Modern European History* 12, no. 2 (2014).

An earlier version of chapter 5 was published as "The Configuration of Orient and Occident in the Global Chain of National Histories: Writing National Histories in Northeast Asia," in *Narrating the Nation: Representations in History, Media and the Arts*, ed. Stefan Berger, Linas Eriksonas, and Andrew Mycock (New York: Berghahn Books, 2008).

An earlier version of chapter 6 was published as "World History Nationally: How Has the National Appropriated the Transnational in East Asian Historiography?," in *Global History, Globally*, ed. Sven Beckert and Dominic Sachsenmaier (London: Bloomsbury Academic, an imprint of Bloomsbury Publishing Plc., 2018).

An earlier version of chapter 7 was published as "The Antagonistic Complicity of Nationalisms—On 'Nationalist Phenomenology' in East Asian History Textbooks," in *Contested Views of a Common Past*, ed. Steffi Richter (Frankfurt: Campus Verlag, 2008).

An earlier version of chapter 8 was published as "The Nationalist Message in Socialist Code: On Court Historiography in People's Poland and North Korea," in *Making Sense of Global History: The 19th International Congress of Historical Sciences Commemorative Volume*, ed. S. Sogner (Oslo: Universitetsforlaget, 2001).

An earlier version of chapter 9 was originally published in *Gender Politics and Mass Dictatorship: Global Perspectives*, eds. Jie-Hyun Lim and Karen Petrone (2011), reproduced with permission of Palgrave Macmillan.

An earlier version of chapter 10 was originally published in Choi Chatterjee et al., eds., *The Global Impacts of Russia's Great War and Revolution, Book 2: The Wider Arc of Revolution, Part 2*, Russia's Great War and Revolution series, edited by Choi Chatterjee et al., vol. 6 (Bloomington, Ind.: Slavica Publishers, 2019).

This work was supported by the National Research Foundation of Korea Grant funded by the Korean government (2017S1A6A3A01079727).

Contents

Acknowledgments ix

Introduction: Between Two Global Easts 1

Part I. Remembering

1 Victimhood Nationalism: National Mourning and
Global Accountability 25

2 The Second World War in Global Memory Space 59

3 Postcolonial Reflections on the Mnemonic Confluence
of the Holocaust, Stalinist Crimes, and Colonialism 92

Part II. Imagining

4 A Postcolonial Reading of *Sonderwege*:
Marxist Historicism Revisited 129

5 Imagining Easts: Cofiguration of Orient and Occident
in the Global Chain of National Histories 151

6 World History as a Nationalist Rationale: How the National
Appropriated the Transnational in East Asian Historiography 179

7 Nationalist Phenomenology in East Asian History Textbooks: On the Antagonistic Complicity of Nationalisms   205

8 Nationalist Messages in Socialist Code: On the Party Historiography in People's Poland and North Korea   226

Part III. Mobilizing

9 Mapping Mass Dictatorship: Toward a Transnational History of Twentieth-Century Dictatorship   251

10 Nationalizing the Bolshevik Revolution Transnationally: In Search of Non-Western Modernization Among "Proletarian" Nations   275

Epilogue: Blurring Dichotomy of Global Easts and Wests in the Age of Neopopulism   300

Index   309

Acknowledgments

The impetus of this book comes from my encounter with transitions. As a transnational historian, I have wandered between Poland and South Korea in the transition to posttotalitarian democracy since 1990. Experiencing two opposite dictatorships of Left and Right in the distant Global Easts kept me critical of the intellectual complacency rooted in the politics of the global Cold War. I thank all my Polish and Korean contemporaries who had lived through the difficult time with good-humored irony.

I have presented earlier versions of these essays at various conferences and in journals and books. I extend my thanks to organizers, editors, and hosts for opening the public discussion of my articles: Aleida Assmann, Sven Beckert, Stefan Berger, Choi Chatterjee, Sebastian Conrad, Paul Corner, Michael Geyer, Frank Hadler, George Iggers, Minoru Iwasaki, Konrad Jarausch, Jürgen Kocka, Satoshi Koyama, Marcin Kula, Alf Lüdtke, Youjae Lee, Matthias Middell, Dirk Moses, Nagao Nishikawa, Karen Petrone, Steffi Richter, Eve Rosenhaft, Dominic Sachsenmaier, Naoki Sakai, Michael Schoenhals, Joanna Wawrzyniak, Michael Wildt. I remember many Polish friends and colleagues, including Michał Śliwa and Jan Piskorski, with delight under the shared motto "think globally, drink locally."

Without Carol Gluck's advice and friendship, I would never have imagined this book. Not only was it her initiative to start a book, but she has also encouraged and supported me to finish this one. By her invitation, I was able to stay at Columbia University to finalize the revision in January and February 2020. Elisabeth Lee gave a diverse collection of essays some unity of style. Caelyn Cobb shepherded the production process expertly and with a masterly touch. Thank you. Dziękuję. 감사합니다.

Global
Easts

Introduction

Between Two Global Easts

Let's build a second Japan here (Poland).

—Lech Wałęsa, September 24, 1980

Experiencing Two Dictatorships Between Seoul and Warsaw

I have been a student of history since 1977. Becoming a history student, under the anticommunist, semimilitary dictatorship in Seoul, was challenging but exciting: the political tension high, the ideological grip tight, the cultural struggle tense, the air rebellious, people anxious, and history disquiet. The developmental dictatorship in South Korea was at its peak, and the anticommunist national security law abusively violated fundamental rights of the freedom of assembly, association, thought, and press. KCIA agents and political intelligence police intruded on the university campus. The self-acclaimed phrase "Korean way of democracy," as the gilded façade of the Park Chung-hee regime, decorated his "developmental dictatorship" that prioritized national security, public safety, social order, and economic development over political freedom and human rights. More than a rhetorical move, Park's philosophy of developmental dictatorship, as elaborated by his political scientists, found legitimation in

German jurist Carl Schmitt's concepts of "sovereign dictatorship," "decisionist democracy," and "state of emergency."[1] In retrospect, my Korean contemporaries in the 1970s had lived in the legacy of the political theology that advocated Nazism as sovereign dictatorship.

At the abstract level, Park's developmental dictatorship never transcended its self-definition: the "Korean way of democracy," "communitarian democracy that is morally superior to the egoistic Western democracy," or "democracy in which the individual selves voluntarily sacrifice themselves for the higher self or absolute ego of nation."[2] The deep memory of the devastating Korean Civil War of 1950–1953, the Cold War conflict between the North and South, and increasingly heightened political tension and countless small military clashes in the DMZ gave robustness to the omnipresent specter of communist North Korea. The Nixon doctrine asking anticommunist Asian allies to tend to their own military defense in 1969 and the rapprochement between the United States and the People's Republic of China, the Strategic Arms Limitation Talks (SALT), and détente between the United States and the Soviet Union in 1972 dramatically altered the international politics of the Cold War. Ordinary South Koreans, apart from critical intellectuals, further internalized an imminent threat from communist North Korea. The shattered Cold War constellation provided the conditions for Park to proclaim a state of emergency, which rationalized the shift from democracy to dictatorship.

A closer look at the conceptual history shatters the antithesis between dictatorship and democracy—an idea rooted deeply in the political common sense of the twentieth century. As the German school of *Begriffsgeschichte* (conceptual history) suggests persuasively, dictatorship in its original usage in the ancient Roman republic meant dictatorial powers endowed to the *tribunus plebis*, provisionally invoked in a state of emergency. Nominated by a consul on the recommendation of the Senate and confirmed by the Comitia Curiata (a popular assembly), a dictator was a temporary tribune with extraordinary executive powers during war and military crises. A dictator's term was set at six months, although he customarily resigned from power as soon as the crisis passed. The original meaning of dictatorship as a temporal form of democracy in the state of emergency prevailed until the nineteenth century. The antonym of dictatorship was not democracy but the normal state, and the antonym of democracy was not dictatorship but monarchy or aristocracy.[3] To nineteenth-century readers, seeing the antithesis of democracy in dictatorship would have been as alien as connecting liberalism with democracy, given the lack of regard liberals had for democracy. A history of the concept of dictatorship raises doubts, therefore, about the Manichean dichotomy between dictatorship and democracy present in the Cold War paradigm. Dictatorship, like democracy, requires its *demos*. As analyzed in part 3 of this book, the term *mass dictatorship* may seem an oxymoron, but at the level of conceptual history, it makes sense as a compound.

Confronting domestic opposition from leftist critical intellectuals and conservative political parties, President Park appealed to a plebiscite to endorse his developmental dictatorship. He put a constitutional amendment for the democracy in the state of emergency to a referendum. Joining rhetoric from Western democracy to the Korean way of democracy, his regime achieved a constitutional coup d'état and established a dictatorship with the support of the people's will. Plebiscites in 1972 and 1975 were designed to give democratic legitimacy to his dictatorship. In a state of emergency, people willingly accepted limits on their fundamental civil rights, including the four freedoms of assembly, association, thought, and press. Both referendums resulted in absolute majorities, with "yes" receiving 91.5 and 74.4 percent, respectively.[4] People's will supported the decisionist democracy at the price of the parliamentary and legal procedures of democracy. Of course, Park's political opponents insisted that some "yes" votes in uniformed organizations like the army and other state sectors were imposed. More important was the democratic façade, decorated by the plebiscites, behind which Park's mass dictatorship resided.

After his election in 1976, U.S. president Jimmy Carter insisted on human rights diplomacy even with American allies, which set up a conflict between his human rights agenda and Park's developmental dictatorship. Against the Carter administration's "Western" universalist human rights diplomacy, the Park regime defended the Korean way of democracy based on the people's will and appeals to "our" national sovereignty. The U.S. human rights diplomacy under the Carter administration was regarded as the Great Power's humiliating intrusion on the sacred national sovereignty of South Korea. Supporters of democratization were branded as naïve pro-Western intellectuals contaminated by unpatriotic and selfish individualism, who had been deprived of national spirit through their embrace of degenerate Western values. They were labeled traitors to the nation—the

South Korean version of the "rootless cosmopolitans" and "fifth columns" denounced in communist Poland and "cultural toadies" (事大主義者) in North Korea. Although on opposite sides of the Cold War, the rightist developmental dictatorship of Park Chung-hee, the "Polish road to socialism" of Władysław Gomułka, and the *Juche* (total subjectivity) of Kim Il-sŏng's ideology all sought the "nationalization of masses" through sociopolitical engineering.[5] Their nationalist discourses all depended on the primordialist concepts of the ethnic nation, social organicism, and filial duties.[6]

As a history student under the developmental dictatorship in South Korea, I had been squeezed between two extremes: anticommunist government propaganda or illegal communist propaganda. Given the strict ban on Marxist books, we had the Korean version of the "second circulation" (*druga obiega—samizdat*) in the 1970s and 1980s.[7] While books in underground circulation in People's Poland (Polska Ludowa) largely had an anticommunist character, the Korean second circulation was replete with Marxist books. Unfortunately, most were Stalinist textbooks and other dogmatic texts in Japanese translation. Among us young underground Marxists prevailed a sort of maximalist attitude that made reading liberal leftist books about alienation, feminism, environment, hegemony, and habitus look like a revisionist deviation. The rightist conservatism of the party *nomenklatura* in communist Poland was hailed as Orthodox Marxism in South Korea, while the conservative anticommunist establishment in South Korea was a parallel of the leftist dissident movement in People's Poland. Right and left swapped places quickly in the seesawing political constellation of the Cold War politics. As an angry young leftist from postcolonial South Korea in the 1980s, I found myself to be a stubborn rightist in postcommunist Poland in the 1990s on account of my international "Luxemburgist" Marxism. Experiencing two opposite dictatorships in the distant Global Easts allowed me to escape the intellectual complacency, be it leftist or rightist, of Cold War politics.

I was lucky to live through the transition in mirage from capitalism to socialism under the developmental dictatorship in South Korea and witness the reversed transition from socialism to capitalism in Poland after the fall of communism in 1989. I was a barefoot historian: the seminar of the dissident underground and street-fighting trained me as a historian of critical thinking rather than as a historian of professional skills. South Korea, benefiting and/or suffering from the "condensed" modernization and developmental dictatorship of the 1970s and 1980s, offered an inspiring social lab for historians. Postcommunist Poland in the radical transformation after 1989 likewise proved a fertile soil for social scientists. Despite profound frustration with poor academic infrastructure and strict censorship, I was consoled by the great English historian Lawrence Stone's confession that he couldn't be confident of his lifework on the English revolution because he had never lived through revolution. Compared to that great British historian, my generation of historians in the Global Easts experienced revolutionary upheaval every minute. We poor historians were fortunate to have the luxury of revolutionary experiences that rich historians cannot dream of.

Marxist Historicism and Red Orientalism

South Korea in the 1970s seemed to reenact the process of primitive accumulation of capital described by Karl Marx in *Das Kapital*. Marxism appealed to me both as a critical insight into the condensed modernization of South Korea and for its *Narodnik* sympathy for the impoverished and oppressed. Fueled by developmental dictatorship, capitalism unfolded in South Korea in patently different ways from those in Western Europe. My contemporaries thought the "Prussian path" of capitalist development would aptly explain the backward peculiarities of South Korean capitalism. The whole range of Prussian peculiarities of this "special path" (*Sonderweg*) potentially applied to Korea: the late development of the nation-state, stubborn vestiges of feudalism, colonial legacy, the aborted bourgeois revolution, political weakness and semifeudal traits of the bourgeoisie, a strange alliance of feudal aristocrats and the bourgeoisie, state-led industrialization, the blocked development of parliamentarianism, the illiberal and antipluralistic political culture, the fascist dictatorship, and immaturity of modern individual subjectivity.[8]

Marxist historicism spurred interest in the history of the capitalist transition in Korea. What peculiarities of Korean history set the Korean process apart from the universal path of Western capitalist development? Problems endemic to Korean society in the 1970s and 1980s—underdevelopment, dictatorship, illiberal political culture, incomplete nation-state formation by the division of North and South Korea, and all other deficiencies in comparison with the model modernity of the West—could be ascribed to the Korean peculiarity in capitalist development. The study of the Korean *Sonderweg* took its intellectual nourishment from the Marxist debate on the transition from feudalism to capitalism, drawing on the Maurice Dobb–Paul Sweezy debate, Japanese Marxian studies of economic history led by the *Kōza-ha* (Lecture faction) and Takahashi Kōhachiro, and the Sonderweg thesis in postwar German historiography. Underlying all these seemingly disparate discussions was a comparative historical approach that held the capitalist development of England as a universal model for gauging the backwardness or peculiarity of capitalist development in the Global Easts.[9]

The problem is that the minute the Global East sees itself reflected in the hegemonic mirror of the West, the singularity of its capitalist history is rendered a negative particularity vis-à-vis Western capitalism's universality.[10] A historical difference, neither superior nor inferior, is forced into a hierarchy, with the West at the top and everyone else placed according to their deviation and distance from the Western universality. The dichotomy of "universality versus particularity" is formulated into the antipodes of a universal-Western-American path and a particular-Eastern-Prussian path in mainstream Marxist historiography. Marx's argument in the preface to *Das Kapital* that "countries that are more industrially advanced only show to the less developed the image of their own future[!]" encapsulates the crux of Marxian "historicism." This unilinear historicism arranges all histories of the world on a global linear time axis. It temporalizes the spatial differences between the West and the East into the evolutionary narratives of forwardness and backwardness in the development of society and economy.

In this historicist scheme, the gap between the advanced West and the backward East is doomed to perpetuate itself. The struggle for recognition, manifested in the effort to show that the Global East can usher in modernity on its own, ironically ingrained a consequential Eurocentrism. Few of my colleagues experienced any "unease about the tension between the European roots of Marx's thoughts and their global significance," the fundamental insight of Indian subaltern scholars described by Dipesh Chakrabarty.[11] What explains this intellectual complacency of the self-Orientalism among Korean Marxists? Whereas Marxism served as a semiofficial ideology in Indira Gandhi's India, it remained forbidden fruit in anticommunist South Korea. South Korean Marxists held fast to the notion that Marxism guarded a devastating truth to be turned on the dictatorial regime, while Indian Marxists could locate Marxism as a semiofficial ideology in a suspect relationship of knowledge and power. It was helpful for those South Korean Marxists that Marx himself had never written about Korea per se—although he wrote a lot on India from the perspective of "imperialism as a pioneer of capitalism" and as a driving force of progress to move Asiatic stagnancy toward capitalist modernity.

Eurocentric Marxism motivated me to choose "Western history" as my specialization in graduate school. The teaching and study of history in postcolonial Korea institutionalized the intellectual legacy of Japanese colonial academia, with a tripartite structure of national history, Oriental history, and Western history. To find and prove the traces of the endogenous development of capitalism in Korea, my thinking went, I needed to have deep historical knowledge of the transition from feudalism to capitalism in England. As the West of the Wests, England was the hegemonic mirror to reflect the peculiarity of Korean history. In the disciplinary politics of Korean academia, national history was the highest historical discipline, given its crucial contributions to the nationalist mobilization of the developmental dictatorship through the bolstering of nationalist subjectivity; alongside the Marxist historicism, criticism of the nationalist instrumentalization inherent to national history guided me into Western history instead of Korean history. Regardless of my motivation, I remained caught up in the Eurocentrism endemic in the unilinear schema of Marxist historicism and red Orientalism. Marxist historicism framed my academic interest in measuring the distance of Korean modernity from the model modernity of the West. More precisely, the unit of measure was calibrated through an amalgam of the Marxist historicism and a Whig history of the English path of capitalist development and parliamentary democracy.[12] In retrospect, the "follow and catch-up" strategy was strongly present at the beginning of historical studies in my youth.

Marxian historicism and Eurocentrism dominated my Ph.D. dissertation of 1988. In the 1980s the underground polemics over the social formation of colonial and postcolonial Korea between the National Liberation (NL) and People's Democracy (PD) factions was a magnetic field that attracted all leftists. Inspired by this debate, I decided to challenge the relationship between Marxism and nationalism in theory and praxis.

Political democratization in Korea, begun in 1987, made it possible for me to submit the following year a dissertation proposal entitled "Marx, Engels and the National Question." In my similarly titled dissertation, I enlisted a newly coined word, *capitalo-centrism*, to advocate for a Marxian Eurocentrism. As long as the advent of socialism required the material basis of mature capitalism, Eurocentrism would be an unwanted companion to capitalo-centrism. Having studied Marx and Engels on the colonial question, which acknowledged colonial British, French, and American contributions to capitalist development by destroying the stagnancy of the "Asiatic mode of production," I accentuated capitalo-centrism as a defense of Marxian Eurocentrism. I tried to show how Marx and Engels had escaped their earlier Eurocentrism in their discussion of the Irish national question since 1867.[13] Still in the orbit of Marxist historicism, red Orientalism, and their steadfast Eurocentrism, I had yet to encounter postcolonialism, post-Marxism, and postmodernism. Common to all five historiographical articles in part 2 of this book, "Imagining," is my self-criticism of Marxist historicism and red Orientalism, written in the wake of my subsequent encounter with these broader critical currents and my experiences as a transnational historian in Poland and Korea.

Displacing East and West

When I first landed in Poland in the winter of 1990, the country was bursting with the excitement of the first democratic presidential election in the postcommunist era. Lech Wałęsa, the legend of the Solidarity Movement and a strong presidential contender, grabbed my attention with his campaign pledge to make Poland "a second Japan."[14] I still have a fresh memory of how puzzled I was at his promise, which sounded like a declaration of "turning the West into the East," namely, "Europe into Asia." It was a stark obverse of the Japanese policy of *datsu-a nyu-o ron* (de-Asianization and pro-Europeanization) of the *Meiji Ishin*—Meiji Regeneration.[15] At that time, my conventional geographical perception placed Poland in the West and Japan in the East. Years later, I recounted this experience while discussing historicism with Sakai Naoki. Sakai offered a trenchant interpretation that not even Wałęsa himself likely realized.[16] In the scheme of historicism inherited from Marx and others that arranged the advanced

West and the backward East along one timeline of world history, Sakai suggested, Poland ended up assigned to the East, Japan to the West. Though Japan may be "East" in terms of the conventional geography, the nation belongs among the economic and social "West" in comparison to Poland. Hence the richness implicit in Wałęsa's campaign promise. Never in my life had I understood more lucidly the incisive power of Edward Said's conceptualization of the East and the West as "imaginative geography."[17]

Living in Poland, as the "East" of "West," awakened me to the politico-historical construction of "West" and "East" or "Europe" and "Asia" as imaginative geography. The geographical categorization of Polish studies in Germany, labeled *Ostforschung* (Eastern studies), is "East," while German studies in Poland, labeled *Studia Zachodnie* (Western studies), is "West." Once national history is placed in a global chain of historical thinking, say, France-Germany-Poland-Russia, the fluidity of the East and the West as imaginative geography becomes clearer. German historical imagination pits German *Kultur* against French *civilisation*, Germany as the East vis-à-vis France as the West. However, Germany became the West vis-à-vis Poland, as the *Ost* in *Ostforschung* of Polish studies implies. In turn, Poland considered itself as the West vis-à-vis "Asiatic" Russia. The diary of Fyodor Dostoyevsky shows the relativity of East and West: "In Europe, we were Tatars, while in Asia we are Europeans too."[18] Japan went so far as to orientalize Russia, positioning itself as the West after victory in the Russo-Japanese War. In Wałęsa's 1980 address, Poland became Japan's East/Asia and Japan Poland's West/Europe.[19]

Far from fixed locations, "West" and "East" are adaptable categories, whose fluidity I came to understand through my experience of investigating Western Europe, Eastern Europe, and East Asia in conjunction with one another, while wandering in the transregional space between Seoul and Warsaw.[20] The unique status of the Polish socialist movement between the reformist platform of the Social Democratic Party of Germany (SPD) and the Bolsheviks' revolutionary voluntarism captured this geographic fluidity well. Stuck between Russia and Germany, Polish socialists could not but feel alienated by SPD's reformist policy, which was an unrealistic luxury for them. At the same time, they did not bother to conceal their strong self-assurance in the face of Lenin's "Tartar Marxism." One can see the germ of the Polish red Orientalism against the Russian Bolshevism in Rosa Luxemburg's labeling of Leninism as "Tartar Marxism."[21] The cultural acceptance of Poland's liminal status is reflected in an excellent volume of studies on the dilemma of Polish socialism, *Między wschodem a zachodem* (Between East and West).[22]

Amid this excitement of wandering between Seoul and Warsaw, I was shaken by an experience that made me realize the deep entrenchment of Eurocentrism in my own thinking. During my stay in Poland, I finished in 1996 a chapter on Poland for *Nationalism, Labour, and Ethnicity 1870–1939*, a book project edited by Stefan Berger and Angel Smith.[23] Angel Smith's feedback on my draft essay frightened me. Referring to my account of the peculiarities of the Polish labor movement as following the Prussian path of capitalist development, he asked me point-blank if I still believed in the validity of the German Sonderweg thesis. At that moment, I became aware that the Polish Marxist historiography I had consulted was the Polish version of that thesis. When Smith, a British historian of the Spanish Civil War, pointed out that my interpretation of the Polish labor history reiterated the Sonderweg thesis, I was at a loss. I suspect that Smith's keen sensibility toward the Sonderweg emanated from his scholarly focus on the history of Spain, another "Orient" of Europe. In retrospect, a crack in the Sonderweg thesis opened by the clashing of historical experiences of diverse peripheries of Korea, Poland, and Spain offered me an exit from the tyranny of Eurocentrism. And yet I was more astounded by how Smith's perspective enabled him to use the Sonderweg thesis as a lever to disengage from the Marxist historicism of the Polish mainstream historiography.

By virtue of this belated recognition of my implicit use of the Polish Sonderweg, I was able to imagine a wide-ranging transversality of historical thinking beyond regional borders and historical specificities. I could contemplate approaching the modern and contemporary history of Central and Eastern Europe from a postcolonial angle. It took me nearly two decades to respond adequately to Smith's comment in my "A Postcolonial Reading of the *Sonderweg*: Marxist Historicism Revisited" of 2014 (chapter 4 of this volume). Postcolonial criticism rescued Eastern European historiography from "the first model of underdevelopment" and the Leninist stereotype of hopelessly undercapitalized and underdeveloped Eastern Europe by labeling it "the Prussian path" of capitalism. *Global Easts*, the title of this book, originated from the displacement of East and West in the historical imagination. "East" in Global Easts is a neither geographically nor historically fixed entity in Oriental history, or East Asia, or Eastern Europe. The "Global East" is a "problem space" where the East remains a problem. The supposed solution for this problem space is to become a "West." This cofiguring of East and West regulates—and limits—our historical imagination. I have to admit, however, that the problem space of Global Easts has a limited scope for its Northern Hemisphere centrism. How to combine, differentiate, and entangle the Global East with the Global South in the global modernity needs to be on the relentless pursuit of answers.

Mass Dictatorship Overcoming Cold War Demonology

Having longed for a transition from capitalism to socialism in Seoul during the 1980s, I witnessed regime change in Warsaw in the opposite direction, from state socialism to wild capitalism. Imagining, participating in, experiencing, and living two opposite transformations in close temporal proximity incited me to challenge the Cold War demonology of right and left alike. In Poland, communism came to be branded as the political Right while anticommunists were labeled as the Left. Many Poles came to regard communism as an ideology that oppressed workers and peasants, a system that had been imposed on their country by Soviet Russia. It is a bitter irony that anticommunist dissidents in People's Poland organized the Committee to Protect Workers (Komitet Obrony Robotników, KOR) against the Polish United Worker's Party (Polska Zjednoczona Partia Robotnicza, PZPR) in 1976. If the anticommunist intelligentsia had to set up a dissident committee to protect workers from the ruling worker's party of the communist regime, socialism as an idea must have been betrayed by its political reality. Throughout the decade of the 1990s, firsthand experience of really existing socialism in Poland made me ponder the surreal reality of socialism.

It was Rosa Luxemburg, a Polish-Jewish Marxist, who inspired my interest in Poland. While reading Luxemburg, I came to learn about the fierce debates over the national question among Polish socialists at the turn of the twentieth century. Looking to the Russian Revolution, the way the Polish Socialist Party (PPS), focused on Polish independence, locked its horns with the Social Democracy of the Kingdom of Poland and Lithuania" (SDKPiL) reminded me in many respects of the Korean Marxist dispute between the National Liberation faction, focused on national reunification, and People's Democracy faction, focused on social revolution in South Korea, as their respective priorities in the 1980s.[24] If late nineteenth-century Poland was Germany's East, late twentieth-century Korea was Japan's East. The sensitivity to the national question among Marxists in both Poland and Korea came from their positions as "Easts" in global modernity. Indeed, Polish Marxists' sharp debates on the national question were unique in the history of the Marxist theory and practice at the turn of the twentieth century. That explains why I was drawn to Polish Marxist thought more than even the most refined version of Western Marxism. Not to mention that the classical Marxists like Rosa Luxemburg, Kazimierz Kelles-Krauz, as well as the gems of postwar Polish (ex-)Marxists, including Oskar Lange, Julian Hochfeld, Leszek Kołakowski, Zygmunt Baumann, Andrzej Walicki, and Adam Schaff, enchanted me for their problematics deeply rooted in the modern and contemporary history of Poland as part of the Global East.

I was dumbfounded, however, by finding out that those great thinkers and interpreters of Marxism had been alienated and even excommunicated from the Communist Party. What surprised me most during my first encounter with the residues of the "really existing socialism" in Poland was that ethnic nationalism had become the ideological pillar of the ruling Polish United Worker's Party (PZPR). The anti-Semitic graffiti on the walls of the ruins of the concentration camp in Oświęcim (Auschwitz) during my first visit in January 1991 horrified me for its appalling antisocialist racism. Later I realized that after 1968, the party launched its racist anti-Semitism under cover of anti-Zionism. The party manipulated Luxemburgism, Western revisionism, national nihilism, social patriotism, objective patriotism, proletarian internationalism, and all other ideological labels for political use. Based on this experience, I recognized how little the history of ideas can convey the reality of a communist regime. I began to have doubts about my own research agenda, namely, the history of ideas of Polish Marxist irredentism. Ironically, the legacy of Rosa Luxemburg attracted me to Poland but rescued me from the *idola teatri* (idols of theater) of Marxism through awakening the reality of the communist regime. I found myself idling on the monograph of theoretical tensions between the social patriotism and proletarian internationalism in the history of the Polish Marxism, which is not finished yet.

Having witnessed the ruins of the "really existing socialism" in People's Poland, I pondered over the fundamental questions of historical transformation, societal change, revolutions, hegemonies, and habitus. The absurdities of "really existing socialism" showed how revolutionary naïveté melted into the air in the historical aftermath of the Bolshevik Revolution. Contrary to the Marxist vision of revolution, the transformation of political institutions, socioeconomic systems, constitution and legal codes, and cultural practices did not guarantee the revolutionary change in the everyday lives of ordinary people. The Marxian prognosis that social revolution would bring a more profound transformation than a political revolution is right—but it does not necessarily guarantee a complete revolution. While Marxian understandings of transformation have inclined toward the structural, my experience with the condensed democratization in Seoul and Warsaw awakened me to the importance of change at the level of everyday life. Problems of condensed democratization originated in a mismatch between institutional democratization and everyday fascism that remained largely unperturbed. Even once dictatorship as a political regime is long gone, the fascist *habitus* often still reigns in everyday practices and influences people's way of thinking.

My theory of "mass dictatorship" was an attempt to bring the issue of everyday fascism into scholarship on dictatorships in the twentieth century.[25] In formulating the concept of mass dictatorship, I was inspired by the thought-provoking essays on People's Poland in *Ofiary czy współwinny* (Victims or accomplices?) (1997). These essays criticized the histories of martyrdom steeped in the people's sublime sacrifices and heroic struggles under the communist dictatorship. While their claim that the masses could be both the victims and the accomplices of dictatorships remained a hypothesis, it provoked a Copernican shift in my approach.[26] The Polish scholarship of the communist dictatorship struck me when I was at a loss with the huge popular nostalgia for the era of Park Chung-hee's dictatorship in the post-totalitarian democracy of South Korea. A project to build a memorial for the dictator Park under Kim Dae-Jung's government occasioned great controversy in 1999. The quarrels revealed how deeply rooted nostalgia for Park's reign remained in the vernacular memory. Reading news coverage that an overwhelming majority of Koreans favored a memorial to Park Chung-hee and that, in a survey of students at the leading universities in Seoul, he was the top-ranked historical figure to emulate, I had to reassess the conventional way of thinking about dictatorship—the traditional definition being a form of government in which a few bad men rule innocent people through the apparatus of coercion and violence.

An uncanny symmetry exists between reactions of Polish right-wing critics to *Victims or Accomplice?* and the responses of Korean leftist intellectuals to the concept of mass dictatorship. My approach to South Korea's developmental dictatorship has met with fierce opposition from the Korean left-wing intellectual establishment, while Havel's and Michnik's stance against the *lustracja* (lustration) provoked angry responses from the anticommunist right-wingers in the Czech Republic and Poland.[27] Fueling their response is the moral inconceivability of popular support for such evil regimes as Poland's experienced socialism or Park's developmental dictatorship. Anticommunist Korean right-wingers and old-fashioned Polish Communists strangely converged in their misuse and abuse of popular nostalgia to excuse the developmental dictatorship and communist regime, respectively. Conversely, Korean leftists and Polish anticommunists denied the reality of the popular nostalgia and shared the same a priori belief that our innocent people could never have supported the political devils.

That bizarre mnemonic companionship of the political rival camps in the global constellation freed me from a demonology obsessed with a simplistic dualism that posits a few vicious perpetrators (the dictator and his cronies) and many innocent victims (the people). Through this transnational experience, I was able to understand dictatorship, leftist and rightist alike, as a response to global modernity—a perception that subsequently developed into understanding mass dictatorship as a transnational social formation. As I came to note the continuity of colonial practice and violence between Western colonialism and mass dictatorship, I could challenge conventional dualities in world history in which democracy and dictatorship line up with such dichotomies between the West and the non-West, the modern and the premodern, and normality and aberration. Western liberal democracy and non-Western mass dictatorship were not so much historical opposites as two sides of the global history of modernity.[28] Part 3 of this volume, "Mobilizing," describes mass dictatorship based on the self-mobilization from below, be it rightist or leftist. Mobilizing is inconceivable without imagining and remembering. The road to the mass dictatorship in the Global Easts was built by historical imagination but paved with collective memory.

From a Historian to a Memory Activist

In 1999 some critical historians, including myself, initiated the organization of the East Asian History Forum for Criticism and Solidarity as a civil alternative to the national history institutions and history textbook conflicts in East Asia. Tumultuous history controversies over the revisionist Japanese history textbook revealed the "antagonistic complicity" of warring nationalisms behind the scenes of open conflicts in East Asia.[29] Instead of making a joint history textbook, the East Asian History Forum aimed at deconstructing the nationalist episteme of history textbooks in the region with a belief that different interpretations didn't really matter if they all stemmed the nationalist antagonism. Differences in interpreting histories, if not antagonistic, were rather desirable in promoting the historical thinking among students. The East Asian History Forum constructed a bridgehead for promoting transnational history. Hindsight showed, however, that the nationalist phenomenology has been deeply rooted not only in history textbooks but also in the memory regime covering the official, vernacular, and personal memories. Increasingly I began to recognize the memory regime as a nationalist stronghold at the grassroots level, which prompted a shift from transnational/global history to transnational/global memory in me. Confronting East Asia as a warring memory space, memory regime change becomes ever more crucial. Entrenched in our everyday lives, films, novels, comic books, TV dramas, museums, galleries, internet games, and social media dominate, maintain, expand, and reproduce the memory regime.

After the disenchantment with communism in People's Poland and a decade-long break, I came back to Polish history with a different set of concerns and problematics. The *Historikerstreit po polsku* (Polish *Historikerstreit* or Polish historians' dispute), ignited in 2000 by Jan Gross's book *Sąsiedzi* (Neighbors), stimulated me to take an interest in the consciousness of victimhood in global memory space. Inspired by Zygmunt Bauman's concept of "hereditary victimhood," I have been developing the working hypothesis of "victimhood nationalism" to understand postwar memory culture in Poland, Germany, Israel, Japan, and Korea. Although the experiences of these countries during the Second World War were not necessarily connected, their memories began to be entangled in the global memory space after the war. Previously isolated local memories, like those of Hiroshima-Nagasaki and Auschwitz; of the Holocaust and colonial genocide; of Stalin's Gulags and Hitler's concentration camps; of *Vertreibung* (the post-1945 expulsion of ethnic Germans from Eastern Europe) and *hikiage* (引揚, the repatriation of Japanese settlers mainly from Manchuria and the Korean peninsula after Japan's defeat in World War II); of Comfort Women and sexual violence in Rwanda and former Yugoslavia; and of *Zwangsarbeit* (the forced labor in the Third Reich) and *Kyouseichouyoyu* (強制徴用, forced mobilization in the Japanese Empire), began to travel in the transatlantic and transpacific memory space, to intermingle and relocate.[30] My concern about the transnational memory of victimhood would be unthinkable without my peregrinations between Korea and Poland.

Globalization has dramatically reconfigured the mnemoscape in the third millennium. The space in which collective memories take shape is no longer national but global, and in the emerging global memory space, memories have become entangled, reconciled, contested, conflicted, and negotiated across borders, connecting historical actors and events across time and space in new ways. Traces of the upheavals and cataclysms that have shaped the modern world, from the primitive accumulation of capital to post–Cold War neoliberalism, form a single palimpsest. Memories of slavery, racism, colonial genocide, nationalism, world wars, holocaust, anticolonial liberation movements, Cold War, the Non-Aligned Movement, the Revolution of 1968, feminist movements, social minority movements, multiculturalism, globalization, postnationalism, and even denialism have become interconnected. To trace the history of this global memory formation and its influence on people's lives, I founded the Critical Global Studies Institute (CGSI) at Sogang University, which launched a transdisciplinary team research project on "Mnemonic Solidarity: Colonialism, War, and Genocide in the Global Memory Space."[31] The project seeks to illuminate how territorialized collective memories of nation-states have been interwoven with one another through the processes and practices of cross-referencing, imitation, confrontation, and competition. Its scholarly focus is the deterritorialization of mnemonic discourse on colonialism, war, and genocide since World War II.

Ultimately, the project seeks to explore the possibilities of coexistence of, and dialogue among, competing memories, to build a global memory space that enables their reconciliation. Thus, alongside the scholarly agenda, the development of new public memory practices is central to achieving the project's objectives. The scholarly work of memory studies needs to be complemented by collaborative exhibitions and public events that expand the possibilities of mnemonic exchange and solidarity. In one way or the other, writers, film directors, producers, actors, historians, sociologists, feminists, performing artists—all cultural practitioners—are memory activists. Echoing this agenda, we researchers at the CGSI curated collectively exhibitions including "Unwelcome Neighbors: Portraits of Sinti and Roma Victims of the Holocaust," in collaboration with Eve Rosenhaft from Liverpool University, January 24–February 28, 2019.[32] Instead of the familiar Holocaust lesson of "never again," we curated it to present the uncanny similarity between the German neighbors' complicity with the Romani holocaust behind the camera lens of Hans Weltzel, a German photojournalist and amateur ethnographer in Dessau-Rosslau in 1930s, and the ordinary Koreans' hostile indifference toward their own unwelcome neighbors—including but not limited to refugees, undocumented immigrants, guest workers, international marriage immigrants—today. As a memory activist, I envisioned the exhibition to be a memorial site where diverse critical memories could dialogue, engage, and cross-reference one another, prompting transnational reflection on ethical and political values.[33] To write history is to activate memory, or vice versa.

Mapping

The three parts of this book, "Remembering," "Imagining," and "Mobilizing," are neither chronologically structured nor in causal relationship but are thematically connected. Any order, direction, or type of reading will be fine. Part 1, "Remembering," is written as a section of memory studies, but with the self-awareness of a memory activist as much as a historian. I posit "victimhood nationalism" as a conceptual tool to explicate competing national memories over the historical position of victims in the memory culture of the Global East. Without a reflection on victimhood nationalism, the transnational memory politics in the postwar era cannot be properly grasped. A transnational history of "coming to terms with past" (*Vergangenheitsbewältigung*) would show that the vicious circle of victimhood nationalisms, based on the antagonistic complicity of nationalisms between the victimizers and victims, has been a rock to any historical reconciliation effort in the Global East. Two other essays, on World War II in the global memory space and the entangled memories of the triple victimhood, raise the question about the hermeneutical value of the cosmopolitanization of the Holocaust. Admitting that the Holocaust has functioned as a memory template in the global memory formation, these essays probe for the nonhierarchical comparability among the Holocaust, colonialist crimes, and the Stalinist terror by exploring global memory formation from the postcolonial perspective. As a conclusion, part 1 suggests "critical relativization" and "radical juxtaposition" as ways of both dehegemonizing and deterritorializing historical memories.

Part 2, "Imagining," consists of five essays on the historical imagination, focusing on the historiography of national histories in Global Easts. The first essay, "A Postcolonial Reading of *Sonderweg*," throws light on Marxist historiographical debates on colonial modernity versus *Sonderwege* and reconciles David Blackbourn and Geoff Eley's criticism of the German Sonderweg with a postcolonial critique of Marxist historicism. By tracing the global chain of national history writings, "Imagining Easts" reveals how the conceptual gradation of Oriental and demi-Oriental was determined by its distance to "West" in the cofiguration of East and West. Neither nationalist nor Marxist historians of Global Easts broke free from the Eurocentric discourse of historicism that projected the "West" as "History." The essay "World History as a Nationalist Rationale" describes the emergence of the "patriotic world history" in the Global East as a result of cultural encounters between East and West. It reveals how people of Global Easts have perceived the collective selves by responding to the conceptual categories brought into play by "Western" modernity. "Nationalist Phenomenology" deconstructs the nationalist episteme of history textbooks in East Asia by unveiling the antagonistic complicity of warring national histories. "Nationalist Messages in Socialist Code" compares the Communist Party historiography of People's Poland and North Korea in conjunction with the communist nationalism adopting the primordialist concept of nation. A critical juxtaposition of the party historiographies in the Global East would explain the conundrum of the Marxist anti-Semitism and American white supremacist leaders' love for North Korea's ideas of self-reliance and the "cleanest race."

Part 3, "Mobilizing," shows how the memory culture and historical imagination could help to consolidate the mass dictatorship regime. Originated in a personal encounter with the memory politics of post-totalitarian democracies in South Korea and Poland, "Mapping Mass Dictatorship" questions the usefulness of totalitarian and Marxist paradigms, both saddled with a simplistic dualism that posits a few vicious perpetrators (the dictator and his cronies) and many innocent victims (the people). By mass dictatorship, I suggest a transnational history of "dictatorship from below." Freed from the Manichean demonology of the Cold War, mass dictatorship focuses on the attempted mobilization of the masses by dictatorships and how these dictatorships frequently secured voluntary mass participation and support. In the continuity of mass dictatorship, "Nationalizing the Bolshevik Revolution Transnationally" analyzes how postcolonial states of the Global East interpreted the Bolsheviks' commitment to socialist subjectivity and collectivism through the lens of radical anticolonialism. A sense of historical backwardness, national humiliation, and the desire to non-Western modernization among the radical nationalists of the Global East created a hybrid socialism as the amalgam of labor mobilization, national liberation, and rapid modernization. *Homo sovieticus* and *homo fascistus* shared a common goal of anthropological revolution to make the individual subject subordinated voluntarily to the collective project, though they were proved to be a delusion, as the failure of the twentieth-century totalitarian experiments attests.

Notes

1. Choi Hyung-ik, "입헌독재론: 칼 슈미트의 주권적 독재와 한국의 유신헌법 [On the constitutional dictatorship theory: Carl Schmitt's sovereign dictatorship and the Korean 'Yushin' Constitution]," *Korean Political Studies* 17, no. 1 (2008): 258–63; Gal Bong Kun, 유신헌법해설 [Commentary on the Yushin Constitution] (Seoul: Gwangmyeongchulpansa, 1975).
2. Park's "Korean way of democracy" was a weird amalgam of the Carl Schmitt's political theory with the prewar Japanese philosophical thought of overcoming modernity. For the idea of "overcoming modernity," see Harry Harootunian, *Overcome by Modernity: History, Culture, and Community in Interwar Japan* (Princeton, N.J.: Princeton University Press, 2000).

3. For the history of concept of dictatorship, see Ernst Nolte, "Diktatur," in *Geschichtliche Grundbegriffe*, ed. Otto Brunned et al. (Stuttgart: Klett-Cotta, 1972), 900–924.

4. Reflection on the experience of Park's developmental dictatorship later led me to the idea of "mass dictatorship," with its focus on dictatorship from below. See chapter 9.

5. George L. Mosse, *The Nationalization of the Masses* (New York: Howard Fertig, 1975). Nishikawa Nagao took the phrase "the nationalization of masses" as a key concept in analyzing nationalism in post-Meiji Japan. See Nishikawa Nagao, 國民國家論の 射程 [The monstrous nation] (Tokyo: Kashiwashobo, 1998).

6. See chapters 7 and 8.

7. "Second circulation" is the Polish term for the underground press in the era of Solidarność in the 1980s.

8. It is intriguing to witness Antonio Gramsci's "passive revolution" still being used as a framework for analyzing the current political topography of Korea: this strand of thinking has been directly passed on to some leftists in today's Korea, who hold that the South Korean bourgeoisie was more like the Italian bourgeoisie in the nineteenth century than the French bourgeoisie in 1798. See chapter 4.

9. Marx's long list of "Asiatic" countries covered India, China, Egypt, Mesopotamia, Persia, Arabia, Turkey, Java, Dutch East Indies, Russia, Mexico, Peru, Etrurians, and even Spain under the Moors. See Umbertto Melotti, *Marx and the Third World* (London: New Left Books, 1977), 77.

10. Gavin Walker, "Postcoloniality and the National Question in Marxist Historiography: Elements of the Debate on Japanese Capitalism," *Interventions* 13, no. 1 (2011): 131–32.

11. Dipesh Chakrabarty, preface to *Provincializing Europe* (Princeton, N.J.: Princeton University Press, 2007), x.

12. See chapters 5 and 6.

13. See Jie-Hyun Lim, "Marx's Theory of Imperialism and the Irish National Question," *Science & Society* 56 (Summer 1992).

14. "Zbudujemy tu drugą Japonię," Polskie Radio, https://www.polskieradio.pl/39/248 /Artykul/684816,Zbudujemy-tu-druga-Japonie, accessed February 16, 2020.

15. See chapter 5.

16. Lim Jie-Hyun and Sakai Naoki, 오만과 편견 [Pride and prejudice] (Seoul: Humanist, 2003).

17. A well-known Korean leftist intellectual confessed privately that he felt discomfited by the sight of white people living in such dire poverty during his East European trip in 1989. What did Poland mean to him? Was it Europe or the East? How different was his perception from that of the Japanese soldiers who confronted Russians in the Russo-Japanese War and the Siberian Intervention?

18. Fyodor Dostoyevsky, *A Writer's Diary*, trans. Kenneth Lantz (Evanston, Ill.: Northwestern University Press, 1993), 1374.

19. When I published a review of *Vergangene Grösse und Ohnmacht in Ostmitteleuropa: Repräsentationen imperialer Erfahrung in der Historiographie seit 1918* (2007), edited by Frank Hadler and Mathias Mesenhöller, in a Korean journal, Hadler told me he was bewildered that a journal named the *Western History Review* (西洋史論) published a review of a book on Central-Eastern Europe. It was an Eastern history for German historians, while East European histories are Western history for their geo-Europeanness in South Korea. Also, Japanese historians working on Eastern Europe and Russian history are categorized as "Western historians" (西洋史家). This episode alludes to the fluidity of East and West in the imaginative geography of historical writing.

20. See chapter 5, and Jie-Hyun Lim, "Displacing East and West: Towards a Postcolonial Reading of 'Ostforschung' and 'Myśl Zachodnia,'" paper prestented at International Konferenz in Kulice, Deutsche Ostforschung und polnische Westforschung 2: Institutionen-Personen-Vergleiche, Szczecin University, Poland, December 8–9. 2006.

21. "Rosa Luxemburg to Leo Jogiches (Quarten, Probably Oct. 08, 1909)," in *The Letters of Rosa Luxemburg*, ed. Stephen E. Bronner (Atlantic Highlands, N.J.: Humanities Press, 1978), 127. It is intriguing to find Clara Zetkin's letter calling Karl Radek and Béla Kun "Turkestans."

22. Paweł Samuś and Andrzej Grabski, eds., *Między wschodem a zachodem: Studia z Dziejów Polskiego Ruchu i Myśli Socjalistycznej* (Lodz: Wydawnictwo Uniwersytetu Łódzkiego, 1995).

23. Jie-Hyun Lim, "Labour and the National Question in Poland," in *Nationalism, Labour and Ethnicity 1870-1939*, ed. Stefan Berger and Angel Smith (Manchester, UK: Manchester University Press, 1999).

24. My studies from that period are "Rosa Luxemburg on the Dialectics of Proletarian Internationalism and Social Patriotism," *Science & Society* 59, no. 4 (Winter 1995/96); and "The 'Good Old Cause' in the New Polish Left Historiography," *Science & Society* 61, no. 2 (Winter 1997).

25. Palgrave Macmillan published the five-volume project under the title of *Mass Dictatorship in the 20th Century*. The volumes are thematically organized into "gender politics," "modernity," "cultural imagination," "politics of memory," and "history of everyday lives." In addition to those five volumes, note the *Palgrave Handbook of Mass Dictatorship*. For further information on the series, see http://www.palgrave.com/de/series/14810.

26. Krystina Kersten, ed., *Ofiary czy współwinni* (Warsaw: Volumen, 1997).

27. For *lustracja* controversies in Poland and Korea, see Piotr Grzelak, *Wojna o lustrację* (Warsaw: Trio, 2005); Lim Jie-Hyun and Kim Yong-Woo, eds., 대중독재 II: 정치종교와 헤게모니 [Mass dictatorship II: Political religion and hegemony] (Seoul: Chaiksesang, 2005), 401–596.

28. See chapter 9, a revised version of Jie-Hyun Lim, "Series Introduction: Mapping Mass Dictatorship: Towards a Transnational History of Twentieth-Century Dictatorship," in *Gender Politics and Mass Dictatorship: Global Perspectives*, ed.

Jie-Hyun Lim and Karen Petrone (Basingstoke, UK: Palgrave Macmillan, 2011), 1–22.

29. See chapter 7 and Lim Jie-Hyun, "東アジア歴史　フォラム" [East Asia history forum], in 植民地近代の視座—朝鮮と日本 [Colonial modernity perspective—Korea and Japan], ed. Miyajima Hiroshi, Lee Sungsi, Yun Haedong, and Lim Jie-Hyun (Tokyo: Iwanami Shoten, 2004), 303–14.

30. See part 1 of this book. Also see Jie-Hyun Lim, "Narody-ofiary i ich megalomania," *Więź*, no. 2–3 (2010): 616–17; Jie-Hyun Lim, "Victimhood Nationalism and History Reconciliation in East Asia," *History Compass* 8, no. 1 (November 2010); Lim Jie-Hyun, "犠牲者意識の民族主義" [Victimhood nationalism], *Ritsumeikangenkobunkagenkyu* 20, no. 3 (2009); and Lim Jie-hyun, "'世襲的犠牲者' 意識と脱植民地主義の歴史学" ["Hereditary victimhood" and postcolonial historiography], in 東アジア歴史対話 ─ 国境と世代を越えて [East Asian historical dialogue—beyond borders and generations], ed. Mitani Hiroshi et al. (Tokyo: University of Tokyo Press, 2007).

31. See Critical Global Studies Institute, http://cgsi.ac/index_eng.php.

32. See Critical Global Studies Institute, http://cgsi.ac/bbs/board.php?bo_table=kor _edu&wr_id=12&page=2.

33. Kyu Dong Lee and Eve Rosenhaft, "Representing/Roma/Holocaust: Exhibition Experiences in Europe and East Asia," *Korean Historical Review* 246 (June 2020): 153–87.

PART I

REMEMBERING

1

Victimhood Nationalism

National Mourning and Global Accountability

Previously, the Jews were envied for their properties, qualifications, positions, and international networks ... today they are envied because of the crematoria.

—Witold Kula, 1996

The Turn Toward Victimhood in Global Memory Culture

We cannot think of victims without perpetrators, or of perpetrators without victims. The dichotomy of victimizers and victims in national terms speaks of the transnationality of nationalism because victim nations and perpetrator nations are interwoven beyond borders. As "the focus in the globalization discourse has shifted from imagination to memory"[1] at the beginning of the twenty-first century, the mnemonic conflict between perpetrating nations and victimized nations plays out in the emerging global memory space. The global memory space has become a battleground in the struggle for international recognition among conflicting national memories. As the struggle for recognition intensifies, victimhood has globally become more valuable in national remembrance. Victimhood, often gendered female, has become preferable to heroship, gendered male, in order to better appeal to the human rights regime inherent to the global memory space. The emergence of the human rights regime consolidated the "moral remembrance," which precipitated the victimhood turn. The "cosmopolitanization of the Holocaust" is most representative of the victimhood turn of the global memory. In the effort to win global recognition of justice, victimhood has become a hereditary element of national heritage. In binding generations together, victimhood becomes constitutive of national identity. The political production, consumption, and distribution of "hereditary victimhood" forge a national memory by promoting mnemonic solidarity among victims and their descendants.[2]

Ernest Renan had the foresight to write that "shared suffering unites people more than common joy, and mourning is better than a victory for the national memory."[3] In Renan's era, however, memories of victimhood were confined inside national borders. Today, memories are entangled, contested, conflicted, and negotiated across borders. The nation-state no longer enjoys a monopoly over collective memories, as memories of national victimhood have paradoxically become ever more contested with the emergence of the global memory space. The advent of the global memory space shaped collective memories. One of the most notable changes in mnemonic topography is a discursive shift from heroic martyrdom to innocent victimhood globally. Feminine victims, hitherto marginalized, began to replace masculine heroes in the national remembrance. The sublimation of victimhood on a global scale in the past two decades has not necessarily resulted in transnational accountability, even for human tragedies such as genocide. On the contrary, nationalist appropriation often taints the trajectories of contested memories of victimhood in the global memory space. Under the assumption that the global public sphere will have more sympathy for innocent victims, nations are desperately mourning in order to win "a distasteful competition over who suffered most."[4]

The binary of collective guilt and innocence has facilitated the turn to victimhood in global memory culture. In the categorical thinking of collective guilt, "people supposedly are guilty of, or feel guilty about, things done in their name but not by them." In Hannah Arendt's thought, collective innocence, paired with collective guilt, contributes to building a strong solidarity among self-proclaimed victims.[5] The judging of culprits not for individual misdeeds but their ethnonational identity builds up robust national memory collectives of victims and perpetrators alike. The particularly strong ties of victimhood within memory collectives monopolize the process of "coming to terms with the past," crowding out other dimensions of that past. Prioritizing victimhood in memory space thus facilitates and justifies the nationalism of nations identifying themselves as victims.

Nation-states now compete to establish themselves as victims of aggressor nations. My working hypothesis of "victimhood nationalism" explains this competition as an emergent phenomenon of regenerated nationalism in the era of globalization of memory.[6] Without a transnational reflection on victimhood nationalisms, we cannot grasp postwar processes of "coming to terms with past," especially because victimhood nationalism has been a significant obstacle to any reconciliation across East and West. Without dismantling victimhood nationalism, we cannot reconcile the past with the present. Any strategy aimed at political transformation without a concomitant change in memory regime has failed in the Global East, where the present and future are held hostage by the past. Transforming the politics of memory in East Asia and Eastern Europe demands more than the mere transfer of political power: it urgently requires a change in memory regime. The first step would be to "victimize" victimhood nationalism.

The most stunning move in victimhood nationalism is the magical metamorphosis of the individual perpetrator into the collective victim. This metamorphosis exonerates individual perpetrators from their crimes. The self-exonerations over time of the Laudański brothers across different political regimes provide a vivid example. As the only living people convicted for the genocide in Jedwabne, they cast themselves as "victims of fascism, of capitalism, of the prewar authoritarian *Sanacja* regime" in the era of communist Poland. After the fall, Stalinism and People's Poland replaced capitalism and the *Sanacja* regime in the Laudański brothers' memories. Even as their alleged perpetrators changed, they honed their status as victims: "like the whole nation we suffered under the Germans, the Soviets, and the People's Poland."[7] Perpetrators turned themselves into collective victims by hiding behind the memory of national victimhood. What underlies this metamorphosis is the obsession with national victimhood in Polish memory, which allows individual perpetrators of the victimized nation to cover up their crimes unjustifiably.[8]

Victimhood nationalism has the sacralization of memories as its epistemological mainstay. Sacralized memories can block the skeptical and critical gaze of the outsiders on "our unique past." A certain degree of sacralization of memory is perhaps inevitable at the individual level, since our personal memory in the deepest sense is intimate and incommensurable with others' experiences. However, a national memory comes into being only when personal memories are shared to some extent through communication, education, commemoration, rituals, and ceremonies en masse. An individual memory thus evoked tends to become fixed in collective memory, which installs itself in the place of personal raw memories.[9] Collective memory should theoretically not be able to be sacralized as it is formed from the social and cultural communication of personal memories. Yet its paradox demonstrates that the properties of a collective can differ from the properties of an individual. Although every individual experience is unique and cannot be fully transferred, "untransferable collective memory" is a contradiction in terms.

Epistemologically, sacralization contributes to the contestation of victimhood nationalism. What politics underlay the discourses of sacralizing victimhood nationalism? The everyday cliché of "you foreigners can never understand our own tragic national past" protects victimhood nationalism against historical scrutiny. By not allowing any comparison, through which outsiders can understand "our unique past," sacralized memories keep a national monopoly on "our own past." Nationalists fashion a mental enclave in this secret past where they can enjoy a morally comfortable position, very often disregarding that the heirs of historical victims have become today's perpetrators. Comparative analysis, in contrast, opens sacralized memories to dialogue with others. In these interactions, seemingly impervious victimhood nationalism can melt away.

Along with the task of desacralizing national memories, analyzing the transnationality of victimhood nationalism demands a multilayered *histoire croisée* approach to comprehend the entangled pasts of the victimized and victimizers. For instance, victimhood nationalism in Poland, Israel, and Korea should be examined with a focus on the interplay with the victimhood nationalism of their perpetrators in Nazi Germany and imperial Japan. Tropes of victimhood nationalism are surprisingly rampant in the vernacular (and official) memories of postwar Germany and Japan; the continuing presence of these tropes in turn justifies and amplifies the victimhood nationalism in Poland, Israel, and Korea. The antagonistic complicity of nationalisms regulates the contour of the transnational memories in the Global East, which further nourishes victimhood nationalism.[10] Of course, the asymmetry of victimhood exists between colonizers and colonized, and between perpetrators and victims, but the asymmetry of their historical positions should not excuse the vicious circle of victimhood nationalisms.

That asymmetry manifests itself in a distinction between the overcontextualization and decontextualization of the past. Victimhood nationalism in underprivileged nations tends to historically overcontextualize their victimhood, which provides them with layers of historical facticity that create a shield memory to deflect from their own wrongdoings and helps to cement their morally comfortable position as a "forever" victim. Individual murderers such as Laudański brothers in Jedwabne could remain victims by overcontextualizing the national victimhood. In contrast, victimhood nationalism among the hegemonic nations is inclined to decontextualize its victimhood from history, to decouple it from the long arm of history, in order to ignore its past crimes. If overcontextualization negates the coexistence of perpetrators, victims, and bystanders within the same nation, decontextualization conceals the past of perpetrators who subsequently became victims under peculiar circumstances of armed retaliation and bloody revenge. In the Polish debates on Jedwabne, Israelis' memory of the Holocaust, and Korean discourses of comfort women, we see the impetus to overcontextualize; in the remembrances of expulsion, repatriation, POWs, Allied bombings, and the A-bombs in the postwar Germany and Japan, we see the inclination to decontextualize.

My goal here is not to re-create a binary of victimizing and victimized nation. By drawing on examples from Poland, Germany, Israel, Japan, and Korea, I want to highlight the transnationality of victimhood nationalism. A multilayered *histoire croisée* reveals blurred complexities of historical reality: a hybridity of plural and contradictory memories at many levels of vernacular, official, personal, and meta-memories among the victimizers and victims, delicate tensions between transitional justices and "liminal justices," victimizers' self-perception as victims, personal victims victimized by the more abstract national victimhood, and the shifting division between victimizers and victims.[11] How do we find a way to dismantle victimhood nationalism in the memory wars of the Global East?

Hereditary Victimhood: Korea, Israel, and Poland

In January 2007 Yoko Kawashima Watkins's autobiographical novella *So Far from the Bamboo Grove* roiled Korean mass media and intellectual circles.[12] Major newspapers in Korea covered this novella for more than a month. In this bildungsroman, the narrator, an eleven-year-old Japanese girl, detailed how her family was faced with threats to their lives, hunger, and fear of sexual assault on their way home to Japan from Nanam, a northern town in Korea, after Japan's defeat in World War II. About 2.27 million Japanese civilian expellees from Manchuria and northern Korea are said to have encountered a similar fate during their repatriation journeys, in an East Asian version of the East European *wypędzenie-Vertreibung* (explusion of Germans from formerly German eastern provinces).[13] In postwar Japan, a wealth of stories about the ordeals of these expellees formed a distinct genre called *hikiage-monogatari*. *So Far from the Bamboo Grove* was not the first piece of Japanese *hikiage* literature translated into Korean. During the Korean Civil War in 1951, a *hikiage* story by Fujiwara Tei, *Nagareru hoshi wa ikite iru* 流れる星は生きている (1949), was translated into Korean, and it has become one of the fifty bestselling books in Korea since 1945.[14] Perhaps it appealed dramatically to Koreans who were suffering from the civil war at the time.[15] Especially Korean War refugees who crossed the border between North and South Korea shared the memory of anxiety and suffering with the Japanese expellees escaping from Manchuria and North Korea under the Soviet occupation.

Translated into Korean in 2005, *So Far from the Bamboo Grove* initially enjoyed a positive, though overall lukewarm, response from the Korean mass media. Media reviewers gave a half-hearted welcome to the Korean translation. On May 13, 2005, the Korean news agency *Yonhap News* reviewed it as "an autobiographical novella that describes the story of Japanese expellees upon Japan's defeat." A book review in the most popular conservative Korean daily newspaper, *Chosun ilbo*, from May 6 reads: "Apart from the nationality of the author, the book can be evaluated as a bildungsroman that calmly describes how the war can be an ordeal for a whole family." These early book reviews suggest that the novella made a positive, if shallow, impression on journalists of the cultural section. In its first year and a half of publication, about three thousand copies were sold, suggesting a sleepy reception in the Korean book market. On January 18,

2007, almost a year and a half after its Korean debut, the novella became caught in the cross-fire of four major Korean newspapers and one news agency, which was followed by an avalanche of attacks on social media.[16] The social pressure was so enormous that the Korean publisher Munhak-dongne, after trying to defend the book in vain, quickly withdrew all copies from bookstores.

It is almost impossible not to suspect some orchestration in this simultaneous fusillade by both the major liberal and conservative print media outlets. On January 16, 2007, the Korean consul in Boston sent a protest letter to the Massachusetts Department of Education. Surprisingly, there was no time lag between the Korean consul's protest in Boston and mass media coverage of *So Far from the Bamboo Grove* in Seoul. According to an article in the *Boston Globe*, the central complaint was that the novella describes Koreans as evil perpetrators and the Japanese as innocent victims.[17] The Korean consul expressed her deep concern that young Americans would be led to believe a "distorted" and "faked" history of East Asia if they read *So Far from the Bamboo Grove* in schools.[18] An archaeological excavation of this uproar reveals a group, Parents for an Accurate Asian History Education (PAAHE), behind this tsunami of long-distance nationalism.

Comprising Korean Americans in the New York City and Greater Boston area, including many well-educated medical doctors and lawyers, PAAHE initiated the trans-Pacific criticism of *So Far from the Bamboo Grove* on January 18, 2007. They were furious that Watkins, widely read in American schools, portrays Koreans as evil perpetrators and Japanese as innocent victims to American students who are otherwise taught little about East Asian history. Their criticism was framed mainly in positivistic terms. PAAHE sought an "accurate Asian history" whose clear-cut contours do not allow complexity and ambiguity. Expressions like "distortion of truth," "fabrication of facts," and "historical lies" dominated their claims. The PAAHE initiative turned the gaze of the Korean press to *So Far from the Bamboo Grove* in January 2007. As those Korean Americans' criticism crossed the Pacific to Korea, the accusations snowballed. A rumor that Watkins's father was a Japanese war criminal, presumably an officer of Unit 731, infamous for its "crime against humanity" level of biowarfare experiments, circulated on social media. Despite PAAHE's obsession with an "accurate" history, their suspicion that Watkins is the daughter of a Japanese war criminal has yet to be proven. It doesn't matter if this is true or not:

suspicion itself is enough to discredit Watkins's story. The insinuation alone conveyed that she could not be an innocent victim.[19]

PAAHE's positivistic criticism of Watkins's *hikiage-monogatari* reflects a naïveté in understanding history. What matters in this transpacific history disturbance is not Asian history, but memory manipulated to upset the balance among the ethnic politics and relationships among Asian Americans. The reversal of the roles of victims and victimizers between Koreans and Japanese most upset the PAAHE members. In their schematic dichotomy of collective guilt and innocence, the Japanese should only be understood as a uniform mass of victimizers. The bitter experience of individual Japanese expellees cannot exist in a vision where the entire Japanese nation is one solely of perpetrators. That schematic memory is central to the nostalgic ethnic self-identity of these Korean Americans.[20] Even more significant is the inherent ethnocentrism expressed through Korean Americans' parental concern for their kids. In a private email excoriating my column on victimhood nationalism in the *Korea Herald*, the English-language Korean newspaper, a PAAHE activist expressed her grave concern that as long as *So Far from the Bamboo Grove* is on school reading lists, Korean American kids will be subject to bullying.

By detaching her story from Japanese colonialism, Watkins may lead Western readers ignorant of East Asian history to understand grassroots revenge or retribution by colonized Koreans as wanton disregard for human dignity and life. Consequently, her novella contrasts Koreans as evil perpetrators with Japanese as innocent victims. Anyone reading the novella would believe that Koreans are cruel and terrible perpetrators who threaten to rape young and innocent Japanese girls. It is likely the American public's ignorance of the history and the suffering of people in East Asia, in contrast to Jewish suffering in the Holocaust, has complicated matters.[21] Entangled memories of war and colonialism in the trans-Asian/Pacific space, not confined to national binaries, could have counterbalanced this naïve decontextualization of history. PAAHE's criticism could have targeted the Eurocentrism in American history education and research. Instead, PAAHE held firm to the schematic dichotomy between Japanese victimizers and Korean victims. Their reasoning, part and parcel of the paradigm of collective guilt, shows how they remain caught in the hegemonic ethnic nationalism of Korea, even as Korea has come to be a multinational and multicultural country long after their emigration. The role of ethnocentrism in the emigrants' long-distance nationalism is stronger than its role in nationalism in Korea itself.

This farcical tumult vividly exemplifies how long-distance nationalism in a diaspora community can promote victimhood nationalism in the home country. Indeed, victimhood comes into relief in the transnational context. What is more, the transnationality of victimhood nationalism regarding Watkins's novella is frequently witnessed on another level, namely, in the frequent emphasis on the historical parallelism between Jews and Koreans as victims. One review of *So Far from the Bamboo Grove* by a Korean American customer on Amazon.com reads: "It is completely distorting the truth about the Japanese WW2 aggressions and atrocities. It makes as if atrocities were committed by the victims rather than the aggressor. . . . If Anne Frank were a German and she were still alive to this day and if she wrote about the mindless rapes committed by Jewish resistance fighters and Jewish American soldiers after WW2 and no mention was made about the Holocaust during WW2. Wouldn't you think that is a DISTORTION of history?" Another customer review reads similarly: "This book is akin to an escape narrative of an SS officer's family running away from Birkenau Auschwitz concentration camp while the heroin [*sic*] daughter of the Nazi officer is running away from cruel and dangerous Jews freed from concentration camps and Poles. Such a narrative is morally irresponsible and disgusting material to force upon innocent children." Those deeply negative book reviews conclude that "this pro-Nazi book must be eradicated from the reading list."[22]

These customer reviews criticize the forgetting and decontextualization of colonial history in the novella of Yoko Kawashima Watkins. If decontextualization is Watkins's narrative strategy, overcontextualization is the counternarrative of victimhood nationalism in Korea. The cited customer reviews show how victimhood nationalism works in the transpacific memory space. Nationalism is peculiarly transnational because nationalist imagination comes into effect, mirroring others. Victimhood nationalism is no exception. One can also note the novella *Year of Impossible Goodbyes* (1991), written by a Korean American writer, Sook Nyul Choi, as an enraged nationalist response against *So Far from the Bamboo Grove* (1986). Choi's novella brings some "poignant, vivid moments" to remind readers of the brutality of the Japanese colonial rule, but it lacks the pacing and power of the Watkins's novella.[23] Choi's novella also did not overcome the nationalist binary by forcing readers to recognize only the Japanese brutality and Korean suffering. In alternative readings, for example, a postcolonial feminist one would point out the narrative of empire appropriating women, family image, and even nostalgia for childhood in *So Far from Bamboo Grove*.[24]

A transnational perspective reveals that the Korean media's angry criticism made *So Far from the Bamboo Grove* even more appealing to Japanese readers. In the rich and thick list of the *hikiage-monogatari* in postwar Japan, Watkins's memoir would not have stood out without the nationalist provocation from the Korean media. When its Japanese translation was published later in 2013, it drew the unduly anxious attention of the Japanese readership. Amazon.co.jp shows that, among 298 ratings, five stars represent 83 percent of scores, and four stars represent 10 percent. Watkins's book enjoys an exceptionally high average rating of 4.7 out of 5 stars, in stark contrast with the low rating of 2.7 stars on average given to the Japanese version of Irish Chang's *The Rape of Nanking*. The "customers who bought this item also bought" information reveals that Japanese readers who bought *So Far from the Bamboo Grove* also bought books by deniers of the comfort women and other Japanese war and colonial atrocities, alongside other *hikiage* books. Broadening the search into "customers who checked this item also checked . . ." reveals numerous denialist books written by Japanese, Zainichi (Korean Japanese), and Koreans.[25]

The deployment of the historical parallelism between Jews and Koreans in customer book reviews needs to be explored further. On the surface, invoking the Holocaust seems a narrative tactic to convince American readers with much better knowledge of European history that the victims are not Japanese but Koreans. The historical parallelism between Jews and Koreans is hardly new, as it was commonly used in Korean nationalist discourse throughout the 1960s and 1970s. However, the discourse focused on Jewish heroism, not victimhood. In the era of development dictatorship under Park Chung-hee, Israelis' Zionism provided a role model for Koreans. The impressive victory of Israel in the Six-Day War, supposedly unexpected, was hailed as a victory of patriotism among young Israelis. Newspapers published never-ending series of extraordinary stories of American Jews who volunteered for Israel's army at the cost of comfortable lives, and honeymooners who canceled their honeymoon to return to the battlefront. They were seen as self-sacrificing heroes rather than passive victims.

Immediately after the military coup in 1962, Park paid a visit to the Canaan Commonwealth, founded by a Presbyterian elder, and had a simple lunch of bread and jam with *kŏnkookcha* (tea of state-building). A few months after Park's visit to Canaan, the "Rural Pioneer Battalion," composed of university students, was founded, with the Israeli Kibbutz as a role model. More precisely, it was a combination of the Israeli Kibbutz and the Pioneer Youth Corps of Manchuria and Mongolia in the Japanese Empire. The Israeli government donated a thousand U.S. dollars for the "National Movement for the Reconstruction" to translate the Kibbutz guide into Korean. Under the development dictatorship, leaders of the New Village Movement and "industrial warriors" were trained regularly at a collective farm named Canaan. Later, this pioneering agrarian farm became the Canaan Farmhand School and educated the first generation of New Village Movement leaders in the high mass dictatorship. Thus the Canaan Farmhand School met Park's expectation for Canaan to bring about the anthropological revolution necessary to transform South Korea. Park Chung-hee's regime justified the self-mobilization system of mass dictatorship in South Korea by modeling it on Israel.[26]

Contrary to common belief, heroism, not victimhood, has dominated postwar Jewish public memory from its inception. Werner Weinberg, whose identity drifted away from a liberated prisoner to a displaced person to a survivor, writes that survivors, including himself, appeared to fellow Israelis as "a museum piece, a fossil, a freak, a ghost."[27] After his visit to the displaced persons (DP) camps in Germany in the fall of 1945, David Shaltiel, Ben Gurion's envoy to Western Europe, said bluntly, "Those who survived did so because they were egoistical and cared primarily about themselves."[28] The slanderous belief of the "survival of the worst," though faded with time, was widespread among worldwide Jewry immediately after the war. Victims were victimized once again by their compatriots. Referred to as "factor" or a "human resource," Holocaust survivors were objectified and instrumentalized in the Zionist discourse. *Yishuv* heroes were immortalized in the Zionist literature of Exodus, while Jewish refugees bore the burden of the clandestine immigration campaign.[29] Zionist Palestine's discourse about Diaspora Jews was suffused with a patronizing rhetoric of pity. A love sermon to the incoming Jewish refugees, "My Sister on the

Beach," by Yitzhak Sadeh, the first commander of the legendary Palmach, tells a story of "male power . . . in the strong, rooted, and brave Israeli Zionism facing a defeated, despairing Diaspora longing to die."[30] Central to this dichotomy of Hebrew heroism in Eretz Israel versus Jewish humiliation in exile was "a sexist reconstruction of history" that feminized the survivors.[31] Survivors remained passive and deprived of agency.

Masculine war heroes often evoked ideals of American Jewry, too. Being victors rather than victims was a cultural code shared widely by American Jewry. American Jews joined the postwar victory celebration, and the Holocaust was not welcome at this celebration.[32] Toward the end of World War II, John Slawson, chief executive of the American Jewish Committee, said explicitly that Jewish organizations "should avoid representing the Jew as weak, victimized, and suffering. . . . There needs to be an elimination or at least a reduction of horror stories of victimized Jewry. . . . War hero stories are excellent."[33] Compared to today's exceptionalist discourse on the Holocaust, it is a striking contrast that leaders of the Anti-Defamation League (ADL) were critical of an ADL film, *The Anatomy of Nazism*, for its overly narrow focus on Jewish suffering.[34] The hero cult in the aftermath of World War II was dominant.

The Cold War inclined the American Jewry toward relative indifference to the Holocaust. Under the pressure of the Cold War, it was more urgent for Jewish organizations in the United States to combat the claims of a broader Jewish-communist connection. Insofar as policy makers in Washington were concerned, with Germany as an essential bulwark against Bolshevism, American Jews were encouraged to hold a realist rather than a punitive and recriminatory attitude toward West Germany. The emphasis was put on Soviet anti-Semitism instead of the Holocaust. The Šlanský trial and the ensuing purge of Jewish communist veterans in Czechoslovakia were deemed to dissociate Jews from communism in the American public mind.[35] The realist attitude of American Jewry about Germans echoed Ben Gurion's calculation that Israel needed to stay close to France and Germany in order to join the "Western" camp. Under these circumstances, "an acute awareness of the Holocaust was not part of the American Jewish experience during the first two decades after the war."[36]

As long as this "historiographical triumphalism" dominated the historical discourse in Israel, the Holocaust was not a popular theme for the national remembrance.[37] When it was remembered in Israel, it was structured by the dualism of focusing on the activist ghetto fighters and questioning Jewish leadership in the ghettoes. Only in 1959 did observation of Holocaust Remembrance Day became mandatory in Israel. Even then, Holocaust commemoration kept its focus on heroic fighters in the Ghetto Uprisings; official references were made to "the Holocaust and the Ghetto Uprisings," "the Holocaust and Heroism," or "Martyrs' and Heroes' Remembrance." While the Ghetto fighters were addressed as "Zionist" or "Hebrew youth," other Holocaust victims were referred to as "Jews." Israeli youth often accused the Jewish victims' behavior as "going like sheep to the slaughter."[38] Historiographical heroism glorified the Masada fighters as ancient Hebrew warriors of national liberation in ancient Rome—a countermodel in opposition to Holocaust victims.[39] Michel Warschawski remembers Israel of the 1960s, where weakness was considered a flaw, and a "savonette" (little soap) was the designated term for a person who was not tough enough.[40]

The Eichmann trial and the Frankfurt Auschwitz trials in the early 1960s marked a turn to victimhood in the collective memory of the Holocaust. With the trial, "a process of identification with the suffering of victims and survivors" occurred among Israelis.[41] Awakened by the 1959 riot of Sephardic Jews, mostly immigrants from Morocco, Israeli leaders badly needed a patriotic national catharsis for national unity. When the hegemony of the Ashkenazic establishment was threatened, the Eichmann trial was used to educate these Sephardic Jews on what happened to Askenazi Jews in the Holocaust. The Six-Day War of 1967 intensified victimhood nationalism. A young soldier's recollection of the war indicates that "people believed we would be exterminated if we lost the war. We got this idea—or inherited it—from the concentration camp. It's a concrete idea for anyone who has grown up in Israel. . . . Genocide—it's a real possibility."[42] By 1992 close to 80 percent of teachers college students in Israel associated Israeli identity with "Holocaust survivors."[43]

Victimhood became hereditary, but victimhood nationalism did not erase Yishuv heroism and the victor's national pride. Victimhood nationalism linked the righteousness of David, fighting against all the Goliaths of human history, to omnipotence and invincibility. Thus they were integrated into a vision of a Yishuvist and Shoah-centric narrative. In this self-contradictory narrative, victimhood nationalism did not necessarily reference real victims. What is at issue is not the agony and anguish of real victims but the idea of victimhood in the abstract. Deployed at a national scale, the victimhood cult went together with the forgetting of the real biographical details of Holocaust victims, who were largely highly assimilated Jews in prewar Europe. The Holocaust, a catastrophe for the assimilationists, was used to justify Zionist desire for an independent state for Jews. The defeat of assimilationism contributed to an ethnocentric perception of nation and history in Israel.[44]

The uniqueness discourse of the Holocaust reinforced the ethnocentric nationalism of the righteous victims and shields them from critical scrutiny. To Ben Gurion, the Holocaust was "a unique episode that has no equal . . . has no parallel in human history." Universalizing the Holocaust would be equivalent to plundering the "moral capital" that Jews accumulated. Menachem Begin responded to the international criticism of Israel's invasion of Lebanon with Holocaust discourse: "After the Holocaust, the international community had lost its right to demand that Israel answer for its actions."[45] Beyond any doubt, the Holocaust is, in many crucial aspects, an unparalleled or singular event. But this does not mean it is unique and cannot be subject to comparative analysis.[46] Apart from Ernst Nolte's problematic juxtaposition of Nazism with Stalinism in the German *Historikerstreit* in 1986–1987, a critical relativization of the Holocaust by the historical parallel of the colonial genocide is crucial to cosmopolitanizing the Holocaust in the global memory space.

Victimhood nationalism cannot exist without opposing forces. Just as victimhood nationalism has been nourished by the antagonistic complicity of nationalisms in East Asia, anti-Semitism has fed victimhood nationalism in Israel. Golda Meir said at the beginning of the 1970s: "Too much anti-Semitism is not good because it leads to genocide; no anti-Semitism at all is also not good because then there would be no immigration (to Israel). What we need is a moderate anti-Semitism."[47] The Jewish stereotype of Polish anti-Semitism that "Poles sucked anti-Semitism with their mothers' milk" evokes the Polish stereotype of Żydokomuna (Judeo-communism), which justifies Polish anti-Semitism. The Polish self-image of the "crucified nation" as the eternal victim of neighbors to the East and West cannot accept the image of themselves as bystanders, let alone perpetrators. The Laudański brothers, victimizers of their Jewish neighbors in Jedwabne, defined themselves as victims by cloaking themselves in the collective memory of victimhood in Poland.

A poll from early April 2001 shows that 48 percent of surveyed Poles did not believe that Poles should apologize to the Jewish nation for Jedwabne, while 30 percent stood for the apology. Some 80 percent did not feel any moral responsibility for Jedwabne, while only 13 percent felt such a responsibility. And 34 percent believed that the Germans were solely responsible for the crime, 14 percent that Germans and Poles were jointly responsible, and 7 percent that Poles were solely responsible. Public opinion did not shift even after the publication of the report of the Instytut Pamięci Narodowej (IPN), which included evidence of the Polish role in the Jedwabne massacre.[48] Jan Gross gingerly describes the dominating debate in Poland on Jedwabne: "an outpouring of thoughtful and searching articles about the need to rewrite Poland's twentieth-century history; about facing up to the larger consequences of anti-Semitism that gave rise also to complicity with Nazi crimes against Jewish neighbors; about the responsibility for misdeeds so difficult to contemplate in a community that was itself victimized by outside oppressors."[49] And yet one cannot fail to detect the Poles' perplexity at finding themselves not victims but victimizers. Poland was by some measures the most heavily devastated country of World War II. It lost more than about five million inhabitants, including three million Polish Jews, which amounts to more than 20 percent of the total population. Elites suffered most. Less than half of its lawyers survived the war. Poland lost two-fifths of its medical doctors and one-third of its university professors and Roman Catholic clergy.

As Rabbi Byron L. Sherwin declared, "The tendency among Jews to stereotype Poles as the perpetrators of the Holocaust not only distorts but obscures the enormous suffering of Poles during the Nazi occupation."[50] It would be much worse to shift the overwhelming responsibility for the genocide away from the Nazis by emphasizing the secondary responsibility and complicity of Poles. Criticizing Jewish stereotypes about Polish anti-Semitism should not automatically justify the Polish obsession with their innocence and propel victimhood nationalism in Poland, in which Auschwitz is cast as a place primarily of Polish martyrdom. The "anti-Semitism without Jews" in today's Poland, though not dominant, should not be ignored either.[51] The Communist Party shared the Polish nationalists' dream of an ethnically pure state, and the nationalist vision that dominated the official party historiography. In a way, the socialist ideal of the ethical and political unity of society reinforced the primordialist concept of the nation, a way of seeing the nation as an organic community and even as a family community.[52] This nationalist narrative has led World War II to be remembered in the Polish memory as a matter between Poles and Germans, with the Jews marginalized.[53] The era of Stalinism repressed and marginalized the memory of the Holocaust since it did not fit Soviet narratives of the anti-Fascist front of the working class and the Great Patriotic War.[54] To cite Michael Steinlauf: "In the essential communist narrative, the Holocaust became an object lesson in the horrors of the last stage of monopoly capitalism.... The site of Auschwitz-Birkenau became a monument to internationalism and commemorated the resistance and martyrdom of 'Poles and other nationalities,' among whom, alphabetically and therefore 'democratically,' Żydzi (Jews) came last."[55]

With the rise of the national communist faction, the genocide of Polish Jews was integrated into the ethnic Polish tragedy. The widely held historical statement that "six million Poles died during the war" promoted the victimhood fantasy that Poles had suffered the most. Jews were integrated into the Polish nation only in the politics of counting victims of Polish citizenship. The Holocaust has even been interpreted as a German-Jewish conspiracy against Poles as an effort to minimize Polish wartime martyrdom and suffering. The Moczar-led "Partisans" launched an attack on *Wielka Encyklopedia Powszechna* (Great universal encyclopedia) in 1967. The division of "concentration camp" (*obozy koncentracyjne*) and "extermination camp" (*obozy zagłady*) in the encyclopedia was criticized as a bias against Polish martyrdom in favor of the suffering of Jews. The exile of the Jewish editor to Sweden was followed by an anti-Zionist campaign in 1968. In the public memory fabricated by the party, Poles were sentenced to annihilation by the Nazis whereas the Jews were relocated. The Warsaw Ghetto Uprising was "a specific kind of fighting of the Polish underground."[56] Witold Kula, a prominent Polish economic historian, remarked sarcastically that Jews are envied because of the crematoria in which they were burned.[57]

Jan Błoński's essay "Biedny polacy patrzą na getto" (Poor Poles look at the ghetto) (1987) brought the repressed memory of the Holocaust to the surface in public memory. Błoński's seminal essay raised the argument not about culpability for what Poles did, but about sins of what they failed to do.[58] It elevated the Polish discussion on the Holocaust beyond legal positivism to ontological ethics. The debate revealed a deep trauma in those

Poles who felt guilty for being helpless bystanders to atrocity. Błoński's eye-opening essay was followed by Jan Gross's book *Sąsiedzi* (*Neighbors*). In the words of Hanna Świda-Ziemba, Jedwabne teaches that "only a thin layer of ice separates innocent prejudices from crime."[59] Despite Gross's unperturbed appreciation of the Polish response to his book, large numbers of Poles were reluctant to admit guilt. To Cardinal Józef Glemp, the primate of Poland, Gross's book was written by commission. In his opinion, Jews were disliked for "their pro-Bolshevik attitude and odd folk customs."[60] The Jedwabne mayor was unable to persuade the townspeople to name the local school after Antonina Wyrzykowska, who rescued seven Jews during the massacre. Stanisław Stefanek, the bishop of Łomża, spoke of an organized campaign by the Jews to extract money from the Poles.

The exculpatory memory of Polish collective victimhood could not accommodate the metamorphosis from innocent Polish victims to the *Homo Jedvanecus*. *Sąsiedzi* received an uncannily similar reception to that for Watkins's book among the Korean audience. Paradoxically enough, Poland suffered the consequences of not having had a Quisling-like collaborationist puppet regime during the Nazi occupation. If it had, anti-Semitism would have remained as a part of a compromised collaborationism.[61] A clean Poland left no room for guilt about the Holocaust, and anti-Semitism remained a staple of patriotism under communism. That complexity is rooted in "a singularly Polish paradox" exemplified by Adam Michnik, where a person could be an anti-Semite, a hero of the resistance, and a savior of Jews since the Polish nationalistic and anti-Semitic right did not collaborate with the Nazis.[62] When the news of the Kielce pogrom spread in 1946, Polish workers were unwilling to condemn its perpetrators publicly and opposed an antipogrom resolution. The Polish Workers' Party (Polska Partia Robotnicza, PPR) had difficulty selling antipogrom propaganda, and workers perceived the PPR as "Jewish" in its opposition to the workers' sentiments.[63]

Victimhood nationalism forces the process of coming to terms with the past into an either/or binary: victims or victimizers. The fury of some Poles against Jan Błoński and Jan Gross echoes Korean Americans' anger against Yoko Kawashima Watkins's *hikiage-monogatari*. Positivistic objections like "a novel with footnotes," "lacking objectivity," "undocumented facts," "made-up lies," and "gross misinterpretation" dominated the immediate response. One customer reviewer was frightened that Gross's book was placed in nonfiction instead of fiction.[64] The Polish self-conception of the "crucified nation," as the eternal victim of its neighbors to the East and West, excludes seeing themselves as bystanders, let alone victimizers. Stressing complexity and ambiguity, these authors disrupt the comfortable dichotomy of innocent victims and evil victimizers. The deployment of historical myths, the making of historical fantasy, are crucial factors in the creation of a nation, which is why more rigorous historical studies often threaten the principle of nationality. To put this fantasy of "hereditary victimhood" under historical scrutiny, to study those victims' complicity and implication in the Holocaust, remained, remains, and will remain blasphemy to some. Europeanization in postcommunist Poland was political and equally cultural transformation. This cultural Europeanization meant locating the local and national memories of Eastern Europe within European memory space, where the Holocaust has become the core issue.[65]

Exculpatory Victimhood: Japan and Germany

A bitter irony in remembering the Second World War in the global memory space is that perpetrators became self-identified victims post facto. In 1950 Hannah Arendt reported on "a deluge of stories about how Germans have suffered" and a delusive emotional analogy of "the expulsion of Adam and Eve from Paradise."[66] Many perpetrators among the *kleine Leute* perceived themselves as victims, explaining apologetically that they were forced to commit crimes. Given the substantial degree of popular backing, self-mobilization, consent from below, and plebiscitary acclamation enjoyed by the regime, people were indeed very likely to be "victims" of their own complicity. Rank-and-file perpetrators alleged they were in the wrong place at the wrong time. Some of them asserted they never fired a shot. Others acknowledged they did, but they claimed implausibly that they were blameless instruments of the alien will of overwhelming power. Like Adolph Eichmann, many a middle-ranking desk murderer claimed, when challenged, that he or she had never pulled the trigger, never killed, never slapped a victim, and even never been an anti-Semite. In a travesty of Kant's categorical imperative, Eichmann claimed that, as a loyal civil servant, he was obeying not only orders but also the law.

What is the secret in the alchemy of turning everyday perpetrators into victims? How was this mnemonic magic possible? Where have all the perpetrators gone if all are victims? Is it possible to imagine a world consisting solely of victims without victimizers? How can we position the individual victimizer within the collective (self-asserted *or* externally acknowledged) of a victimized nation, class, gender, or race? Conversely, by what standard might we discern an individual victim among the collective victimizers? Who bears responsibility for what happened? Is it possible for the same person to be simultaneously victim and victimizer? Where is the dividing line between victims and victimizers? What if the dividing line runs through each individual? Is it the only victimizer's half in each individual who is responsible? What about the other victimized half in each individual? How can we settle the relationship between the victim and victimizer within one individual or any single collective?

The cliché that victimizers also suffer from war is at best a pat answer. Immediately after the Second World War, the Japanese, Germans, and Italians were mourning defeat and suffering, while their victims of wars of aggression, massacres, and genocide were celebrating the liberation and war victory. Paradoxically, victimizers had a more urgent need to explore the experience of being victimized, as it potentially would exonerate them for their crimes. For instance, Japanese atrocities committed against the POWs of the Western Allies were thought to be counterbalanced by the suffering and massive death of Japanese POWs in the Siberian gulags. Emphasizing the killing of German civilians in Allied bombings and the suffering of German expellees from the East seems an attempt at self-exculpation to countervail Germans' culpability. Guilt and victimhood are inherently asymmetrical. Victimhood nationalism among perpetrators accordingly requires more sophisticated and pedantic arguments. Real victims do not need to vindicate their victimhood by using Kant's categorical imperative, as Eichmann tried.[67] Victimhood nationalism doth protest too much.

Japan, as "the only nation ever atom-bombed (*yuiitsu no hibakukoku*)," could secure a privileged position in the competition for victimhood. Decontextualized from the history of the fifteen years of the Sino-Japanese and Asia-Pacific war, the catch phrase *yuiitsu no hibakukoku* is replete with the single-minded assertion that the Japanese were the victims of the atomic bomb.[68] Various American writers' remarks on "Auschwitz and Hiroshima as terrible twin symbols of manmade mass death," especially after the Soviet Union's acquisition of the first nuclear weapon, seemed to manifest Japanese victimhood.[69] Radhabinod Pal, the Indian judge at the Tokyo trial, confirmed Japanese victimhood by suggesting that the American use of the atomic bomb was the closest counterpart to Nazi atrocities in the war.[70] In the public memory of postwar Japan, however, Japanese military leaders victimized innocent Japanese even before the A-bomb. Fire bombings, hunger, the repatriation of Japanese civilians from Manchuria and Korea, and military oppression on the home front have all been used to substantiate Japanese victimhood. John Dower explains, "It became commonplace to speak of the war dead themselves—and indeed, of virtually all ordinary Japanese—as being victims and sacrifices."[71]

The public memory of war to mythicize ordinary Japanese as innocent victims of a system rather than as accomplices of war atrocities was not only self-generated. The Supreme Command of the Allied Powers (SCAP) encouraged this morally comfortable tale from another direction. SCAP worked under the assumption that the Japanese people had been slaves of feudal habits of subservience to authority. A secret report by the Psychological Warfare Branch of the U.S. Army reads: "The Japanese personally have contributed their full measure to the war effort and fulfilled their obligation to the Emperor. All their effort is to no avail because their military leaders have betrayed them. The people are not to be blamed for their suffering. . . . The military clique has practiced false indoctrination."[72] With this patronizing approach to the Japanese people, SCAP exempted ordinary Japanese from war responsibility and guilt. This discursive amnesty was paid for by dismissing the agency of average Japanese. Ordinary Japanese became passive subjects, blindly loyal to authority, and thus innocent of the nation's various transgressions done in their names and with their participation. Victims, deprived of agency, cannot be held accountable for the misuse of power. Both left-wing activists and right-wing politicians appropriated Japanese victimhood for their own purposes. They could either blame the Cold War U.S.-Japan security alliance or detach themselves from the legacy of militarism and war responsibility.[73]

The term "Pacific War," imposed by SCAP, was another deliberate conceptual tool to dismiss Japanese war responsibility to its Asian neighbors. SCAP substituted the "Pacific War" for the "Great East Asia War," which paired with the "Great East Asia Co-Prosperity Zone," the Japanese total war system coined to legitimize Japanese invasion of its Asian neighbors.

With its focus on the conflict between America and Japan, the term "Pacific War" downplayed Japanese military aggression against its Asian neighbors. "Pacific War" emphasized Japanese attacks against Americans or Europeans, including the maltreatment of Allied POWs. By omitting Asia in the Asia-Pacific War, Japanese military transgressions such as Unit 731's biological warfare, forced labor mobilization through Asia, comfort women, and other violations of human rights in Asia fell into oblivion. This shift explains partly why "the Japanese people don't have much consciousness of having invaded China and have a tendency to emphasize only the suffering they bore in the Pacific War."[74] Without a doubt, exculpating the Japanese people from a sense of war guilt contributed to building victimhood nationalism in postwar Japan.

It was in antinuclear pacifism that Japanese war victimhood was most easily detached from Japanese wartime atrocities. Japan's exceptionalism as "the only nation ever atom-bombed" decontextualized this traumatic tragedy from its historical background. Hiroshima and Nagasaki epitomized all the anguish and agony that Japanese people suffered. Hiroshima, as an absolute evil, was often compared with the Holocaust. A popular novella singled out the Japanese and Jews as the archetypal victims of white racism.[75] SCAP censorship had repressed the public memory of the atomic bombing of Hiroshima and Nagasaki. By the early 1950s the bombings were treated more or less as an unexpected natural disaster. Only through the Lucky Dragon Incident on March 1, 1954, did atomic bomb victimhood develop into victimhood nationalism, under a pacifist umbrella. Thus "Hiroshima became an icon of Japan's past as an innocent war victim and a beacon for its future as a pacifist nation."[76] The antiwar pacificist movement generated a collective memory that provide a fertile cultural matrix for the victimhood genre of *hikiage-mono*. In the historically structured complicity of antagonistic nationalisms in East Asia, Japan's preoccupation with atomic bomb victimhood spurred on victimhood nationalism in Korea. "A distasteful competition over who suffered most" became inevitable in East Asia, too.

Although the victimhood memory generally came to the forefront over Japanese wartime aggression, even the remembrances of more conventional Japanese war atrocities seemed relatively insignificant compared to the apocalyptic hell of atomic destruction. The story of the aesthetic origins of the Hiroshima Peace Memorial Park is intriguing in this respect.

The design for the park, selected through a public competition in 1949, has a nearly identical ground plan to the Commemorative Building Project for the Construction of Greater East Asia projected in 1942 as a theatrical Shintoist memorial zone to be built on an open plain at the foot of Mt. Fuji. World-renowned architect Tange Kenzō designed both projects. The striking parallels between the imperial project commemorating the Great East Asia Co-Prosperity Sphere and the Hiroshima memorial site for peace and mourning of the victims of the atomic bomb are symptomatic of the Japanese exculpatory memory based on the shift from victimizers to victims.[77] Yamahata Yosuke, who became world famous for his picture of a Nagasaki A-bomb child victim, campaigned with the Japanese Army in China as a war photographer during the "Fifteen-Year War" and had taken lots of photos of innocent Chinese children smiling with Japanese soldiers.[78]

In the bitter memories of the Nazi past in Germany, ordinary Germans remained either Hitler's first victims or his last victims, or both. The position of "Hitler's first victims" was vulnerable because of the competition from Austrians. The Moscow Tripartite Conference in 1943 interpreted the annexation of Austria on March 15, 1938, as an imposed action and thus "null and void." The Allied Powers recognized Austria as the "first free country to fall victim to Hitlerite aggression." The Moscow Declaration on Austria shows how the Allies connived to create the myth of Austrian victimhood. A small band of Austrian exiles had been eager to blame "Prussia" or "Nazi-Prussia," even though many Austrians had supported the *Anschluss* and the absorption of Austria into the *Ostmark*. Though the "delirious enthusiasm" and "boundless popular jubilation" for the *Anschluss* had faded, especially after the battle at Stalingrad in 1943, Austrians' "emotional bond of loyalty to Hitler" remained mostly intact. The figures for Austrian participation in Nazi crimes are telling. While Austrians made up only 8 percent of the population of Greater Germany, they constituted 14 percent of the *Schutzstaffel* (SS) and 40 percent of those involved in killing operations, from the euthanasia program of people with disabilities to Auschwitz.[79] The Vienna Philharmonic Orchestra had a higher ratio of Nazi members than the Berlin Philharmonic.

The illusion of Austrian victimhood reflects a particular historiosophical approach shared by the Allies. Winston Churchill took the initiative in making Austrians into Hitler's first victims. In his address on February 19, 1942, Churchill promised to liberate Austria from the "Prussian yoke." For

British with fresh memories of World War I, the Prussians remained the arch-enemy. Churchill even wished to treat southern Germans more mildly than Prussians in the North. In Churchill's mind, Nazi tyranny and Prussian militarism had to be destroyed. To some extent Russians in the Soviet Union shared Churchill's perception of the Prussian enemy. The Junkers were central villains in the communist demonology of the Nazi regime. Communist historiography equated Junkers with Nazis, a connection that resonated with Leninist conception of the "Prussian path to capitalism historiographically." Implicitly, Churchill's "Prussian yoke" and Lenin's "Prussian path" shared a vision of the peculiarities of German history, which eventually facilitated the triumph of fascism in Germany. The postwar German historiography of the *Sonderweg* had similar implications. The peculiarities of German history were summed up as "Prussianness," a deviation from a presumed liberal democratic normality that (in this analysis) accounted for the failure of Weimar democracy and the rise of Nazism.[80] It implied a distinction between evil Junker-Prussian Nazis and good, ordinary, non-Prussian Germans.

Paradoxically, a focus on Prussia-as-Germany could exonerate ordinary Germans in the same way that American Orientalism cast ordinary Japanese as servile to imperial power and victims of the military leadership. In this historical scenario, a handful of evil Junker-Prussian Nazis were alone responsible for the war and the Holocaust. They victimized ordinary Germans. The claim to victimhood colored the self-image of West Germany in the period of Konrad Adenauer's chancellorship (1949–1963). In this view, a handful of evil Junker-Prussians used terror and propaganda to coerce otherwise good Germans. Emphasizing the suffering of ordinary Germans at the hands of their international enemies complemented this national victimhood. There existed a long list of German suffering, including allied bombing, the expulsion of East Prussian and Sudeten Germans, rape of German women by Red Army soldiers, plunder, and revenge on the part of the Slavic Easterners.

The thesis of "Hitler's last victims," represented by Oliver Hirschbiegel's film *Der Untergang*, is no less problematic than the thesis of Hitler's first victims. In this profoundly problematic film, "perpetration and victimhood are played out within the national collective, between evil Nazis and good Germans, thus (almost) excluding memory of Jewish suffering."[81] With the fall of the Berlin Wall, Germans could confront their complicated history without the ideological constraints of the Cold War, and a new emphasis on German suffering emerged, including Allied bombing and the expulsions from the East. Günther Grass's novel *Im Krebsgang* (2002) represents the more nuanced and balanced understanding of the war complexities without self-exculpation. While the novel focuses on the tragic fate of about eight thousand German civilian refugees on the *Wilhelm Gustloff*, which was torpedoed and sunk by a Soviet submarine, Grass is careful to give historical context by alluding to ship's service in the Nazi's "Strength Through Joy" campaign, the Nazi career of its dedicatee, the transportation of the Luftwaffe unit that bombed Guernica in the Spanish Civil War, the highest rate of pro-Nazi political support among German refugee victims in the East, and the presence of suspicious noncivilians onboard.[82]

Grass's balanced contextualization of the tragedy of the *Wilhelm Gustloff* details the suffering of the German expellees without losing the sight of the collusion, collaboration, and complicity of East Prussian Germans with the Nazis. It is in stark contrast with the decontextualized history in Yoko Kawashima Watkins's narrative, exclusively focused on the suffering of the Japanese repatriates. Grass's novella opened the door to public dialogue on German suffering, freed from the Cold War dichotomy of victims and victimizers. Embedded within it was his critique of revisionist historiography of the 1990s that decontextualized German victims of Allied bombing and expulsion. The novel depicts the thousands of German victims onboard the *Wilhelm Gustloff* in consideration of their roles as Nazi collaborators-victimizers. The historical meandering implied in the title ("Crabwalk") warns about the dangers of a naïve dichotomy of victimizers and victims on the abstract level and in absolute terms. It does not necessarily produce a new victims' discourse.

Indeed, Grass's cautious handling of contextualization seems a world apart from Jörg Friedrich's account of the Allied bombing. Friedrich relativizes the Holocaust by comparing the suffering of the German civilians with the suffering of European Jews through linguistic association: "Friedrich refers to Bomber Command 5 as 'task force (*Einsatzgruppe*)'; cellars and bomb shelters are described as 'crematoria' and the bombing victims are being 'exterminated (*vernichtet*).' "[83] Friedrich's victimhood narrative seems intentionally to decontextualize. The historical contextualization, as shown in *Im Krebsgang*, seeks not to justify the Allied bombing as a punishment for historical culprits but to reveal historical complexity and ambiguity incompatible with the categorical dichotomy between victimizers and victims. Very often, being ahistorical, either decontextualized or overcontextualized, makes one vulnerable to politicization.

Victimhood has been selective in both Germanies. In West Germany, the suffering of expellees from Eastern Europe and German POWs imprisoned in the Soviet Union were collectively mourned. Their personal and vernacular memories structured the public memory of communist brutality and the loss of the German East. The "Documents of Expulsion" were replete with countless reports of terror, rape, plundering, family separation, forced deportations, starvation, slave labor, and killings. Robert Moeller explains, "The editors of documentation projects claimed that what Germans had suffered under Communists was comparable in its horror only to what Jews had suffered under Nazis."[84] Discursively, it was a continuation of Goebbels's attempts to Orientalize Russians as subhuman Asian hordes. In East Germany, the expulsion of Germans from brotherly communist countries was erased from the official memory. The rape of German women by Red Army soldiers was a taboo subject. Instead of criticizing the heroic Red Army, the Allied bombing of East German cities like Dresden was interpreted as a devious plan to sabotage future socialist building in the German Democratic Republic (GDR). GDR citizens had primarily been victims of the Allied imperialists' criminal bombing. At times the suffering of bombing victims in the GDR area was equated to the suffering of Jews in the Holocaust.[85]

As Germany unified, so did German victims who had politically differentiated historical memories. Tensions developed around how to compare victimhood between unified Germany and its Slavic neighbors. The polemics of the past became more heated between Germans and their Slavic neighbors as German expellee organizations demanded compensation. Under post–Cold War circumstances, leaders of the expellee organizations appealed to Polish courts to return their properties confiscated by the communist regime. A loud outcry was heard that Free Poland should not advocate the oppressive policies of that regime.[86] Erika Steinbach, the president of Der Bund der Vertriebenen (BdV), has been more aggressive in her assertion. She urged the German government to set the annulment of the Beneš Decree as the precondition for the Czech Republic and Poland to enter the European Union. Steinbach is not reluctant to use the terms "forced labor, the extermination camp, and genocide" (Zwangsarbeits und Vernichtungslager, Genozid) to describe the internment camps of German expellees from what are now parts of the Czech Republic and Poland. "Genocide of more than 15 million people" was her estimation of the number of victims among German expellees. She equated the suffering of German expellees with the suffering of Jewish victims of the Holocaust.[87] In other words, Poles and Czechs who victimized these expellees were equivalent in crucial ways to the Nazi perpetrators of the Holocaust. Indeed, in an interview with Passauer Neue Presse in March 2007, Steinbach compared the rightwing Polish government with the neo-Nazis in Germany due to its indifference to the question of expulsion.[88]

Poles and Czechs undeniably victimized German refugees and expellees upon Germany's defeat in the Second World War. On June 30, 1945, Czechs shot twenty-two Sudeten Germans and one Czech woman in the Czech town of Teplice (Wekelsdorf). In the graveyard of Łambinowice (Lamsdorf), the bodies of 1,137 Germans, mostly women, children, and the elderly, were consecrated in September 2002. They died of starvation and hard labor in a work camp run by Poles with Soviet permission. On July 31, 1945, the Czech militia and civilians threw more than fifty Germans into a river and opened fire on them in Ustí nad Labem (Aussig). The list is too long to be enumerated here. It is also true that these German expellees were hardly innocent of responsibility for Nazism. The Sudeten Germans were strong Nazi supporters who voted for the Nazi-style Sudeten German Party with an overwhelming majority of 90 percent. Nazis enjoyed popularity in East Prussia, too. The decontextualization of German expellees' victimhood by Steinbach and others gave rise to a furious response from their counterparts who were victims of Nazism. Poles and Czechs are responding to the decontextualization of German victimhood with overcontextualization, in an apparent effort to justify their violent acts against the German expellees. What is left is again the competition over which victims suffered most, sharpened by the antagonistic complicity of victimhood nationalisms.

Victimhood was also dominant in the collective memory of fascism and war in post-Fascist Italy. Benedetto Croce represented apologetic and exculpatory memory by inserting fascism in a parenthesis of the Italian history, something alien to the history of the real and authentic Italy. In his account, fascism was a short episode imposed by foreign infiltrators. He presented Italian fascism as benign in comparison with Nazism. Perpetrators alien to the national body politics of Italy—German soldiers, drug addicts, homosexuals, and sadists at large—committed all the pure brutality or physical atrocities. Stressing the Italian anti-Fascist tradition and exalting the role of the Italian Resistance in the years 1943–1945 helped distance Italy from its Fascist past and established an implicit distinction between "good Italians" and "bad Fascists." Croce's account facilitated the shift away from collective responsibility and guilt for the Fascist atrocities on the part of ordinary Italians. Only a collective self-image of a victimized nation remained from the Fascist past. No wonder that there was no Italian Nuremberg, and "Fascism disappeared—conveniently for many—into a black hole."[89]

Victimhood nationalism is ahistorical because it dwells in the realm of overcontextualization and decontextualization. If the overcontextualization inherent in historical contextualism gives rise to historical conformism of whatever happened in history, the decontextualization results in the form of ahistorical justification of the historical aftermath. The specters of decontextualization and overcontextualization hovering over the victimhood controversy make historical reconciliation vulnerable to politicization. The Japanese expellees became victims of Koreans, and German expellees suffered from retaliation from Poles and Czechs upon the defeat in World War II. Japanese and German expellees were hardly innocent of atrocities resulting from colonialism and Nazism. With its unilateral emphasis on victimhood, the decontextualization at play in Japanese and German victimhood nationalism gives rise to a furious response from their counterparts who had been victimized before and during World War II. They respond to Japanese and German decontextualization with overcontextualization, which appears to justify their violence against Japanese and German civilian expellees. The competition for exclusive victimhood between opposing victimhood nationalisms begins this way. All that remains is the antagonistic complicity of victimhood nationalisms among unequal victims.

Responsibility: From Whom to Whom?

Collective memories are not fixed. They are continuously negotiated between available historical records and current social and political agendas. But historical responsibility does not float. In English dictionaries, one finds an interesting synonym of responsibility, namely, *answerability*—an ability to answer. Indeed *Verantwortung, odpowiedzialność, responsibilité*, as equivalents of "responsibility" in other European languages, have the same connotation. The word *answerability* sounds very casual. When the pointed question of "answerability to whom?" arises, the term suddenly becomes profoundly charged. Answerability presupposes an ability to listen to the voices of others. If we remind ourselves of the Derridean idea of the Other as one's own justice, listening to others is a substantial part of my justice and yours. The voice of others is very often a dissenting one. Listening to the outrageous comments, distressing stories, and moaning of others is often disturbing and painful. Historical responsibility means listening and answering to the crying, groaning, and whimpering of others who passed away in the brutal past. Unfortunately, under undemocratic political circumstances, historians pretend to hear nothing. Shamans, not historians, are healing victims by recalling the dead souls through religious rituals. By listening, shamans of Jeju Island in South Korea, who suffered from the anticommunist political genocide and brutal suppression of the memory of victims, have been memory activists more than others.

Ontologically, nobody can be blamed or convicted for what one did not do. One can be responsible only for what one did. In other words, "only the murderer is responsible for the murder." Collective guilt or innocence cannot help us to come to terms with the complex and tragic past of the dark modernity. Focusing on collective guilt or innocence only encourages people to perceive reality in national terms that serve to justify their own victimhood nationalisms. The perpetrators' principle of "a reductive selectiveness" would remain intact. It would signify a posthumous victory for the oppressors. Denying collective guilt does not, however, mean denying the existence of "cultural collective," constructed from a sense of participation in a shared past spanning throughout many generations.[90] Adam Michnik's confession intuitively captured this distinction: "I do not feel guilty for those murdered, but I do feel responsible. . . . I feel guilty that after they died they were murdered again, denied a decent burial, denied tears, denied truth about this hideous crime, and that for decades a lie was repeated."[91]

If responsibility means answerability to the voices and pains of others, historical responsibility implies the responsibility for the present memory of the past. We, as historians, are responsible for the exculpatory memory of victimhood nationalism. The proclivity, even desire, of national historians to lend the hereditary victimhood and the sacrificial aura to their own nations bears historical and historiographical irresponsibility, for it facilitates the posthumous victory of perpetrators in the form of victimhood nationalism. Historians need to "victimize" victimhood nationalism. It would be the first step toward a memory regime change capable of producing mnemonic solidarity beyond national borders. Memorial collectives are still in the making, with us all doing our parts.

Notes

1. Aleida Assmann and Sebastian Conrad, introduction to *Memory in a Global Age: Discourses, Practices, and Trajectories*, ed. Aleida Assmann and Sebastian Conrad (Basingstoke, UK: Palgrave Macmillan, 2010), 1.
2. I borrow the term "hereditary victimhood" from Zygmunt Bauman, *Modernity and the Holocaust* (Ithaca, N.Y.: Cornell University Press, 2000), 238.
3. Ernest Renan, 민족이란 무엇인가 [*Qu'est-ce qu'une nation?*], trans. Shin Haeng-sun (Seoul: Chaeksesang, 2002), 81.
4. Antony Polonsky and Joanna Michlic, introduction to *The Neighbors Respond: The Controversy Over the Jedwabne Massacre in Poland*, ed. Polonsky and Michlic (Princeton, N.J.: Princeton University Press, 2004), 9.
5. Hannah Arendt, *Eichmann in Jerusalem: A Report on the Banality of Evil* (New York: Penguin Books, 1994), 278, 297–98.
6. Jie-Hyun Lim, "Victimhood Nationalism: Compelling or Competing?," *Korea Herald*, April 9, 2007; Jie-Hyun Lim, "희생자의식 민족주의 [Victimhood nationalism]," *Bipyung*, no. 15 (Summer 2007): 154–76.
7. Anna Bikont, "We of Jedwabne," in Polonsky and Michlic, *The Neighbors Respond*, 294; Anna Bikont, *The Crime and the Silence: Confronting the Massacre of Jews in Wartime Jedwabne*, trans. Alissa Valles (New York: Farrar, Straus and Giroux, 2015), 10–17.
8. In turbulent debates on Jewish massacres in Jedwabne, a seventy-year-old ordinary Pole admitted that "we were taught as children that we Poles never harmed anyone. A partial abandonment of this morally comfortable position is very, very difficult for me." See Polonsky and Michlic, introduction to *The Neighbors Respond*, 1.
9. Primo Levi, *The Drowned and the Saved* (New York: Vintage Books, 1989), 24.
10. Jie-Hyun Lim, "The Antagonistic Complicity of Nationalisms: On Nationalist Phenomenology in East Asian History Textbooks," in *Contested Views of a Common Past: Revisions of History in Contemporary East Asia*, ed. Steffi Richter (Frankfurt: Campus Verlag, 2008), 205–22. See also chapter 7 in the present book.
11. Lisa Yoneyama, *Cold War Ruins: Transpacific Critique of American Justice and Japanese War Crimes* (Durham, N.C.: Duke University Press, 2016), 43–80.

12. Yoko Kawashima Watkins, 요코이야기 [*So Far from the Bamboo Grove*], trans. Yun Hyeonju (Seoul: Munhakdongne, 2005).

13. Ara Takashi, ed., 日本占領 外交關係資料集 [Diplomatic documents of the Japanese Occupation], vol. 3 (Tokyo: Kashiwa shobō, 1991), 304. Cited in Lori Watt, *When Empire Comes Home: Repatriation and Reintegration in Postwar Japan* (Cambridge, Mass.: Harvard University Press, 2009), 2, 39. Among them, 110,000 expellees from Manchuria and 17,690 repatriates from the Korean peninsula perished in years of 1945 and 1948. See Yamata Yōko, 図説 満洲—日本人の足跡をたどる [Traces of the Japanese in Manchuria—an illustrated history] (Osaka: Umeda Shuppan, 2011), 80–98.

14. The story was translated into English by Nana Mizushima as *Tei: A Memoire of the End of War and Beginning of Peace* (N.p.: Tonnbo Books, 2014).

15. Yoon Sang In, "수난담의 유혹 [Alluring stories of the suffering]," *Bipyung*, no. 15 (Summer 2007): 197–98.

16. I subscribe to two politically opposite dailies, the conservative *Chosun* and liberal *Kyunghyang*, to check their reports and editorials against each other. I still have a vivid memory of that morning when I found both dailies united in attacking Yoko Kawashima Watkins's novella. It was the last thing I expected from the Korean media, and it fired my curiosity about the novella and its reception. Kang Youngsoo, "'한국인이 일 소녀 강간' 미 교재 파문 확산" [Koreans raping a Japanese girl], *Chosun ilbo* online, January 17, 2007, https://www.chosun.com/site/data/html_dir/2007 /01/17/2007011700119.html and https://www.chosun.com/site/data/html_dir/2007 /01/17/2007011700765.html; Kim Yongsuk and Kim Jaemoon, "'요코 이야기'美 교재사 용 파문확산" [A scandalous reading list in America—Yoko Monogatari], *Kyunghyang shinmun* online, January 17, 2007, http://news.khan.co.kr/kh_news/khan_art _view.html?artid=200701171812301&code=970201 and http://news.khan.co.kr/kh _news/khan_art_view.html?artid=200701171342061&code=970100.

17. "Controversial Book to Remain in Classes," *Boston.com*, January 3, 2007, http:// archive.boston.com/news/local/massachusetts/articles/2007/01/03/controversial _book_to_remain_in_classes/.

18. Lee Gichang, "지영선 인터뷰:요코이야기는 인종차별, 논리적 대처 필요" [Interview with Ji Youngsun: Yoko monogatari's racism], *Yonhaptongshin* online, January 17, 2017.

19. Choi Woosuk, "일본 역사왜곡 소설, 미국 중학교재로 사용" [A Japanese novella distorting history], January 18, 2007, *Chosun ilbo* https://www.chosun.com/site/data /html_dir/2007/01/18/2007011800085.html; Choi Woosuk, "잘못된 요코이야기 못 배 운다" [I won't learn from Yoko], *Chosun ilbo*, January 19, 2007, https://www.chosun .com/site/data/html_dir/2007/01/19/2007011900855.html.

20. It is in the same vein that members of the Chinese diaspora in the United States have seized on the Nanjing Massacre to solidify an ethnic identity. Many American Jews likewise cling to the sanctity of the Holocaust as basic to their identity. See Joshua A. Fogel, ed., *The Nanjing Massacre in History and Historiography* (Berkeley: University of California Press, 2000), 3. Isn't victimhood a mainstay of the long-distance nationalism among the diaspora communities in the United States?

21. Lisa Yoneyama, "아시아계 미국인과 일본의 전쟁범죄" [Asian-Americans and Japanese war crime], paper presented to 4th Symposium of Korean-Japanese Solidarity 21, July 14, 2007.

22. Customer reviews of *So Far from the Bamboo Grove*," Amazon.com, accessed April 13, 2007, http://www.amazon.com/review/product/0844668109.

23. Martha Parravano, "For Intermediate Readers—*Year of Impossible Goodbyes* by Sook Nyul Choi," *Horn Book Magazine* 68, no. 1 (January 1992): 69.

24. Je Boon Yu, "Anarchy of Empire and Empathy of Suffering: Reading of *So Far from the Bamboo Grove* and *Year of Impossible Goodbyes* from the Perspectives of Postcolonial Feminism," *Journal of English Language and Literature* 58, no. 1 (2012): 163–84.

25. "So far away from bamboo grove," amazon.co.jp reviewer's corner, accessed on January 16, 2020.

26. "박의장, 청경우독을 남기고" [Chairman Park urging diligent work with study], *Kyunghyang shinmun* 3, 1962.02.10; "만평개간한 농사혁명" [On the agrarian revolution] *Kyunghyang shinmun* 3, 1962.02.10; "박정희 의장 눈감고 기도" [Chairman Park is praying], *Dong-A ilbo* 3, 1962.02.10; "농촌을 위한 박의장의 지시를 보고" [About Chairman Park's instruction for rural communities], *Kyunghyang shinmun* 3, 1962.02.11. See also chapter 9.

27. Werner Weinberg, *Self-Portrait of a Holocaust Survivor* (Jefferson, N.C.: Mcfarland, 1985), 152.

28. Idith Zertal, *From Catastrophe to Power: Holocaust Survivors and the Emergence of Israel* (Berkeley: University of California Press, 1998), 217.

29. Zertal, 221.

30. Zertal, 263.

31. Ilan Pappe, "Critique and Agenda: The Post-Zionist Scholars in Israel," in "Israel Historiography Revisited," special issue, *History and Memory* 7, no. 1 (1995): 72. A sexist reconstruction of history can also be broadly found in the Korean nationalist discourse of the comfort women.

32. Alan Mintz, *Popular Culture and the Shaping of Holocaust Memory in America* (Seattle: University of Washington Press, 2001), 5.

33. Quoted in Peter Novick, *The Holocaust and Collective Memory* (London: Bloomsbury, 2001), 121.

34. Novick, 116.

35. Novick, 91, 98, 116, 121, and passim.

36. Mintz, *Popular Culture*, 6. See also Alvin Rosenfeld, *The Americanization of the Holocaust* (Ann Arbor: University of Michigan, 1995); Hilene Flanzabaum, ed., *The Americanization of the Holocaust* (Baltimore: Johns Hopkins University Press, 1999); Henry L. Feingold, *Bearing Witness: How America and Its Jews Responded to the Holocaust* (Syracuse, N.Y.: Syracuse University Press, 1995).

37. Dan Diner, "Cumulative Contingency: Historicizing Legitimacy in Israeli Discourse," in "Israel Historiography Revisited," special issue, *History and Memory* 7, no. 1 (1995): 153.

38. Yael Zerubavel, "The Death of Memory and the Memory of Death: Masada and the Holocaust as Historical Metaphors," *Representations* 45 (Winter 1994): 80–81.

39. Diner, "Cumulative Contingency," 74–78.

40. Michel Warschawski, *On the Border*, trans. Levi Laub (Cambridge, Mass.: South End Press, 2005), 153–54.

41. Tom Segev, *The Seventh Million: The Israelis and the Holocaust*, trans. Heim Watzman (New York: Owl Books, 2000), 361.

42. Segev, 389. It should be also noted that in the international arena Israeli officials and American Jewish political activists have tried to increase public awareness of the Holocaust to generate sympathy and support for Israel. See Novick, *The Holocaust*, 156–57.

43. Segev, *The Seventh Million*, 516.

44. Diner, "Cumulative Contingency," 155–57.

45. Novick, *The Holocaust*, 156; Segev, *The Seventh Million*, 399–400.

46. For an excellent analysis of the uniqueness discourse, see Alan Rosenbaum, ed., *Is Holocaust Unique? Perspectives on Comparative Genocide* (Boulder, Colo.: Westview Press, 2001).

47. Quoted in Warschawski, *On the Border*, 154.

48. Polonsky and Michlik, introduction to *The Neighbors Responded*, 39; Jan Gross, *Neighbors: The Destruction of the Jewish Community in Jedwabne, Poland* (New York: Penguin Books, 2002), 120.

49. Gross, *Neighbors*, 123.

50. Quoted in Joshua D. Zimmerman, ed., *Contested Memories: Poles and Jews During the Holocaust and Its Aftermath* (New Brunswick, N.J.: Rutgers University Press, 2003), 9.

51. It is striking that 40 percent of respondents in a nationwide public opinion survey in 2004 declared that Poland is still being governed by Jews. See Jan Gross, *Fear: Anti-Semitism in Poland After Auschwitz* (New York: Random House, 2006).

52. Jie-Hyun Lim, "Nationalist Message in Socialist Code: On Court Historiography in People's Poland and North Korea," in *Making Sense of Global History*, ed. Solvi Sogner (Oslo: Universitetsforlaget, 2001), 373–80.

53. Barbara Engelking-Boni, "Psychological Distance Between Poles and Jews in Nazi-Occupied Warsaw," in *Contested Memories: Poles and Jews During the Holocaust and Its Aftermath*, ed. Joshua D. Zimmerman (New Brunswick, N.J.: Rutgers University Press, 2003), 48.

54. It is symptomatic that reprinting of the Polish version of Władyslaw Szpielman's *Pianist* in the era of People's Poland has not been allowed, on the grounds that the book can give readers the wrong impression that Polish Jews suffered more than ethnic Poles.

55. Michael Steinlauf, "Teaching the Holocaust in Poland," in *Contested Memories: Poles and Jews During the Holocaust and Its Aftermath*, ed. Joshua D. Zimmerman (New Brunswick, N.J.: Rutgers University Press, 2003), 264.

56. Steinlauf, 265–66.

57. Witold Kula, *Rozdziałki* (Warsaw: Wydawnictwo Trio, 1996), 213.

58. Jan Błoński, *Biedny Polacy Patrzą na Getto* (Kraków: Wydawnictwo literackie, 1996).

59. Hanna Świda-Ziemba, "The Shortsightedness of the Cultured," in Polonsky and Michlic, *The Neighbors Respond*, 103.

60. "Interview with the Primate of Poland, Cardinal Józef Glemp, on the Murder of Jews in Jedwabne, 15 May 2001," in Polonsky and Michlic, *The Neighbors Respond*, 167.

61. Gross, *Fear*, 130.

62. Adam Michnik, "Poles and Jews: How Deep the Guilt?," in *The Neighbors Respond*, 435.

63. Gross, *Fear*, 120–22.

64. W. Wierzewski, "We Don't Know the Facts Yet," customer review of *Neighbors*, Amazon.com, November 14, 2001, https://www.amazon.com/review/RGCUHD PXATM1F/ref=cm_cr_srp_d_rdp_perm?ie=UTF8&ASIN=0142002402.

65. "Gespräch zwischen Micha Brumlik und Karol Sauerland," in *Umdeuten, Verschweigen, Erinnern: die späte Aufarbeitung des Holocaust in Osteuropa*, ed. Micha Brumlik and Karol Sauerland (Frankfurt am Main: Campus, 2010), 8, 11.

66. Hannah Arendt, "The Aftermath of Nazi Rule: Report from Germany," *Commentary* (October 1950): 342–43.

67. Jie-Hyun Lim, "Victimhood," in *The Palgrave Handbook of Mass Dictatorship*, ed. Paul Corner and Jie-Hyun Lim (London: Palgrave Macmillan, 2016), 427–44.

68. James J. Orr, *The Victim as Hero: Ideologies of Peace and National Identity in Postwar Japan* (Honolulu: University of Hawai'i Press, 2001), 1.

69. Novick, *The Holocaust*, 112.

70. John W. Dower, "An Aptitude for Being Unloved: War and Memory in Japan," in *Crimes of War: Guilt and Denial in the Twentieth Century*, ed. Omer Bartov, Atina Grossmann, and Mary Nolan (New York: New Press, 2002), 226.

71. Dower, 228.

72. Quoted in Orr, *The Victim as Hero*, 16.

73. Orr, 7, 14, 15, 32.

74. Orr, 32.

75. Ian Buruma, 아우슈비츠와 히로시마 [*The Wages of Guilt: Memories of War in Germany and Japan*], trans. Jeong Yonghwan (Seoul: Hangyoreh Shinmun, 2002), 119–26.

76. Orr, *The Victim as Hero*, 52.

77. Lisa Yoneyama, *Hiroshima Traces: Time, Space, and the Dialectics of Memory* (Berkeley: University of California Press, 1999), 1–3.

78. Tessa Morris-Suzuki, 우리안의 과거 [*The Past Within Us: Media, Memory, History*], trans. Kim Kyoungwon (Seoul: Humanist, 2006), 127–33.

79. Evan Burr Bukey, *Hitler's Austria: Popular Sentiments in the Nazi Era 1938-1945* (Chapel Hill: University of North Carolina Press, 2000), 43.

80. See chapter 4.

81. Bill Niven, introduction to *Germans as Victims*, ed. Bill Niven (Basingstoke, UK: Palgrave Macmillan, 2006), 16.

82. Günther Grass, 게걸음으로 가다 [*Im Krebsgang*], trans. Jang Huichang (Seoul: Minumsa, 2002).

83. Stefan Berger, "On Taboos, Traumas and Other Myths," in Niven, *Germans as Victims*, 219–20.

84. Robert G. Moeller, "War Stories: The Search for a Usable Past in the Federal Republic of Germany," *American Historical Review* 101, no. 4 (October 1996): 1013, 1017, 1027.

85. Berger, "On Taboos," 215.

86. Bartosz Wieliński, "Czego żąda owiernictwo pruskie," *Gazeta Wyborcza*, December 19, 2006.

87. Jan Piskorski, *Vertreibung und Deutsch-Polnische Geschichte* (Osnabrück: Fibre Verlag, 2005), 37, 42ff.

88. "Steinbach: Polski rząd jak niemieccy neofaszyści," *Gazeta Wyborcza*, March 7, 2007.

89. Paul Corner, ed., *Popular Opinion in Totalitarian Regimes: Fascism, Nazism, Communism* (Oxford: Oxford University Press, 2009), 122–23.

90. David Engel, introduction to the Hebrew edition of *The Neighbors Respond*, 413.

91. Michnik, "Poles and Jews," 435.

2

The Second World War in Global Memory Space

Holocaust Meets the Postcolonial

On March 8, 2013, International Woman's Day, officials unveiled a monument to Korean "comfort women" in front of the Bergen County courthouse in New Jersey. This memorial stone took its place outside the courthouse in the county's "ring of honor," alongside four monuments commemorating the victims of African American slavery, the Holocaust, the Armenian genocide, and the Irish potato famine.[1] Commemorating the comfort women in the same category with these other horrific events came from extensive work and lobbying by the various groups of memory activists on the transpacific memory space. The memory of Korean comfort women—the euphemism used by the Japanese military for sexual slaves—began migrating to the United States early in the twenty-first century. Korean American Civic Empowerment (KACE) was one of the early promoters of the transpacific migration of the memory of comfort women to the United States. KACE sponsored two monuments in Palisades Park and Bergen County and lobbied successfully for H.Res. 121 (2007), asking the Japanese government to "formally acknowledge, apologize, and accept historical responsibility." The efforts of KACE to preserve the memory of comfort women included the art exhibition *Come from the Shadows: The Comfort Women* in New York City in 2011.

In New York, for their transpacific memory campaign, KACE collaborated with the Kupferberg Holocaust Center of Queensborough Community
College. The two groups jointly organized a meeting of Korean comfort
women and Holocaust survivors in the auditorium of Queensborough
Community College on December 13, 2011; the meeting received broad
media coverage in Korea. Subsequently, they launched the North Asian History Internship, a jointly operated program designed to teach American
college students about atrocities committed by Japanese imperial armed
forces. The program has focused on the violation of women's rights by highlighting the experiences of comfort women.[2] The Holocaust and comfort
women mnemonically encountered each other a posteriori in the transnational memory space, though de facto the two groups of victims never
directly overlapped. The mnemonic confluence of the Holocaust and comfort women, facilitated by the transatlantic and transpacific migration of
memory, epitomizes the extraterritoriality of the global memory of World
War II. The performativity of wartime memory is shifting from the national
to the transnational.

About a year after the Queensborough meeting, a similar transnational
memory performance took place on December 6, 2012, in Melbourne, Australia. In front of the German consulate, eighty-four-year-old Alf Turner
read a petition from Australian Aborigines denouncing Nazi persecution
of the Jewish people. Then he handed over the document to a German consul. Two hundred supporters, including Holocaust survivors and members
of the Jewish community, watched this transfer. The ceremony reenacted
William Cooper's protest against the Nazis in 1938, just weeks after *Kristallnacht*. Cooper, the seventy-seven-year-old secretary of the Australian
Aboriginal League, an Aboriginal elder of the Yorta Yorta tribe and Alf
Turner's grandfather, had led a delegation to deliver the petition condemning the Nazi persecution of Jews to the German consulate in Melbourne.[3]
The Aboriginal communities had suffered from white Australian settlers'
quest for *Lebensraum* and racist discrimination. Their analogous historical
experience sensitized them to the Nazi persecution of the Jews and inclined
them toward solidarity with Jewish victims.[4] Cooper's show of solidarity
with German Jews in 1938 is in stark contrast with postwar "White Australia" policy that denied entry visas to Oriental Jews. Cooper's unique
protest against the Nazis came to prominence in the twenty-first century,
reflecting the confluence of postcolonial and Holocaust memory in the

global memory space. Eurocentrism and racism had delayed the recognition of the first protester, William Cooper, until the beginning of the twenty-first century.

Holocaust survivors, comfort women, and Australian Aborigines constructed a striking mnemonic solidarity across the globe, even though their stories remained unconnected throughout World War II. Their memory is entangled, even as their history is not. Denial discourses and nationalists' exculpatory memories have become globally connected, too. Australian law professor Martin Krygier, son of a Polish-Jewish refugee, persuasively showed the parallels between the nationalist denial of the Jedwabne massacre in Poland and the racist defense of the forced removal of Aboriginal children ("Stolen Generations") from their families in Australia.[5] Krygier's taxonomic approach could also be applied to the diverse deniers of the suffering of comfort women, the Nanjing massacre, the *Wehrmacht* atrocities, South African apartheid, military massacres at My Lai and No Gun Ri, and the Holocaust itself. Exculpatory memories of egocentric nationalism have built new connections among groups that had no direct historical interactions. New alliances, even if not explicit, are evident, as in the case of the Jedwabne massacre and the *Wehrmacht* exhibition.[6]

Denial discourse occupies a wide spectrum, ranging from the victim-izers' outright denial of past genocide to the victims' consequential denial by banalizing the genocide as an omnipresent reality. Holocaust denial has become an industry.[7] Holocaust denial now provides a more general template for denying and negating a broad array of atrocities, including the Jedwabne massacre in Poland, stolen Aborigine children in Australia, comfort women in the Japanese Imperial Army, Armenian genocide, and other colonial genocides and atrocities. An international conference held in Tehe-ran in December 2006, Review of the Holocaust: Global Vision, revealed a strange alliance between the Islamic theocracy with the American racist Ku Klux Klan (KKK) by inviting David Duke, the former grand wizard of the KKK, as a keynote speaker. Iranian theocracy used Holocaust revision-ism to delegitimize the state of Israel, while the extreme right of the First World needed an alliance with Third World Islam to present itself as more acceptable "white separatist," instead of "white supremacy."[8] We might characterize the undeniable phenomenon of generalizing Holocaust denial into negationism of genocide writ large as "Deniers' International." Deniers are connected organizationally or discursively over the globe.

Mnemonic connectivity across the globe occasions the clash of two opposing mnemonic performativities—critical and exculpatory. The remembrance of the Second World War has been shaped by varied and frequently conflicting perspectives and positionalities—the memories of victims and perpetrators, victimhood and agency, bystanders and accomplices, victory and defeat, resistance and collaboration, empires and colonies, occupation and liberation, dictatorship and democracy, coercion and consent, heroes and villains, men and women, captors and prisoners, soldiers and civilians, and other sets of contestants. For most of the second half of the previous century, coming to terms with World War II remained a national project, often leading to national apologetic memory. While considered exclusively within national borders, contested memories were often formulated in a system of binaries. As Carol Gluck describes, the result was "a memory of a *world* war with the *world* left out."[9] This chapter tries to rescue the memory of World War II from *la tyrannie du national.*[10] This endeavor demands more than a compilation of national memories. Rescuing memory from the nation is a "moral business" requiring the articulation of the global performativity in remembering World War II. This moral business creates a reconcilable, or at least symbiotic, global memory culture through a critical comparison of the fragmented memories of war, dictatorship, colonialism, and genocide.

Nationalization of Memory

Sakai Naoki's anecdote about the Japanese translation of the German word *Nationalsozialismus* dates back to the early 1990s. At the request of the *Asahi Journal*, Sakai submitted an essay to the journal, but his manuscript was repeatedly turned down. Sakai had translated *Nationalsozialismus* as *kokumin shakaishugi* (socialism of the nation) instead of *kokka shakaishugi* (socialism of the state). Sakai's term was unacceptable to the left-wing editor of the journal. In German, as in English, the word for "nation" can mean anything from a group of people with a shared government and territory (*Staatsnation*) to a people of shared ethnic heritage (*Kulturnation*). It has been rendered most frequently in Japanese as *kokumin* (nation) or *minzoku* (ethnicity or ethnic nation). "Nation" was also translated as *kokka* (state), though rarely. Many Japanese left intellectuals believed that the word "nation" in *Nationalsozialismus* signified *kokka* (state). By using the term *kokka shakaishugi* (state socialism), they could rescue *kokumin* (nation) from Nazism. The *Shōwa-shi* (Shōwa history) debate in 1955 reconfirmed the sacralization of *kokumin*. The nation-centered dichotomy of *kokumin* (nation) and *hi-kokumin* (non/anti-nation) in the *Shōwa-shi* debate foreclosed the potentiality of *hi-kokumin* demanding historical responsibility of *kokumin*.[11] Postwar democracy in Japan was inclined to democratize, rather than problematize, the nation.

For many Japanese intellectuals, interrogating Japan's responsibility for war remained a solely national business—and was supposed to remain so. The *kokumin*'s ethnocentric worldview is closely connected with the ironic memory of the Japanese Empire as the colonized, not the colonizer. This inverted memory of empire allowed the Japanese to adopt a postcolonial rather than postimperial positionality.[12] The history of modern Japan, from 1853 when Perry's American ships landed in the bay of Uraga to 1952 when American occupation forces left the country, was periodized as the "Hundred Years War" against the West and "White Pacific."[13] The Second World War was just one episode in the century-long epic struggle between Asia and West, between the colonized and colonizers, and between White Pacific and Asian Pacific.[14] Insofar as the Japanese self-identification as the postcolonial state is dominant, the forgetting of the histories of the colonized Koreans, Taiwanese, and Chinese as "third country nationals" remains in effect. This transformation of the colonizers into the colonized is key to understanding why *kokumin* (nation) has been so cherished in the collective memory of colonialism and war in Japan. Japanese colonial amnesia was diplomatically endorsed when Japan, instead of its former colonies like Korea and Taiwan, was invited to Bandung Conference of 1955 to launch a Non-Aligned Movement opposing colonialism and neocolonialism.

Sukarno got into the weeds of Japanese translation of nation. The Indonesian leader, a self-identified left nationalist, perceived National Socialism as *kokumin shakaishugi* (nation-socialism) and, therefore, good. When he received an honorary degree from the University of Indonesia on February 2, 1963, Sukarno delivered a speech on nationalism and leadership. Benedict Anderson vividly remembered Sukarno's address in praise of Hitler on that day: "Wah, Hitler was extraordinarily clever really. . . . This Third Reich would really and truly bring happiness to the people of Germany."[15] On other occasions, Sukarno frequently described Sun Yixian (Sun

Yat-sen), Kemal Atatürk, Gandhi, and Ho Chi Minh as on par with Hitler. When Dutch colonizers compared Sukarno's government with the pro-Nazi Quisling regime, and the young Indonesian independence fighters with the Hitler Youth and the SS, their gaze was no less obscene than Sukarno's. They failed to remember Anton Mussert, führer of the Dutch National Socialist Movement, who argued for Dutch access to German *Lebensraum* in the Slavic East, where they could bring to bear their colonial experience in Java and Sumatra.[16]

In contrast to national collective memories, many individual memories challenge *kokumin* (nation)-centered remembrance. Upon the unconditional surrender of Japan, about six hundred Japanese soldiers joined Sukarno's Indonesian independence fighters in the "Hundred Years War" against the "West." Those who fell in the fight were buried in the national cemetery, to be remembered as Indonesian national heroes. Chil-sung Yang, or Komarduin, a Korean who contracted with the Japanese Army to guard the Allied POW camp, was one of those fallen heroes. Captured in the Garut basin in November 1948, he was executed as a war criminal on August 10, 1949, for fighting alongside Indonesian fighters against Dutch colonialism. Though he has been remembered as a national hero in Indonesia and buried in the national cemetery in Garut, postcolonial Korea consigned him to oblivion for his collaboration with the Japanese Army. The diversity of memories across half the globe concerning Yang Chil-sung cannot be captured by any one national memory: Dutch war criminal, Indonesian national hero, Japanese colonial collaborator, Korean national traitor, and innocent colonial victim by his fate.[17]

Europeans also spared no effort in nationalizing war memory. The widespread silence about nonnational victims was most pervasive in the first decade of the postwar period. First of all, Jews were ousted from the national memory of war across Europe. Jewish persecution and the Holocaust were either nationalized or excluded from the patrimony. The Gendarmerie Nationale reported on a demonstration by about three hundred people shouting "France for the French" in the fourth *arrondissement* of Paris on April 19, 1945. The protest was triggered by the expulsion of a person occupying the apartment of a Jew who had returned to Paris. When Netty Rosenfeld applied for a job at "Radio Herrijzend Nederland," run by the Dutch resistance after liberation in 1944, she was told that her Jewish surname was not suitable for public broadcasting. A reader's letter to *De*

Patriot, a former Dutch resistance paper, insisted that Jews had a duty to thank those who fell victim on behalf of Jews. In Belgium, "the patriot clause," initiated by the Catholic opposition, sought to exclude Jews from national reparations because they had been deported for being Jews, not for being resistance fighters.[18]

Jewish survivors were excluded from the national memory of war in Germany, too. While many Germans were forced to acknowledge Nazi atrocities under Allied occupation, repentance could not be made compulsory. A survey in November 1946 showed that 37 percent of Germans thought "the extermination of Jews and Poles and other non-Aryans was necessary for the security of Germans." Almost the same ratio of Germans agreed to a proposition that "Jews should not have the same rights as those belonging to the Aryan race." In a 1952 poll, 37 percent of West Germans affirmed that it was better for Germany not to have Jews in its territory. Adenauer's reparation plan faced opposition from all political camps. The Christian Democratic Union (CDU) opposed payments to Jewish victims, claiming it would only fuel anti-Semitism among those who objected to preferential treatment for Jews. The Communist Party (KPD) likewise opposed the plan, but for a different reason. It claimed that only capitalists and financiers in Israel would benefit from the reparation project.[19] The collective memory in Germany and many other Western European countries was imbued with a national bigotry reminiscent of the division of *kokumin* and *hi-kokumin* in Japanese memory.

A series of *Kameradenschinder* (comrade abuse) trials between the late 1940s and early 1960s in West Germany is most telling.[20] Some returned POWs were criminally charged for denouncing and abusing their "comrades" while in Soviet POW camps. Unlike the leniency shown toward Nazi criminals in the 1950s, the West German judiciary eagerly prosecuted German POWs who had collaborated with their Soviet captors. These collaborators were accused of victimizing fellow Germans. While West German public opinion tended to exonerate convicted Nazi war criminals because they were simply following orders, POWs accused of Soviet collaboration did not receive such tolerance. Aiding Soviet authorities was a more serious crime than being a Nazi. Some verdicts maintained that defendants had violated the bonds of "comradeship" and the soldierly ideal of masculine virtues—the very ideals that had improved the efficiency of "quality work" of German soldiers—soldiering in genocidal warfare.[21] West

German courts were keener to castigate "crimes against nation" than to punish "crimes against humanity."

The memory of Jewish suffering was also repressed and marginalized in communist Eastern Europe. It simply did not fit Soviet narratives of the antifascist front of workers and the "great patriotic war." East European communists openly gave voice to their anti-Semitism with their use of the phrase "rootless cosmopolitanism." In the GDR, the party launched an anti-Semitic campaign, purging "cosmopolitans" alongside "German fascists" and capitalists as traitors to the nation. The party rejected Jewish restitution for the same reason as the Belgian Catholic Party. Władysław Gomułka in "People's Poland" resolutely fought against national nihilism and proclaimed the mono-ethnic nation state as the goal. Later, in his antirevisionist campaign in 1956–1958, Kim Il-sŏng defended his dictatorship by criticizing "national nihilism." Kim was as proud of being a nationalist as he was of being a communist. The legitimacy of his *Juche* (collective subjectivity/sovereignty) dictatorship came from the public memory of Kim's anti-Japanese partisan struggle.[22] Marxists in the West also disregarded Jewish suffering under the banner of socialist universalism, a heritage with roots in the Dreyfus Affair. Jules Guesde claimed that the struggle to advocate for Dreyfus meant defending a wealthy bourgeois military officer—a deviation from the class struggle principle.[23]

Contrary to the official propaganda of proletarian internationalism, communist regimes were a hotbed for the memory of the nationalist episteme. The socialist ideal of the ethical and political unity of society reinforced the primordial concept of nation as an organic community. No wonder the grassroots memory of anti-Semitism in the interwar period continued under the regime of People's Poland. Top-down orders for the fair treatment of Jewish citizens often were blocked by prejudiced, low-ranking local bureaucrats. The Polish Workers' Party's (PPR) central committee instructors were at a loss when they realized that workers were unwilling to publicly condemn perpetrators of the Kielce pogrom of 1946. Many factory workers and organized peasants opposed a resolution condemning the pogrom and began to perceive the PPR as "Jewish," in opposition to native workers. An anonymous reporter submitted an account of the meeting of Stanisław Mikołajczyk's opposition activists: "The third speaker . . . put out a resolution that Jews should also be expelled from

Poland, and he also remarked that Hitler ought to be thanked for destroy-ing the Jews (tumultuous ovation and applause)."[24]

Anti-Semitism alone in Poland cannot explain the postwar resistance to condemning wartime crimes against Jews and postwar continuation of calls to expel them. Vichy France and the Netherlands killed almost as large a percentage of their Jewish population as Poland, where Nazi occupation policy was more pervasive and intense: approximately 80 percent of Jews were exterminated in the Netherlands. Anti-Semitism in Poland, however, has its own peculiarities. While anti-Semites of other countries under Nazi occupation often became Nazi collaborators, Polish anti-Semitic national-ists were not compromised. They fought against the Nazis and even risked their lives to rescue Jews by joining the Żegota, the underground organi-zation to save Jews. Thus a patriotic Pole could be a hero of resistance, an anti-Semite, and a savior of Jews. Those anti-Semitic saviors of Jews saved Jews so as to save the honor of the Polish nation. In this Polish paradox, the nation was deified and the memory of anti-Semitism remained a part of the patriotic memory in postwar Poland.[25] Jews could be Poles posthu-mously because "dead Jews make good Poles." Jews were integrated into the Polish national memory only through the politics of counting victims on the basis of citizenship.

Across Europe, Jews were not the only victims alienated from patriotic memory. Foreign slave workers were excluded from the German repara-tion scheme until August 2, 2000, when the Bundestag passed the law to recompense foreign slave workers. POW returnees were greeted with silent disdain in all warring countries. Their capture signified cowardice rather than brave resistance; thus they had to bear the burden of national defeat and responsibility for the calamitous war. Some were suspected of national treason. West German courts' eagerness to prosecute former POWs who had collaborated with Soviet authorities was in contrast with their relative unwillingness to prosecute Nazi crimes in 1950s.[26] Sinti and Roma were stigmatized under laws permitting their surveillance and incarceration as justified measures for preserving public order. As supporters of another totalitarian regime, communists were also ineligible for individual com-pensation. The West German judiciary found it necessary for the mainte-nance of social order to place asocials in protective custody, imprison them, and even sterilize those previously categorized as "asocials" by the

Third Reich. Discriminatory compensation practices, based on ethnicity, race, ideology, and sexuality, went along with the nationalization of memory.

The nationalization of memory also codified gender discrimination. Paragraph 175 of the Nazi criminal code, which criminalized male homosexuality, was deemed compatible with the West German democratic constitution and remained part of the criminal code. "Aryans" punished for violating Nazi racial codes for sex, especially women punished for having sexual relations with foreign POWs, did not qualify as victims.[27] Until the early 1990s, comfort women had been silenced and their memories erased from the national and regional memories in postcolonial Korea and East Asia. Though the Batavian court convicted the Japanese for forcing Dutch women POWs into prostitution, the conviction turned on it being racial transgression rather than sexual exploitation.[28] Even when a former comfort woman publically testified in 1991, the experiences of comfort women remained a matter of "nationalized sexuality." Memory activists of comfort women proposed building a monument at Independence Hall of Korea in the same year, but it was turned down on the pretext of lack of space in the most spacious memorial site in Korea. The heroic narrative of Independence Hall had no room for victims. The dominant patriarchal memory of postcolonial Korea marginalized and suppressed the memory of comfort women.[29]

The Sublime Victimhood

A bitter irony of the war memory across the globe initially was the perpetrators, the Axis powers, becoming self-proclaimed victims. Paradoxically, victimizers had a more urgent need to explore the experience of being victimized, as if any transgressions of their victims could exonerate their war atrocities, massacres, and genocidal crimes. Given the substantial degree of popular backing, voluntary self-mobilization, and the high level of plebiscitary acclamation for the regime, the *kleine Leute* in the Axis powers were more likely "willing victims" than innocent ones. When perpetration and victimhood are played out within the national collective—between evil Nazis and good Germans, between *hi-kokumin* and *kokumin*, between resistance fighters and collaborators, then the mnemonic magic of turning petty perpetrators or accomplices into innocent victims becomes possible. Thus this mnemonic magic excludes the memory of suffering by nonnational others, such as Jews, foreign slave workers, comfort women, alien Slavic communists, homosexuals, and colonized subalterns.

Among Axis powers, Japan has led the competition for victimhood because of the atomic bombing that remains beyond comparison. Hiroshima as an absolute evil is often compared with the Holocaust. Auschwitz and Hiroshima are often named as twin symbols of man-made mass death and even singled out as two archetypical examples of white racism.[30] The word *holocaust* was translated and used as early as 1945 in Japan. Takashi Nagai, a Catholic medical doctor known as the saint of Urakami Church, addressed Nagasaki victims as "the lamb without blemish, slain as a whole-burnt offering on an altar of sacrifice, atoning for the sins of all the nations during World War II." It is intriguing to find the word *hansai* (燔祭), the Japanese translation of "holocaust" from chapter 22 of Genesis, in Nagai's funeral address for Japanese A-bomb victims in Nagasaki.[31] It is a surprise to find the earliest recorded public use of "Holocaust" in the postwar world in Nagai's funeral speech in 1945, which is much earlier than "Yad Vashem" in Jerusalem or "Żydowski Instytut Historii" in Warsaw. But it did not receive due attention globally because it was in the East Asian language translation.[32] For Nagai, Catholic martyrs in Nagasaki were the worthy sacrifice for world peace and the atomic bomb became a harbinger of peace. Catholics in Nagasaki called the devastation of the atomic bomb *go-ban kuzure* (fifth persecution).[33]

With its biblical semiotics, *hansai* facilitated the nationalist sublimation of victims (*higaisha*) into sacrifices (*giseisha*). Especially for Japanese nationalists, including the Tsukurukai (New History Textbook Society) devotees, the *hibakusha*, the radiation-exposed victims, are equivalent to the dead of Auschwitz: both are victims of absolute evil.[34] Victimhood nationalism, as a political religion, comes into being in the sublime transition from victims to sacrifices. By transposing *pro domino mori* into *pro patria mori*, it could sacralize fallen soldiers and national suffering.[35] For those victims, however, sublimation was nothing other than humiliation. Disregarding their will, abstract ideas instrumentalized and thus revictimized victims. One A-bomb survivor wrote bluntly that people in Hiroshima did not like to be treated as "data" in the political movement that utilized their misery. The suicide of Kikuya Haraguchi, a poet and A-bomb victim, remains a poignant memory in this regard. He chose to die by his own hand instead of dying from radiation exposure. Committing suicide was his last resort to save his subjectivity and human dignity.[36] With his death, Haraguchi protested against the victimhood narrative that instrumentalized A-bomb survivors. The story did not end here, however.

Fire bombings, *hikiage* (the repatriation of Japanese civilians), the suffering of Japanese POWs in the Soviet Union, and the wartime misery of hunger and military oppression also were emphasized in order to vindicate Japanese victimhood. By projecting guilt and responsibility onto a handful of evil militarist-perpetrators, the majority of ordinary Japanese could remain victims. If Japanese military leaders were totally responsible, then ordinary Japanese became innocent victims who were exempt from war accountability. Japanese war crimes, guilt, and responsibility were sanitized by emphasizing the victimhood of ordinary Japanese people.[37] The transgressions of others could absolve them of their own crimes. Non-Japanese parties also contributed to the creation of the public memory of Japanese victimhood. The Supreme Command of the Allied Powers (SCAP) assumed that military leaders deceived the Japanese people. If they were deceived, they could not be guilty. SCAP's Orientalist view exempted poor, ordinary Japanese from war culpability by depriving them of agency: ordinary Japanese were innocent of the nation's transgressions done in their names and with their participation. That explains how Japanese history textbooks could implicitly link the Japanese people and Asian peoples together as common victims of the Japanese military.[38]

The historical self of the Japanese people thus came to be totally redefined. The politics of memory in postwar Japan meant that, consciously or unconsciously, many Japanese abandoned their prewar awareness of themselves as active supporters of the total war efforts by the state. They reconstructed themselves as passive, unwilling, and forced collaborators. Remembering Hiroshima and Nagasaki became a way of forgetting the Nanjing massacre, comfort women, the maltreatment of POWs, and countless other war atrocities. Conventional war atrocities also seemed insignificant compared to the apocalyptic hell of Hiroshima and Nagasaki. By segregating war victimhood from war aggression, antinuclear pacifism provided "a high moral ground of the victim who cannot be held responsible for the misuse of power."[39] On March 16, 2008, the Associated Press wired a report covering the commemoration ceremony for the fortieth anniversary of the My Lai Massacre in Vietnam and quoted a message from Shimoharu Fujio, an atomic bomb survivor of Nagasaki, who said, "I'm very angry about the indiscriminate killings both here in My Lai and in Hiroshima and Nagasaki. I came here to send a message of peace to the world." Japanese *hibakusha* delegates called attention to the inhumanity of indiscriminate killings of civilians by pointing out the similarities between the suffering of victims of the atomic bombings and that of the victims of the My Lai Massacre.[40]

Iris Chang's tactic of naming the "Nanjing Massacre" as the "forgotten Holocaust" and "Pacific Holocaust" is considered a deliberate response to the universal victimology of Hiroshima and Nagasaki. By claiming in her best seller that the Japanese in Nanjing outdid "the Romans of Carthage (*only* 150,000 died in that slaughter)," Chang made a diachronic hierarchy of victims in world history.[41] The phrases "forgotten Holocaust" and "Poland's Holocaust" have been used in Polish historiography in defense of the national righteousness of Poland. The "forgotten Holocaust" defined Poles as "the first people in Europe to experience the Holocaust." In this historiography, the Ukrainian, Belarusian, Lithuanian, German, and Jewish nationalists in interwar Poland constituted a grave danger to the survival of Poland and a barrier to nation building. As a result, interwar Poland remained a "state of nationalities" (*państwo narodowościowe*) instead of a nation-state. What is unforgettable and unforgivable is that many of these ethnic minorities sided with either the Soviet Union or Nazi Germany and collaborated in killing and oppressing ethnic Poles. In this framework, Poles became "the first people in Europe to experience the Holocaust," and "the treatment of Poles by the Germans was even worse than that of Jews" in the Polish self-righteous memory of war.[42]

The conjunction of self-exculpatory and justificatory memory with victimhood nationalism in Japan raises a serious epistemological question concerning the decontextualization of history. Yoko Kawashima Watkins's *hikiage-mono* (repatriation story), as analyzed in the chapter 1, represents a good example of how to decontextualize one's own victimhood. Decontextualized memories of victimhood are rampant. Yonehara Mari, a veteran simultaneous translator between Japanese and Russia, tells intriguing stories. In Tokyo in 1990, a symposium on Japanese POWs was filled with indignation, insults, and heckling. It was the first official meeting of the Japanese POWs who were detained in Soviet Union, now old, and the Soviet delegates. An uproar began when a historian in the Soviet delegation said the Soviet troops "entered" Manchuria. "How can you say they simply 'entered,' when they invaded, violating the Neutrality Pact?" Amid the pandemonium, the Soviet historian resumed speaking: "Shut your mouth, where were you then? Are you saying Manchuria was your territory?" The room went silent at once.[43] Another story is about a dialogue between a painter and Noda Masaaki. The painter gave a passionate speech about his bleak experience as a detainee in Siberia—dead comrades' faces, severe cold, starvation, hard labor, and the decrepit condition of the camp. When Noda asked about his experience in Northeast China, i.e., Manchuria, the eloquent painter was suddenly at a loss for words. An experience of perpetration leaves one anxious to bury the memory into oblivion.[44]

Cross-referencing of Holocaust, atomic bombing, and allied bombing is an effective instrument to decontextualize the victimhood in memory culture of postwar Germany and Japan. Apart from the twin evils of Auschwitz and Hiroshima in the Japanese memory, Jörg Friedrich's account of the Allied bombing equated the suffering of German civilians with the suffering of European Jews through linguistic associations of "Einsatzgruppe," "Gaskeller," "vernichtet," and "Zivilisationsbruch."[45] Friedrich's account of the German suffering from the Allied bombing is quite a contrast to Günther Grass's Im Krebsgang (Crabwalk, 2002). As mentioned before, the latter is careful to give historical context by alluding to the ship's service in the Nazi's "Strength Through Joy" campaign, the Nazi career of its dedicatee, the transportation of the Luftwaffe unit that bombed Guernica, the highest rate of pro-Nazi political support among German refugee-victims, and the presence of noncivilians onboard.[46] Indeed, Grass succeeded in keeping the balanced contextualization of the tragedy of the Wilhelm Gustloff. Instead of equating the suffering of the guilty German expellees with the innocent Jewish victims, he never misses the points of the collusion, collaboration, and complicity of East Prussian Germans with the Nazis in the course of the Second World War.

Criticizing Friedrich's narrative for decontextualizing history does not mean justifying Allied bombings as a punishment for historical culprits. Instead, it means locating German suffering in its historical context. Friedrich insists that Luftwaffe records regarding the "Battle of Britain" provide no indication that the Germans had a deliberate plan to bomb civilian targets. The Luftwaffe's air raid on Wieluń, a small Polish town, in the morning of September 1, 1939, was outside his scope. The command for this air raid, which marked the beginning of World War II, was *"direkt auf den Marktplatz!"* The bombing of the market square killed an estimated 1,200 Polish civilians and destroyed roughly 70 percent of the town. The commandant in charge of the air raid on Wieluń was Major General Wolfram Freiherr von Richthofen—the same officer who had commanded Condor Legion to bomb Guernica during the Spanish Civil War on April 26, 1937. Wieluń was Poland's Guernica.[47] While including Nagasaki, Friedrich's story of bombing excluded Guernica and Wieluń.

In West Germany, the East Prussian and Sudeten German expellees and German POWs interned in the Soviet Union were collectively mourned. In the Cold War, their personal memories structured the public memory of communist brutality and the nostalgic loss of the German East. Politicians in West Germany often compared what Germans had suffered under the communists with what Jews had suffered under the Nazis. The argument that German expellees were driven from their historic homelands because of their ethnicity were of a stripe with Nazi racist crimes. Germans subject to brutal retaliation in internment camps modeled on Nazi concentration camps were regarded as victims of "a crime against humanity." German POWs in Soviet camps were claimed as victims of the ethnic hatred and racial prejudices of the Russians. In the cinematic imagination, they were described as "Anne Frank behind the Urals." Discursively, these framings continued Goebbels' effort to Orientalize Russians as subhuman Asian hordes.[48] Although the worst offenders were soldiers from Belorussia and the Ukraine thirsty for revenge, the stereotype of Asian Tartar soldier as sexual looters also circulated widely. Nazis' "Brown Orientalism" persisted in postwar Germany.

The Cold War divided the memory of victimhood in two Germanies. In the GDR, the expulsion of Germans from brotherly communist countries was hardly questioned and was referred to as *Umsiedlung* (resettlement), not *Vertreibung* (expulsion). It was taboo to discuss the rape of German women by Red Army soldiers. Instead, the Allied bombing of East German cities was emphasized and interpreted as a devious plan to sabotage socialism. GDR citizens were first and foremost victims of criminal Allied bombings. Official ideologues openly equated the suffering of bombing victims in the GDR area with the suffering of Jews in the Holocaust. Walter Ulbricht fashioned himself as the leader of a future-oriented, German anticolonial revolt against American imperialism. Just as the Japanese nation metamorphosed themselves into victims of colonization within the Pacific War narrative, East Germans ensconced themselves in a morally comfortable position as innocent victims of American imperialism within a Cold War narrative. At first they were victims of the Nazis and capitalists who were traitors to the national interest of the German people. Then, Germans were threatened by American imperialism, which sought to colonize Germany and enslave the German people and, above all, the working class.[49]

In 1961 Hans Bonn, the mayor of the East German city of Dresden, wrote to the mayor of Hiroshima suggesting "a partnership in the fight for peace and against rising militarism to transcend the divisions of East and West." Bonn's letter echoed the leftists of both Germany and Japan, who claimed they were now victims of American occupation, multinational corporations, and the international capitalist order. The mayor of Hiroshima, however, did not welcome the suggestion from Dresden.[50] Then Walter Weidauer, a GDR historian, wrote about a witness of the planning of an atomic attack on Germany, who says that Dresden was designated the target of the first atomic bombing even before Hiroshima.[51] The ideological yoke of Cold War demonology suffocated any initiative challenging its essential binary. The Japanese Foreign Ministry denied passports to the Japanese organizers of the Hiroshima-Auschwitz Peace March in 1962–1963 by citing the "unfair discrimination by going to a site of genocide by German soldiers in Auschwitz but not the one committed by Soviet soldiers in the Katyń forest."[52] The ministry's concern was not groundless. Jan Frankowski, who initiated and suggested the Hiroshima-Auschwitz Peace March, was a founding member of PAX—a Catholic organization closely associated with the Polish Communist Party (PZPR), a parliamentary member in the Sejm, and the founder of Social-Christian Association (ChSS) under communist rule.[53]

The Hiroshima-Auschwitz Peace March exemplifies how blaming American imperialism in parallel with Nazism could reveal the intriguing interconnectedness of *hibakusha* victims and Holocaust victims. The mnemonic juxtaposition of Auschwitz and Hiroshima has been one mainstay of the memory culture in Japan. Yumie Hirano, a "memory keeper" in Hiroshima, mentioned explicitly that "many Jews were killed because of racial discrimination, and innocent civilians were killed in Hiroshima. I want to convey how human rights are abused at a time of war."[54] The Japanese obsession with Anne Frank marks another nationalist appropriation of the Holocaust memory. "The Anne Frank–Japan connection is based on a kinship of victims" between Auschwitz and Hiroshima/Nagasaki.[55] The Holocaust had become a metonym for national victimhood. But the Japanese nationalists don't think of the countless Anne Franks their troops had victimized in neighboring Asian nations. From a trans-Asian perspective, the mnemonic nexus of Auschwitz and Hiroshima/Nagasaki has worked as a screen memory to cover Japanese perpetration and atrocities in neighboring countries. A walking exemplar of this conjunction, the right-wing philologist Watanabe Shōichi, argues that "atomic bombings of Japan—for which US never apologized—constitute a human rights issue in comparison to which the problem of comfort women could be defined as only a commercial act."[56]

In the post–Cold War era, the German victimhood narrative exceeded all limits of international political constraints. Erika Steinbach, the former president of Der Bund der Vertriebenen (BdV), never hesitated to describe the suffering of German expellees using the terms "forced labor, extermination camp, and genocide." While she equated the misery of German expellees with the suffering of Jews in Holocaust, the Poles and Czechs who victimized these expellees were equated with the Nazi perpetrators of the Holocaust.[57] In Steinbach's decontextualized world of victims, it did not matter if these German expellees bore responsibility for Nazism. Just like the self-justificatory memory in Japan, Steinbach seems to stick to "an age-old strategy of self-exculpation, one guilt is set against the other and thereby reduced to zero."[58] A perverse feedback loop of mutually reinforcing victimhood nationalisms ensued. Japanese and German use of victimization narratives to exculpate themselves prompted furious responses from the victims of Nazism and Japanese colonialism, which then further strengthened victimhood nationalism in Japan and Germany.

Historikerstreit Globally

The year 2000 was formative in global memory space. Transnational, self-reflexive, critical, alien- and gender-sensitive memories arose simultaneously. On January 27–29, 2000, twenty-three heads of state, fourteen deputy prime ministers, and other representatives from forty-six countries gathered in Stockholm to discuss Holocaust education, remembrance, and research. At the end of this history-summit meeting, all attendees signed the "Stockholm Declaration," which proposed remembering the Holocaust as a transnational civic virtue. In May 2000 the publication of Gross's *Sąsiedzi* (*Neighbors*) triggered "*Historikerstreit po polsku*" (Polish Historiker-streit). As Poles greeted Leszek Kołakowski's warning about an incipient, painful *Historikerstreit* in Eastern Europe,[59] the heated controversy over the Jedwabne massacre brought "a genuine moral revolution" to postcom-munist Poland and awakened its sleeping complicity. On August 2, 2000, the Bundestag passed the law to recompense foreign slave workers for their wartime labor. Last but not least, the "Women's International War Crimes Tribunal on Japan's Military Sexual Slavery" was convened in Tokyo in December 2000. Transnational memory activists focused on comfort women convicted the dead emperor Hirohito of "crimes against humanity."

From the viewpoint of transnational memory, all *Historikerstreite* in the postwar era incubated the conflict between the critical and the self-justificatory memory. Compared to 1950s and 1960s, the global memory landscape in 2000 revealed a sea change. Indeed, "past is more difficult to predict than future." In an article in 2014 on the Fritz Fischer controversy (the *Historikerstreit* on World War I), *Der Spiegel* described justificatory mem-ory as a *Zeitgeist* in 1960s Germany. Reacting to Fischer's thesis on German culpability even for the First World War in 1961, conservatives in the Bund-estag were resolved "to combat and eradicate the habitual, negligent and deliberate distortions of German history and Germany's image today, distortions that are sometimes made with the intention of dissolving the Western community."[60] The German Foreign Ministry tried to pre-vent Fischer from traveling to the United States for a series of lectures in 1964. The reaction is in stark contrast to the German public's enthusi-astic reception of Daniel Goldhagen in 1996, regardless of his essentialist interpretation of German anti-Semitism.

The Eichmann trial and the Frankfurt Auschwitz trial in the early 1960s awakened the repressed memories of war, genocide, dictatorship, and colo-nialism. Politically correct history is impossible, because one cannot turn the clock back. But politically correct memory is possible, because mem-ory is in the making now. One cannot change what happened in the past, but one can change the way of remembering that past. That explains why the generation of 1968 launched the memory war against self-exculpatory memory. Reactions to the American-Vietnam War detonated the bomb of critical memory globally. Drawing on the idea of the Nuremburg tribunal, Bertrand Russell used his citizen's tribunal to accuse the United States of genocide. Later the Women's International War Crimes Tribunal on Japan's Military Sexual Slavery of 2000 would be modeled on his efforts. Telford Taylor, the American prosecutor in Nuremburg, expressed his agreement in his *Nuremburg and Vietnam: An American Tragedy.* Jean-Paul Sartre associated the American genocide in Vietnam with France's bloody war against the Algerian anticolonial fighters. Jewish student activists contributed Holocaust analogies that buttressed the antiracism in the Vietnam-genocide discourse. The Vietnam War prompted young revisionist historians in Greece to see the UK and the United States not as saviors of Greece from communist tyranny but as imperialists that crushed a popular radical movement.[61]

American atrocities in Vietnam also fueled Japanese interest in exposing their own atrocities in the Fifteen Years' War (1931–1945). After chronicling American war atrocities in Vietnam as a journalist for the *Asahi shimbun*, Honda Katsuichi came to reflect on this matter. In summer 1971 he spent forty days traveling across the path of Japanese military aggression in China to collect eyewitness accounts and other evidence. He wrote a series of travel reports in the *Asahi shimbun*, later published as a book, *Chūgoku no tabi* (Travels in China). Meeting Honda's book on the Nanjing massacre with angry criticism, conservatives denied and minimized the massacre by naming it the "Nanjing *Incident.*" Maoist China had been indifferent to the Nanjing massacre per se because its "present significance" was to prevent American imperialists' remilitarization of Japan. Only much later, on August 15, 1985, was the "memorial for the compatriot victims in the Nanjing massacre by the Japanese invading troops" completed. It was renovated and expanded again in 1997, the same year Iris Chang's *Rape of Nanking* was published.[62]

Epistemologically, a shift from documents to testimonies underlies the global emergence of critical memory. If Nuremburg is marked as "the victory of the written over the oral," the Eichmann trial freed victims to speak and opened the era of witnesses. Raul Hilberg's thorny question, "Is it not equally barbaric to write footnotes after Auschwitz?," epitomizes that shift. Hilberg's question reads as a warning to pompous positivist historians.[63]

The dilemma is that perpetrators and rulers monopolize narrative and history while victims have only experiences and voices. Testimonies are important and sometimes the only sources, but victims' memories are incomplete, imbalanced, and often incorrect. Conventional historians interrogate and interrupt witnesses and dismiss testimony for its inaccuracy, as if memory is a game of truth or dare. As the Eichmann trial showed, the K-Zetnik witnesses did not prove facts but rather transmitted affects. Their task was to transmit the untransmissible.

In his convincing psychoanalytic account of a survivor's memory about "four chimneys blown up," Dori Laub pointed out the gap between intellectual memory and deep memory. While the formal historical record reveals that one chimney at Auschwitz actually blew up, the survivor-witness's deep memory of four chimneys reflects the reality of the unimaginable occurrence of a Jewish armed revolt. Both the survivor-witness and the record are right in "the aporia of Auschwitz," illustrating the "non-coincidence between facts and truth, between verification and comprehension."[64] Ignoring the epistemological bite of such challenges, positivistic historians of denial are insistent. They never comprehend the aporia of Auschwitz and keep interrogating as if the slightest inconsistency invalidates the entire testimony. In scouring meandering testimonies, deniers can easily find inconsistencies in logic, factual inaccuracies, and petty textual faults. Then they ask, "Why weren't we told before if it were true?" But the truth is they didn't listen. The right question should be, "Why weren't we listening before?"[65] Even Jan Gross took four years to accept the testimony of Szmuel Wasersztajn as a source for his book on Jedwabne—a powerful illustration that the hierarchy of the written over the oral remains strong even among advocates of critical memories.[66]

The task of transmitting the untransferable risks the sacralization of memory. A certain degree of sacralization of memories is inevitable for individuals, as it makes one's past unique, incommensurable with others' experiences. On the national level, however, collective memory comes into being through communication, education, commemoration, rituals, and ceremonies among the masses. By nature, such a collective memory cannot be sacralized. Rather it comes to be through political contestation. The generic *Historikerstreit* shows that the sacralization of traumatic memory is the epistemological foundation of exculpatory memory, because it prevents the critical gaze of the outsiders from "our unique past." Sacralized memories are the preserve of nations—nations deny outsiders the right to understand their distinctive national pasts, much less to study or interrogate them. In a profound irony, the uniqueness of the Holocaust validates and reinforces the global space of individual national justificatory memories. Arguments about the Holocaust's uniqueness hew so close to the colloquial thesis of "you foreigners can never ever understand our tragic national past" that in the generic *Historikerstreit* there is no effective difference.

Thematically the topic of "complicity/collaboration" is the most salient and global issue in the *Historikerstreit* concerning war, genocide, dictatorship, and colonialism. Once liberated from the Manichean Cold War binary between a few bad victimizers and many innocent victims, the complicity/collaboration issue gained traction. Postcolonial criticism, the political project of democratizing democracy in the postdictatorial regimes, and *Vergangenheitsbewältigung* (coming to terms with the past) in postcommunist Eastern Europe accelerated the debate in three dimensions: (post)colonial guilt, genocidal complicity, and agency and responsibility.

First, postcolonial criticism broke the repressive connection between history and the nation and thus shook the binaries of national resistance and colonial collaboration and of colonial continuity and postcolonial discontinuity. In the East Asian memory space, Manchukuo, the Japanese puppet state in Manchuria, provides a good example. Though critical to postcolonial East Asia, Manchukuo faded from the East Asian memory space after 1945. This long absence raises suspicions. Both the rightist and leftist dictatorship in the two Koreas inherited from Manchukuo historical legacies of the defense state, military mobilization, national ceremonies, big sports festivals, and even Confucianism as the official ideology. The strange amalgam of the American Taylor system, social engineering, and mobilization in the total war system of interwar Germany and Japan, planned economy and industrial warriors of Soviet Union likewise flowed into the developmental dictatorship in South Korea through Manchukuo.[67] Manchukuo, as memory of colonial guilt, had no place in the postcolonial nationalist narrative.

Postcolonial criticism pays attention also to the continuity of guilt between colonial genocide and the Holocaust. Viewed from postcolonial perspectives, the colonial (dis)continuity between German colonialists' genocide in the Herero and Nama wars in 1904–1907 and the Holocaust could be better explained in the memory of Euro-colonialism. As a group of Black radical intellectuals sharply pointed out, Western European colonialism, fascism, and Nazism shared practices, methods, and objects.[68] The Nazi utopia of a racially purified German empire mimicked Western colonialism, "turning imperialism on its head and treating Europeans as Africans."[69] German Nazis must have felt a kind of "white men's burden" vis-à-vis Slavic people as "white negroes." And "the Slavs would be the German equivalent of the conquered native populations of India and Africa in the British empire."[70] Indeed, "Western" colonialism provided an important historical precedent for the genocidal thinking of the Nazis.

The Holocaust is an unparalleled or singular event. But it is also of a kind with other genocides and thus can be subject to comparative analysis. A discourse of uniqueness that forbids any comparison is an ideologically driven attempt to preserve the Holocaust as a kind of sacred entity. The emergence of the global memory space shattered the illusion of the Holocaust's uniqueness and its sacred aura. Before the German Nazis' Holocaust, colonial powers of Western Europe had wrought terror on indigenous peoples worldwide for nearly five hundred years. The claim of the uniqueness of the Holocaust, however, rises from the Eurocentric belief that the Holocaust stands apart from other genocides since it was committed in the heart of civilized Europe rather than in "primitive or barbaric" societies.[71] Much worse than Eurocentrism, the Holocaust's uniqueness, consciously or unconsciously, creates the conditions of possibility for denying other historical genocides. It is appalling to find eminent Holocaust scholars arguing that, unlike the Holocaust, the Rwandan genocide was pragmatic and Nazis' mass killing of Roma and Sinti were solutions to social problems.

The second issue is genocidal complicity. Individual memories of the genocide prove the dictum that "structure does not kill, but individuals do." Ordinary men and women, making improvisational and face-to-face decisions under local conditions, implemented and supplemented the mass killings. Murderers were flesh-and-blood human beings just like us. We should consider an existential-ethical question such as Christopher Browning's: "If the men of Reserve Police Battalion 101 could become killers under such circumstances, what group of men cannot?" In other words, "placed in comparable situations and similar social constituencies, you or

I might also commit murderous ethnic cleansing."[72] Noda Masaaki's psychoanalysis of Japanese veteran perpetrators is poignant in this regard. Despite acknowledging their wrongdoings, most perpetrators could not remember the faces of their victims. As the interview progressed, however, at the instant of genuine repentance, the face of his victim returned to one veteran soldier's memory.[73] Masaaki's finding echoes Zygmunt Bauman's reflection on "the emancipatory role of the feeling of shame" in the *Historikerstreit* in Poland.

On the macro level, genocidal complicity resonates with the denationalization of memory. For example, deconstructing the patriotic memory of resistance revealed the collaboration and genocidal complicity in the Vichy regime. Paradoxically speaking, the "de-Resistantialization" made it possible to criticize French collaboration and complicity in deporting Jewish neighbors. Critical engagement with the memory of genocidal complicity did not stop with the "Vichy syndrome." Soon the "Algerian syndrome" followed. Maurice Papon on trial personified the twin genocidal complicity: the roundup and deportation of the Jews from Bordeaux in Vichy France and bloody killing of Algerian immigrant-demonstrators on October 17, 1961. Yet he was convicted and sentenced only for the crime committed against Jews.[74] The memory of genocidal complicity in France and other European countries was denationalized but not yet de-Europeanized.

The third issue, "agency and responsibility," overlaps with issues of colonial continuity and genocidal complicity. Neologisms from the 1990s—"mass dictatorship," *Fürsorgediktatur* (welfare dictatorship), *Konzensdiktatur* (dictatorship of consent), "everyday fascism," and "palingenetic consensus"—indicate how the study of dictatorship has shifted from a focus on coercion to one of consent. Paradoxically, that shift promoted the critical memory of dictatorship by focusing on the agency of *kleine Leute* who supported the dictatorship from below. They cannot be exonerated from responsibility and culpability. What is more complicated is that no line clearly divided victimizers and victims. Rather, it ran through each individual. Not everyone was an accomplice, but everyone was in some measure responsible for what had been done. The Japanese historians' debate on the total war system, in which voluntary participation and self-mobilization were discussed, tells the same story. The change from the justificatory memory of *kokumin* victims to the critical memory of self-mobilized historical actors made it impossible for ordinary Japanese to be exempted from accountability for the war.[75]

Like the *Historikerstreit* in Eastern Europe, the Korean *Historikerstreit* on "mass dictatorship" debated the responsibility and complicity of the masses in conformity with the dictatorship. The political experience of democratization in South Korea shows that the Fascist habitus still reigns in everyday practices and influences people's way of thinking, even long after the developmental dictatorship. At heart in the debate was how to explain the obstinate Fascist habitus and the strong nostalgia for developmental dictatorship among democratic citizens and how to democratize the democracy haunted by the legacy of the dictatorship. Though the thesis of mass dictatorship has been caught in the crossfire between leftist-liberal historians and sociologists, the moral implication of the "mass dictatorship" could not be more divergent from justificatory memory. The hoary myth, central to the old antifascist demonology, of the working masses as resistance fighters and innocent victims validated self-justification and exculpatory memory. Adam Michnik's critical self-reflection of "whether we are not all children of totalitarian communism, whether we do not all carry inside ourselves the habits, the customs, and the flaws of that system," stands on the same terrain.[76]

"Multidirectional Memory"

The Museum of Occupations in Tallinn, Estonia, installed two massive mockup trains at the gateway to the back half of the exhibition, one bearing the Nazi swastika, the other the Soviet red star. The two locomotives in the center of the museum represent the political symmetry between two totalitarian regimes—Nazism and Stalinism. They evoke Andrzej Wajda's film *Katyń*, which begins with scenes of the dramatic encounter between two bands of Polish refugees in the middle of the bridge near Kraków. Nazi Germans are chasing the one group fleeing to the east, while the Red Army is pursuing the other band toward the west. The Prague Declaration on European Conscience and Communism, signed on June 3, 2008, reflects this bitter wartime memory of "nowhere to go" among East Europeans. The Prague Declaration calls for "the equal treatment and non-discrimination of victims of all the totalitarian regimes" based on the recognition that the Nazis and communists both committed crimes against humanity. The declaration recommends the "establishment" of the day of the signing of the Molotov-Ribbentrop Pact on August 23 as "a day of remembrance of the victims of both Nazi and Communist totalitarian regimes."[77] It reflects Eastern European intellectuals' concern that an excessive emphasis on the Holocaust can obscure the Stalinist-communist crimes against non-Jewish East Europeans. Once the East European countries secured membership in the European Union and NATO, suppressed antipathy against the Stockholm decision on Holocaust education, a precondition of the East European countries' entry to those institutions in 2000, surfaced.

The Prague Declaration soon encountered opposition. The "Seventy Years Declaration" signed on January 20, 2012, the seventieth anniversary of the Wannsee Conference of 1942, criticized the Prague Declaration's "attempts to obfuscate the Holocaust by diminishing its uniqueness and deeming it to be equal, similar or equivalent to communism" and advocated "distinct days and distinct programs to remember the Holocaust and other victims of other twentieth-century totalitarian regimes."[78] The clash between the two declarations reflects differences in historical experiences during and after World War II. While Eastern Europeans tend to emphasize the similarities between communism and Nazism as totalitarian regimes, Western Europeans maintain the uniqueness of the Holocaust. Since the slogan of "no hierarchy between victims" that challenges the Holocaust's uniqueness frequently appear at some neo-Nazi rallies, the confrontation is all the more complicated.

I agree with the principle of "agreeing to disagree," which promotes multiple memories, recognition of cultural difference, and empathy with others. We need, nevertheless, to problematize here the essentialist perception of the Holocaust. Uniqueness and comparability are not either/or questions but bound to the specific historical context. If the relativization of the Holocaust contributed to the exculpatory memory in the German *Historikerstreit*, the discourse of Holocaust uniqueness chokes critical memory in Israel. The so-called new historians' criticism of the Zionist appropriation of the Holocaust in Israel would never mean to endorse necessarily the self-exculpatory memory in Germany or Holocaust denial in Iran. Whether to be critical or to be justificatory depends on the discursive loci of the uniqueness and relativism of the Holocaust in specific historical contexts.

As Michael Rothberg points out, memory is not a zero-sum game.[79] The recognition of suffering of one party does not deny the suffering of another party. On the contrary, the interaction, negotiation, confluence, cross-references, and conjunction of different historical memories across the globe empowers the performativity of critical memory vis-à-vis exculpatory memory. The Australian aborigine leader William Cooper's protest action against Nazi persecution of Jews in 1938 is a good example. The swift response by African Americans to the "Genocide Convention" of 1948 is another landmark step toward global critical memory. In a petition delivered to the UN—*We Charge Genocide*—in 1951, American Black radicals pinpointed parallels between Nazi perpetrators and racist perpetrators in the United States. Concerned about gaining support for the UN's Genocide Convention from the United States, Raphael Lemkin did not endorse the petitioners in print.[80] The General Assembly did not adopt their petition. However, the UN's official denial and Lemkin's criticism did stop W. E. B. Du Bois from recalling "the scream and shots of a race riot in Atlanta and the marching of the Ku Klux Klan" during his visit to the ruins of the Warsaw ghetto in 1949. Du Bois confessed, "The result of these three visits, and particularly of my view of the Warsaw ghetto, was not so much a clearer understanding of the Jewish problem in the world as it was a real and more complete understanding of the Negro problem."[81]

The migrant archive of the Holocaust in contemporary Germany inspires multidirectional memory too: the Kurdish-German staging of an adaptation of Holocaust survivor Edgar Hilsenrath's novel about the Armenian genocide, Şenocak's novel that places the Holocaust into contact with the Armenian genocide and dislocates ethnicity radically in the person of its German-Turkish-Muslim narrator, and the engagement of a multiethnic collective with the Holocaust through the *Stadtteilmütter* project. All this experimental memory activism in the migrant archive deconstructs the discourse of Holocaust uniqueness, which has been increasingly used to discipline non-Jewish minorities.[82] The mnemonic confluence of the Holocaust and comfort women appears to signify the extraterritoriality of global memory and the potentiality of postnationalist, solidaristic memory communities. "Cosmopolitan memory," however, does not necessarily guarantee the deterritorialization of memory. The Holocaust, as cosmopolitan memory, can be marshaled to persuade the global audience of national suffering; the Holocaust thus can serve as a weapon of reterritorializing memory.

From the standpoint of multidirectional memory, problematizing today's East European memory does not mean criticizing the deconstruction of Holocaust uniqueness but rather the sublimation of national victimhood. The East European *Historikerstreit*, including the Jedwabne controversy in Poland and *Vergangenheitsbewältigung* in Baltic countries, shows that the obsession with national victimhood blinds Eastern Europeans to their complicity in perpetrating the Holocaust. No less problematically, the East European *Historikerstreit* never confronted postcolonial criticism of the Eurocentricity of debates over victimhood. In his bestselling history textbook for high school students in 2004, Wojciech Roszkowski, a popular anticommunist Polish historian in the "second circulation" under martial law and a cosignatory of the Prague Declaration, writes that the nineteenth century saw the expansion of the European civilization to the rest of the world, and thus that Eurocentrism is inevitable to some degree.[83] To develop global critical memory, the East European *Historikerstreit* must provincialize European memory through the multidirectional negotiation of the memories of the Holocaust, the two totalitarian regimes of Nazism and Stalinism, and postcolonial criticism of colonial violence.

Notes

1. "美정부 1호 위안부기림비 뉴저지서 제막식" [Unveiling the first comfort women monument in USA], *Chosun ilbo* online, March 9, 2013, http://news.chosun.com/site/data/html_dir/2013/03/09/2013030900651.html.

2. KACE, "Compilation of Korean News Articles on Comfort Women Survivors and Holocaust Survivors' Meetings," December 21, 2011, http://kace.org/2011/12/21/compilation-of-news-articles-on-comfort-women-survivors-and-holocaust-survivors%27-meeting/.

3. Dan Goldberg, "An Aboriginal Protest Against the Nazis, Finally Delivered," *Haaretz*, October 10, 2012, http://www.haaretz.com/jewish-world/jewish-world-features/an-aboriginal-protest-against-the-nazis-finally-delivered.premium-1.483806.

4. Gary Foley, "Australia and the Holocaust: A Koori Perspective," accessed January 20, 2020, http://www.kooriweb.org/foley/essays/pdf_essays/australia%20and%20the%20holocaust.pdf.

5. Martin Krygier, "Letter from Australia: Neighbors: Poles, Jews and the Aboriginal Question," *East Central Europe* 29 (2002): 297–309.

6. Piotr Forecki, *Od Shoah do Strachu: spory o polsko-żydowską przeszłość i pamięć w debatach publicznych* (Poznań: Wydawnictwo Poznańskie, 2010), 309.

7. Paul Behrens, Nicholas Terry, and Olaf Jensen, eds., *Holocaust and Genocide Denial: A Contextual Perspective* (New York: Routledge, 2017), 2.

8. William F. S. Miles, "Indigenization of the Holocaust and the Tehran Holocaust Conference: Iranian Aberration or Third World Trend?," *Human Rights Review*, no. 10 (2009): 507; George Michael, "Mahmoud Ahmadinejad's Sponsorship of Holocaust Denial," *Totalitarian Movements and Political Religions* 8, (September/December 2007): 667–69.

9. Carol Gluck, "Operations of Memory: Comfort Women and the World," in *Ruptured Histories: War, Memory, and the Post-Cold War in Asia*, ed. Sheila Miyoshi Jager and Rana Mitter (Cambridge, Mass.: Harvard University Press, 2007), 48.

10. Pieter Lagrou, *The Legacy of Nazi Occupation: Patriotic Memory and National Recovery in Western Europe, 1945-1965*, Studies in the Social and Cultural History of Modern Warfare, book 8 (Cambridge: Cambridge University Press, 1999).

11. Naoki Sakai, "History and Responsibility: On the Debates on the *Shōwa History*," in *Mass Dictatorship and Memory as Ever Present Past*, ed. Jie-Hyun Lim, Barbara Walker, and Peter Lambert (Basingstoke: Palgrave Macmillan, 2014), 120–21. Stalin banned the term "National Socialism" in 1931-1932, perhaps because of the ideological ventriloquism of Stalinism and Nazism. GDR leaders seemed to prefer the term "German fascism" to Nazism too.

12. Gluck, "Operations of Memory," 51.

13. Hayashi made a comparison between the Jean d'Arc-led French-English Hundred Years War and the Japanese hundred years war against the Western imperialism. Hayashi Husao, 大東亞戰爭肯定論 [Legitimizing the Great East Asia War] (Tokyo: Chuobunko, 2014), 7, 19, 149, 248.

14. Sebastian Conrad, "The Dialectics of Remembrance: Memories of Empire in Cold War Japan," *Comparative Studies in Society and History* 56 (2014): 13, 17–18.

15. Benedict Anderson, *The Spectre of Comparisons: Nationalism, Southeast Asia and the World* (London: Verso, 1998), 1–2.

16. Michael Burleigh, *The Third Reich: A New History* (New York: Hill and Wang, 2001), 425.

17. Utsumi Aiko, 朝鮮人 BC 級戰犯の記録 [Records of the Korean BC class war criminals] (Tokyo: Keisōshobō, 1982); Utsumi Aiko and Murai Yoshinori, 赤道下の朝鮮人叛亂 [Korean rebellion on the equator] (Tokyo: Keisōshobō, 1980).

18. Pieter Lagrou, "Victims of Genocide and National Memory: Belgium, France and the Netherlands 1945-65," *Past & Present* 154 (1997): 182, 193, 198–99; Ian Buruma, *Year Zero: A History of 1945* (New York: Penguin Press, 2013), 134–35.

19. Tony Judt, *Postwar: A History of Europe Since 1945* (New York: Penguin Press, 2005), 58–59; Robert G. Moeller, *War Stories: The Search for a Usable Past in the Federal Republic of Germany* (Berkeley: University of California Press, 2001), 26–27.

20. Frank Biess, "Between Amnesty and Anti-communism: The West German Kameradenschinder Trials, 1948–1960," in *Crimes of War: Guilt and Denial in the Twentieth Century*, ed. Omer Bartov, Atina Grossmann, and Mary Nolan (New York: New Press, 2002), 138–60.

21. See Alf Lüdtke, "Soldiering and Working: Almost the Same? Reviewing Practices in Industry and the Military in Twentieth-Century Contexts," in *Work in a Modern Society: The German Historical Experience in Comparative Perspective*, ed. Jürgen Kocka (New York: Berghahn, 2010), 109–30.

22. Jeffrey Herf, *Divided Memory: The Nazi Past in the Two Germanys* (Cambridge, Mass.: Harvard University Press, 1997), 33–36; see also chapter 8 of the present volume.

23. Robert Cherry, "Holocaust Historiography: The Role of the Cold War," *Science & Society* 63 (Winter 1999–2000): 459–60; Norman Geras, "Marxists Before the Holocaust," *New Left Review* 224 (1997): 37–38; Pierre Vidal-Naquet, *Assassins of Memory: Essays on the Denial of the Holocaust*, trans. Jeffrey Mehlman (New York: Columbia University Press, 1992), xxi.

24. Jan T. Gross, *Fear: Anti-Semitism in Poland After Auschwitz* (New York: Random House, 2006), 98, 120–22, 225–26.

25. Adam Michnik, "Poles and the Jews: How Deep the Guilt?," in *The Neighbors Responded: The Controversy Over the Jedwabne Massacre in Poland*, ed. Adam Polonsky and Joanna Michlic (Princeton, N.J.: Princeton University Press, 2004), 435–36.

26. Biess, "Between Amnesty and Anti-communism," 140–42, 149–152; Frank Biess, *Homecomings: Returning POWs and the Legacies of Defeat in Postwar Germany* (Princeton, N.J.: Princeton University Press, 2006).

27. Moeller, *War Stories*, 28–29.

28. Gluck, "Operations of Memory," 67.

29. Yang Hyunah, "한국인 군위안부를 기억한다는 것" [Remembering Korean Comfort Women], in *Dangerous Women*, ed. Elaine H. Kim and Chungmoo Choi, trans. Park Eun-mi (Seoul: Samin, 2001), 175.

30. Ian Buruma, 아우슈비츠와 히로시마 [*The Wages of Guilt: Memories of War in Germany and Japan*], trans. Jeong Yonghwan (Seoul: Hangyŏreh Shinmusa, 2002), 119–26; John W. Dower, "An Aptitude for Being Unloved: War and Memory in Japan," in *Crimes of War: Guilt and Denial in the Twentieth Century*, ed. Omer Bartov, Atina Grossmann, and Mary Nolan (New York: New Press, 2002), 226.

31. Takahshi Tetsuya, 국가와 희생 [State and sacrifice], trans. Yi Mok (Seoul: Chaekgwahamkke, 2008), 72–83; John W. Dower, "The Bombed: Hiroshima and Nagasaki in Japanese Memory," *Diplomatic History* 19 (Spring 1995): 285.

32. American officers, rank-and-file soldiers, and other World War II participants used the term *Holocaust* in their private correspondence but not in the public memory or commemoration. See Steve Friess, "When 'Holocaust' Became 'The Holocaust,'" *New Republic*, May 18, 2015, https://newrepublic.com/article/121807/when-holocaust-became-holocaust; Sean Warsch, "A 'Holocause' Becomes 'the Holocaust,'" *Jewish Magazine* (October 2006), http://www.jewishmag.com/107mag/holocaustword/holocaustword.htm.

33. Gwyn MaClelland, "Guilt, Persecution, and Resurrection in Nagasaki: Atomic Memories and the Urakami Catholic Community," *Social Science Japan Journal* 18, no. 2 (2015): 239.

34. Tetsuya Takahashi, "The Emperor Showa Standing at Ground Zero: On the (Re)configuration of a National 'Memory' of the Japanese People," *Japan Forum* 15, no. 1 (2003): 6.

35. It is difficult to catch this semantic sublimation in the German *Opfer* and the Polish *ofiara*, signifying victim and sacrifice simultaneously, but the division between victim and sacrifice is rather clear in English and East Asian languages. For victimhood nationalism, see chapter 1.

36. Kenzaburo Oe, *Hiroshima Noto* [*Hiroshima Notes*] (Tokyo: Iwanami Shoten, 1965), 6, 8.

37. Dower, "An Aptitude for Being Unloved," 228.

38. James J. Orr, *The Victim as Hero: Ideologies of Peace and National Identity in Postwar Japan* (Honolulu: University of Hawai'i Press, 2001), 9, 14–16, 33.

39. Orr, *The Victim as Hero*, 36, 44,

40. Hiroshi Fujimoto, "Towards Reconciliation, Harmonious Coexistence and Peace: The Madison Quakers, Inc. Projects and the Hibakusha's Visit to My Lai in March 2008," *Nanzan Review of American Studies* 37 (2015): 14–15.

41. Iris Chang, *The Rape of Nanking: The Forgotten Holocaust of World War II* (New York: Basic Books, 1997), 5–6.

42. Tadeusz Piotrowski, *Poland's Holocaust: Ethnic Strife, Collaboration with Occupying Forces and Genocide in the Second Republic, 1918–1947* (Jefferson, N.C.: McFarland, 1998); Richard C. Lukas, *Forgotten Holocaust: The Poles Under German Occupation*, rev. ed. (New York: Hippocrene Books, 2005).

43. Yonehara Mari, 마녀의 한다스 [Witch's thirteen essays], trans. Lee Hyunjin (Seoul: Maumsanchaek, 2009), 105.

44. Yonehara Mari, 대단한 책 [Extraordinary book], trans. Lee Ōnsook (Seoul: Maumsanchaek, 2007), 126. .

45. Jörg Friedrich, *Der Brand: Deutschland im Bombenkrieg 1940-1945* (Munich: Propyläen Verlag, 2002).

46. Günther Grass, 게걸음으로 가다 [*Im Krebsgang*], trans. Jang Huichang (Seoul: Minumsa, 2002).

47. Tadeusz Olejnek, *Wieluń. Polska Guernika* (Wieluń: BWTN, 2004). The legendarily arrogant Richthofen later led the Luftwaffe to invade Greece, Yugoslavia, and Russia. His bombers carpet-bombed Stalingrad, as his diary notes: "My two-day major assault on Stalingrad with good incendiary effects right from the start." Anthony Beevor, *The Second World War* (New York: Little, Brown, 2012), 337.

48. Moeller, *War Stories*, 78–82, 161–64.

49. Jeffrey Herf, *Divided Memory: The Nazi Past in the Two Germanys* (Cambridge, Mass.: Harvard University Press, 1997), 35, 109–10.

50. Ran Zwigenberg, "Never Again: Hiroshima, Auschwitz and the Politics of Commemoration," *Asia-Pacific Journal: Japan Focus* 13, no. 3 (January 19, 2015): 6.

51. Bas von Benda-Beckmann, *A German Catastrophe? German Historians and the Allied Bombings, 1945-2010* (Amsterdam: Amsterdam University Press, 2010), 132–33.

52. "Hiroshima-Auschwitzu Heiwa Koshin," newsletter no. 1, Hiroshima Peace Memorial Park Archive, Kawamato Collection, box 38, folder 1, no. 911, p. 10. Cited in Zwigenberg, "Never Again," 7.

53. "Jan Frankowski," *Słownik biograficzny katolicyzmu społecznego w Polsce*, vol. 1, A–J (Lublin: Towarzystwo Naukowe Katolickiego Uniwersytetu Lubelskiego, 1994); Ariel Orzełek, "U genezy Chrześcijańskiego Stowarzyszenia Społecznego. Powstanie i rozpad pierwszego zespołu redakcyjnego tygodnika [Za i Przeciw],' " *Kwartalnik Historyczny* 126, no. 4 (2019): 723, 727–28, 730.

54. Sakiko Masuda, " 'Memory Keeper' Yumie Hirano to Visit Poland in May, Convey Survivors' Experiences of Atomic Bombing," *Chugoku shimbun*, April 18, 2016, http://www.hiroshimapeacemedia.jp/?p=59331.

55. "Why Are the Japanese So Fascinated with Anne Frank?," *Haaretz*, January 22, 2014, https://www.haaretz.com/jewish/anne-frank-the-japanese-anime-1.5314070.

56. Karoline Postel-Vinay with Mark Selden, "History on Trial: French Nippon Foundation Sues Scholar for Libel to Protect the Honor of Sasakawa Ryōichi," *Asia-Pacific Journal: Japan Focus*, April 26, 2010, https://apjjf.org/-Mark-Selden/3349/article.html.

57. Jan Piskorski, *Vertreibung und Deutsch-Polnische Geschichte* (Osnabrück: Fibre Verlag, 2005), 37, 42ff.

58. Aleida Assmann, "On the (In)compatibility and Suffering in German Memory," *German Life and Letters* 59 (April 2006): 194.

59. Leszek Kołakowski, "Amidst Moving Ruins," *Daedalus* 121, no. 2 (Spring 1992): 56.

60. Dick Kurbjuweit, "World War I Guilt: Culpability Question Divides Historians Today," *Der Spiegel*, February 14, 2014, http://www.spiegel.de/international/world/questions-of-culpability-in-wwi-still-divide-german-historians-a-953173.html.

61. Berthold Molden, "Vietnam, the New Left and the Holocaust: How the Cold War Changed Discourse on Genocide," in *Memory in a Global Age: Discourses, Practices, and Trajectories*, ed. Aleida Assmann and Sebastian Conrad (Basingstoke, UK: Palgrave Macmillan, 2010), 79–96; Mark Mazower, "The Cold War and the Appropriation of Memory: Greece after Liberation," in *The Politics of Retribution in Europe: World War II and Its Aftermath*, ed. István Deák, Jan T. Gross and Tony Judt (Princeton, N.J.: Princeton University Press, 2000), 224–25.

62. Daqing Yang, "The Malleable and the Contested: The Nanjing Massacre in Postwar China and Japan," in *Perilous Memories: The Asia-Pacific War(s)*, ed. T. Fujitani, Geoffrey M. White, and Lisa Yoneyama (Durham, N.C.: Duke University Press, 2001), 50–86.

63. It echoes more significant because Hilberg himself is very much an archive-based historian. Raul Hilberg, "I Was Not There," in *Writing and the Holocaust*, ed. Berel Lang (New York: Holmes & Meier, 1988), 17, 20, 25.

64. Marianne Hirsch and Leo Spitzer, "The Witness in the Archive: Holocaust Studies/Memory Studies," *Memory Studies* 2 (2009): 156, 159, 161.

65. Martin Krygier, "Letter from Australia," 300.

66. Jan Gross confessed that he could not at first trust the testimony of Szmuel Wasersztajn—one of the main sources for his book on Jedwabne. He and his ex-wife Irena thought that Wasersztajn was insane. It took four years for him to understand what happened in Jedwaben after having encountered Wasersztajn's testimony. See *Jan Tomasz Gross w rozmowie z Aleksandrą Pawlicką* (Warsaw: Wydawnictwo b, 2018), 137–40; Jan T. Gross, *Neighbors: The Destruction of the Jewish Community in Jedwabne, Poland* (New York: Penguin Books, 2002), 6.

67. Suk-Jung Han, "The Suppression and Recall of Colonial Memory: Manchukuo and the Cold War in the Two Koreas," in *Mass Dictatorship and Memory as Ever Present Past*, ed. Jie-Hyun Lim, Barbara Walker, and Peter Lambert (Basingstoke: Palgrave Macmillan, 2014), 172–74.

68. Cedric J. Robinson, "Fascism and the Intersection of Capitalism, Racialism and Historical Consciousness," *Humanities in Society* 3 (Autumn 1983), 325–49; Jürgen Zimmerer, "Die Geburt des Ostlandes aus dem Geiste des Kolonialismus: Die nationalsozialistische Eroberungs- und Beherrschungspolitik in (post-)kolonialer Perspektive," *Sozial Geschichte* 19, no. 1 (2004); Benjamin Madley, "From Africa to Auschwitz: How German South West Africa Incubated Ideas and Methods Adopted and Developed by the Nazis in Eastern Europe," *European History Quarterly* 35, no. 3 (2005); Enzo Traverso, *The Origins of Nazi Violence* (New York: New Press, 2003); Robert Gerwarth and Stephan Malinowski, "Der Holocaust als kolonialer Genozid? Europaeische Kolonialgewalt und nationalsozialistischer Vernichtungskrieg," *Geschichte und Gesellschaft* 33 (2007).

69. Mark Mazower, *Dark Continent: Europe's Twentieth Century* (New York: Vintage Books, 1998), xiii.

70. Ian Kershaw, *Hitler, 1936–45: Nemesis* (New York: Norton, 2001), 400, 405.

71. Dan Stone, "The Historiography of Genocide: Beyond Uniqueness and Ethnic Competition," *Rethinking History* 8, no. 1 (2004): 129, 131–33. See also Dirk Moses, "Conceptual Blockages and Definitional Dilemmas in the 'Racial Century': Genocides of Indigenous Peoples and the Holocaust," *Patterns of Prejudice* 36, no. 4 (2002); Mazower, *Dark Continent*.

72. Christopher Browning, *Ordinary Men: Reserve Police Battalion 101 and the Final Solution in Poland* (New York: Harper Perennial, 1993), 189; Michael Mann, *The Dark Side of Democracy: Explaining Ethnic Cleansing* (Cambridge: Cambridge University Press, 2005), 9.

73. Noda Masaaki, 戰爭と罪責 [War and guilt] (Tokyo: Iwanami Shoten, 1998).

74. Joan B. Wolf, *Harnessing the Holocaust: The Politics of Memory in France* (Stanford: Stanford University Press, 2004), 189–98.

75. See the five volumes of the Palgrave series of "Mass Dictatorship in the 20th Century" (2011–2014); Konrad H. Jarausch, ed., *Dictatorship as Experience: Towards a Socio-Cultural History of the GDR* (New York: Berghahn Books, 1999). For the Japanese case, see Yasushi Yamanouchi, J. Victor Koschmann, and Ryūichi Narita, eds., *Total War and Modernization* (Ithaca, N.Y.: Cornell East Asian Series, 1998).

76. Lim Jie-Hyun and Kim Yong-woo, eds., 대중독재 II [Mass dictatorship II] (Seoul: Chaeksesang, 2005), 401–615; Adam Michnik, *Letters from Freedom: Post-Cold War Realities and Perspectives*, ed. Irena Grudzińska Gross (Berkeley: University of California Press, 1998), 152. When the late dictator Park's daughter was elected to the presidency in December 2012, criticism of mass dictatorship evaporated into thin air.

77. Senate of the Parliament of the Czech Republic, "Prague Declaration on European Conscience and Communism," June 3, 2008, http://www.praguedeclaration.eu/.

78. "The Seventy Years Declaration," January 20, 2012, *Defending History* 13, 4434, http://defendinghistory.com/70-years-declaration/29230.

79. Michael Rothberg, *Multidirectional Memory: Remembering the Holocaust in the Age of Decolonization* (Stanford, Calif.: Stanford University Press, 2009), 23; Rothberg, "From Gaza to Warsaw: Mapping Multidirectional Memory," *Criticism* 53, no. 4 (2011): 523.

80. Ann Curthoys and John Docker, "Defining Genocide," in *The Historiography of Genocide*, ed. Dan Stone (Basingstoke, UK: Palgrave Macmillan, 2010), 16–21. Lemkin has been invoked in the contemporary Israeli-Palestinian conflict. To critics of Israeli treatment of Palestinians, it was an irony that the law of genocide was created by a Jewish Holocaust survivor. See James Loeffler, "Becoming Cleopatra: The Forgotten Zionism of Raphael Lemkin," *Journal of Genocide Research* 19, no. 3 (2017): 341.

81. Eric J. Sundquist, *The Oxford W. E. B. Du Bois Reader* (Oxford: Oxford University Press, 1996), 471.

82. Michael Rothberg and Yasemin Yildiz, "Memory Citizenship: Migrant Archives of Holocaust Remembrance in Contemporary Germany," *Parallax* 17 (2011): 37–41.

83. Anna Radziwiłł and Wojciech Roszkowski, *Historia dla Maturzysty. Wiek XIX* (Warsaw: Szkolne PWN, 2004), 7.

3

Postcolonial Reflections on the Mnemonic Confluence of the Holocaust, Stalinist Crimes, and Colonialism

Thaw of the Cold War Memory

With the fall of communism, the interaction of global memory formation and local mnemonic sensitivities became more complicated in the 1990s. The thaw of the Cold War set off an avalanche of vernacular memories of the Stalinist terror that replaced the official memories of the communist regimes of Eastern Europe. In releasing the oppressed memories of Stalinist terror and Nazi collaboration in Eastern Europe, the thaw of these memories triggered an East European version of the *Historikerstreit*. The fall of communism likewise melted the mnemonic ice around the atrocities of the Western colonial powers in Asia, Africa, and Latin America. The West could no longer marginalize the memories of colonial genocide and atrocities, because the propagandistic imperative to defend Western civilization against Soviet communism had lost its historical force. Freed from the ideological constraint of the Cold War, the triple victimhood of the Holocaust, colonial genocides, and Stalinist crime together became entangled globally in the post–Cold War era. This new mnemoscape means far more than the agglutination of a greater range of repressed memories.[1]

As the triple victimhood became globally intertwined, the struggle for international recognition of one's national grievance intensified, and historical authenticity became a battlefield. The mnemonic confluence of the triple victimhood has structured global memory formation in the post–Cold War era. Oscillating between the global template of victimization and local sensitivities, global memory formation is always in a state of becoming. By this I mean neither the global memory space as a fact or a condition nor the simple compilation or comparative juxtaposition of separate memories within it. *Formation* here denotes process rather than structure, and scrutiny of how this triad of victimhoods has become entangled can shed new light on the dynamics of that process in the twenty-first century. I hereby propose the phrase *global memory formation* to stress this process of becoming, in contrast to the static sense of "global memory space." Focusing on global memory formation after the "fall" in 1989, this chapter adopts a postcolonial perspective to analyze how victimhood memories arising out of these experiences have become entwined globally. Against the flat model of the cosmopolitanization of the Holocaust, I will argue for the nonhierarchical comparability of historical traumas. As a conceptual tool of dehegemonizing and decentering universal memories and deconstructing mnemonic nationalism, I will propose "critical relativization" and "radical juxtaposition" in concluding remarks.

Cosmopolitanization, Vulgarization, and Nationalization

One of the most salient features of postwar global memory formation is how the Holocaust became a generic memory template for genocides and human traumas across the globe.[2] The absolute horror of the Holocaust made it nearly impossible to think and speak of evil and victimhood without reference to it. The Holocaust has become a template for remembering American slavery, the genocide of the indigenous nations of the New World, countless colonial atrocities in the Global South, the Japanese A-bomb victims, the Nanjing Massacre, American war crimes in Vietnam, and the Korean comfort women. In Eastern-Central Europe, painful memories of the Allied bombing and *Vertriebene* in Germany, mass killing, enslavement of the Slavs in "Germany's Wild East," Ukrainian *Holodomor*, and all other Stalinist crimes in former communist countries invoked the Holocaust. Even Polish nationalist historians used "forgotten Holocaust" and "Poland's Holocaust" to stress Polish victimhood around World War II; according to them, Poles were the first nation to experience the Holocaust.[3] Allegedly,

"the treatment of Poles by the Germans was even worse than that of Jews."
In this estimation, "Poles were even more exposed than Jews to arrest,
deportation, and death," especially during 1939–1941.[4] Paradoxically, the
Holocaust memory is employed rhetorically to make the case for Polish victimhood nationalism and to marginalize the Holocaust, thereby establishing a hierarchy among victims. The nationalist appropriation of the
Holocaust is not the Polish peculiarity but a widespread phenomenon of
global memory formation.

In global memory formation, many local memories interact with the
Holocaust as the mnemonic touchstone of "absolute meaning" of evil.
The Holocaust becomes a metonym for every crime against humanity. This
globalized Holocaust tacitly denies the uniqueness of the Holocaust.[5] As
the Holocaust became an ethical template, a way to think about genocides
and other crimes in the global memory space, it ceased to be an exclusively
Jewish experience. Not just ethics, politics, or rhetoric, the Holocaust is
also aesthetic. Artists employ ever more transgressive techniques to generate strong emotional reactions to the Holocaust and its global analogs.
This omnipresence of the Holocaust in the global memory space has
brought "an ostensible Holocaust fatigue." The appropriation of the Holocaust as an analog to different historical events by local memory activists
necessitates banalizing historical specificity to make the comparison fit.
This cosmopolitanization of the Holocaust often happened only through
anachronistic and superficial comparisons. The mechanically symmetrical reciprocity in memory formation can project "a too simplistic vision of
the world."[6] At the absurd extreme, the "de-Judaization of the Holocaust" became necessary to keep the remembrance of the Holocaust alive
globally.[7] The distance between cosmopolitanization and vulgarization of
the Holocaust memory is much shorter than we have imagined.

The ubiquity of the Holocaust as a memory template is not confined to
the synchronous but also applies to the diachronous. Giorgio Agamben's
Homo Sacer found a trope of the Holocaust in the ancient Roman Empire.[8]
In the religious imagination, the medieval fundamentalisms linking divine
salvation to mass murder are now seen as pointing to a forthcoming Holocaust. Some church historians referred to First Crusaders' massacre and
looting in Jerusalem in 1099 and the Albigensian crusade against the
Cathars in 1209–1229 as the first Holocausts. An American indigenous rights
activist has compared Christopher Columbus to Heinrich Himmler. Apart

from activists, scholars have made similar claims about the comparability (or not) of the indigenous genocide by European colonialism, American slavery, and the Holocaust.[9] Raphael Lemkin, the initiator of the UN's Genocide Convention, suggested comparing the Holocaust with the persecution of the Cathars, Japanese Catholics in the Tokugawa Shogunate, Muslims in medieval Spain, and the Herero in German Namibia.[10]

To make the Holocaust comparable to other crimes triggers decontextualizing or, worse, ahistoricizing it into a political instrument. Japanese right-wing nationalists frequently make a grossly simplified comparison between the Holocaust and A-bomb victims. Equating Holocaust victims and the East European victims of the Stalinist terror under the slogan of "no hierarchy among victims" ignited a competition over "who suffered most," rather than animating mnemonic solidarity in Central-Eastern Europe. The projection of the Holocaust children victims onto the "stolen children" in Australia, the capricious reference to Anne Frank in Japan, East Asia, and apartheid South Africa overly synchronizes and instrumentalizes the Holocaust memory in the postcolonial context. What is obscene is the comparison of the Israeli Army to the Nazi German Army in the "anti-Zionist" propaganda publications of the Polish United Worker's Party (PZPR) in 1968. The communists achieved and did what prewar generations of Polish nationalist anti-Semites had dreamt of and tried to do.[11] Cosmopolitanization and vulgarization are the head and tail of the same coin of the Holocaust memory and dual components of global memory formation.

Nevertheless, the political instrumentalization and indigenization of the Holocaust memory does not necessarily confirm Alon Confino's judgment that global memory of the Holocaust is "imprecise," "inaccurate," and "misleading" because it has "no real resonance" outside of Europe, Israel, and the United States.[12] In fact, its very resonance sets the global memory space ringing as Benjamin Netanyahu exploits the Holocaust to brutalize the Palestinians by stripping them of basic human rights in the name of the survivors of the Holocaust; Holocaust memory has been instrumentalized, vulgarized, and abused in Israel too.[13] Israeli politicians have used the moral capital of the Holocaust to reinforce the Israel's ethnocentric nationalism of the righteous victims.[14] The Holocaust has been conjured to justify anticommunist liberal democracy in the United States or multicultural integration in Britain. Antiabortionists called the legalization of abortion the "American Holocaust," gay activists appealed to the public about the AIDS holocaust, and animal rights activists coined the slogan "Buchenwald for animals." In advertisements, the National Rifle Association conspicuously noted that the Warsaw Ghetto uprising burst out with only ten pistols.[15] The vulgarization of the Holocaust culminated in Ben Carson's remark that "if Jews had owned guns, the Holocaust wouldn't have happened."[16]

Daniel Levy and Natan Sznaider's observation that, by transposing the Holocaust memory onto other memories of genocide and atrocities, "*Never again Auschwitz* provided the foundation for emerging cosmopolitan memories" is both right and wrong.[17] In the twenty years since their essay was written, it has become clear that Holocaust discourse is increasingly providing the mnemonic leverage for the reterritorialization and nationalization of collective memory.[18] The cosmopolitanization of the Holocaust entailed the reterritorialization or renationalization of global memory formation through simplistic comparison and vulgarization of the Holocaust. Alongside historical revisionism, national commemoration, and contests over comparative victimhood, the Holocaust discourse is increasingly leveraged to reterritorialize global memory formation. Often, transcultural memories of the Holocaust lead to the "calamatization of politics" rather than a universal human rights regime. People have invoked the Holocaust to prophesize genocide, which justifies "the terroristic political action in the form of pre-emptive strikes and anticipatory self-defense to forestall feared destruction."[19] All over the globe, Holocaust memory has been conjured up as a magical cross-reference to evince and universalize "our own" victimhood nationalism.

The performativity of the Holocaust paved the road to Serbian nationalists claiming the similarity between Jewish and Serbian suffering. They even tried to rehabilitate the Chetnik-Serbian collaborators by leveraging this mnemonic alliance.[20] Postcommunist politicians in Eastern Europe have appropriated the memory, symbols, and imagery of the Holocaust to stress their respective national victimhoods at the hands of Stalinists. They elevate the crimes of communists to the level of the Holocaust and delegitimize communist efforts in the fight against fascism.[21] In so doing, they cleared the path for resurgent nationalism, whose extreme wing can be traced back to the Nazi collaborators. In the most literal sense, it is not Holocaust denial. But, effectively, the nationalization of Holocaust memory by the local politics of the East European postcommunist regimes involves

Holocaust denial. The paradox that nationalization of Holocaust memories in local politics promotes the historical normalization of the fascist movement by delegitimizing the communist antifascist movement shows the complexity of Holocaust remembrance in the global memory space.[22]

Warsaw, Auschwitz, and Black America

Amid the refugee crisis that shook Europe in September 2015, Polish historians engaged in sharp polemics over on how to interpret East European apathy or even antipathy toward Islamic refugees, mainly from Syria. *Gazeta Wyborcza* reported that Jan Gross sparked the controversy. In his contribution to *Die Welt*, he claimed that the hostility of East European countries, including Poland, toward the Islamic refugees originated in the failure to come to terms with the past of the Holocaust. Gross argued that a self-reflexive critique of East European complicity with Nazis in killing Jews might have yielded more empathy toward alien refugees. He asserted that Poles murdered more Jews than Germans, which challenged the myth of the unified Polish resistance movement under the German occupation.[23] In his article, Gross continued his efforts to show Polish complicity in the Holocaust. Even so, his thesis that the sins of the current regime arose out of a failure of memory practices merits further examination. Particularly in the Baltics and Poland, the Holocaust had long been considered peripheral to national suffering under Stalinist oppression. At best, the Holocaust has been located in the political symmetry between the Nazi occupation and Stalinist oppression.[24] Paradoxically, a widespread racist joke that "we are ready to accept refugees, because we always have had concentration camps" gave more credence to Gross's insight into the discursive connectivity of anti-Semitism and Islamophobia in contemporary Poland.[25]

Polish historians Marcin Zaremba and Aleksander Smolar, among others, refuted Gross's claims by pointing out that Poland and other East European countries have no colonial past. In *Gazeta Wyborcza*, they argued that Poles had no opportunities to learn how to cohabitate with the colonized of a different culture, religion, and race. Poland had never been a colonial power with experience with a colonized Other.[26] Zaremba and Smolar argued that Western Europe, including Germany, should be more welcoming to Islamic refugees. For its colonial past, Western Europe has been familiar with those refugees as colonial subjects. Implicit was the criticism that "You are guilty of colonialism, but we are innocent. So the refugee problem is yours only." A cursory look at the history of the partitioning of Poland by Russia, Austria, and Prussia, the tragic trajectories of national irredentism, and the suffering of the Polish nation at large might give credence to the image of Poland as innocent of colonialism. But Poland, even as it was being colonized by German settlers, could have been considered a colonizer by its Lithuanian and Ukrainian neighbors in the borderland. While subaltern vis-à-vis Germany and the "West," Poland was also an empire, with its local agents fully incorporated in the global structure of domination.[27] Poles' contempt for their eastern and western Slavic neighbors has likewise been shaped by the characterization of Poland as the first model of underdevelopment and a "neglected suburb of Europe." Poles have never been free from "the intellectual project of demi-Orientalization" by the West.[28]

Viewed from the postcolonial perspective, Poland was not innocent of internal colonialism and its colonial practice. The Second Republic in interwar Poland was a multiethnic state, where ethnic Poles formed only about 68.9 percent of the population. The rest were Ukrainians (13.9 percent), Jews (8.7 percent), Belorussians (3.1 percent), Germans (2.3 percent), and others. Polish nationalists regretted that the Second Republic of Poland remained "not a nation-state but a state of nationalities."[29] The Sanacja regime responded to the multicultural demands of various ethnic minorities by setting up the internment camp at Bereza Kartuska in 1934. Internal colonialism against national minorities, demi-Orientalism against the *kresy* (borderlands) and Eastern Slavic neighbors, and anti-Semitism combined with the anti-Bolshevism inherent to *Żydokomuna* in the Sanacja regime colluded rhetorically with Nazi anti-Slavic and anti-Semitic colonialist propaganda. Polish nationalism was no exception to the "ambivalent hybrid" of desire and resentment of subaltern imperialists. The ambivalent position of Poland as a subaltern empire provided an excuse for Vladimir Putin's anti-Polish World War II revisionism, culminating in the seventy-fifth anniversary of the liberation of Auschwitz in January 2020. On September 1, 2019, the Russian Ministry of Foreign Affairs tweeted that the text of the nonaggression treaty between Nazi Germany and Stalin's USSR (1939) was preceded by the German-Polish treaty (1934). Putin's anti-Polish revisionism whitewashed Stalin's handshake with Hitler and erased the first two years of World War II, between 1939 and 1941.[30]

Poland has lacked not colonial experience per se, but critical awareness about internal colonialism. In the communist era, hundreds of thousands of Vietnamese guest workers flowed into East Germany, Poland, Czechoslovakia, and Baltic Soviet Republics. In this "global socialist ecumene," a transnational exchange of ideas, knowledge, and cultural artifacts and transnational movement of people flowed on a quite significant scale. The global socialist ecumene did not end after the collapse of the communist bloc. The Polish government's acceptance of one hundred thousand Chechen refugees and exiles since 1996 refutes the idea of Islamophobia as a characteristic of postcommunist Poland. The large scale of Chechen refugees in Poland is impressive, even if motivated by Russophobia. Yet Polish attitudes toward Chechen refugees shifted dramatically from empathy to apathy in the recent refugee crisis.[31] Living shoulder to shoulder with the "other" was not sufficient experience to engender empathy or respect for different cultures, religions, and lifestyles. Gross's criticism that Polish hostility against Islamic refugees represents its failure of coming to terms with the past of the Holocaust makes sense, if one recognizes that the dispute is fundamentally an epistemological one, not a factual one.

This is only part of the story. The unvarnished insensitivity toward Islamic refugees, even among critical intellectuals, equally springs from the absence of postcolonial self-criticism in postcommunist Poland.[32] The collective guilt of anti-Semitism and the colonial innocence compete to be the narrative template for the "collective memory" of postcommunist Poland. As previous chapters on the *Historikerstreit* in Poland show, the memory of colonial victimization under Nazism and Stalinism has worked as a screen memory to repress the memory of the political complicity and sinful repentance in the Holocaust perpetrated in Poland. "*Historikerstreit po polsku*," the heated debate around the Jan Błoński's seminal essay "Biedny polacy patrzą na getto" (Poor Poles are looking at the ghetto) in 1987 and Jan Gross's book *Sąsiedzi* (*Neighbours*) in 2000 brought "a genuine moral revolution" to postcommunist Poland by breaking thorough the screen memory and surfacing the suppressed guilt. A drastic metamorphosis of Polish self-definition from innocent victim to *Homo Jedvanecus* in the postcommunist *Historikerstreit* did not produce the postcolonial criticism. The mnemonic confluence of the postcolonial critique and the Holocaust memory is yet to be found in the *Historikerstreit*.

The postcolonial view of the Holocaust reveals that the Nazi invasion and occupation of the Slavic East was a colonialist project. The discursive link between colonial genocide and the Holocaust is tangible. The historical continuity between the German colonial genocide, the Nazis' Eastern occupation policy, and the Holocaust can be explained in terms of Euro-colonialism.[33] The *"Generalplan Ost"* stood on the assumption that the SS would run the latifundia exploiting "native" Slav labor until the Germans were numerous and mechanized enough to do without them. To German settlers, pioneering in the East is "colonial work," like work under the African sun.[34] Quoting Nazis, the "Volga is Germany's Mississippi," "the Slavs would be the German equivalent of the conquered native populations of India and Africa in the British empire," "Asia begins in Poland," and "Slavs were white Niggers."[35] Nazism was the intra-European colonialism. The Nazi occupation of Poland was a colonial project, an uncanny mimicry of Western colonialism by "turning imperialism on its head and treating Europeans as Africans."[36] Nazis' anti-Semitism and anti-Slavic racism had to be extreme because it had to turn a white-and-white into a white-and-black issue in its racist imagination. The colonial proximity made the Nazi anxiety of racial containment more pronounced, because dividing lines between German and Pole were uncertain.[37]

This absence of obvious outward traits enabling discrimination is akin to the horror of the English colonizers confronting the colonized Irish. By blaming the primitiveness of Poland on Jewish influence, some Nazis merged the rationale of Germany's civilizing mission of Poland with anti-Semitism. Europeans have profoundly resisted situating Nazism and the Holocaust within the context of global colonialism. Eurocentrism demands that the Holocaust stand out "from other genocides because it was committed in the heart of civilized Europe rather than in the midst of (supposedly) primitive or barbaric societies."[38] It echoes Zygmunt Bauman's warning that Holocaust-style genocide is a logical outcome of Western modernity, not of premodern barbarity.[39] Aimé Césaire pinpointed the Eurocentric intellectuals' dilemma as such: every European bourgeois "has a Hitler inside him . . . and what he cannot forgive Hitler for is not the crime in itself, the crime against man, it is not the humiliation of man as such, it is the crime against the white man, and the fact that he applied to Europe colonialist procedures which had until then been reserved exclusively for the Arabs of Algeria, the 'coolies' of India, and the 'niggers' of Africa."[40]

The Polish translation of the Césaire's *Discours sur le colonialisme* was published in the socialist era of People's Poland in 1950 to criticize both the

Nazi occupation of Poland and Western imperialism in Asia and Africa. The communist postcolonialism in postwar Poland saw an analogy between the Slavic East under Nazi occupation of the "Third Europe" and postcolonial states of the "Third World,"[41] which is absent among postcommunist liberal historians. The anxieties of the nineteenth-century Polish intelligentsia dominate their mentalité, which originated in the ambivalences of envy, admiration, and distrust toward Western Europe. Poland's tripartite identity as a former colony, as a former colonizer, and as a subject of Western hegemonies had more layers than mere colonial ambivalence. Whereas István Deák, an eminent American-Hungarian historian, could suggest the similarity between Jedwabne and the massacre of innocent blacks in Tulsa, Oklahoma, in May 1921, the lack of the postcolonial perspective among Polish historians is regrettable.[42]

The postcolonial criticism about the Holocaust explains why some African American intellectuals saw parallels between Nazi perpetrators and the American white racist-nationalists.[43] The confluence of anti-Semitism and racism can be found in W. E. B. Du Bois's remembrances of his trip to Galicja in 1890. When a cart driver in a small Galician town asked if Du Bois wanted to stop "Unter die Juden," a local hotel run by a Jew, Du Bois realized an additional facet of the race problem. To that person, Du Bois, an African American, was no other than a Jew. Du Bois was surprised to find that Polish university teachers and students in Kraków were hardly aware of their own anti-Semitism. The identities of Galician Jews and African Americans in the late nineteenth century constantly overlapped before Du Bois's eyes. From his experience in Germany, Galicja, and Poland, Du Bois found that racism is more than color prejudice.[44] He was not the first person who recognized the transatlantic entanglement of Jews and Africans. The Black Atlantic slave communities gave themselves strength and hope by seeing the African diaspora through the lens of the Moses-led Jewish exodus from the Egyptian Pharaoh. That comparison gave the Afro-American diaspora's suffering a redemptive quality.[45]

The Yiddish version of Uncle Tom's Cabin, Di Shklaferay, is another good example of this entanglement. Adapting the novel to Jewish circumstances, Ayzik-Meyer Dik made the master a Jew, who helped "Uncle Tom" escape to freedom in Canada. Di Shklaferay became a best seller among Jews immigrating to America in the late nineteenth century. In 1897 Forverts, the oldest Yiddish newspaper founded in New York, compared the emancipated

American slaves with the Jewish Exodus from Egypt and urged American Jews to watch *Uncle Tom's Cabin* (1927). Radical Jews sent their children to unsegregated summer camps. The spirit of solidarity between African Americans and Jews continued with the participation of liberal and radical Jews in NAACP activities. Louis Harap, the managing editor of *Jewish Life*, invited Du Bois to a "Tribute to the Warsaw Ghetto Fighters" on the ninth anniversary of the Warsaw Ghetto Uprising, on April 16, 1952. He asked Du Bois to speak on the "significance of the ghetto fight for the Negro people in the United States today in relation to cooperation with their allies, the Jewish people and the common people of America."[46] Du Bois's talk eventually appeared in *Jewish Life*. Du Bois described remembering "the scream and shots of a race riot in Atlanta and the marching of the Ku Klux Klan" during his visit to the ruins of the Warsaw ghetto in 1949. He recognized he could get a "more complete understanding of the Negro problem" through a "clearer understanding of the Jewish problem in the world."[47]

Earlier, the New Negro movement had taken notice of Japan's race-conscious defiance against the United States at the Paris Conference of 1919. Japan's defiant demand for racial equality cast it as a race rebel and a racial victim, which led to an iconography of the Japanese as the New Negro of the Pacific. Black activists expected they would be able to win the racial war against the whites "with the aid of Japan on the side of Negroes." The Universal Negro Improvement Association, led by Marcus Garvey, invited Japanese speakers to their meetings to reinforce the idea of a racial war. African Americans' imagined solidarity with peoples of Asia sustained their uncompromising critique of white supremacy.[48] Du Bois, the man of the Jewish-Black mnemonic nexus, imagined the Black-Asian nexus in the coming racial war to challenge white domination.[49] This Black-Asian nexus hints at the potential of connecting Asian memory to Eastern Europe, the Holocaust, and Black America. For many Black activists, including Du Bois, speaking critically about Japan as a "colored imperium" was rare. As Taketani Etsko has shown, one author argued in 1932 that " 'White Supremacy' was slain in Manchuria" by the Japanese. An essay in the *Afro-American* stated: "The little brown men of Nippon are taking weapons of western world exploitation and are beating the Westerners at their own game."[50] C. L. R. James was exceptional among Black-Asian activists for his criticism of the Japanese Empire.

Blacks and Jews also found common ground in apartheid South Africa. Many prominent antiapartheid activists treasured *The Diary of Anne Frank*; handwritten copies circulated in the notorious apartheid-era prison Robben Island. In one of his public addresses as president of the postapartheid democratic South Africa, Nelson Mandela remembered that Anne's diary had kept his spirits high and reinforced his confidence in the invincibility of the cause of freedom and justice. Antiapartheid activists in South Africa drew on the analogy to Nazi Germany to mobilize international support for the antiapartheid movement as the most critical moral battle in the postwar world.[51] The three successive exhibitions of "Nazisme in Zuid-Afrika" held at the Anne Frank House in Amsterdam in the early 1970s, jointly organized by Pluto (the Dutch–South African student group) and the Anti-Apartheids Beweging Nederlands (Dutch Anti-Apartheid Movement, AABN), brought together postcolonial and Holocaust memory. Visitors could see the banner declaring "Nazism=Apartheid" and a life-size papier-mâché doll of Prime Minister B. J. Vorster holding a swastika.[52]

For Black Germans, there was an organic connection between their treatment by the Nazis and Germany's colonial and early postcolonial history. First-generation colonial migrants first arrived in Germany as performers in ersatz "native villages" in the *Völkerschau*, which the Nazis adapted to racist ideological practice. Eve Rosenhaft has argued that interestingly—maybe it's obvious—black writers and film-makers outside of the United States and especially in Europe seem to be more committed than either African Americans or white Europeans to seeing themselves in Holocaust history and using their findings to reflect on the issues of race and identity particular to them.[53] Black British critic Paul Gilroy's *Black Atlantic* and *Between Camps* sought to recover the history of dialogue between Blacks and Jews. The postcolonial is significant in the transatlantic nexus of memories.

Nagasaki, Hiroshima, and Auschwitz

"Stunned by the intense air of death" during his first visit to Auschwitz in 1987, Nakatani Takeshi now gives tours at Poland's national museum at Auschwitz-Birkenau. After passing the strict tour guide examination, he started working there in 1997. He hopes his tour guiding will help Japanese visitors to understand "the suffering of victims and the importance and fragility of peace." However, he does not see the museum "from the perspective of relations between Japan, China, and the Korean peninsula."[54] Yumie Hirano, who serves as a "memory keeper" of the A-bomb experience in Hiroshima Peace Memorial Park, has a different approach. The city of Hiroshima launched a program for ordinary citizens to share the stories of aging A-bomb survivors and their desire for peace in 2012. Hirano has subsequently visited Peru, Mongolia, and Iceland to share A-bomb survivors' accounts. In an interview before her visit to Poland in 2015, she said, "Many Jews were killed because of racial discrimination, and innocent civilians were killed in Hiroshima. I want to convey how human rights are abused at a time of war."[55]

The two Japanese curators of memory hold different, almost opposite, views on the mnemonic connectivity and historical comparability of Auschwitz and Hiroshima. If the Auschwitz tour guide insists on the incommensurability of the Holocaust, the Hiroshima memory keeper sees them as meaningfully commensurable. The different training in Auschwitz in Poland/Israel and Hiroshima in Japan might account for some of the difference. Nakatani Takeshi's training as an official Auschwitz tour guide represents the official memories of Poland and Israel, while Yumie Hirano's practice as a voluntary memory keeper in Hiroshima epitomizes the dominant discourse of the A-bomb victimhood in Japan. This critical divergence indicates that connecting Auschwitz and Hiroshima is a complicated subject.

In "Year Zero," 1945, the A-bomb in Japan already invoked the Holocaust. The first entanglement is found as early as November 23, 1945, in Nagasaki. In a memorial mass for the A-bomb Catholic victims in Nagasaki, congregant Takashi Nagai delivered a funerary message to six hundred local Catholic survivors holding eight thousand small white crosses signifying the number of Catholic victims of the A-bomb. The speech moved all participants to bitter tears. The text of Nagai's address reads: "The atomic bomb was originally destined for the prefectural offices at the center of Nagasaki. But because of weather conditions, the wind carried the plane north to Urakami, and the bomb exploded above the cathedral there . . . we want to believe that Urakami church was chosen not as a victim but as a pure lamb, to be slaughtered and burned on the altar of sacrifice to expiate the sins committed by humanity in the Second World War."[56] The redemptive discourse, shown through the analogy of Jewish exodus used in the African diaspora, reappears in postwar Nagasaki.

In his funeral oration, Nagai continued, "We want to believe that only the sacrificial victim of Urakami could bring the war to an end; by this sacrifice, billions who would otherwise have fallen victims to the ravages of war have been saved." Nagai then used *hansai* (燔祭), the Japanese translation of "Holocaust" from chapter 22 of Genesis, to illustrate the sublime world-redemptive suffering of the Japanese *hibakusha*, A-bomb victims. "How noble, how splendid was that holocaust of 9 August, when flames soared up from the cathedral, dispelling the darkness of war and bringing the light of peace!"[57] Nagai's speech is one of the earliest recorded public uses of the "Holocaust" in the postwar global memory space. "Holocaust" was not widely used even in Israel and the "West" until the late 1950s. One can find random uses of "holocaust," as in the letter Dr. David Wilsey, who served the 116th Evacuation Hospital of the U.S. Army, wrote to his wife on March 23, 1945, or in a top rabbi's telegram in Palestine on "holocaust synagogues in Germany" after Kristallnacht, 1938. There were only sporadic uses of "Nazi holocaust," "European holocaust," and "Hitler holocaust" in the 1950s, but "holocaust" had yet to become the "Holocaust."[58] What characterizes Nagai's usage of *hansai* (Holocaust) is the sublimation of the death of innocents into a sacrifice for humanity.

Nagai's use of "Holocaust" is not directly related to Auschwitz, although it was a word in motion that linked Auschwitz and Hiroshima. With their provenance in biblical semiotics, *hansai* and Holocaust facilitated the nationalist sublimation of victims (*higaisha*) into sacrifices (*giseisha*). It sacralized death into holy sacrifice to atone for the sins of humankind and the salvation of the world. A biblical sublimation of the victim made a person subjected to oppression, suffering, and injury into an eternal life sacrificed to something sacred. Political religion comes into being by conferring a holy status on earthly entities like the nation, state, class, history, and race. Civic or political religion binds the individual to the sacralized secular body through ethical and social commandments.[59] Once political religion elevates the nation into a form of religious deity, it evokes the latent "victimhood nationalism" inherent in the suppressed memories of victims.[60] Takashi Nagai's thesis of "Urakami Cathedral in the Holocaust" gave psychological texture to Japanese victimhood nationalism.

Later, Auschwitz and Hiroshima were frequently cited as twin symbols of mass death and as archetypical examples of white racism.[61] The attentive Japanese press coverage of the Eichmann trial provided a mnemonic nexus to associate Hiroshima and Nagasaki with the Holocaust. The Japanese poet and peace activist Kurihara Sadako made an incisive analogy between Auschwitz and Hiroshima: "Of the world's two great holocausts, Auschwitz was a major atrocity carried out by the enemies of the victorious Allies; Hiroshima/Nagasaki was a major atrocity carried out by Allies." She insinuated that Hiroshima was worse than Auschwitz because A-bomb survivors had to suffer from the long-term effects of radiation exposure while Auschwitz ended.[62] Relatively untouched by the sporadic scandals over anti-Semitism and Holocaust denial,[63] the analogy of Auschwitz and Hiroshima never faded from the Japanese mnemoscape.

Ron Zwigenberg sees the Hiroshima-Auschwitz Peace March of 1962–1963 as a precedent for cosmopolitan memory. In March 1962 four Japanese memory agents cum antinuclear peace activists left Hiroshima to participate in the eighteenth anniversary of the liberation of Auschwitz on January 27, 1963. Satō Kyōtsū, a Buddhist monk and a veteran of the Japanese Imperial Army, led this lengthy peace pilgrimage from Hiroshima to Auschwitz. Their aim was "to deepen the connection between these two places of utmost suffering and tragedy in World War II." En route to Auschwitz, they visited memorial sites from World War II in Vietnam, Singapore, Israel, Greece, Yugoslavia, and Hungary. It was likely the first mnemonic pilgrimage on a global scale covering the Euro-Asian memory space.[64] The Hiroshima-Auschwitz Peace March was in truth more an obstacle course. Japanese authorities, agents of Cold War ideology, denied those very Japanese activists passports for their alleged bias in visiting Auschwitz rather than the site of a Soviet massacre of military and civilian Poles in Katyń. From the perspective of the Polish Communist Party, Hiroshima symbolized the crimes of American imperialism, so they welcomed the Japanese peace activists. For them, the peace march potently connected American imperialism and Nazi Germany. *Dziennik Polski*, a local newspaper in Kraków, reported on the Hiroshima peace delegates at the eighteenth-anniversary ceremony of the liberation of Auschwitz camp. It stressed the Buddhist monk Sato's advocacy of the Polish government agenda of an A-bomb-free Central Europe.[65]

National histories proved stubbornly robust against the establishment of cosmopolitan memory. In the inverted memory of the Japanese Empire, Japan occupied the postcolonial rather than postimperial position. The "Pacific War" between Japan and the United States was just one episode of Japan's century-long struggle against and defeat of the colonialism of the Western Great Powers.[66] Within this frame, Japan could fashion itself as an innocent victim as it came to terms with its actions during the Second World War. The American A-bombing and subsequent occupation reinforced the Japanese postcolonial position. Accordingly, the misery and suffering of the Taiwanese, Korean, Chinese, Vietnamese, Indonesian, Philippines, and other Asian neighbors were largely ignored or forgotten. Hiroshima-Auschwitz Peace March participants regarded themselves as the most victimized party and as pacifist heroes until confronted, in the course of their pilgrimage, with the accusations and memories of the Japanese war atrocities against their Asian neighbors. Even so, these pilgrims did not radically change their views. Many of them remained negative toward Koreans who, in striving for revenge, were unable to forgive Japan.[67]

The "cosmopolitan" memory arising out of the Hiroshima-Auschwitz peace pilgrimage thus had a much more limited makeup in that it marginalized ethnically non-Japanese *hibakusha* victims. Even Oe Kenzaburo, perhaps one of the most sensitive writers and intellectuals on minorities, confessed that he initially disregarded Korean A-bomb victims in his reporting on antinuclear pacifism and memory in Hiroshima.[68] The ethnocentric memory of identifying themselves as victims blinded many Japanese to their Asian neighbors' suffering incurred by the Japanese invasion. Remembering Hiroshima and Nagasaki quickly became a way of forgetting Nanjing, Bataan, comfort women, and countless other Japanese atrocities.[69] In other words, the Japanese antinuclear pacifism has been "less interested in dwelling on Japan's past sins than in promoting its future unity as a pacifist nation." Hiroshima became "an icon of Japan's past as an innocent war victim and a beacon for its future as a pacifist nation."[70] On a more abstract level, "the claim to posit a universal category of humanity as the subject of memorialization serves to obstruct condemnation of Japanese nationalism and ethnocentrism."[71]

One cannot but be reserved about the "cosmopolitan memory" connecting Hiroshima and Auschwitz in the 1960s. The death diplomacy of exchanging the ashes of unidentified victims vulgarized the *memento mori* of the genocide. It epitomized the nationalist appropriation of the Holocaust by the Japanese and ideological instrumentalization of Hiroshima by the Polish. The cosmopolitan memory of the Hiroshima pacifism in the Euro-Asian space, consciously or unconsciously, worked as a screen memory covering the Asian neighbors' suffering from the Japanese colonial invasion. The Japanese obsession with Anne Frank functioned similarly. Almost every Japanese has read about her, be it her book, manga comic book adaptations, or anime cartoon. As Alain Lewkovitz explains, "the Anne Frank–Japan connection is based on a kinship of victims" in Auschwitz and Hiroshima/Nagasaki. Few Japanese contemplated that their military actions might have perpetrated crimes against countless Anne Franks in Asia.[72] As discussed earlier, the Serbian nationalists likewise activated the universalist Holocaust memory as a screen memory to cover up Serbian war crimes and atrocities during the Yugoslavian civil war in the 1990s.

Saint Maksymilian Kolbe, like Anne Frank, captured the postwar Japanese imaginary. Martyred at Auschwitz, he was later canonized. The Japanese depictions of St. Kolbe seized on his missionary work in Nagasaki between 1930 and 1936 to link the Holocaust to the nuclear bombings of Japan. The Auschwitz-Nagasaki link became another critical piece of this global memory formation that meant experience of a Holocaust-like event could expiate past sins. The Saint of Nagasaki himself, Takashi Nagai, who came up with the term *hansai* in his funeral oration for Nagasaki victims, had paid a visit to Father Kolbe during his mission at the Hongochi monastery in Nagasaki. He would later write of how miraculous it was Father Kolbe could be so active, with his lungs heavily damaged by tuberculosis. Father Kolbe's missionary work in Nagasaki, the very site of Japanese Catholic martyrdom on August 9, 1945, and his own martyrdom as a Catholic acquired considerable and powerful symbolic capital in postwar Japan. The mnemonic nexus of Father Kolbe as the Auschwitz-Catholic martyr and Nagasaki A-bomb victims strengthened in the A-bomb memory in postwar Japan. In retrospect, it was a coincidence that Saint Kolbe, a future Polish Catholic martyr in Auschwitz, had engaged in the missionary work between 1930 and 1936 in Nagasaki, the historic center of the Japanese Catholic martyrdom. Once again, it is an extraordinary coincidence that the atomic bomb detonated in the sky over the Immaculate Conception

Cathedral in Nagasaki on August 9, 1945. Saint Kolbe committed to the ideas of the Immaculate Conception Cathedral by founding the monastery of Niepokalanów.

Father Kolbe's beatification in 1971 and canonization in 1982 became the occasions to strengthen the mnemonic nexus of Kolbe and Japanese A-bomb victims in Nagasaki.[73] Endō Shūsaku, a famous Catholic liberal novelist in Japan, published a serial novel about Father Kolbe in the popular progressive daily newspaper *Asahi shimbun* in 1980–1982. This novel wove together a Japanese kamikaze war victim and Father Kolbe's martyrdom at Auschwitz. That strange juxtaposition gave the impression that providence rather than of coincidence resulted in the deaths of the Nagasaki A-bomb victims and Father Kolbe; they sacrificed themselves for the peaceful future of humankind. Endō Shūsaku's short essay "Miracle," about the story of Kolbe as the Auschwitz martyr, was published in a high school literature textbook and is still widely read among Japanese teenagers. By his estimation, the highest form of love is to sacrifice one's own life to save another's. This kind of love deserves to be called a "miracle."[74]

Sono Ayako, one of Prime Minister Abe's informal brain trustees, provoked online fury by writing that South Africa's apartheid policies of racial separation had been good for whites, Asians, and Africans. She has praised apartheid as a model of how Japan could expand immigration.[75] Sono's ultranationalist and racist public remarks are well-known, but less known is her commitment to celebrating Father Kolbe. In 1971 she wrote a documentary biography, *Kiseki* (*Miracles*), retracing Kolbe's trajectory to Poland when he was beatified. Sono's "miracle" is no different from that of the liberal Endō Shūsaku in its emphasis that the highest love means sacrificing one's own life to save another's. Sono Ayako perceived Kolbe's death as a pure aesthetics in the form of transcendentalism.[76] She was also fascinated with the patriotic myth of Kolbe and his family, which was not the case in Endō's love for Kolbe.[77]

The obsessive attention to Father Kolbe, especially the lacunae, suggests political instrumentalization. A Polish Catholic martyr of Auschwitz became entangled with the history of the persecution of Japanese Catholics in Nagasaki. The absolute silence about the Kolbe's anti-Semitism raises questions about his remembrance in Japan, even among radical progressive Catholic intellectuals there. At Kolbe's beatification in 1971, Jan Józef Lipski raised the issue of anti-Semitism in Kolbe's journal *Mały Dziennik*. The uproar about Kolbe's anti-Semitism was not confined to Poland.[78] His canonization in 1982 reignited the controversies over his anti-Semitism, which were widely covered in the *New York Times*, *Washington Post*, and elsewhere.[79] The reasons for Japanese Catholics' silence about this issue remain unclear. Answering this question would be a way of mapping Japanese memory culture in the postwar period.

Comfort Women, Armenian Americans, and Performative Nationalism

If a meeting of Korean comfort women and Jewish American Holocaust survivors in the auditorium of Queensborough Community College in 2011 symbolizes the mnemonic confluence of the Holocaust and comfort women, the comfort women statue in Glendale, California, tells a different story. On July 9, 2013, the Glendale City Council voted 4 to 1 to approve plans for a monument to Korean comfort women. Despite the Japanese nationalist lobby against the statue, the council was determined. Two council members of Armenian heritage, Ara Najarian and Zareh Sinanyan, voted for the plan. Glendale is the second biggest Armenian settlement in the world after Yerevan, the capital city of Armenia: some eighty thousand Armenian Americans comprise nearly 40 percent of Glendale's population of two hundred thousand.[80] In 2016 the *Atlantic* reported that Armenians in Glendale could live comfortably and profitably without speaking a word of English because Armenian television stations, restaurants, churches, and schools are ubiquitous.[81]

Council member Najarian called the unveiling "a moment of pride for the City of Glendale" and expressed his hope that the monument could be "a part of the healing process" for the Korean comfort women victim-survivors. In another speech, Sinanyan, the first Armenian-born politician to be seated on the City Council and the grandson of an Armenian genocide survivor, explained, "Everything I do in life is shaped by the fact that 98 years ago my people were slaughtered, expelled, raped and subjected to all kinds of horrors. . . . Denial of a mass crime leads to only bad things. An apology would go a long way, an admission, a sense of remorse would go a long way to establish a more normal, peaceful and loving relationship between nations."[82] Sinanyan implied that his own awareness of the Armenian genocide made him sensitive to Korean comfort women.

Presumably, the political calculation of appealing to twenty thousand Korean American residents in Glendale stood behind his speech, too.

Designed to explore and reflect on major human atrocities, the ReflectSpace Gallery in the Glendale Central Library has hosted an impressive series of exhibitions on cosmopolitical memories. Its inaugural exhibition, "Landscape of Memory: Witnesses and Remnants of Genocide," in May–June 2017 reflected on the Armenian genocide through the cross-disciplinary work of witnesses, survivors, and artists. The second exhibition, "Do the Right Thing: Commemoration of Comfort Women," from July 20 to September 3, 2017, was dedicated to the memory of comfort women. Armenian American photographer and curator Ara Oshagan and Korean American curator Jun Hye Yeon Monika cocurated works of twelve international documentarians and artists. Their exhibition's theme of "tension between the inability to speak about personal trauma and the deep human urge to tell" could be found among all genocide victim-survivors. Subsequent exhibitions—"Wake: The Afterlife of Slavery," "i am: Narratives of the Holocaust," "in/visible—Negotiating the US-Mexico Border," and "Nonlinear Histories—Transnational Memory of Trauma"— show explicitly the gallery's dedication to critically exploring the global memory space.[83]

The reactions of the Japanese American community in Southern California contrast sharply with those of Japanese American right-wing nationalists. Japanese deniers of the comfort women and nationalist memory activists, both abroad and at home, had begun to travel in the transpacific memory space. They appealed to the White House, Congress, and local governments to demolish comfort women monuments in the United States. They petitioned the Barack Obama administration to "remove the monument and not to support any international harassment related to this issue against the people of Japan." These deniers argued that purported Japanese crimes against comfort women were simply commercial transactions that Korean nationalists were lying about in order to dishonor the Japanese nation. The United States became a battlefield of the struggle for the recognition of competing memories in East Asia. The memory war of the forced labor and comfort women issue in the transpacific memory space harms the regional anticommunist alliance among South Korea, Japan, and the United States, as indicated by the tumbling General Security of Military Information Agreement (GSOMIA) crisis among Korea, Japan, and United States in 2019.[84]

In contrast to the reactions of Japanese American right-wingers, *Rafu shimpo*, the Japanese American community newspaper in Little Tokyo in Los Angeles, published a very sympathetic report on the unveiling ceremony of the Glendale monument to comfort women. Nikkei for Civil Rights & Redress (NCRR), in close collaboration with *Rafu shimpo*, has supported commemorating comfort women in the United States. NCRR was founded in 1980 to call for compensation and redress for 120,000 Japanese Americans imprisoned in internment camps during World War II. The group helped many camp inmates to testify at the congressional hearings of the Commission on Wartime Relocation and Internment of Civilians in 1981. At the same time, it strenuously supported comfort women memory activism in the United States. After September 11, NCRR established a committee to collaborate with the Muslim Public Affairs Council, the Council on American-Islamic Relations, and the American Arab Anti-discrimination Committee.[85]

The surprising collaboration of the Armenian American community and Japanese Americans in NCRR on the commemoration of Korean comfort women in Glendale seems to be a genuine grassroots cosmopolitan memory. Compared to the European cosmopolitan memory imposed by transnational elites, this vernacular Armenian-Jewish-Korean-Japanese-American cosmopolitan memory sounds enchanting. Mnemonic solidarity finally looks attainable and within reach. A closer look, however, reveals a different story. Zareh Sinanyan had to apologize for posting racist, homophobic, and vulgar comments on YouTube, "many of which appeared centered around Armenia's geopolitical enemies."[86] His online comments contradicted his speech about the mnemonic solidarity of Armenian genocide and Korean comfort women at the commemoration ceremony in Glendale. Also, in a private talk with Korean American memory activists, leading Armenian American politicians in Glendale disagreed with one who compared the Armenian genocide and crimes against comfort women.[87] Reading between the lines, for them, only the "Armenocide," and not lesser crimes like those against comfort women, can be compared with the Holocaust. Mnemonic solidarity is still writhing in competitive agony.

Without mnemonic solidarity—incipient, ersatz, or transactional—global recognition of comfort women is impossible. Until the early 1990s, comfort women had been silenced and their memories erased from the national and regional memories in postcolonial Korea and East Asia. Global awareness of comfort women came through the revelation of the sexual violence in former Yugoslavia and Rwanda. Scenes of horror transmitted via satellite from Rwanda and former Yugoslavia appalled the global public sphere, which had become sensitized to sexual violence. A reckoning of the sexual abuse in former Yugoslavia sharpened the awareness of women's rights as an inalienable, integral, and indivisible part of human rights. The International Criminal Tribunals for the former Yugoslavia and Rwanda (ICTY and ICTR) included rape as a crime against humanity.[88] In December 2000 the "Women's International War Crimes Tribunal on Japan's Military Sexual Slavery" convened in Tokyo. Gabrielle Kirk McDonald, former president of the International War Crimes Tribunal on the Former Yugoslavia, and Patricia Viseur-Sellers, legal adviser for gender-related crimes in the Office of the Prosecutor for the International Tribunal for the Former Yugoslavia and the Rwanda Tribunal, acted as judge and chief prosecutor, respectively. Eight regional prosecutorial teams, including a joint team from South and North Korea, presented cases on behalf of the former comfort women.[89]

Modeled on the citizen's tribunal created by Bertrand Russell during the Vietnamese War, the Women's International War Crimes Tribunal on Japan's Military Sexual Slavery did not have legally binding force, but its conviction of the Japanese state and the deceased emperor, Hirohito, for "war crimes and crimes against humanity" sent shockwaves around the world. The final judgment reads: "The crimes committed against the survivors remain one of the great unremedied injustices of the Second World War. There are no museums, no graves for the unknown comfort woman, no education of future generations, and no judgment days, for the victims of Japan's military sexual slavery. Many of the women who have come forward to fight for justice have died unsung heroes."[90] As the global public sphere has become more conscious of sexual war crimes, it has become possible to shift from "apology and compensation" to "punishment and responsibility." Carol Gluck argues, "Just as the Holocaust became a global example of genocide, so did the comfort women become a touchstone for new international law relating to the violence against women in war."[91]

In September 2016 Suwon mayor Yeom Tae-young proposed to send a comfort woman statue to Freiburg mayor Dieter Salomon. Initially, Mayor Salomon agreed because a gift is a customary gesture of international friendship between sister cities. A committed Green Party politician, Salomon stood for critical *Vergangenheitsbewältigung*. He had to withdraw his decision, however, after people protested that building a comfort woman statue without any memorial to the victims of the German sexual violence in the SS brothels in the concentration camps and on the Eastern front was scandalous. The mayor of Matsuyama, Freiburg's sister city in Japan, also complained about receiving massive amounts of email from Matsuyama inhabitants, which contributed to Salomon's reversal.[92] On November 20, 2016, the Korean Council for the Women Drafted for Military Sexual Slavery by Japan, a Korean nationalist-feminist NGO, awarded Mayor Yeom a special prize for his contribution to "erect a memorial for the victims of the military sexual slavery" statue. Yeom is the first winner of this special prize designed for local governors who promote and globalize the issue of comfort women.[93]

Thanks to his tireless efforts, on March 8, 2017, International Women's Day, a replica of the comfort woman statue in front of the Japanese Embassy in Seoul was unveiled in the Nepal-Himalaya-Pavilion in Wiesent, a small Ostbayern village of fewer than 2,500 people.[94] Neither German nor Korean media report explain why this site was chosen for the statue. The statue was out of context, out of history, and out of memory. The audience was less likely the citizens of Wiesent than Koreans in South Korea. Around the same time, the provincial assembly of Gyunggi-do province, in which Mayor Yeom's Suwon city is located, passed a resolution to erect a comfort woman statue in Dokdo/Takeshima, a small rock under territorial dispute between Korea and Japan. As the chairperson of Gyunggi-do Provincial Assembly stressed the principle of "human rights" in this resolution,[95] the comfort women statue in Wiesent revealed the open secret of how mnemonic nationalism appropriates and vulgarizes the cosmopolitan memory. The global memory space provided the quixotic Korean nationalists with a brand new front. Korean victimhood nationalism, deeply rooted at the local government level, became a player in the global memory space. Reinforced by the memory activists of the comfort women, victimhood nationalism has become more performative, visualized, intimate, and entrenched in the everyday life of postcolonial Korea.

The Critical Relativization in Postcolonial Perspectives

The mnemonic confluence of the triple victimhood—the Holocaust, colonial genocides, and Stalinist terror—characterizes global memory formation in the post–Cold War era, where the "multidirectional memory" is not yet free from hegemonic memory politics.[96] A postcolonial reflection on the ways of globally connecting memories of Auschwitz and the gulag, of Holocaust and atomic bombing, of the Armenian genocides and the comfort women, reveals that global memory formation has been subject to the conflict of remembrance, official or vernacular, between deterritorialization and reterritorialization. Any mere juxtaposition of triple victimhood would not necessarily produce a cosmopolitan memory. In the postwar period, emergent national memories have competed for the hegemony of global memory formation and to establish themselves as the most victimized. This has resulted in the creation of a hierarchy of victimhood. The closer to Holocaust, the higher the position of victimhood. As shown in postcommunist Eastern Europe and in Asia, Africa, and South America, a cosmopolitanized Holocaust has been appropriated to serve mnemonic nationalism.

Victimizers have appropriated the Holocaust and made it local in order to recast themselves as victims. They use this indigenized Holocaust as an aegis against scrutiny of their own crimes. Under the specific circumstances, where victims and victimizers overlap, the indigenized Holocaust remembrance worked as a screen memory to veil the dark history of the victims' crimes and atrocities. Many local appropriations of the Holocaust created a cosmopolitan Holocaust in the ever-forming global memory space. Contrary to expectation, this cosmopolitan memory is not free from nationalist appropriation. It provides narrative dominance with morally persistent leverage, thus intensifying the struggle for narrative dominance among conflicting national memories. Arguably, the Holocaust as cosmopolitan memory is more vulnerable to nationalist appropriation, perhaps because it occupies the position of absolute morality.[97] It is disturbing, for example, to witness the efforts of the Jasenovac Committee of the Synod of Bishops of the Serbian Orthodox Church since the end of the Balkan civil wars to rehabilitate the Serbian-Chetnik collaborators as concentration camp victims—in close collaboration with the World Holocaust Remembrance Center at Yad Vashem.[98]

It is a paradox that the Holocaust as cosmopolitan memory is frequently misused and abused to justify nationalist remembrance in Eastern Europe and East Asia in the post–Cold War era. It is not because the Holocaust has "no real resonance" outside of Europe, Israel, and the United States.[99] Israel, the United States, and Western Europe have never been reluctant to politicize, instrumentalize, and abuse the Holocaust memory. The victim-survivors' existential authenticity in "Western" countries could authenticate, justify, and facilitate the politicization of the Holocaust memory more conveniently. Often, the cosmopolitanization of the Holocaust intensified mnemonic nationalism with its banner of mnemonic solidarity in global memory formation. When Walter Ben Michaels, frustrated by the absence of commemoration of slavery on the Mall in Washington, D.C., asked if "commemoration of the Nazi murder of the Jews on the Mall [might not] in fact [be] another kind of Holocaust denial,"[100] he pointed out the political mobilization of the cosmopolitan memory of Holocaust as a screen memory covering the painful remembrance of American slavery.

Zygmunt Bauman's warning that the Holocaust is a logical outcome not of premodern barbarity but of Western modernity gives us a clue to how to connect the postcolonial criticism to global memory formation in the post–Cold War era. His postmodernist critique of the Holocaust disquieted "the moral comfort of self-exculpation" of the non-German West by shattering the complacent binary of brutal perpetrators and innocent victims. If it is a "legitimate outcome of the civilizing process" in modern society, the Holocaust becomes "our" problem, beyond the German-Jewish problem.[101] In the same way, a postcolonial criticism can alert us to the mnemonic nationalism of the triple victimhood. A postcolonial critique of anticolonial nationalism as an accomplice, not just an alternative, to colonialism points out the ambivalence of colonialist desire and frustration among the colonized. It can help us to rescue the memory of colonial victimhood in former colonized areas from mnemonic nationalism. The critical gaze of postcolonialism can be extended to Eastern Europe, where the analogy between the Slavic East under the Nazi occupation of the "Third Europe," the socialist satellite states under the Russian Stalinist communism, and the postcolonial states of the "Third World" was already familiar. A postcolonial entanglement of the triple victimhood is one of the keys to understanding the global memory formation in the post–Cold War era.

To conclude this chapter, I propose a "critical relativization and radical juxtaposition" to countervail the nationalist appropriation of the cosmopolitan memory. This differs from the advocative relativization in the German *Historikerstreit* in the late 1980s, which cast Bolshevik Russia as an Eastern "Other," an existential threat, to Christian Western Europe. Ernst

Nolte and other right-wing historians denied the uniqueness of the Holocaust by treating it as a copy of communist "annihilation therapy." Nolte viewed the Holocaust as the "Asiatic deed," which the Nazis learned from the Bolsheviks in 1917–1921.[102] Nolte's one-sided emphasis of Nazism as a response to Bolshevism in the European and global civil war brought about a kind of exoneration and sanitization of Nazism by blaming Nazi crimes on Bolshevism. The denial of uniqueness and relativization of the Holocaust became a trademark for the nationalist apologists of the Nazi past. In the history of historiography, however, comparative recontextualization has been a repository of a critical methodology in deconstructing the nationalist historiography. Although the relativization of the Holocaust opened the way to self-exculpation in the wake of the *Historikerstreit*, "comparability cannot really exculpate."[103]

As Nolte showed, relativizing the political responsibility of the Holocaust exculpates the Nazi perpetrators by treating the Russian Bolsheviks as the prime mover in a global chain of "annihilation." Sharing Nolte's opinion, Jarosław Kaczyński, head of Poland's ruling Law and Justice Party, stressed the comparability of communism as a "genocidal system" to German Nazism. In this bizarre rapprochement between Nolte and Kaczyński, the problem is neither a comparison nor juxtaposition, but the "political relativization of responsibility."[104] Criticizing political relativization does not mean we must essentialize the Holocaust, which "tends to free other, less universally abhorred aspects of Nazism (like the crimes against labor), let alone other parts of the killing program (like the murder of gypsies, Poles, Soviet P.O.W.s, homosexuals, and so on) from attention."[105] The political absolutization is no less problematic than political relativization of responsibility. Jan Grabowski criticizes that German *Tätergeschichte* (the history of the perpetrators), by focusing on "how the Holocaust was solely and uniquely perpetrated by Germany," is now in danger of leading to the distortion, even falsification, of the history of the Holocaust."[106] Good and well-intended Germans, "eagerly taking all the blame" for the Holocaust, expunge East European collaborators from Nazis' genocidal actions. Viewed from the transnational perspective of critical relativization, Germans' goodwill of taking exclusive political responsibility would deny *Homo Jedvabnecus*. It is similar to Japanese "conscientious intellectuals" (良心的知識人) unconsciously helping to promote nationalisms in Korea and China. Critical relativization of history, not political relativization of responsibility, can rescue the global memory from those overcontextualizing falsifications.

The memory war in postcommunist Eastern Europe and the postcolonial tri-continent represents a second wave of the *Historikerstreit* globally. Memories and narratives of the past became more diverse, contradictory, localized, and multiplied than the ideological binary of the Cold War. The cosmopolitanization of Holocaust memory is a phenomenon of the post–Cold War era. Global memory formation is more than the mere transposition of the Holocaust memory onto colonial genocide and Stalinist terror. A "critical relativization" and "radical juxtaposition" of different memories, even unconnected, makes possible a nonhierarchical comparison in the global memory space.[107] Global memory formation is in the process of forming and of becoming and, as such, responsive to the critical gaze. Neither denial of uniqueness nor the essentialization of the Holocaust are viable paths forward. Critical relativization and radical juxtaposition engenders empathy and helps us resist prioritizing our own victimhood. Deploying the critical relativization and radical juxtaposition is to criticize the reterritorialization and national hierarchization of victimhood in global memory formation.

Notes

1. See chapter 2.
2. Daniel Levy and Natan Sznaider, "Memory Unbound: The Holocaust and the Formation of Cosmopolitan Memory," *European Journal of Social Theory* 5, no. 1 (2002); Daniel Levy and Natan Sznaider, *The Holocaust and Memory in the Global Age*, trans. Assenka Oksiloff (Philadelphia: Temple University Press, 2006).
3. See Richard C. Lukas, *Forgotten Holocaust: The Poles Under German Occupation* rev. ed. (New York: Hippocrene Books, 2005); Tadeusz Piotrowski, *Poland's Holocaust: Ethnic Strife, Collaboration with Occupying Forces and Genocide in the Second Republic, 1918-1947* (Jefferson, N.C.: McFarland, 1998).
4. Lukas, *Forgotten Holocaust*, 34–35.
5. Amos Goldberg, "Ethics, Identity, and Anti-fundamental Fundamentalism: Holocaust Memory in the Global Age," and Haim Hazan, "Globalization Versus Holocaust," in *Marking Evil: Holocaust Memory in the Global Age*, ed. Amos Goldberg and Haim Hazan (New York: Berghahn Books, 2015), 20–21, 31.
6. Michael Rothberg, "From Gaza to Warsaw: Mapping Multidirectional Memory," *Criticism* 53, no. 4 (2011): 535.

7. Julia Lange and Marius Henderson, introduction to *Entangled Memories: Remembering the Holocaust in a Global Age*, ed. Marius Henderson and Julia Lange (Heidelberg: Universitätsverlag Winter, 2017), 8.

8. Giorgio Agamben, *Homo Sacer: Sovereign Power and Bare Life*, trans. Daniel Heller-Roazen (Stanford, Calif.: Stanford University Press, 1998).

9. Ward Churchill, "American Holocaust: Structure of Denial," *Socialism and Democracy* 17, no. 1 (2003): 26. Churchill's argument reads more like a manifesto of an activist than a scholarly work. For more nuanced debates on the comparability of genocide of indigenous people and the Holocaust, see Steven T. Katz, "Comparing Causes of Death in the Holocaust with the Tragedy of the Indigenous Peoples of Spanish America: The View of David E. Stannard," *Journal of Genocide Research* 22, no. 3 (2020): 373–90, doi: 10.1080/14623528.2020.1718360; and David E. Stannard, "True Believer: The Uniqueness of Steven T. Katz," *Journal of Genocide Research* 22, no. 3 (2020): 391–409, doi: 10.1080/14623528.2020.1719734. For the comparability of slavery and the Holocaust, see Jan Burzlaff, "The Holocaust and Slavery? Working Towards A Comparative History of Genocide and Mass Violence," *Journal of Genocide Research* 22, no. 3 (2020): 354–66, doi: 10.1080/14623528.2020.1718355; Steven T. Katz, "Response to Jan Burzlaff's Review of Steven T. Katz, The Holocaust and New World Slavery," *Journal of Genocide Research* 22, no. 3 (2020): 367–72, doi.1080/14623528.2020.1718357. See also A. D. Moses, "Conceptual Blockages and Definitional Dilemmas in the 'Racial Century': Genocides of Indigenous Peoples and the Holocaust," *Patterns of Prejudice* 36, no. 4 (2020): 7–36; and Roberta Pergher, Mark Roseman, Jürgen Zimmerer, Shelley Baranowski, Doris L. Bergen, and Zygmunt Bauman, "Scholarly Forum on the Holocaust and Genocide," *Dapim: Studies on the Holocaust* 27, no. 1 (2013): 40–73.

10. A. Dirk Moses, "The Holocaust and World History," in *The Holocaust and Historical Methodology*, ed. Dan Stone (New York: Berghahn Books, 2012), 273.

11. Ian Buruma, *The Wages of Guilt* (New York: Vintage, 1995), 92–111; Benoît Challand, "1989, Contested Memories and the Shifting Cognitive Maps of Europe," *European Journal of Social Theory* 12, no. 3 (2009): 398–402; Martin Krygier, "Letter from Australia: Neighbors: Poles, Jews and the Aboriginal Question," *East Central Europe* 29, part 1–2 (2002): 297–309; Shirli Gilbert, "Anne Frank in South Africa: Remembering the Holocaust During and After Apartheid," *Holocaust and Genocide Studies* 26, no. 3 (2012): 366–93; William F. S. Miles, "Indigenization of the Holocaust and the Tehran Holocaust Conference: Iranian Aberration or Third World Trend?," *Human Rights Review* 10 (2009); Dariusz Stola, "Anti-Zionism as a Multipurpose Policy Instrument: The Anti-Zionist Campaign in Poland, 1967–1968," *Journal of Israeli History* 25, no. 1 (March 2006): 183, 191; and special issue on "The Holocaust/Genocide Template in Eastern Europe," *Journal of Genocide Research* 20, no. 4 (2018).

12. Alon Confino, "The Holocaust as a Symbolic Manual," in Goldberg and Hazan, *Marking Evil*, 56.

13. Hagai El-Ad, "Netanyahu Exploits the Holocaust to Brutalize the Palestinians," *Haaretz*, January 23, 2020, https://www.haaretz.com/israel-news/.premium -netanyahu-exploits-the-holocaust-to-brutalize-the-palestinians-1.8437715/.

14. Tom Segev, *The Seventh Million: The Israelis and the Holocaust*, trans. Heim Watzman (New York: Owl Books, 2000), 399–400; Peter Novick, *The Holocaust and the Collective Memory* (London: Bloomsbury, 2001), 156.

15. Jean-Marc Dreyfus and Marcel Stoetzler, "Holocaust Memory in the Twenty-first Century: Between National Reshaping and Globalisation," *European Review of History* 18, no. 1 (February 2011): 74–75; Novick, *The Holocaust*, 241.

16. Jay Michaelson, "Why Ben Carson's Rant About Gun Control and the Holocaust Is So Dangerous," *Forward*, October 9, 2015, https://forward.com/opinion/national /322394/why-we-shouldnt-ignore-ben-carsons-rant-about-gun-control-and-the -holocaust/.

17. Daniel Levy and Natan Sznaider, "Memory Unbound: The Holocaust and the Formation of Cosmopolitan Memory," *European Journal of Social Theory* 5, no. 1 (2002): 99.

18. One should note that the cosmopolitanization of the Holocaust has as its neces- sary complement a process of "decosmopolitanization" or "renationalization" of German identity. See S. Welch and R. Wittlinger, "The Resilience of the Nation State: Cosmopolitanism, Holocaust Memory and German Identity," *German Politics and Society* 29, no. 3 (2011): 38–54.

19. A. Dirk Moses, "Genocide and the Terror of History," *Parallax* 17, no. 4 (2011): 91.

20. See Lea David, "Holocaust Discourse as a Screen Memory: The Serbian Case," in *History and Politics in the Western Balkans*, ed. Srdan M. Jovanovic and Veran Stance- tic, *OPAL* 1–2 (October 10, 2013): 65, 67, 69, 71, 79.

21. Jelena Subotić, *Yellow Star, Red Star: Holocaust Remembrance After Communism* (Ithaca, N.Y.: Cornell University Press, 2019), 5–11.

22. For the nationalization of Holocaust memory in other East European countries, see Micha Brumlik and Karol Sauerland, eds., *Umdeuten, verschweigen, erinnern: Die späte Aufarbeitung des Holocaust in Osteuropa* (Frankfurt: Campus Verlag, 2010); Aro Velmet, "Occupied Identities: National Narratives in Baltic Museums of Occupa- tions," *Journal of Baltic Studies* 42, no. 2 (2011).

23. Jan Gross, "Die Osteuropäer haben kein Schamgefühl," *Die Welt*, September 13, 2015, https://www.welt.de/debatte/kommentare/article146355392/Die-Osteuropaeer -haben-kein-Schamgefuehl.html.

24. Siobhan Kattago, "Agreeing to Disagree on the Legacies of Recent History Mem- ory, Pluralism and Europe After 1989," *European Journal of Social Theory* 12, no. 3 (2009): 382; Martin Evans, "Memories, Monuments, Histories: The Re-thinking of the Second World War Since 1989," *National Identities* 8, no. 4 (December 2006): 320.

25. "Dyskusja: czy to nasza sprawa?," *Więź*, no. 662 (2015): 42.

26. Bartosz t. Wieliński, " 'Polska nie chce uchodźców, bo nie rozliczyła się ze zbrodni na Żydach.' Oburzenie po tekście Grossa," *Wyborcza.pl*, September 15, 2015, http:// wyborcza.pl/1,75968,18817369,skandalista-gross.html; Aleksander Smolar, "Smolar:

Gross szokuje," *Wyborcza.pl*, September 16, 2015, http://wyborcza.pl/1,75968,1882 4173,smolar-gross-szokuje.html.

27. I am still thinking of the possibility of applying the concept of "subaltern empire" to the Polish-Lithuanian Commonwealth and interwar Poland. See Viatcheslav Morozov, "Subaltern Empire? Toward a Postcolonial Approach to Russian Foreign Policy," *Problems of Post-Communism* 60, no. 6 (November–December 2013); Jordan Sand, "Subaltern Imperialists: The New Historiography of the Japanese Empire," *Past and Present*, no. 225 (November 2014).

28. Lucy Mably et al., " 'Other' Posts in 'Other' Places: Poland Through a Postcolonial Lens?," *Sociology* 50, no. 1 (2016): 66; Larry Wolff, *Inventing Eastern Europe: The Map of Civilization on the Mind of the Enlightenment* (Stanford, Calif.: Stanford University Press, 1994), 9; Jerzy Jedlicki, *A Suburb of Europe: Nineteenth-Century Polish Approaches to Western Civilization.* (Budapest: Central European University Press. 1999), xiii.

29. Janusz Pajewski, *Budowa Drugiej Rzeczypospolitej 1918–26* (Kraków: PAU, 1995), 164.

30. Anshel Pfeffer, "In New Battle Over Auschwitz Legacy, Poland Falls Victim to Holocaust Geopolitics," *Haaretz*, January 22, 2020, https://www.haaretz.com/israel -news/.premium-auschwitz-75-years-israel-yad-vashem-poland-victim -holocaust-geopolitics-putin-1.8432285; Ofer Aderet, "The Dirty Politics Behind Israel's Capitulation to Putin's WWII Revisionism," *Haaretz*, January 16, 2020, https://www.haaretz.com/israel-news/.premium-the-dirty-politics-behind -israel-s-capitulation-to-putin-s-wwii-revisionism-1.8406565.

31. See the witness of Malika Abdoulvakhabova, a Chechen refugee resident in Poland, "Dyskusja: czy to nasza sprawa?," 36, 38, 39.

32. It is in stark contrast with the socialist postcolonialism in People's Poland, where Aimé Césaire's classical text of "Discourse on Colonialism" was translated immediately after the original publication in 1950. See Adam Kola, *Socjalistyczny postkolonializm: Rekonsolidacja pamięci* (Toruń: NCU Press, 2018).

33. Juergen Zimmerer, "Die Geburt des Ostlandes aus dem Geiste des Kolonialismus: Die nationalsozialistische Eroberungs- und Beherrschungspolitik in (post)kolonialer Perspektive," *Sozial Geschichte* 19, no. 1 (2004); Benjamin Madley, "From Africa to Auschwitz: How German South West Africa Incubated Ideas and Methods Adopted and Developed by the Nazis in Eastern Europe," *European History Quarterly* 35, no. 3 (2005); Enzo Traverso, *The Origins of Nazi Violence* (New York: New Press, 2003); Robert Gerwarth and Stephan Malinowski, "Der Holocaust als kolonialer Genozid? Europaeische Kolonialgewalt und nationalsozialistischer Vernichtungskrieg," *Geschichte und Gesellschaft* 33 (2007); A. Dirk Moses, "Empire, Colony, Genocide: Keywords and the Philosophy," in *Empire, Colony, Genocide*, ed. A. Dirk Moses (New York: Berghan Books, 2008).

34. David Furber, "Near as Far in the Colonies: The Nazi Occupation of Poland," *International History Review* 26, no. 3 (2004): 541, 544, 549.

35. Ian Kershaw, *Hitler, 1936–45: Nemesis* (New York: Norton, 2001), 400, 405.

36. Mark Mazower, *Dark Continent: Europe's Twentieth Century* (New York: Vintage Books, 1998), xiii. See also Mark Mazower, *Hitler's Empire: How the Nazis Ruled Europe*

(New York: Penguin Press, 2008); Furber, "Near as Far in the Colonies," 541–79; Juergen Zimmerer, "Die Geburt des Ostlandes aus dem Geiste des Kolonialismus. Die nationalsozialistische Eroberungs- und Beherrschungspolitik in (post-) kolonialer Perspektive," *Sozial Geschichte* 19, no. 1 (2004); Madley, "From Africa to Auschwitz"; Mably et al., "'Other' Posts in 'Other' Places," 60–76.

37. Kristin Kopp, *Germany's Wild East: Constructing Poland as Colonial Space* (Ann Arbor: University of Michigan Press, 2012), 78.

38. Dan Stone, "The Historiography of Genocide: Beyond 'Uniqueness' and Ethnic Competition," *Rethinking History* 8, no. 1 (2004): 133.

39. Zygmunt Bauman, *Modernity and the Holocaust* (Ithaca, N.Y.: Cornell University Press, 2000), xi–xii, 28, 152, and passim.

40. Aimé Césaire, *Discourse on Colonialism*, trans. J. Pinkham (New York: Monthly Review, 2000), 36.

41. Kola, *Socjalistyczny Postkolonializm*, 2–3.

42. István Deák, "Heroes and Victims," in *The Neighbors Responded: The Controversy Over the Jedwabne Massacre in Poland*, ed. Adam Polonsky and Joanna Michlic (Princeton, N.J.: Princeton University Press, 2004), 422.

43. Eric J. Sundquist, *The Oxford W. E. B. Du Bois Reader* (Oxford: Oxford University Press, 1996), 471; Cedric J. Robinson, "Fascism and the Intersection of Capitalism, Racialism and Historical Consciousness," *Humanities in Society* 3 (Autumn 1983): 325–49.

44. W. E. B. Du Bois, "The Negro and the Warsaw Ghetto," in Sundquist, *The Oxford W. E. B. Du Bois Reader*, 470.

45. Paul Gilroy, *The Black Atlantic: Modernity and Double Consciousness* (London: Verso, 1993), 207–8.

46. "Letter from Jewish Life to W. E. B. Du Bois, February 13, 1952," W. E. B. Du Bois Papers (MS 312), Special Collections and University Archives, University of Massachusetts Amherst Libraries, http://credo.library.umass.edu/view/full/mums312-b137-i103.

47. Du Bois, "The Negro and the Warsaw Ghetto," 471; see also chapter 2 of this book.

48. Yuichiro Onishi, "The New Negro of the Pacific: How African Americans Forged Cross-Racial Solidarity with Japan, 1917–1922," *Journal of African American History* 92, no. 2 (Spring 2007), 192–94, 199.

49. For the Black-Asian nexus, see Bill Mullen, *Afro-Orientalism* (Minneapolis: University of Minnesota Press, 2004); Yuichiro Onishi, *Trans-Pacific Anti-racism: Afro-Asian Solidarity in 20th-Century Black America, Japan, and Okinawa* (New York: New York University Press, 2013); Etsuko Taketani, *The Black Pacific Narrative: Geographic Imaginings of Race and Empire Between the World Wars* (Hanover, N.H.: Dartmouth College Press, 2014).

50. William Pickens, "Reflections: 'White Supremacy' Is Dead," *New York Amsterdam News*, March 9, 1932, 8; and William Jones, "Day by Day: Japan Again Thumbs Nose," *Afro-American*, November 26, 1932, both quoted in Taketani, *The Black Pacific Narrative*, 50.

51. Gilbert, "Anne Frank in South Africa," 366, 374.

52. Otto Frank, who actively used Anne Frank's legacy to fight racism and apartheid, protested the "Nazism=Apartheid" banner on the grounds that the two were not comparable. See Gilbert, 375.

53. Eve Rosenhaft, "Beyond Multidirectional Memory: Tracking the Holocaust in the Black Diaspora," in *Mnemonic Solidarity: Global Interventions*, ed. Jie-Hyun Lim and Eve Rosenhaft (London: Palgrave Macmillan, 2021), 52.

54. Toshihisha Onishi, "Auschwitz Guide Works to Enlighten Japanese Visitors," *Japan Times*, March 5, 2015, https://www.japantimes.co.jp/news/2015/03/05/national /history/auschwitz-guide-works-to-enlighten-japanese-visitors/#.

55. Sakiko Masuda, " 'Memory Keeper' Yumie Hirano to Visit Poland in May, Convey Survivors' Experiences of Atomic Bombing," *Chugoku shimbun*, April 18, 2016, http:// www.hiroshimapeacemedia.jp/?p=59331.

56. Konishi Tetsuro, "The Original Manuscript of Takashi Nagai's Funeral Address at a Mass for the Victims of the Nagasaki Atomic Bomb," *Journal of Nagasaki University of Foreign Studies*, no. 18 (December 2014), 55, 58, 61.

57. Tetsuro, 58, 62.

58. Dr. Wilsey, an anesthesiologist in the 116th Evacuation Hospital of the U.S. Army, wrote to his wife on March 23, 1945, that "we were (are) in a nightmarish holocaust . . . Holocaust! After Holocaust! After Holocaust." See Steve Friess, "When 'Holocaust' became 'The Holocaust,' " *New Republic*, May 18, 2015, https://newrepublic .com/article/121807/when-holocaust-became-holocaust. See also Sean Warsch, "A 'holocaust' Becomes the Holocaust," Jewish Magazine (October 2006), http:// www.jewishmag.com/107mag/holocaustword/holocaustword.htm; "John Petrie Investigates the Etymology of the Word 'Holocaust' " (1999), http://www.fpp.co .uk/Auschwitz/docs/HolocaustUsage.html.

59. Emilio Gentile, "The Sacralisation of Politics: Definitions, Interpretations and Reflections on the Question of Secular Religion and Totalitarianism," *Totalitarian Movements and Political Religions* 1 (Summer 2000).

60. See "Victimhood Nationalism in Contested Memories–National Mourning and Global Accountability," in *Memory in a Global Age: Discourses, Practices and Trajectories*, ed. Aleida Assmann and Sebastian Conrad (Basingstoke, UK: Palgrave Macmillan, 2010), 138–62. See also chapter 1 of this book.

61. Ian Buruma, 아우슈비츠와 히로시마 [*The Wages of Guilt: Memories of War in Germany and Japan*], trans. Jeong Yonghwan (Seoul: Hangyŏreh Shinmusa, 2002), 119–26; John W. Dower, "An Aptitude for Being Unloved: War and Memory in Japan," in *Crimes of War: Guilt and Denial in the Twentieth Century*, ed. Omer Bartov, Atina Grossmann, and Mary Nolan (New York: New Press, 2002), 226.

62. Sadako Kurihara, "The Literature of Auschwitz and Hiroshima," *Holocaust and Genocide Studies* 7 (March 1993): 86, 87.

63. Rotem Kowner, "Tokyo Recognizes Auschwitz: The Rise and Fall of Holocaust Denial in Japan, 1989–1999," *Journal of Genocide Research* 3, no. 2 (2001): 257, 259, and passim.

64. Ran Zwigenberg, "Never Again: Hiroshima, Auschwitz and the Politics of Commemoration," *Asia-Pacific Journal* 13, issue 3, no. 1 (January 19, 2015). See also Ran Zwigenberg, *Hiroshima: the Origins of Global Memory Culture* (Cambridge: Cambridge University Press, 2014).

65. "Pierwszy dzień wolności," *Dziennik Polski*, January 29, 1963.

66. Sebastian Conrad, "The Dialectics of Remembrance: Memories of Empire in Cold War Japan," *Comparative Studies in Society and History* 56 (2014): 13, 17–18.

67. Zwigenberg, "Never Again," 10–11.

68. Later, Oe made a self-criticism that he did not consider the Korean and Okinawan victims in the original version of the "Hiroshima Note." See Kenzaburo Oe, preface to the English edition in *Hiroshima Notes*, trans. D. L. Swain and T. Yonezawa (New York: Marion Boyars, 1995), 9. Its original Japanese version was written in 1963.

69. John Dower, "The Bombed: Hiroshima and Nagasaki in Japanese Memory," *Diplomatic History* 19, no. 2 (Spring 1995): 281.

70. James J. Orr, *The Victim as Hero: Ideologies of Peace and National Identity in Postwar Japan* (Honolulu: University of Hawai'i Press, 2001), 52.

71. Lisa Yoneyama, *Hiroshima Traces: Time, Space, and the Dialectics of Memory* (Berkeley: University of California Press, 1999), 25.

72. JTA, "Why Are the Japanese So Fascinated with Anne Frank?," *Haaretz*, January 22, 2014, https://www.haaretz.com/jewish/anne-frank-the-japanese-anime -1.5314070.

73. For Maksymilian Kolbe and Nagasaki Hibakusha, see Jie-Hyun Lim, "Critical Juxtaposition in the Postwar Japanese Mnemoscape: Saint Maksymilian Kolbe of Auschwitz and the Atomic Bomb Victims of Nagasaki," in *Memory and Religion from a Postsecular Perspective*, edited by Zuzanna Bogumił and Yuliya Yurchuk (London: Routledge, 2022).

74. Endō Shūsaku, "コルベ神父" [Father Kolbe],『新編國語總合』改訂版 (Tokyo: Daishukan Bookstore, 2018), 186.

75. Elaine Lies and Takashi Umekawa, "Japan PM Ex-adviser Praises Apartheid in Embarrassment for Abe," *Reuters*, February 13, 2015, https://www.reuters.com /article/us-japan-apartheid/japan-pm-ex-adviser-praises-apartheid-in -embarrassment-for-abe-idUSKBN0LH0M420150213.

76. Phillip Gabriel, *Spirit Matters: The Transcendent in Modern Japanese Literature* (Honolulu: University of Hawai'i Press, 2006), 51.

77. Sono Ayako, *Miracles: A Novel*, trans. Kevin Doak (Portland, Me.: MerwinAsia, 2016), 15, 63, 68, 101–2.

78. Jan Józef Lipski, "Ojciec Kolbe i *Mały Dziennik*," *Tygodnik Powszechny*, no. 38 (1182), 19. IX. 1971.

79. Richard Cohen, "Sainthood," *Washington Post*, December 14, 1982, https://www .washingtonpost.com/archive/local/1982/12/14/sainthood/899d8e06-3209-4fd6 -90de-d6798f76ee57/; Henry Kamm, "The Saint of Auschwitz Is Canonized by Pope," *New York Times*, October 11, 1982, https://www.nytimes.com/1982/10/11/world/the

-saint-of-auschwitz-is-canonized-by-pope.html; David Binder, "Franciszek Gaj-owniczek Dead; Priest Died for Him at Auschwitz," *New York Times*, March 15, 1995, https://www.nytimes.com/1995/03/15/obituaries/franciszek-gajowniczek-dead -priest-died-for-him-at-auschwitz.html; John Gross, "Life Saving," *New York Review of Books*, February 17, 1983, https://www.nybooks.com/articles/1983/02/17/life -saving/; Daniel Schlafly, Warren Green and John Gross, "Kolbe and Anti-Semitism," *New York Review of Books,* April 14, 1983, https://www.nybooks.com/articles/1983 /04/14/kolbe-anti-semitism-2/.

80. Rafu Staff Report, "Glendale Approves Comfort Women Memorial," *Rafu shimpo,* July 15, 2013, http://www.rafu.com/2013/07/glendale-approves-comfort-women -memorial/.

81. Chris McCormick, "Armenian Exceptionalism," *Atlantic,* April 4, 2016, https://www .theatlantic.com/business/archive/2016/04/glendale-armenians/475926/.

82. Rafu Staff Report, "Glendale Approves Comfort Women Memorial."

83. "Past Exhibitions," ReflectSpace Gallery, Glendale Central Library, https://www .reflectspace.org/past-exhibits (accessed January 12, 2021).

84. Choe Sang-Hun, "South Korea Resists U.S. Pressure to Improve Ties with Japan," *New York Times*, November 15, 2019, https://www.nytimes.com/2019/11/15/world /asia/south-korea-japan-intelligence-sharing.html.

85. Nikkei for Civil Rights and Redress, http://www.ncrr-la.org/about.html, accessed March 9, 2020.

86. Brittany Levine, "Glendale Councilman Zareh Sinanyan Apologizes for Racist Post-ings," *Los Angeles Times*, May 1, 2013, http://articles.latimes.com/2013/may/01 /local/la-me-ln-glendale-councilman-apologizes-20130501.

87. General secretary of KACE in discussion with the author, KACE office, Flushing, N.Y., July 4, 2014.

88. Maki Kimura, *Unfolding the "Comfort Women" Debates: Modernity, Violence, Women's Voices* (Basingstoke, UK: Palgrave Macmillan, 2016), 6–8.

89. Rumi Sakamoto, "The Women's International War Crimes Tribunal on Japan's Mil-itary Sexual Slavery: A Legal and Feminist Approach to the "Comfort Women" Issue," *New Zealand Journal of Asian Studies* 3 (June 2001): 49–50.

90. Judges of the Women's International War Crimes Tribunal on Japan's Military Sex-ual Slavery, "Transcript of Oral Judgment," December 4, 2001, http://iccwomen .org/wigjdraft1/Archives/oldWCGJ/tokyo/summary.html.

91. Carol Gluck, "What the World Owes the Comfort Women," in Lim and Rosenhaft, *Mnemonic Solidarity*, 79.

92. Esther Felden, "Freiburg und die Trostfrau," *Deutsche Welle*, September 21, 2016, http://www.dw.com/de/freiburg-und-die-trostfrau/a-19563885.

93. Yi Minu, "염태영 수원시장 정대협 특별상 수상" [Mayor Yeom wins special prize from the Korean Council for Women Drafted for the Military Slavery by Japan], *Newspeak*, November 21, 2016. http://www.newspeak.kr/news/articleView.html?idxno=116422.

94. Stefan Gruber, " 'Trostfrau' mahnt zum Frieden," *Mittelbayersicshe Zeitung*, March 12, 2017, https://www.mittelbayerische.de/region/regensburg-land/gemeinden

/wiesent/trostfrau-mahnt-zum-frieden-21411-art1496089.html. Special thanks to Tanja Vaitulevich for information about this bizarre event.

95. Hong Yong Duck, "경기도의회 올해안에 독도에 평화의 소녀상 세우기로" [Kyŏnggido local council resolves to build the comfort women statue in Dokdo this year], *Hankyoreh*, January 16, 2017, http://www.hani.co.kr/arti/society/area/778893.html.

96. See Michael Rothberg, *Multidirectional Memory: Remembering the Holocaust in the Age of Decolonization* (Stanford, Calif.: Stanford University Press, 2009).

97. The verdict of the European Court of Justice on December 17, 2017, that denying the Armenian genocide belongs to the domain of freedom of speech, while denial of the Holocaust is a crime transcending freedom of speech, alludes to why the Holocaust remains the most popular leverage to justify "our own national suffering." See Ofer Aderet and Reuters, "European Court: Denying Armenian 'Genocide' Is No Crime," *Haaretz*, December 19, 2013, https://www.haaretz.com/european -court-no-crime-to-deny-armenian-genocide-1.5301268.

98. Jovan Byford, "When I Say 'the Holocaust' I Mean 'Jasenovac': Remembrance of the Holocaust in Contemporary Serbia," *East European Jewish Affairs* 37, no. 1 (2007): 51–74.

99. Confino, "The Holocaust as a Symbolic Manual," 56.

100. Walter Ben Michaels, "Plots Against America: Neoliberalism and Antiracism," *American Literary History* 18, no. 2 (2006): 289–90.

101. Bauman, *Modernity and the Holocaust*, xii, 28.

102. See Siobahn Kattago, *Ambiguous Memory: The Nazi Past and German National Identity* (Westport, Conn.: Praeger, 2001), 56–62; Geoff Eley, "Nazism, Politics and the Image of the Past: Thoughts on the West German Historikerstreit 1986–1987," *Past & Present*, no. 121 (November 1988): 173.

103. Charles Maier, *The Unmasterable Past: History, Holocaust and German National Identity*, 2nd ed. (Cambridge, Mass.: Harvard University Press, 1997), 1.

104. Maier, xii.

105. Eley, "Nazism, Politics and the Image of the Past," 174.

106. Jan Grabowski, "Germany Is Fueling a False History of the Holocaust Across Europe," *Haaretz*, June 22, 2020, https://www.haaretz.com/world-news/.premium-germany -is-fueling-a-false-history-of-the-holocaust-across-europe-1.8938137.

107. For critical juxtaposition of things without providing connectives, see Susan Stanford Friedman, "Planetarity: Musing Modernist Studies," *Modernism/Modernity* 17, no. 3 (2010): 493–94.

PART II
IMAGINING

4

A Postcolonial Reading of *Sonderwege*

Marxist Historicism Revisited

Why Wasn't Germany England?

"Why wasn't Germany England?" By posing this question, Ralf Dahrendorf reveals the underlying assumption of the German Sonderweg thesis.[1] Dahrendorf's question assumes the dichotomy of "England as the West" versus "Germany as the Rest." He posits English history as the universal, normal, democratic yardstick by which to measure the particular, abnormal, fascist aberration of German history. Jürgen Kocka explained that, "through comparisons with England, France, the United States, or simply 'the West,'" historians "attempted to identify the peculiarities of German history which . . . hindered the long-term development of liberal democracy in Germany and eventually facilitated the triumph of fascism."[2] To be peculiar is to be aberrant, to have taken an alternate, lesser path—a Sonderweg. Historians of German modernity have explained these peculiarities in numerous ways: the belated nation (*die verspätete Nation*), the aborted bourgeois revolution, the feudalization of the bourgeoisie, aristocrat-led industrialization, the blocked development of parliamentarianism, the illiberal and antipluralistic political culture, and so forth.[3]

In the global trajectory of Marxist historical thought, however, one finds many *Sonderwege* instead of *the Sonderweg*. Even before the World War II, the *Kōza* faction of Japanese Marxist historiography laid the foundation for the postwar Sonderweg thesis by using idioms such as the semifeudal serf-dom, parasitic landlordism, "arrested development" of the bourgeoisie, militarist form of finance capital, patrimonial role of the state, delayed civil society, collectivist society, and immature modern subjectivity.[4] Modern historiographies of China and Korea likewise have been standardizing their accounts of the Eastern courses of historical development as Sonder-wege, deviations from the West.[5] These East Asian Sonderwege fed off one another, all the while reinforcing the central premise of the Sonderweg, that is, there's the West and then the rest. Supporting the Comintern the-sis of the Chinese revolution (1927), the Japanese Sonderweg echoed Stalin in stressing how Chinese capitalism involved the coexistence of the devel-oping merchant capital and the feudal vestiges in villages.[6] However, the Japanese Sonderweg was both similar to and different from Asian Sonder-wege. Uniquely among East Asian nations, Japan was able to break free and establish a Sonderweg closer to that of the West. Japan's victory over Rus-sia in the Russo-Japanese War of 1905 established its Western-style nation-building bona fides. Since then, Japan has had a variant of Sonder-weg closer to the West's.[7] Japan's position fluctuated between the East and West in the world history narrative.

East European historiography drew on accounts of German peculiari-ties through the optic of "the first model of underdevelopment." Under this perspective, peasant Eastern Europe was hopelessly undercapitalized and underdeveloped.[8] The world-renowned postwar Polish economic historian Witold Kula insisted on the distinctiveness of the East European Sonderweg by quoting Friedrich Engels's warning against trying to bring "Patagonia's political economy under the same laws as are operative in present-day England."[9] Larry Wolff explains that Eastern Europe was the West's "first model of underdevelopment."[10] The peculiarity of East European his-tory continued in the party historiography that took the Leninist term the "Prussian path" of capitalism as a structural default to explain the East European modern.[11] Ottoman Turkey was thought to be another example of the Prussian path of "half-baked failed modernity."[12]

In the global project of Marxist historiography, Sonderwege in the "Rest" localized historical equivalents of the German peculiarity, the "Prussian path," into a network of "particularities" of diverse regions and states. In the Marxist schema of the world economy, capital occupies the position of the universal, while other local conditions equal the particular.

In the shift from Sonderweg to Sonderwege, "singularity" of every nation becomes the "particularity" characteristic of a class of nations.[13] Much as the East European peculiarity has been explained "in terms of *isolation from* versus *exposure to*" fundamental developments in the West,[14] the Sonderwege of East Asian histories have been constructed "through the dynamics of attraction to and repulsion from the West."[15] Once translated into the generic "particularity," individual "singularities" are reduced to their relative deviation from the developmental narrative of Europe.[16]

If we wish to interrogate the transmutation of German peculiarity into the "particularity" in the global chain of states and regions, we must undertake a critical review of the temporalization of historical spaces in a linear historical development. The Sonderweg thesis accommodates the global historicist time in a twisted form of "first in England, then in Germany."[17] Treating Germany as the East casts its history as a history of deviation from England, taken to be the West. East and West become temporalized as past and future, as premodern and modern. The Eurocentric vision of the Sonderweg thesis consigned more dictatorial and less developed Germany/East to "an imaginary waiting room of history" on the way to the Anglo-American/Western democracy and development. This argument serves as the historical alibi of the modernist West because fascism and dictatorship are reduced to manifestations of the generic particularity of the premodern "Rest." Thus "West" is exempted from association with fascism defined *ab initio* as premodern. "To become modern, it is still said, is to act like the West."[18]

A postcolonial reading of Sonderwege demands that we put Dahrendorf's question in the sequential chain of global history: "Why wasn't Germany England?" ramifies into "Why wasn't Poland Germany? Why wasn't Poland even Japan? Why wasn't Japan England?, etc."[19] In each of these scenarios, Germany takes a different positionality. When compared to England, it occupies the imaginary "East"; when compared with Poland, it finds itself as the "West." As Norbert Elias's analysis of French "civilization" versus German "culture" shows, German *Kulturwissenschaft* imagined France as its own West.[20] In contrast, German East Europeanists called Polish studies *Ostforschung*, namely, Eastern studies. Using an Orientalist discourse, *Ostforschung* essentialized Poland as an East. In Poland, German studies were called *Studia Zachodnie*, or Western studies. Arguably the strategic position of Germany in the global history has oscillated between

East and West in the "imaginative geography." Even Prussia remained a part the imagined Orient of German Orientalism. Konrad Adenauer, a post-war German chancellor from the western Rheinland, muttered "Asia" every time his train crossed the Elbe into Prussia.[21]

"East" and "West" are not geopositivistic but relational concepts. Thus "Western civilization" loses its essentialized authenticity. If West signifies the normal route to modernization, East represents a deviation from the model course. The strategic locations of the East and the West as well as individual nations in the historical discourse vary, depending on how they are cofigured discursively. For example, Japan is posited as East in cofiguration with England, France, and maybe Germany. Vis-à-vis Korea, China, and even Poland, however, Japan's strategic location shifts to West. East and West implies a sequential order of evolution. The sequential order from East to West connotes the temporalization of historical spaces in a linear development scheme. To quote Dipesh Chakrabarthy, "Historicism is what made modernity or capitalism look not simply global but rather as something that became global *over time*, by originating in one place (Europe) and then spreading outside it. This 'first in Europe, then elsewhere' structure of global historicist time was historicist."[22]

In this self-Orientalizing schema, the West represented by England has achieved the maturation of the unique historical conditions for science, rationalism, industrialism, freedom, equality, democracy and human rights. To overcome the dichotomy of the backward East and advanced West, historians in the East have tried to find the missing ingredients such as the middle class, cities, political rights, rationalism, and, above all, the endogenous development of the capitalist mode of production in their own histories.[23] The Eurocentric vision of the Sonderweg thesis consigned the dictatorial and less developed Germany/East to "an imaginary waiting room of history" on the way to the Anglo-American/Western democracy and development. The argument serves as the historical alibi of the modernist West, because fascism and dictatorship are reduced to manifestations of peculiarities of the premodern Rest, and thus West is exempted from association with a barbarism defined *ab initio* as premodern. In problematizing the Sonderweg thesis, I will show that both colonial modernity and Sonderwege have been constructed on the Marxist dichotomy of the "American path" versus the "Prussian path" to capitalist development, while questioning the dominant narrative of the world history that locates the origins of capitalist modernity entirely within the West and makes the historical experiences of capitalist Western Europe the imposing standard for all human history. A postcolonial reading of Sonderweg subjects the Eurocentric conception of the "Prussian path" to the complexity of hybrid modernity, which disrupts linear narratives of modernization and Euro-capitalism.[24] At the same time, it critiques both Eurocentric Marxism and Third Worldism, which retain the assumptions of Marxist historicism. Then I will bring new light to the Marxist historiographical debate on colonial modernity versus Sonderwege by reconciling David Blackburn and Geoff Eley's criticism of the German Sonderweg with the postcolonial critique of Marxist historicism.

Eurocapitalism and Colonial Modernity

The main current of Marxist historians has been captive of the Eurocentric historicism that projects the West as "History."[25] The Marxist concept of unilinear development of history with European capitalist development as the universal model in world history was the fertile ground for the Sonderweg thesis. Geoff Eley's remark on "the ironies of a British Marxist invoking anti-Marxist revisionist historiographies of the English and French Revolutions against West German anti-Marxists relying on discredited Marxist constructions of British and French history" pinpoints the hermeneutical complicity of the Marxist and Whig historiography of the bourgeois revolution.[26] It gives us a clue to understanding why the Russian bourgeoisie, more than any other class, welcomed *Das Kapital* as a scientific blueprint for promoting capitalism in Russia.[27] Despite their political antagonism, rooted in class differences, both Marxist and Whig interpretations envision an ideal bourgeoisie who would bring forth the revolution from below and accelerate nation-building, centralized state formation, democracy, and industrialization.

The Sonderweg thesis has both Marxist and Whig historiographies underlying its comparative perspective. A. J. P. Taylor's Whig interpretation of German history, combined with German social historians' Whig conception of English history, birthed the Sonderweg thesis. Marxian descriptions of the bourgeois revolution and the transition from feudalism to capitalism resonated with Whig models of the development of capitalism and parliamentary democracy. In Marxist historicism, the "capitalo-centric" seems to overshadow the "Eurocentric" as an organizing principle.[28] However, the capitalo-centric cannot be disentangled from the Eurocentric, as the rise of capitalism is considered quintessentially a European story. Europe remains the universal metric.

Although the late Marx recognized the possibility of alternative developments of capitalism, the West remained the model for normative capitalist development. Marx's frequent use of the prefix "pre" in the precapitalist mode of production tips his hand. Marxist historicism tends to temporalize the historical space on a linear timeline with the capitalist West at the endpoint. Marx's proclamation in the preface to *Das Kapital* that the "country that is more developed industrially only shows, to the less developed, the image of its own future(!)" eloquently represents the unilinear temporalization of space.[29] While Marx deleted the exclamation mark from this passage in the second edition of *Das Kapital* in 1873, it did not mean he denied the temporalization of space.[30] Despite the logical possibility of multilinear development of history in Marx, in his work different paths of human evolution pursue, aim, converge, flow, and meet in a confluence of universal Eurocapitalism. To quote Timothy Mitchell, "the use of the idea of a singular historical time to reorganize the dispersed geographies of modernity into stages of Europe's past finds its first clear expression in the work of Marx."[31]

In the Marxian historical schema, the spatial difference between Germany/East/Periphery and England/West/Center coincides with the developmental difference between backwardness and forwardness. The Marxist controversy over the transition from feudalism to capitalism in *Science & Society* (1950–1953) confirmed the universality of the Eurocapitalism in arguing for the endogenous development of the capitalist mode of production in Western Europe. In his *Studies in the Development of Capitalism* (1946), which initiated these debates over transition, Maurice Dobb sought to find the genesis of industrial capital through the particularities of the English agriculture, with a focus on the rise of yeomanry and the land expropriation of small peasants.[32] Participants in the debate made extensive exegeses of Marx on the genesis of capitalism to convince readers of their argument. Whether through European agrarian forces (Dobb) or European commercial one (Paul M. Sweezy), the rise of capitalism arose, nevertheless, out of Eurocapitalism.

The Marxist Sonderweg comes into being in the womb of Eurocapitalism. The Japanese Marxist economic historian Takahashi Kōhachirō expanded on Dobb's "two ways" of capitalist development by contrasting "the classical bourgeois revolution of Western Europe" of England and France with "the erection of capitalism under the control and patronage of the feudal absolutist state" in Prussia and Japan.[33] Takahashi's interest in this transition, shared by the Weberian Ōtsūka Hisao, was sparked by the idea that eighteenth-century Europe provided a yardstick for the development of Japanese society, specifically Japanese capitalism. Both Takahashi and Ōtsūka believed that the purest and most classical forms of the developmental stages of history were found in Western Europe.[34] In other words, the question of "why wasn't Japan England?" drove their study on capitalism in the West. Korean Marxist historians likewise traced capitalist development in premodern eighteenth-century Korea against European models.

Years before the Marxist controversy over the transition from feudalism in the 1950s, Lenin had elaborated "two ways" of capitalist development. The Leninist formulation of the Prussian path of a "bourgeois-Junker landlord economy" and the American path of a "bourgeois farmer economy" complemented the Marxist *Sonderweg* thesis as well.[35] For Lenin, the Prussian path epitomized the peculiarity of capitalist development in Russia. Considering that Russia was the Great Power with the Third World economy in the late nineteenth century, the Prussian path may recapitulate capitalist development in "the Rest." Later, Marxists generalized Lenin's formula to contrast the Prussian path as the aberrant capitalism in "the Rest" with the American path as the model capitalism in the West. While Lenin was essentially asking, "Why wasn't Russia England?," through his elaboration of two paths of capitalist development, Antonio Gramsci tacitly asked, "Why wasn't Italy France?," by designing "passive revolution" to capture the Italian bourgeoisie's "revolution-restoration." Like the feudalized bourgeoisie in Germany and Japan, the Italian bourgeoisie tried to reform from above to prevent the revolution from below.[36] It is captivating to read that many Marxist intellectuals in both postcolonial Korea and India have conjured up the "passive revolution" as a theoretical lever to define the contemporary political situation. In postcolonial India, the ideological construct of the "passive revolution of capital" has been conjured up to incorporate the "entire structures of precapitalist community taken in their existential forms" into the hegemony.[37]

Marxist historicism shaped by the Sonderweg discourse can be traced back to Marx and Engels. In contrast to the Leninist national self-determination and Maoist Third World revolution, Marx's writings on the periphery of global capitalism seem to indicate the negligence of the disenfranchised colonial subjects and an endorsement of the role of colonialists in bringing about modernization simultaneously. Engels was no less enthusiastic than Marx in advocating for colonialism as a locomotive of modernization. For instance, Engels saw the failure of the "hopeless" uprising led by the Algerian leader Abd-el Kader against French colonialism as "an important and fortunate fact for the progress of civilization."[38] Engels also advocated for the American conquest of Mexico "in the interest of civilization," mainly because the "energetic Yankees" rather than the "lazy Mexicans" would give a new stimulus to world trade.[39] In his capacious sense of "Asiatic" countries, Marx included India, China, Egypt, Mesopotamia, Turkey, Java, Tartars Persia, Russia, Mexico, Peru, Etrurians, and even Spain under the Moors.[40]

One can add the Slavs as "historyless people," labeled by Engels in 1848, to Marx's list of Asiatic countries. As an analyst of contemporary politics, Engels predicted that the victory of the Slavic national movements by the Czechs, Croatians, and other Southern Slav minorities would subordinate the civilized West to the barbaric East. Trade, industry, knowledge, and civilization would be subject to the primitive agriculture of the Slavic serfs.[41] Poles were the exception because a Polish uprising would prevent reactionary Russia from interfering in the European revolution. Although Marx and Engels undeniably shared the German Orientalism against Slavic neighbors, it would be far-fetched to include Marx and Engels with the Nazis' Eastern policy on the Slavic question, as have some argued in the past.[42] What is to be problematized is that the definition of the Slavs as "historyless people" was justified in the interest of civilization, trade, industry, and progress.

When news of the Taiping Rebellion reached Europe in 1850, Marx and Engels were pleased by the social upheaval in "the oldest and least perturbable kingdom on earth." According to them, the forthcoming Chinese revolution was not an endogenous but an exogenous revolution that the British bourgeoisie brought about and that would incorporate a reluctant barbaric people into world trade and the civilized world.[43] In their eyes, the Taiping Rebellion might serve as a catalyst for the European revolution; by causing a financial crisis for both the Indian colonial government and the British Empire, it would accelerate the economic crisis in Britain. Marx saw the rebellion in Asia as religious in nature. The political revolutions in Asia were considered to be no more than a destructive action in the form of grotesque terror with no hope for the social revolution.[44] The fundamental change in Asia was thought to be brought about by British colonialism.

Though Marx was critical of British colonial atrocities, the brutality of British capital was deemed a historical necessity to destroy the transformation-resistant idyllic village communities in precolonial India. Marx explained, "England . . . was the unconscious tool of history in bringing about a social revolution."[45] Marx's analysis of British rule in India addresses the inevitability of colonialism and its world-historical necessity. Capitalist development in India supposedly required colonialism to destroy the stagnation of the Asiatic mode of production.[46] Despite his critical views on colonial brutality, Marx preferred the "scientific barbarism" of British colonialism to the "barbaric egoism" of the Mughal Empire or other forms of "naïve" Indian rule.[47] Bill Warren's argument for "imperialism as the pioneer of capitalism" seems a better heir of Marx than the Leninist theory and practice of national liberation.[48]

Rosa Luxemburg likewise argued that national liberation movements in (semi-) colonies and less developed countries cannot be a driving force toward capitalist progress.[49] From the Trotskyist angle, Nigel Harris sharpened the Marxian critique of the Leninist principle of national self-determination, dependency theory, socialist autarky, and Third Worldism. He noted that, upon this nationalist turn, Marxism has become an ideology to advocate for the accumulation of capital by the nation-state.[50] Harris's critique echoes Warren's warning about the twisting of Marxism into a "modernizing nationalism" and "a more suitable industrializing ideology than the ideologies of eighteenth- and nineteenth-century capitalist industrialization" at the periphery.[51] In colonial and semicolonial places, Marxist historicism shaped by Sonderweg particularism recapitulated Marx and Engels on "Asiatic" countries.

Ironically, some colonial Marxists in Korea treated the Eurocentric unilinear conception of history as a "weapon of criticism" against red

Orientalism to save colonial Korea from the stagnant "Asiatic mode of production." For instance, Namwoon Paik, the most prominent Marxist historian in colonial Korea, periodized Korean history as corresponding exactly with the Marxist development stages of the primitive commune, slave economy, (Asiatic) feudalism, and capitalism. He sought to show the course of Korean history in step with the Western model history.[52] By relying on the unilinear schema of world capitalist development, Paik celebrated the autogenous capitalism of colonized Korea to contest the Japanese colonizer's view of Korea as a stagnant Asiatic mode of production. Motivated by the desire to overcome the Marxist Eurocentrism of the Asiatic mode of production, Paik invoked a "consequential" Eurocentrism.

It is a historical paradox that liberal developmental economists—rather than contemporary Marxists—in postcolonial Korea have adopted a view closer to Marx and Engels on historical development in Asia. Confronted by rapid capitalist growth in South Korea, especially since the 1960s, developmental economists envisioned the colonial modernization under Japanese rule as a precondition for the advent of semiadvanced capitalism in postcolonial Korea. Through a comparative approach, they identified two factors that explain the peculiarity of the swift capitalist development in South Korea: the small peasant economy in traditional societies and the experience of modernization under Japanese colonial rule.[53] Their arguments that Japanese colonialism spurred modern capitalist development echo Marx and Engels on the formative effect of British colonial rule in India for the development of capitalism. According to the developmental economists, "the historical DNA of the rational management accumulated in the small peasant economy" was the driving force behind colonial modernization and the rise of Korea to the Asian Newly Industrialized Countries (NICs) in the postwar era.[54]

So broad is the political and ideological spectrum of such colonial-modernity narratives that it enlists different, conflicting, and even symmetrically opposing Marxist schools. All parties involved in the polemic over colonial modernization shared the capitalo-centric perspective despite their differences about endogenous and exogenous capitalism. The shared commitment to a linear developmental trajectory of a Eurocapitalism in the transition from feudalism to capitalism enables this unlikely symbiosis. The capitalo-centric view immanent in Marxist historicism, whether it involves a unilinear or a multilinear development scheme of the history of humankind, gives rise to Eurocentrism. Eurocentrism is inevitable in the capitalo-centric view that capitalism grows organically and evolves peacefully from feudalism in Europe and then diffuses to the "Rest." The hermeneutical complicity of the Marxist and Whig historiography of capitalism has been nurtured on this capitalo-centric terrain.

All these colonial modernity and modernization narratives, be they Marxian, liberal, or colonialist, share the same fundamental flaw: they deny agency to the colonized subalterns; they attribute the agency of colonial modernity exclusively to the external force, namely, colonialism. Very often they treat colonial subjects who are opposed to Western colonialism as "prepolitical" or "subpolitical" historical actors, ignorant of and even resistant to progress and development in this modernist narrative.[55] "Asiatic" social movements could be disregarded as archaic and antithetical to progress such as capitalist development, mechanization of the labor process, industrialization, centralization of the power, the rise of the nation-state, and privatization. When "history from below" thrusts colonial modernity into a harsh light in terms of modernist dominance and power, the Sonderweg thesis, Eurocapitalism, and colonial modernity begin to reveal the rot at the roots of progress and development.[56]

Dependency and the Colonial Sonderweg

Marx and Engels allude to the colonial Sonderweg in their writings on colonialism. Their ambiguity concerning the colonial question reveals not a straight but a crooked line between colonial modernity and the colonial Sonderwege. For instance, Engels changed his mind concerning the "hopeless" religious uprising in Algeria to pay homage to Abd-el Kader's valor in 1857 and explicitly sympathized with the Bedouins' independence movement. At the same time, he raised doubts about the revolutionary potential of the English proletariat. The embourgeoisement of the English proletariat shattered Marx and Engels's belief that the socialist revolution in Britain would drive out all forms of human oppression. The vision that the victory of the English working class would bring freedom to India died when the prospect of proletarian revolution in Britain faded away.

Engels's encounter with Irish realities opened the gate to reformulating the solution to colonial questions. What he witnessed during his travel to Ireland in 1856 was different from his and Marx's own forecast that British colonialism would bring progress to colonies. At the start of his journey, Engels recognized that British colonialism destroyed emerging Irish local industries and kept Ireland as a pure agrarian country by forcing its people to be suppliers of raw materials for English industry as well as be markets for English commodities. More than that, the profit from colonial exploitation could bribe the English working class into accepting the reformist agenda of the capitalist regime. Thus social revolution in England could no longer be a precondition for Irish independence. Instead, after 1867, Marx and Engels had to posit national liberation in Ireland as a necessary condition for English emancipation.[57]

"Dependency" theoreticians and Third World Marxists began to reinterpret the Marxian legacy of national emancipation. Dependency theoreticians were desperate to find the moment of overcoming red Orientalism in the later development of Marx and Engels's thoughts on the "Rest": the abandonment of the idea of "England as the model," overcoming the prejudice against the small peasantry, the recognition of the colonized subjects as agents in their own history, and thus escape from Eurocentrism.[58] Engels saw in Ireland the unrequited transfer of capital and surplus from the colony to the metropole through the process of unequal exchange between center and periphery. Dependency theoreticians have emphasized colonial plundering over colonial modernization. They have maintained that the surplus appropriation from the colony to the metropole lies at the heart of colonialism. Capitalist development or modernization of colonies followed a twisted path represented by "comprador capitalism." Comprador capitalists of (semi)colonies enabled and collaborated with their colonizers in the same way the Sonderweg thesis claims, as when the German bourgeoisie who "become culturally subordinated within a traditional, authoritarian and aristocratic value system."[59]

Comprador capitalism was a colonial "Prussian path" toward capitalist development; the comprador capitalist was the colonial equivalent of the feudalized bourgeoisie of Prussia. Lenin's conception of "the bourgeois revolution without bourgeoisie" seemed to fit the colonial situation, where the comprador capitalist lost the revolutionary will to fight. According to Lenin, the Russian bourgeoisie was neither willing to abolish feudal serfdom nor able to lead the bourgeois revolution. Thus the Russian proletariat should bring about the bourgeois-democratic revolution under the banner of a democratic republic on behalf of and in spite of the bourgeoisie. Through the emphasis on the feudalization of the bourgeoisie, the primacy of premodern traditions, bourgeois monarchist, and semifeudal backwardness in analyzing contemporary Russia, Lenin tried to characterize capitalist development in Russia as a typical Prussian model. His arguments for the Russian Sonderweg could be easily applied to the colonial Sonderweg. Colonial Marxists had translated the Leninist Sonderweg into the agenda of the national liberation, bourgeois democratic revolution, and capitalist transformation to be performed by the proletariat.

Instead of the term "colony," Polish historiography uses "under occupation" (*pod zaborami*), but functionally the Polish Sonderweg shared many characteristics of the colonial Sonderweg. The Polish Sonderweg thesis can be traced back to Rosa Luxemburg, Lenin's theoretical opponent on the national question, who pointed out that the Polish bourgeoisie became true to "the throne and altar" because of the "organic integration" of Polish capitalism into the Russian market.[60] Polish Sonderweg is a hybrid of colonial and Russian Sonderweg. Polish Sonderweg is a middle way between Russian and colonial Sonderweg. A Polish Marxist historiography reasserts Lenin's thesis of 1907 that the Polish proletariat and the peasants had to perform the tasks of the bourgeois-democratic revolution and nation-building for, and in spite of, the bourgeoisie.[61] The Sonderweg of "the bourgeois revolution performed by the proletariat" came out of the delayed capitalist development and feudalization of the bourgeoisie. The peculiarities of the Polish bourgeoisie under the Partition who compromised with the foreign absolutist powers can be summed up as the "Prussian path" of Polish capitalism.[62] One could argue that Polish Sonderweg originated in the second serfdom and feudal reaction in the late sixteenth century and the tsar's peasant emancipation in 1864.

Colonial Sonderweg theoreticians in Korea argued that Japanese colonial rule arrested, deviated, and deformed capitalist development with the complicity of Korean parasitic landlordism. According to the colonial Sonderweg theory, Japanese colonialism imposed a miserable deviation from the normal course of capitalist development, and the developmental military dictatorship in South Korea arose from Japanese colonial rule that deformed the normal capitalist development and bourgeois liberal democracy. The theoreticians argue that the peculiarity of the colonial dependency lies in the uneven division of labor between metropole and

colony, the absence of the bourgeois revolution, disabled national economy, burlesque modernization, bureaucratic capitalism, and residues of
the feudal structure.[63] The peculiarity of capitalist development in colonial Korea is similar to the peculiarities of the German Sonderweg and the
"Prussian path" in Leninist terms. Also, colonial Sonderweg of Korea resonates well with the Japanese Marxist Sonderweg, which attributes Japanese fascism to "pathological factors peculiar to Japan, usually interpreted
via a theory of pre-modern particularism versus modern universalism."[64]

The premise that the Japanese colonial presence caused Korea to swerve
from the usual capitalist course presupposed the prior existence of a normal endogenous development of capitalism. On a meta level, one could see
how this reverses the usual historical order of events laid out by Marx and
Engels such that colonial plundering leads to a precolonial emergence of
capitalism. Even so, this reverse chronology relies on Eurocapitalism as the
norm, which, as with the work of Paik discussed earlier, led to "consequential" Eurocentrism. Opponents of this Eurocentric vision of Korean history
championed a different path of noncapitalist development, also, ironically, Eurocentric. They were accused of being proponents of a model of
development that requires Asian stagnation to be remedied through colonial modernization. The "Asiatic mode of production" was in line with Marx
and Engels's classic account of how colonialism, through the destruction
of the stagnancy of "oriental" societies, would bring about the material
basis for European capitalism. This red Orientalism, however, would neu-
ter the Korean nationalist critique of Japanese colonialism by denying the
existence of precolonial, nascent, homegrown capitalism.

To preserve the anticolonial critique, many Marxist and nationalist historians in postcolonial Korea tried hard to preserve the colonial Sonderweg through evidence of the polarization of the rural population and the
emergence of large-sized farms—the very course of seventeenth- and
eighteenth-century English capitalism. They discovered the commercial
production of specialized crops, the wholesale commerce, handcraft industries subject to the merchant capital and putting-out system, mercantilism, and modernist thought. All this will be familiar to anyone who has
read Marxist economic histories of Europe. Japanese colonialism trampled
the sprout and endogenous development of capitalism and perverted the
standard capitalist development from the late Chosŏn period onward. This
Korean historiographical turn exemplifies how "Marx's theory of the mode

of production goes in parallel with the nation-state's ideology of modernity and progress," as Gyan Prakash argued.[65]

In a historical framework, the particularism of the colonial Sonderweg can exist only alongside the universalism of precolonial capitalist development. Modern Indian historiography also illustrates the coexistence of particularism and universalism in the historical imagination of modernity. Both conservative imperialists and their nationalist opponents in Indian historiography showed "a continued effort to produce a rule of colonial difference within a universal theory of the modern regime of power."[66] By referring to the same framework of universal history, the history of Britain incorporates the history of India. With its narrative of capitalist development running from the precolonial past to the postcolonial present, the theory of indigenous capitalism marginalized the role of colonialism and magnified the endogenous development of capitalism. However, it adhered to the explanatory hegemony of Eurocapitalism by jumping voluntarily into the orbit of the capitalo-centric world history.

In Korea, the colonial Sonderweg discourse likewise seeks to strip colonialism of its centrality to the modernizing process. The Korean Sonderweg does this by identifying two distinctive modernities: the modernity of technology and the modernity of emancipation. "Technological modernity" encompasses industrialization, economic growth, and political engineering, whereas "emancipatory modernity" includes democracy, political freedom, human rights, and disenchantment. This binary of modernities mirrors that of the "Prussian path" versus "American path." Even though the colonial Sonderweg denies that only colonialism can usher in modernity by teasing out the technological and emancipatory, it still swings back to the Whig interpretation of the bourgeoisie, capitalism, and modernity. Despite its anticolonialist impetus, the colonial Sonderweg discourse still literally uses the terms of Eurocentric discourse—nation-state, capitalist development, and modernity—in its analysis of colonialism.

Despite its Eurocentricity, the colonial Sonderweg thesis took shape from a Third World Marxist discourse seeking to find an alternative path to modernity that bypasses capitalism altogether. In this Marxist view, the socialist path brings about the modernity of emancipation; a colonial-capitalist path only ushers in the modernity of technology.[67] Reducing colonial modernity to the technical modernization, the colonial Sonderweg implies the idea of socialism as an anti-Western modernization project. Socialism, in this sense, becomes a means of attaining a modern industrial society and an autonomous nation-state more effectively and justly than capitalist modernization. If capitalism connotes a modernization imposed by Western colonialism, socialism would mean endogenous modernization combined with national liberation. Thus socialism became the ideology for the rapid economic development of countries in which the conditions of normal capitalist development do not exist.[68] Stalin called socialism the "follow and catch up" strategy of peripheries in spelling out the connection between the First Five-Year Plan and strategic concerns of the Soviet regime; leaders of Third Worldism, such as Jawaharlal Nehru, Julius Nyerere, Mao Zedong, and Kim Il-sŏng, shared many of these views.[69]

Twisted by dependency theory, socialist autarky, and Third Worldism, Marxism became an ideology that advocates the accumulation of capital by the state. Marxist historicism made it possible for Third World Marxism to be an ideological weapon to justify the "socialist accumulation of capital" by the state and the "follow and catch up" strategy of the peripheries. The nationalist vision of socialism in the colonial *Sonderweg* thesis embedded the Eurocentric view of civilization within anti-Western visions of world order. Colonial Sonderwege never denied the dichotomy between the Western model and the Eastern deviation. However anti-Western its political message, the "follow and catch up" strategy remains Eurocentric to its core. This strategy presupposes the spatio-temporal progression from East to West in sequence and the "first in Europe, then elsewhere" structure of global historicist time. In the final instance, the colonial Sonderweg thesis is a Eurocentrism that is comparable to colonial modernity and Eurocapitalism.

From the National to the Transnational

Colonial modernity and colonial Sonderwege involve sharply diverging positions on the role of colonialism in pioneering capitalism, colonial modernization, the sprout of capitalism, small peasant economy, enlarged scale farming, the Asiatic mode of production, and the agency of colonial subjects. For all these differences, they share the theoretical-historical dichotomy of the "American path" versus the "Prussian path." The strategic dominance of the West as a model and the East as a deviation in the global historical discourse remains unshaken. The question, "Why wasn't Germany England?"—ubiquitous in historiographical debates in the postcolonial states—exemplifies the translatability of "singularity" into "particularity" within Eurocentric "universality." Even viewing Eurocapitalism from the place of "underdevelopment" does not guarantee an alternative discourse to Eurocentric history. The implicit comparative analysis of the German Sonderweg takes the nation-state as its unit of analysis. Historical peculiarities, identities, borders, cultures, and collectives are all looked at through the nation-state. The essentialization of national history results in the hierarchization of national histories in the single unified trajectory of world history.

In the German Sonderweg thesis, the dichotomy of the West as the model versus the East as the deviation determines the basic hierarchy that recapitulates world history with a Eurocapitalist telos. So long as world history merely aggregates national histories, this telos seems inevitable. Even new forms of comparative history remain subject to its conception of history. In his critique of the Sonderweg, Jürgen Kocka sought to rescue the asymmetrical historical comparison central to the German Sonderweg.[70] A decade later, he suggested combining comparative history with newer forms of entangled and connected history. This version of comparative history goes beyond comparison to comprehend historical encounters, interactions, relations, and transfers through comparison.[71] However methodologically experimental, these efforts ultimately locate each national history in a Eurocentric trajectory of development and hierarchy of global modernity. The kind of entangled histories Kocka suggested can be possible only through a sustained critique of historicism itself.

A postcolonial reading of the German Sonderweg demands a radical break with the "authoritarian universalization" of comparative history that makes "the cultural and historical patterns of capitalist Western Europe the established standards for all human history and culture."[72] Replace comparative national history with entangled world history as the unit of analysis; with world capitalism rather than the national economy. A global history of capitalism gives a vivid account of Eurocapitalism as a product of interactions between the "West" and the "Rest." Not a fixed entity, world capitalism is a dynamic unit of analysis, influenced by the transfer, interchange, interaction, and mutual relationship.[73] Marx saw the bloody dawn of capitalism in the formation of the global colonial system.

He adumbrated a history of primitive accumulation, full of conquest, enslavement, robbery, murder, and all forms of violence, which was peculiar to Eurocapitalism as a model course in the West.[74]

All arguments of non-Western origins of modernity, from capitalism's Caribbean origin, monitorial schooling's Bengal origin, constructing English literature in colonial India, to the invention of the panopticon in Russia's colonization of Ottoman territory, deny the Eurocentric diffusionism in making the world capitalism. Rather, the interpretation of modernity as a product not of the West but of its interaction with the non-West is a way of overcoming the Eurocentrism.[75] The historical formation of modernity should instead be grasped under the perspective of transnational and transregional interaction. Scrutinizing world capitalism through a transnational point of view invalidates the dichotomy of West versus East, American path versus Prussian path, the original versus the derived, model versus deviation, universality versus particularity, normality versus peculiarity. While the Sonderweg thesis as a "singularity" in the context of German history might be a dead herring, a postcolonial reading of Sonderwege as "particularities" is still worth pursuing.

Notes

1. Quoted in David Blackburn and Geoff Eley, *The Peculiarities of German History* (Oxford: Oxford University Press, 1984), 7, 164.
2. Jürgen Kocka, "Asymmetrical Historical Comparison: The Case of the German *Sonderweg*," *History and Theory* 38, no. 1 (1999): 41. In historiography, *Sonderweg* has been translated as peculiarity. Pairing the German peculiarity with the English universality, however, demands rearticulating the English word "peculiarity" as "particularity." In this chapter, peculiarity and particularity will be used interchangeably.
3. Kocka, 40–50.
4. See Sebastian Conrad, *The Quest for the Lost Nation: Writing History in Germany and Japan in the American Century* (Berkeley: University of California Press, 2010); Yasushi Yamanouchi, J. Victor Koschmann, and Ryūichi Narita, eds., *Total War and Modernization* (Ithaca, N.Y.: Cornell University Press, 1998).
5. See Paul Cohen, *Discovering History in China: American Historical Writing on the Recent Chinese Past* (New York: Columbia University Press, 1984); Lim Jie-Hyun and Lee Sungsi, eds., 국사의 신화를 넘어서 [Beyond the myth of national history] (Seoul: Humanist, 2004); Jie-Hyun Lim, "The Configuration of Orient and Occident in the Global Chain of National Histories: Writing National Histories in Northeast Asia,"

in *Narrating the Nation: Representations in History, Media and the Arts*, ed. Stefan Berger, Linas Eriksonas and Andrew Mycock (New York: Berghahn Books, 2008).

6. Gavin Walker, "Postcoloniality and the National Question in Marxist Historiography: Elements of the Debate on Japanese Capitalism," *Interventions* 13, no. 1 (2011): 124–26.

7. Lim, "The Configuration," 295–96. For the Japanese version of Orientalism, see Stefan Tanaka, *Japan's Orient: Rendering Pasts Into History* (Berkeley: University of California Press, 1993).

8. Robin Okey, *Eastern Europe 1740-1985* (London: RKP, 1992), 69–74; Józef Chlebowczyk, *On Small and Young Nations in Europe* (Wrocław: Ossolineum, 1980), 176; Miroslav Hroch, *Social Preconditions of National Revival in Europe* (Cambridge: Cambridge University Press, 1985), 134.

9. Witold Kula, *An Economic Theory of the Feudal System: Towards a Model of the Polish Economy 1500-1800*, trans. Lawrence Garner (London: NLB, 1976), 10.

10. Larry Wolff, *Inventing Eastern Europe: The Map of Civilization on the Mind of the Enlightenment* (Stanford, Calif.: Stanford University Press, 1994), 9.

11. Feliks Tych, *Socjalistyczna Irredenta* (Kraków: Wydawnictwo Literackie, 1982); Feliks Tych, "Some Conditions and Regularities of Development of the Polish Working Class Movement," *Acta Poloniae Historica* 22 (1970); Tadeusz Łepkowski, "O narodzie i polskiej świadomości narodowej w epoce reform i powstań XVIII i XIX wieku," *Nowe Drogi* 20, no. 5 (1966); Witold Kula, *Historia Zacofanie Rozwój* (Warsaw: Czytelnik, 1983), 63–76.

12. See Selcuk Esenbel and Meltem Toksöz, "Deconstructing Imperial and National Narratives in Turkey and the Arab Middle East," paper presented to the conference "Global History Globally," Berlin, October 20–21, 2011.

13. Walker, "Postcoloniality," 131–32.

14. Monika Baár, *Historians and Nationalism: East-Central Europe in the Nineteenth Century* (Oxford: Oxford University Press, 2010), 277.

15. Naoki Sakai, *Translation and Subjectivity: On "Japan" and Cultural Nationalism,* (Minneapolis: University of Minnesota Press, 1997), 50.

16. Polish *myśl zachodnia* (Western thought, which is de facto German studies) argued that the gap between Poland and Germany is narrower than the gap between Germany and its west. See Jie-Hyun Lim, "Displacing East and West: Towards a Postcolonial Reading of 'Ostforschung' and 'Myśl Zachodnia,'" Internationale Konferenz in Kulice, Deutsche Ostforschung und polnische Westforschung 2: Institutionen-Personen-Vergleiche, Szczecin University, Poland, December 8-9. 2006

17. It is a parody of the phrase of "first in Europe, then elsewhere" from Dipesh Chakrabarthy, *Provincializing Europe: Postcolonial Thought and Historical Difference* (Princeton, N.J.: Princeton University Press, 2000), 7.

18. Timothy Mitchell, "The Stage of Modernity," in *Questions of Modernity*, ed. Timothy Mitchell (Minneapolis: University of Minnesota Press, 2000), 1.

19. Particularly Lech Wałęsa's promise to make Poland a second Japan confirms this seemingly weird question. In Wałęsa's remarks, Poland occupies the strategic

position of the East while Japan represents the West. Lech Wałęsa, "Poland should become a second Japan" in his speech on September 24, 1980, "Zbudujemy-tu-drugą-Japonię," Polish radio archive, https://www.polskieradio.pl/39/248/Artykul/684816,Zbudujemy-tu-druga-Japonie.

20. Nishikawa Nagao, 國境を越える方法 [How to cross the national border] (Tokyo: Heibonsha, 2001), chap. 6.

21. Ian Buruma and Avishi Margalit, *Occidentalism* (New York: Penguin Press, 2004), 52.

22. Chakrabarthy, *Provincializing Europe*, 7.

23. Partha Chatterjee, *The Nation and Its Fragments: Colonial and Postcolonial Histories* (Princeton, N.J.: Princeton University Press, 1993), 30.

24. Mitchell, "The Stage of Modernity," 7; Vasant Kaiwar and Sucheta Mazumdar, "The Coordinates of Orientalism: Reflections on the Universal and the Particular," in *From Orientalism to Postcolonialism*, ed. Sucheta Mazumdar, Vasant Kaiwar, and Thierry Labica (London: Routledge, 2009), 32–33.

25. Gyan Prakash, "AHR Forum: Subaltern Studies as Postcolonial Criticism," *American Historical Review* 99 (1994): 1475.

26. "Forum," *German History* 22, no. 2 (2004): 234.

27. See Albert Resis, "*Das Kapital* Comes to Russia," *Slavic Review* 29 (June 1970).

28. Ephraim Nimni suggested the term *capitalo-centric* in "Marxism and Nationalism," in *Marxist Sociology Revisited: Critical Assessments*, ed. Martin Shaw (London: Olympic Marketing, 1985), 107.

29. Karl Marx, *Capital*, vol. 1, trans. Ben Fowkes (Hammondsworth, UK: Penguin, 1990), 91.

30. For the traces of the sophisticated change in Marx on the capitalo-centric position, see Haruki Wada, "Marx and Revolutionary Russia," in *Late Marx and the Russian Road: Marx and the Peripheries of Capitalism*, ed. Teodor Shanin (London: RKP, 1983), 40–75.

31. Mitchell, "The Stage of Modernity," 9.

32. For the debates, see Maurice Dobb, *Studies in the Development of Capitalism* (London: RKP, 1963); and Georges Lefebvre et al., *The Transition from Feudalism to Capitalism*, with an introduction by Rodney Hilton (London: Verso, 1978).

33. Kōhachirō Takahashi, "A Contribution to the Discussion," in *The Transition from Feudalism to Capitalism*, 94–96.

34. Conrad, *The Quest for the Lost Nation*, 176.

35. V. I. Lenin, "The Agrarian Programme of Social-Democracy in the First Russian Revolution, 1905–1907," in *Lenin Collected Works*, vol. 13 (Moscow: Progress, 1972), 239–41.

36. Antonio Gramsci, *Selections from the Prison Notebooks* (New York: International Publishers, 1971), 59, 106–14.

37. Chatterjee, *The Nation and Its Fragments*, 213.

38. F. Engels, "French Rule in Algeria," in *Karl Marx on Colonialism and Modernization: His Despatches and Other Writings on China, India, Mexico, the Middle East and North Africa*, ed. Shlomo Avineri (Garden City, N.Y.: Double Day, 1969), 43.

39. F. Engels, "Die Bewegungen von 1847," in *Marx-Engels-Werke (MEW)* (Berlin, 1975), 4, 501; Engels, "Der demokratische Panslawismus," in *MEW* 6, 273.

40. Umberto Melotti, *Marx and the Third World*, trans. Patricia Ransford (London: Macmillan, 1977), 77.

41. For Engels on the Slavic peoples, see Roman Rosdolsky, "Friedrich Engels und das Problem der geschichtlosen Völker," *Archiv für Sozialgeschichte* 4 (1964).

42. H. M. MacDonald, "Karl Marx, Friedrich Engels and the South Slavic Problem in 1848–49," *University of Toronto Quarterly* 8 (1939), 457.

43. Marx, "Revolution in China and in Europe," in *Karl Marx on Colonialism*, 62, 64–65, 67–69.

44. Marx, "Chinese Affairs," in *Karl Marx on Colonialism*, 418.

45. Marx, "The British Rule in India," in *Karl Marx on Colonialism*, 89.

46. Marx, "Parliamentary Debate on India," and "The British Rule in India," in *Karl Marx on Colonialism*, 77, 79, 86, 88.

47. Marx, "The British Rule in India," in *Karl Marx on Colonialism*, 88.

48. Bill Warren, *Imperialism: Pioneer of Capitalism* (London: Verso 1980), 7.

49. Jie-Hyun Lim, "Rosa Luxemburg on the Dialectics of Proletarian Internationalism and Social Patriotism," *Science and Society* 59, no. 4 (Winter 1995/96).

50. Nigel Harris, *The End of the Third World: Newly Industrializing Countries and the Decline of an Ideology* (Harmondsworth, UK: Penguin, 1987).

51. Warren, *Imperialism*, 6.

52. Bang Gijung, 한국근현대사상사연구 [Studies in modern and contemporary history of ideas in Korea] (Seoul: Yoksabipyungsa, 1992).

53. Ahn Byeongjik, 근대조선공업화연구 [A study of industrialization of modern Korea] (Seoul: Ilchogak, 1993); Ahn, 근대조선의 경제구조 [The economic structure of modern Korea] (Seoul: Bibongchulpansa, 1990).

54. Ahn Byeongjik and Yi Younghoon, 대담 [Dialogue] (Seoul: Giparang, 2007), 78–94, 142–50.

55. Eric J. Hobsbawm used the categories of "prepolitical" and "subpolitical" in *Primitive Rebels: Studies in Archaic Forms of Social Movement in the 19th and 20th Centuries* (New York: Norton, 1959), 2, 5, 13, and passim. The title and subtitle by themselves are very suggestive.

56. If modernity means the state-of-being that comes from the long-term interaction of colonizer and colonized, modernization is more top-down nuanced in the process of colonization.

57. For the change in Marx and Engels's thoughts on the colonial and national question, see Jie-Hyun Lim, "Marx's Theory of Imperialism and the Irish National Question," *Science & Society* 56, no. 2 (1992).

58. For some attempts to save Marx from the suspicion of Eurocentrism by referring to Marx and Engels on Ireland and the late Marx on Russia, see August Nimtz, "The Eurocentric Marx and Engels and Other Related Myths," in *Marxism, Modernity and Postcolonial Studies*, ed. Crystal Bartolovich and Neil Lazarus (Cambridge: Cambridge University Press, 2002), 65–80; Pranav Jani, "Karl Marx, Eurocentrism, and the 1857

Revolt in British India," in *Marxism, Modernity and Postcolonial Studies*, 81–97; Aditya Mukherjee, "Empire: How Colonial India Made Modern Britain," paper presented at the conference on Making Europe: The Global Origins of the Old World, FRIAS, May 27–29, 2010.

59. Blackburn and Eley, *The Peculiarities of German History*, 75.

60. Lim, "Rosa Luxemburg on the Dialectics," 498–530.

61. Tych, "Some Conditions," 159.

62. Jie-Hyun Lim, "Labour and the National Question in Poland," in *Nationalism, Labour and Ethnicity 1870-1939*, eds. Stefan Berger and A. Smith (Manchester, UK: Manchester University Press, 1999), 124.

63. Park Hyun-Chai, 박현채전집 [Collected works of Park Hyun-Chai] (Seoul: Haemil, 2006), 3:730–31, 745–47.

64. J. Victor Koschmann, introduction to the English edition of Yamanouchi, Koschman, and Narita, *Total War and "Modernization*," xi–xii.

65. Gyan Prakash, "Subaltern Studies as Postcolonial Criticism," *American Historical Review* 99 (1994): 1475–90.

66. Chatterjee, *The Nation and Its Fragments*, 32.

67. Chung Yeontae, "식민지근대화론 논쟁의 비판과 신근대화론" [Debates on colonial modernization and new colonial modernity], *Changjakgwa Bipyung* 103 (Spring 1999): 371–72.

68. Eric J. Hobsbawm, "Out of the Ashes," in *After Fall: The Failure of Communism and the Future of Socialism*, ed. Robin Blackburn (London: Verso, 1992), 318.

69. See chap. 10.

70. Kocka, "Asymmetrical," 45.

71. Jürgen Kocka, "Comparison and Beyond: Traditions, Scope and Perspectives of Comparative History," in *Comparative and Transnational History: Central European Approaches and New Perspectives*, ed. Heinz-Gerhard Haupt and Jürgen Kocka (New York: Berghan Books, 2009).

72. Kolja Lindner, "Marx's Eurocentrism: Postcolonial Studies and Marx Scholarship," *Radical Philosophy* 161 (May/June 2010): 28.

73. Whether the late Marx saw capitalism as "a changing ensemble of worldwide relations that assumes different forms in specific regional and national contexts" is beyond the scope of this chapter. Lindner, "Marx's Eurocentrism," 37.

74. Marx, *Capital*, 1:895.

75. Mitchell, "The Stage of Modernity," 2–3.

5

Imagining Easts

Cofiguration of Orient and Occident in the Global Chain of National Histories

MAURICE: Bereźnica Wyżna . . .
MAGNUS: Is it in Europe?. . . Finland?
MAURICE: . . . No, it is not in Finland. A bit lower, much lower. . . . I am
from the country which is located in the West from East and in the
East from West.

—Sławomir Mrożek, 1986

Encapsulating National History in Eurocentric "Tunnel History"

National history is a biography of nation-state. It is a teleological history of describing the development of historical necessity that inevitably leads to the present nation-state. The academic shine of "objectivity" and "science" conferred by national history legitimizes the nation-state. "History" became the scientific apologia for the nation-state, and the people looked to national history to illuminate the course of human progress that culminated in the nation-state.[1] "History" invoked the desire of the ordinary people to be positioned in the course of national history and subjected them to the hegemony of state power. When Jules Michelet defined a historian as Odysseus, who teaches the dead how to interpret and decipher the meaning of their own language and deeds not known to themselves, he revealed how the historian appropriates the dead for the cause of the nation-state.[2] The present historical order of national history is "a curious inversion of conventional genealogy" that begins from the "originary present." The nation's biography cannot but be written "uptime" because there is no Originator.[3] In this reverse causality, the nation-state becomes the ancestor of all its historical precedents.

The "originary present" as the firm footing of national history or a nation's biography is intrinsically Eurocentric, because it reviews the past retroactively from the present world order, an order that has been overwhelmed by the European powers. The demise of national histories with an increasing Europeanization of historical writing in Western Europe after 1945 does not mean the end of the national history paradigm. Instead, this Europeanization "brings also a danger of new ideological closures, of erecting new borders and building new boundaries" between Europe and non-Europe, and constructs "a homogenized European path" superior to other non-European experiences.[4] In claiming that "Europe itself is a *raison d'état*," Richard von Weizsäcker broadened the scope of the national history paradigm from the individual nation-state to the European Union.[5] The national history encapsulated in the Eurocentric tunnel history during the imperialist age remains unshaken in this postcolonial era, leaving the episteme of the national history paradigm intact.

The Eurocentric "tunnel history" within the boundaries of the EU builds on the myth of the European miracle, holding that facets of ancient and medieval Europe established the unique historical conditions for its self-generating modernization in comparison with the "Rest."[6] Europe, as a self-contained historical entity, implies European exceptionalism. Only European civilization, in this view, promulgated rationalism, science, equality, freedom, human rights, and industrialism in world history. The Eurocentric mode of historical thought in European exceptionalism is endorsed by an evolutionary historicism that comprehends both the narrative and the concept of development in a homogenous and unified time of history. Citing Dipesh Chakrabarty, "Historicism is what made modernity or capitalism look not simply global but rather as something that became global *over time*, by originating in one place (Europe) and then spreading outside it. This temporal structure of 'first in Europe, then elsewhere' over the globe was historicist."[7]

The "first in Europe, then elsewhere" construction of historicism meant a temporalization of space, which gave rise to Eurocentric diffusionism. In the temporalized space of the world, culture, civilization, innovations, and the modern flowed out from the European to the non-European sector.[8] European history became the hegemonic mirror with which non-Europeans viewed themselves. The Eurocentric mode of historical thought created the illusion that the stages of progress and development in Europe ought to have equivalents in Global Easts, though with temporal gaps. The historian's task in the Global East has been to find the symmetrical equivalents to European history. As Sakai Naoki remarked succinctly, "The attempt to posit the identity of one's own ethnicity or nationality in terms of the gap between it and the putative West, that is, to create the history of one's own nation through the dynamics of attraction to and repulsion from the West, has, almost without exception, been adopted as a historical mission by non-Western intellectuals."[9]

The same was true in Eastern Europe. If the West theorized the Orient by essentializing Middle Eastern, Asian, and North African societies as static and underdeveloped, it invented Eastern Europe as "an intellectual project of demi-Orientalization." Even before Asia, Eastern Europe became the West's "first model of underdevelopment," and, in turn, the nineteenth-century Polish intelligentsia defined Western Europe by contrast and positioned themselves as mediators between Europe and the Orient.[10] The Balkans were also the bridge between the East and West. The Balkans "invoked labels such as semideveloped, semicolonial, semicivilized, semi-oriental."[11] As the Count de Ségur, the French ambassador to Russia, traveled through Poland in 1784, he could not escape the thought that he had "left Europe entirely," and other "Western" travelers discovered the great barrier between Asiatic and European manners in Poland. Europeans were in contradistinction to the Balkans, too.[12] The conceptual gradation of Oriental and demi-Oriental was determined by its distance to "West." The shorter the distance, the less Oriental.

The Eurocentric national history paradigm consigned less-developed nations to "an imaginary waiting room of history." Non-European nations saw their indigenous history as a history of "lack" in comparison with Europe.[13] Both nationalist and Marxist historians of Global Easts have tried to overcome this lack by finding the middle class, cities, rationalism, science, equality, freedom, human rights, industrialism, and, above all, the capitalist mode of production in their own history. Their keenness to prove their belonging among the genuinely historical nations led them to endeavor to make their histories intelligible to a Western readership by finding Western elements and explaining the history of Global Easts in terms of European history. To achieve this goal, the East and West, and the Orient and Occident, had to be cofigured in a way that satisfied the historical imagination and intellectual curiosity of Western readers. The result was misery for the East because the cofiguration of East and West in the Eurocentric historical scheme inevitably reaffirmed Occidental superiority and Oriental inferiority.

Neither nationalist nor Marxist historians of Global Easts broke free from the Eurocentric discourse of historicism that projected the West as "History."[14] Nationalist and Marxist historians both have been imprisoned by the idea of unilinear development of history, which views the European path as the sole universal model. The underlying presumption of modern historiography that European colonialism and third-world nationalism had shared in common was the universalization of the nation-state as the most desirable and natural form of political community. This mode of thought forms a global chain that ties together national histories on a worldwide scale, which feeds Eurocentrism and Orientalism. National histories of Global Easts became the epistemological twins of the Eurocentric national histories of the West by sharing the Orientalist value-code in the form of "anti-Western Orientalism."[15] Fernand Braudel's insight that Europe invented historians and then made good use of them to promote their national interests at home and elsewhere in the world demonstrates this phenomenon in a very convenient way.[16]

Demi-Orientalism: Inventing Orient in Invented Orient

The first national history of Japan, *A Brief History of Japan* (日本史略), appeared in 1878, at the request of the Paris Bureau of International Expositions. Its revised version of 1888, *View of National History* (國史眼), became the official textbook in the newly created history department of Tokyo Imperial University. The first Japanese national history and official history textbook had "Western readers" as its primary audience.[17] Its main purpose was to present to the West the unbroken imperial line as the source of Japan's political sovereignty and legitimacy. The textbook was resonant with the revived interest in ancient history and the growing emphasis on the legitimacy of the imperial lineage at home. Itō Hirobumi, the architect of the modern Japanese constitution, insisted on the discovery and maintenance of the scattered and forgotten tombs of the emperors. The imperial house's historical legitimacy, invented or rediscovered, he believed, would provide the grounds for his struggle to revise the unequal treaties with the Western powers.[18] With the establishment of a legitimate imperial genealogy, the Japanese national "geo-body" took shape as a natural and organically integrated territorial unit that extended back throughout historical time, and its contours were firmly drawn in the second half of the nineteenth century. A comprehensive effort to "Japanize" the periphery—internally colonize the locals—and construct a Japanese organic geo-body began with the first Japanese national history, which was designed to create the official image of a united and centralized nation-state.[19]

A legitimate imperial genealogy and the organic geo-body of the Japanese nation, however, were not enough to construct Japan's national history. Japan's "own, indigenous, and peculiar" cultural tradition had to be invented to make the national history more convincing and appealing to Western readers. That explains why Kume Kunitake, coauthor of *View of National History,* revived the almost forgotten tradition of No (能)—a masked dance drama—and made it a national heritage. Iwakura Domomi had selected and reinvented old practices of Japanese imperial rituals, in the hope of using them in diplomatic protocols with Western powers. He left the invented imperial rituals open to any change for diplomatic considerations. Itō Hirobumi, Kume Kunitake, and Iwakura Domomi were among the forty-eight delegates who visited the United States and several European countries in 1871–1873.[20] Based on the models they saw in the United States and Europe, they tried to construct Japanese national history and tradition. Thus Japanese history was rendered intelligible to Western readers. The first book on the history of Japanese art, *Histoire de l'art du Japon* (稿本日本帝国美術略史), was also published originally in French upon the request of the Paris Bureau of International Expositions in 1900.[21] The motivation to write this book was to glorify the Japanese state by highlighting its national heritage and encouraging "our own artistic spirit" to keep abreast of the European standard.

Around the same year, Okakura Tenshin lectured on the history of Japanese art in the Tokyo Fine Arts Academy. He categorized cultural properties into a hierarchy, with national treasure at its top, and classified them into sculptures, paintings, and crafts, according to European classifications of art. Buddhist statues shifted from religious objects to artifacts for aesthetic appreciation. They became the equivalents of classic Greek sculptures when Okakura compared Buddhist statues from the Nara period with the ancient figures of Greek sculptures.[22] Okakura defined "Suiko" art as the starting point of Japanese national art history, which was mostly either imported from mainland China and the Korean peninsula or created by migrants from Baekje, the ancient kingdom that had been located in the southwestern part of the Korean peninsula. He appropriated the fine arts created by migrants or neighbors for Japanese national history. He was not reluctant to make a Buddhist statue imported from Tang China in Kyoto's Toji Temple into one of Japan's most cherished national treasures. This is just one of many imported goods in the long list of Japan's national treasures.[23]

Before Okakura came Ernest Fenollosa, a converted American Buddhist. Fenollosa helped found the Tokyo Fine Arts Academy and the Imperial Museum and served as its director in 1888, and he made the first inventory of Japan's national treasures. Later he became the curator of Oriental arts at the Boston Museum of Fine Arts and founded the Japan Society in Boston. In a sense, Okakura summarized what Fenollosa had discovered and defined as Japanese art. While the first Japanese national history had Europeans as its target readership, Japanese art history had the American Orientalist as its first historian. Explicit and implicit references to the West construed indigenous Japanese identity through national history and art. The cofiguration of East and West, Orient and Occident, was inevitable in either case. Once tied to the global chain of national histories by mimetic desire, historical writings of the Global Easts cannot but be discursive prisoners of Eurocentrism and Orientalism. If "Orientalism is better grasped as a set of constraints upon and limitation of thought than it is simply a positive doctrine,"[24] it is not difficult to imagine how this Orientalist set of constraints had influenced the construction of the first Japanese national history and art history. In short, the first national history books in Japan indicate the self-subjection of the Japanese to the putative West because of their desire for Western recognition of their own cultural and national authenticity.

In 1887, Tokyo Imperial University hired twenty-six-year-old Ludwig Riess, an alleged student of Leopold von Ranke, who taught history and historical methodology in the newly established history department. According to Tsuda Sōkichis reminiscence, Riess introduced a scientific history and methodology with the emphasis on the "objectivity" of Rankean history.[25] It is not clear whether he conveyed the Rankean defense of Prussian authority as part of God's design, but Ranke's historical methods were not wholly new to some Japanese scholars, trained primarily in the tradition of the textual analysis school (koshogaku). Their rigorous textual criticism and devotion to gathering facts and compiling chronologies were similar to the Rankean methodology. Rankean history, however, never meant apolitical historiography. Encouraging national sentiments and patriotism went hand in hand with promoting objective historical study. Japanese modern historians tried to modernize and refresh the storytelling of the Japanese past, and they were not shy about tipping their political hand. Kuroita Katsumi, contrary to today's estimation of him as the founder of the positivist history school in the 1880s and 1890s, did not hesitate to say that historical sites deserved to be protected regardless of their historical authenticity as long as such sites could stimulate patriotism. Kuroita was deeply affected by patriotic historical sites in Europe. The Wilhelm Tell site, in particular, captivated him. He thought that Tell's story of being a model patriot inspired patriotism among ordinary Swiss.[26]

Japanese positivistic historiography, influenced by Rankean methods, developed in parallel with a political commitment to the nation-state. Japanese modern historiography tried to establish Japan's equivalence with Europe while simultaneously highlighting its differences from the rest of Asia. It aimed at saving Japan from the invented Orient by identifying European elements in Japanese history while inventing its own Orient of China and Chosŏn (Korea). The more they became familiar with European history, the wider the gap grew between Japan and Europe. When historicism changed the vertical evolutionary time into the horizontal space of "imaginative geography," Japan discovered that it lagged behind the unilinear development scheme of world history, and it had to be placed in the Orient in comparison with Europe. The more Japanese historians tried to find a symmetrical equivalent to the history of the West, the more they suffered from the sense of lack. Inventing an Orient, Asian neighbors served to make up for that sense of deficiency. By inventing Japan's own Orient, Japanese historians could let China and Chosŏn take the place of Japan and allow Japan to join the West in the imaginative geography.

Japanese Orientalism or sub-Orientalism toward its neighbors can be summed up in a new geopolitical entity called *toyo* (東洋). It means literally "Eastern Sea," but it was Japan's peculiar formulation of the "Orient." The establishment of *toyoshi* (Oriental history) as a separate academic field gave the historical and scientific authenticity to the new entity of toyo. In 1894 Naka Michiyo proposed a division of world history into Occidental and Oriental history for the middle school curriculum, and the Ministry of Education accepted his proposal in 1896. Toyoshi was established against the background of the Sino-Japanese War, which amplified Japanese national pride in its victory over a Great Power. The Russo-Japanese War of 1905 further solidified the disciplinary position of toyoshi. The Japanese victory over Russia seemed to justify the Japanese peculiarity—whose historical development course is far from Asia and close to Europe (*datsu-a nyu-ō ron*, de-Asianization and pro-Europeanization). After 1905, anticolonial intellectuals of Global Easts could use the Japanese success to invalidate the discourse of white man's superiority and his burden to civilize Asia.[27]

In the discourse of toyoshi, the Japanese term for China changed from *chugoku* (literally meaning a central state) to *shina*. Japanese nativist scholars in the nineteenth century used *shina* to separate Japan from the traditional Sinocentric worldview with its duality of barbarian versus civilized that the term *chugoku* implies. In early twentieth-century Japan, *shina* emerged as a word to pick out China as a troubled place in contrast to Japan, a modernized nation-state.[28] If *chugoku* represents Sinocentric China, *shina* has the Orientalist implication of making China a peripheral nation. Joining the Western imperialist block by colonizing Taiwan (1894) and Korea (1910) reinforced the Japanese Orientalism implicit in toyoshi. *Shinajin* (China-man), together with *chosenjin* (Korean), connote an oppressed and victimized people in contemporary Japanese usage. No longer ethnic terms, they serve as metonyms for alienated citizens in today's Japan.

Japanese historians of toyoshi borrowed conceptual tools from the West to make their arguments sound reasonable. Shiratori Kurakichi, the principal architect of toyoshi, argued that China reached the most advanced level of fetishism, the first stage in the Comtean framework of the three stages of fetishism, theology, and positivism. In his attempts to work within the Comtean framework and European Orientalism, he never signaled that he shared the same purpose with them. By placing Japan in a more advanced position than China, he tried to exempt Japan from European Orientalism. He was also keenly aware that "Occidentals are apt to fall into self-indulgent arrogance and conceit."[29] In his work, toyoshi had implications for Japanese Orientalism as well as for Occidentalism. Patronizing Eastern neighbors and essentializing the "West" as the model is the head and tail of the same coin. Toyoshi discourses became increasingly antagonistic toward the West while retaining the modernist approach to history. Equipped with Rankean scientific methods, toyoshi has been deployed as a disciplinary strategy to distance Japan from both the dark parts of Asia and an atomized Western modernity and to place it in-between. Toyoshi stamped not only China and Chosŏn but also the West as the Japanese "Other."

A vulgarized version of Orientalist toyoshi discourse, "studies of colonial policies" drew a line between Japan as the civilized state and China and Chosŏn as barbarian states. If toyoshi focused mainly on China, the main target of studies of colonial policies was Chosŏn-Korea. While historians nurtured toyoshi, social scientists led the studies of colonial policies. Fukuta Tokujo, a pioneer of social policies in Japan, argued that Japan had developed along the historical path formulated by Karl Bücher and that its national economy had reached the final stage of economic progress. To make the image of Japanese development more salient, he needed a mirror to reflect Japanese superiority. With its backward economy, Chosŏn-Korea provided an ideal mirror. Much like European Orientalists, Fukuta positioned himself as an expert on the economic history of Asia who considered himself as a non-Asian when he stressed the contrast between East and West with a presupposition that Japan is outside the East.[30]

What one finds among the works of Japanese scholars of colonial policies studies is a representation of Asia in the language of European Orientalists. The negative images of Chosŏn represented in these works are strikingly similar to the national attributes of Chosŏn that Isabella Bird Bishop enumerated in her account of travel to Chosŏn in the late nineteenth century: obstinate, narrow-minded, suspicious, lazy, shameless, brutal, and childish. These studies provided historical justification for the Japanese mission to civilize Korea. They resonated with European Orientalist generalizations of the role of colonialism in destroying the stagnant economy of the "Asiatic mode of production" and modernizing the colonies by introducing civilization or the capitalist mode of production in Marxist terms. The discourse on Korea typifies the invention of the Orient within an invented Orient. This Orientalist strategy for writing colonial histories led to the establishment of Japanese exceptionalism. The discursive location of Japanese exceptionalism in the thought of Japanese Orientalists was a sweet spot between Orientalism and Occidentalism that would conceal their inferiority complex toward the West and exalt a sense of superiority over Asian neighbors.

The discourse on Japanese feudalism provide Japan's de-Asianization and pro-Europeanization as evidence of its exceptionalist road to modernization. Unlike its Asian neighbors, it claimed, Japan had a feudalistic society comparable to European feudalism, and this distinction enabled it to succeed in its rapid modernization. Once established, after the Russo-Japanese War, the exceptionalist narrative of Japanese feudalism quickly became normalized. The most widely read East Asian history text among English readers, *East Asia: Tradition and Transformation*, dedicates a chapter entitled "Feudal Japan: A Departure from the Chinese Pattern" to this topic.[31] This title illustrates the vital role that the discourse of Japanese feudalism played in making Japan a member of the Occident and distancing it from the Orient. This line of historical inquiry expresses the Japanese aspiration to be identified with the West. Japanese Orientalists may despair that Puccini's *Madama Butterfly* is more popular among Westerners than Fairbank, Reischauer, and Craig's *East Asia*. Their strategy of inventing an Orient to escape from European Orientalism has been most successful among the Japanese, less successful among other Asians, and least successful among Westerners.

The distinctive Western quality of Japanese feudalism likewise structured the Marxist controversy over the Meiji Ishin (Meiji Restoration) of 1868 between the *Koza-ha* (Lecture's faction) and the *Rono-ha* (Labor-Peasant faction). The debate concerned where on the Western path to locate the Meiji Restoration. While the *Koza-ha* saw it as the culmination of the absolutist state, the *Rono-ha* interpreted it as a bourgeois revolution. Despite this discord, their arguments rested on the same grounds as the European Marxists' analysis of feudalism, absolutism, and the bourgeois revolution and thus were tainted with "red Orientalism."[32] The Japanese Marxists' unusual concern with the Asiatic mode of production is related to the Japanese version of "red Orientalism." Japanese Marxist historians, arguing for the Asiatic mode of production, contrasted Japan's path to European capitalism with the Asiatic stagnancy of Asian neighbors. Not a deviation from Marxism at all, the account of the Asiatic mode of production by the Japanese Marxists was akin to Marx's analysis of India and China from the 1850s.[33] Moreover, this Marxist historiographical approach accorded with the civilizing mission of Japanese colonialism.

Postwar Japanese historiography, for all its heterogeneity, has a strong continuity with prewar historiography, especially regarding the discourse of the Orient and the Occident. Little has changed in the images of Japan invented by the West for the West. In critiquing the total war system or Japanese fascism, both liberal and Marxist historians still blame "premodern" residues and Japan's "deviated modernity." They both assume that the Japanese catastrophe could be attributed to "pathological factors peculiar to Japan, usually interpreted via a theory of pre-modern particularism versus modern universalism."[34] This was the Japanese Sonderweg thesis: the West is taken as the absolute reference, while Japan sought to align itself with the West by differentiating itself from its more "Eastern" neighbors. The Japanese Orientalists invented their own Orient to free themselves from European Orientalism.

This Japanese Orientalism is reminiscent of German *Ostforschung*. In the East Asian context, the German word *Ostasien* merely had a geographical meaning, unlike the pejorative Orientalist sense of the Anglo-French word "Orient." The Japanese imperial dream of making the Greater East Asia Co-Prosperity Sphere (大東亞共榮圈) used the word *toa* (東亞), translated from the German *Ostasien*, instead of *toyo* (東洋), the Japanese translation of the English word Orient.[35] The neutral valence of the term of *toa* (東亞) suggests the more virulent strain of Orientalism did not blossom in Germany because Germans did not build up a colonial empire, in contrast with the vast colonial empire of Britain and France. But German historical discourses have not been free from Orientalist bias. Postcolonial perspectives lead us to see the dialectical interplay of Orientalism and Occidentalism on a global scale. The German usage of "Ost" indicates the peculiar ambivalence of German Orientalism. Germany identified itself "East" vis-à-vis France, as its putative "West"; it identified itself as "West" vis-à-vis its Slavic neighbors. Anglo-French Orientalism suffered no such relativistic oscillation, as England and France embodied the West.

The literal translation of the German *Ostforschung* would be "Eastern studies," but its contents were "Polish studies." Seen from a postcolonial perspective, the *Ostforschung* was a conceptual tool to Orientalize its Slavic neighbors as Germany's Orient in German historical thought and imagination. German Orientalism frequently used analogies between the colonization of the "Wild West" in America and the medieval Eastern colonization in East Prussia to justify Germany's civilizing mission in Eastern Europe: "California is to the U.S.A. what Bohemia was to Germany in the medieval period." According to Johann Gustav Droysen, the interethnic mixing of Slavic and German blood was as rare as its counterpart was "among the American redskins and [white] settlers." In his well-known essay on the Teutonic Knights, Heinrich von Treitschke articulated the most extreme version of German Orientalism, referring to the rights of the German *Kulturvölker* over Slavic barbarians.[36] For those founding fathers of modern historiography in nineteenth-century Germany, the Eastern territory colonized by Germans was a "no man's land," or "European Third World."

One can easily find the discursive links between the Polish frontier and German colonialism overseas within the framework of Eurocentric diffusionism. For German Orientalists, the border zone between Poland and Germany was the German *Kulturboden* (cultural ground), which was degraded by its primitive Asiatic inhabitants. In the realm of forestry, the scientific colonizers viewed East European and African *Urwald* (primeval forests) alike as obstacles to social and economic development.[37] *Ostforschung* was the German version of Orientalism, seeing its Slavic Eastern neighbors as the Oriental "Other," which nourished the Nazi's historical imagination of the colonial expansion to Eastern Europe. Hitler's invasion of Eastern Europe and Russia made that Orientalist imagination violently manifest through war, colonial expansion, and genocide.[38] In their letter to German colleagues in 1965, Polish Catholic bishops made a far-fetched link between the medieval Teutonic Knights and the Nazi invasion of Poland.[39] Also, Poles' grave concern over the postwar Oder-Neisse borderline between Germany and Poland reflects their historic fear of the German colonialism of *Drang nach Osten* (drive toward East).

The Orientalist perception of the Slavic East was deeply engrained in the grass-roots mind, too. When a German soldier, stationed in Poland, wrote in his war diary in 1939 that "the soul of an Eastern man is mysterious," it suggests the ineffectiveness of the Polish strategy of incorporating itself as Western by Orientalizing Russia.[40] The *Wehrmacht* soldiers' letters from the Eastern front complained of Poland as "land of Jews," where lice and mystical minds of Easterners would greet the traveler. The Baedeker travel guide to the *Generalgouvernment* systematically injected racist prejudice against the Poles, akin to the stereotypical denizens of the Wild West of the United States: "For those travelling from the East to the Reich, the General Government is already a powerful, homely, charming entity, but for those travelling from the Reich to the East, it is already the first greeting of an eastern world."[41]

Factual national peculiarity matters less than how a nation is positioned in the imagined geography. In contrast to its self-portrayal as the "East" vis-à-vis France, Germany cast itself as the "West" in relation to its Slavic neighbors. *Studia Zahodnie*, the literal meaning of "Western studies" in Polish, bolstered German Orientalism by affirming Germany as the "West." The cofiguration of East and West in the historical imagination does not stop at the German-Polish border. Posited as the "East" by Germans, Poles regarded themselves as "Europeans" against the "Asiatic" Russians. In turn, Russians, underprivileged as "Tartars" in Europe, represented themselves as Europeans confronting Asian neighbors. As Dostoyevsky said, "In Europe, we were hangers-on and slaves, while in Asia we shall be the masters. In Europe, we were Tatars, while in Asia, we are Europeans too."[42] With its victories in the Sino-Japanese and Russo-Japanese Wars, Japan simultaneously established its equality with the West and confirmed Russia's affinity with the East. The global chain of East and West in the historical imagination has forged the Orientalism, demi-orientalism, and self-orientalism over the globe.

Global Easts: Inventing Nation in Invented Orient

The year 1895 saw a paradigm shift in Korean historical writing. The concept of national history and national language appeared for the first time among the reformist government policies in the aftermath of the modernist reform of 1894. Reformists emphasized the necessity of teaching national history and national language. The reformist government made Korean history textbooks for primary and junior high schools. These textbooks changed the names of Korea's neighboring countries and reshaped the geographic imaginary. China was changed from *Hwa* (華, meaning "splendor") to *Jina* (支那, Korean equivalent of *Shina*). Korean reformists changed the name of Japan from the contemptuous *Wae* (倭) into *Ilbon* (日本: Korean equivalent of Nippon, which the Japanese prefer).[43] This reversal in the place of China and Japan in the hierarchy of states occurred in the wake of the Sino-Japanese War. This departure from the traditional Sinocentric world order marked a decisive political and discursive realignment of the East.

Korean reformers even started to Orientalize China in their journalistic writings. A decentered and provincialized China was a barbarous nation characterized by laziness, idleness, corruption, and premodern stubbornness. Orientalizing China was a process of making boundaries of inside/ outside and inclusion/exclusion. Chinese immigrants in Korea were blamed for allegedly harming the Korean people. Rumors of Chinese cannibalism— kidnapping Korean babies and eating human flesh—began to spread among the Korean masses. China was no longer seen as "Middle Kingdom," occupying the center of the world, but was decidedly on the periphery. It was anything but civilized and was demoted to the periphery, which even Denmark would soon shame. The reform of the nation was bound to "Westernization" as a way of making the nation strong. One editorial compared a "Western farmer" with a "Korean farmer," the latter as five hundred years behind the Western counterpart. A typical Eurocentric historicism to temporalize Europe and Asia in the sequential order of development and progress was underlying that editorial.[44] Later, this trend to demote China in comparison with the Western model developed into an expansionist argument to justify *Drang nach Manchuria*—the drive toward Manchuria.

The cofiguration of China and the West in the Korean Enlightenment led to a new national awakening. By decentering, provincializing, and demoting China, Korean Enlightenment intellectuals essentially followed the same strategy of Japanese Orientalism by inventing China as an Orient. Inventing the Orient in an invented Orient was a means of civilizing in the style of the West.[45] A dozen world history books, including general histories like *A History of the Independence Movement in Italy, A History of the*

Fall of Poland, the *Modern History of Egypt*, and biographies of national heroes such as Napoleon Bonaparte, George Washington, and Bismarck spurred a national awakening and encouraged the formation of national consciousness during the reformist period.[46] Except for these books, it was almost always Japan that represented the West in Korean historical discourse. Due to the influence of Social Darwinism, a form of racial pan-Asianism dominated among Korean Enlightenment intellectuals by the early twentieth century. Pan-Asianism argued that the opposition between the yellow peoples and the white peoples is the real historical struggle. Interpreting the Japanese concept of *toyo* (Orient) in an Occidentalist way, it stressed regional solidarity and Japanese leadership. This pan-Asianism helped to satisfy the burgeoning national aspiration to break away from the traditional Sino-centric world order.

After Japan imposed a protectorate on Korea in 1905, pan-Asianism became a weapon wielded against Japanese colonialism for violating the ideals of Asian solidarity and for shirking Japan's leadership responsibilities. Even so, the strategic position of Japan as the West in the Korean nationalist imagination remained unshattered. Despair and disillusionment with pan-Asianism led to an increasing emphasis on the national soul, national essence, and national culture in Korea. The ethnic concept of the nation began to prevail in Korean historiography. The ethnolinguistic preoccupation of Korean historians led them to generate a vision of authentic Korean culture and pure ethnic identity formed from a blood lineage unbroken for five thousand years, descending from the mythic figure Tan'gun.[47] This ethnic invention based on a spiritual firmament was not unique to Korea. One can find this burgeoning ethnic sense of national being throughout the historiographies of the Global Easts: the nineteenth-century German advocacy of *Kultur* against French *civilisation*; Russian Slavophiles' assertion that "inner truth" based on religion, culture, and moral convictions is much more important than "external truth" expressed by law and state; and Indian nationalist discourse of the superiority of the spiritual domain over the material domain.[48]

The ethnic perception of a nation asserts the nation's sovereignty and the indissolubility of its national spirit, even when the state is in the hands of a colonial power. Nationalist historians created an organic concept of the nation, which views the nation as the eternal reality and collective destiny of every individual. Staying true to the nation-state demands the total subordination of the individual to the national community. Perhaps this collectivist orientation explains the populist or communalist elements present in many postcolonial states.[49] The primordialist view of the nation has prevailed in Korean historiography until now. It tends to essentialize the nation by subordinating all historical events to the development of the nation. Agency belongs to the nation; all other individual actors are subsumed under the collective subject. Nation is the eternal reality that survived numerous challenges even before the era of nation-states. Even when discussing ancient history, "our nation" and "our country" remain, anachronistically, the subjects of history. Combined with the discourse of the "fatherland" and "national legitimacy," this narrative replaces various nonnational historical communities with the imagined nation. Insofar as the imagined nation is the foremost historical agent, an individual's allegiance, including loyalty, contributions, and self-sacrifice for the national unity, becomes the measure of historical judgment.[50]

Lee Ki-baek, the author of A New History of Korea, the most widely read Korean history book for university students and general readers both at home and abroad, claimed that "love for the nation and belief in the truth is the head and tail of the same coin."[51] His statement is even more astonishing given his stress on the Rankean approach to history, known as "positivist historiography" in Korean and Japan. Ranke himself created a contradiction of the scientific method and Prussian statism. During his study in colonial Japan, Lee Ki-baek must have recognized how the Japanese Rankean disciples of "positivistic historiography" could be in harmony with the political commitment to the nation-state. In both Japan and Korea, the modern scientific historiography of Rankean methodology could coexist with a history designed to promote patriotism. Interestingly, Korean national identity was closely intertwined with Japanese writings about Korean culture and history. Korean efforts to "invent the nation" in Korea owe much to the "invented nation" produced by Japanese Orientalists.[52] In particular, the survey of custom practices in Korea, conducted by the Japanese Government-General just after the annexation of Korea in 1910, was an ideal opportunity to invent Korean traditions by adjusting and deforming realities for the convenience of colonial policies. The details of inventing traditions during this survey would show the extent to which Korean historians and ethnologists have used this survey to make Korean traditional practices.

Sekino Tadashi, who was an assistant professor in the engineering department of Tokyo Imperial University, carried out archaeological and historical research on Korea in 1902 at the request of the Japanese government. In his reports, Sekino classified and graded his discoveries of Korean art according to the European model applied to Japanese art history. With his high appraisal of the art of the Unified Silla period (676–918 CE), he contrasted the remarkable development of Silla art with the decline of traditional art in the Chosŏn period (1392–1910 CE).[53] Since Sekino, the Orientalist image of contrasting "ancient glory and present misery" has been reiterated in many writings on Korean art history. The image of flourishing art represented at its finest by the pagodas at Bulguk-sa Temple and the Buddhist sculptures in the nearby Sŏkkuram Grotto, built in the year 751, figures prominently in postcolonial contemporary Korean historiography, including history textbooks. The large archaeological excavation projects of Kyŏngju, the capital of the Silla Kingdom, were sponsored by the state in the early 1970s with an aim to discover the glorious indigenous artistic heritage in tune with the Zeitgeist of national subjectivity and the "Korean way of democracy" advocated by the dictatorship. Indigenous Korean art, as invented and discovered by the Japanese colonizers, remained a useful tool for inventing national art in postcolonial Korea.

Yanagi Muneyoshi discovered the artistic value of white porcelain in the Chosŏn dynasty. Despite his sympathy for Korean art and criticism of Japanese colonialism, he described white porcelain pieces of the Chosŏn dynasty with feminizing tropes. The colonizer's masculine view informs his definition of traditional Korean color as the "innocently pure white" and of the quintessence of Korean culture as "her" melancholy of tears and regrets. By contrasting "the youthful, dynamic, and colourful" Japanese art and "natural, irrational, and monochromatic" Korean art, Yanagi posited a masculinized Japan as the subject of estimation and a feminized Korea as the object of observation. Considering that "support for a particular kind of gender relations was used as a justification for colonial domination,"[54] Yanagi's sympathy for Korean art cannot be free from the charge of Orientalism. Amusingly enough, one can find Yanagi's discourse of "Han—tears and regrets" conjured up in contemporary Korean mass culture like cinema whenever it is presented to a Western audience. As the pioneer of the Mingei (folk craft) Movement, Yanagi Muneyoshi wrote the book William Blake: Life, Art, Thought in 1914. It suggests that Yanagi could discover Japanese folk craft through the gaze of Blake's Western romanticism. Otherwise, those folk crafts would have remained just goods of everyday life.

The practice of discovering native culture by cofiguring East and West is also found in the folklore and modern literature of colonial Korea. For example, the most popular short story of nativist aesthetics was produced by Yi Hyosŏk, who was a typical "modern boy." He could find and describe the beauty of native Korea, not because he was familiar with native culture, but because he could approach the native culture through the gaze of Western culture. Having studied English literature at Kēzo Imperial University, the modern boy embodied Western modernism in everyday life.[55] He loved to drink espresso, a very rare beverage at that time, with bread and butter. He also loved to socialize with the Russian émigré women in Harbin, then the most European city in Manchuria. Lyrical nativism was possible only in comparison with the West. In fact, the tradition was "a reconstructed image that is organized under the new categories and assumptions of the modernist discourse."[56] The colonial nativist culture was aesthetically complicit with the colonizers' modernist discourse.

Marxist historiography has never been an exception to the practice of cofiguring East and West in historical thinking and writing. When Marx said that the "country that is more developed industrially only shows, to the less developed, the image of its own future,"[57] he articulated the guiding principle of Marxist historicism. It projected the spatial distance between East and West onto the evolutionary time difference between backwardness and forwardness in a unilinear scheme of human history. Marx's frequent use of the prefix "pre" in the "precapitalist mode of production" in the non-West reaffirms the temporalization of the space. Any Marxist historical narrative regarding the precapitalist mode of production or Asiatic mode of production has a built-in historicism. Marxist historicism incentivized the revolutionary nationalists to adopt Marxism as an ideological weapon for the "follow and catch up" strategy of the peripheries.[58] Many of them looked to Marx as a theorist of capitalist modernity. The dominant Marxist historical narrative in Korea is the thesis of "the sprouts and endogenous development of capitalism." Korean Marxist historians tried very hard to find the polarization of the rural population and the emergence of "enlarged scale farming," a historical process that they argued produced an agrarian bourgeoisie and proletariat. They sought a historical footprint for a sort of European capitalist development including commercial production of specialized crops, the formation of the national market, the emergence of the wholesale commerce on the national scale, domestic handicraft industries under the control of merchant capital in the putting-out system, mercantilism, and modernist thought.

Along with emerging capitalist relations of production, this line of historical inquiry traces back to ancient and medieval history to find a slave and feudal society. They had to find evidence of the sprout of capitalism by finding evidence of medieval feudalism, which should be preceded by slavery in ancient history. This is a familiar landscape and spectacle to readers of Marxist economic histories of Europe. However, it is far from a creative application of Marxism and is more akin to the mechanical application of Marxist narratives of European history to Korean history. Historians who promoted a discourse that ran contrary to this Eurocentric scheme of Korean history and insist on a different path, such as arguing that state landownership may have been an obstacle for economic development, are labeled as theorists of the Asiatic mode of production and thus proponents of the stagnation thesis of Korea. It shows how "Marx's theory of the mode of production goes in parallel with the nation-state's ideology of modernity and progress."[59]

If one sees Marx as a theorist of modernity, one may quickly find that "Marx's account of modernization was inextricably a description of Westernization, and therefore that his view of global history was a general history of the West."[60] At the moment when Korean Marxists and Japanese Marxists began to stress universal history or the universal laws of world history, they became dependent on Eurocentric historical narratives and plunged into the discursive pool of "red Orientalism." On the other hand, the location of Korean history in Marx's Eurocentric universalist scheme was the result of a desperate effort to deny the stagnancy of the Asiatic mode of production. It is a genuine paradox of Korean Marxist historians to deny Marx's own prognosis of colonialism "to fulfill a double mission in India: one destructive, the other generating—the annihilation of old Asiatic society, and the laying of the material foundations of Western society in Asia."[61] They preferred the Marxian universalist schema to the Asiatic mode of production to avoid justifying Japanese colonialism. However, neither the Asiatic mode of production nor the Eurocentric universalist schema could escape the charge of "red Orientalism."

From the viewpoint of the cofiguration of East and West, the *Drang nach Westen*—the drive to the West—in Polish historiography can be understood in a broader sense of world history. Poles, Czechs, Hungarians, and Slovakians in the "Visegrád Four" preferred the term "Central Europe" to "Eastern Europe" because they did not want to be categorized as "East." Polish Occidentalism disregarded "Europe Orientale" on the ground that this simple geographic categorization of "Eastern Europe" has no historical, civilizational, economic, or cultural meaning in Poland. The notion of Europa Słowiańska (Slavic Europe) is also suspect because there exists no racial and cultural unity of Slavic peoples.[62] The Czech writer Milan Kundera and the Hungarian philosopher Mihály Vajda also claimed a central European status. The result was a bizarre Europe "with a west and a center, but no east."[63] "Center" and "Central Europe" were preferred terms because of their linkage to Western civilization. However, Polish intellectuals could not unreservedly use "Central Europe" because historically "Mittel Europa" implies German hegemony in the region.

The valences of terms posed a serious dilemma for Polish intellectuals: their word choices had potential implications for Polish Occidentalism. Confronting this dilemma of being preferable and inappropriate, Jerzy Kłoczowski and other Polish historians proposed Europa Środkowo-Wschodnia (Central-Eastern Europe) as a solution.[64] In the civilizational constellation of the Cold War, Oskar Halecki first constructed the idea of the Europa Środkowo-Wschodnia as an alternative to the British, French, and German perceptions of Eastern Europe. Halecki tried to distinguish Poland from the Russian Empire and other Eastern Slavic neighbors by emphasizing the civilizational rupture between Poland and the Soviet Russia. This political motivation to separate Poland historically from the communist bloc led Halecki, the anticommunist émigré historian, to the idea of Europa Środkowo-Wschodnia. In the interwar period, Oskar Halecki located the historical position of Poland as "between the oppositional powers of Germany and Asia." Alongside Poland, Russia and Lithuania were also squeezed between the German invasion from the west and the aggression of the barbarous Asiatic hordes from the east.[65]

For a Polish historian of the post–Cold War generation, the concept of Europa Środkowo-Wschodnia provided the "potential not to lose the global history or European history." At the very least, Poland could stay within the periphery of the West.[66] The post–Cold War generation of Polish historians continued to embrace Halecki's idea of Europa Środkowo-Wschodnia. The breakup of the Soviet Union temporarily relieved them of the fear of Russia, and the threat of the German hegemony was real. A short history of the shift of Poland from Eastern to Central-Eastern reflects a desperate desire to escape the image of the Orient invented by the German *Ostforschung*. By joining the European Union, the "Visegrád Four," including Poland, could bid farewell to their past as the invented East of German Orientalism. The post–Cold War generation's conception of Europa Środkowo-Wschodnia, however, does not necessarily mean a profound negation of the West-East hierarchy implicit in German Orientalism. Their obsession with "central" reflects the long anxieties of Polish intellectuals, who regarded Poland "as a poor and neglected suburb of Europe, a suburb that looked at the Metropolis with contradictory feelings of envy, admiration, and distrust."[67] The use of "Central" is an attempt to reverse Poland's place in the hierarchical world history while leaving the underlying logic of Orientalism intact. Using a postcolonial perspective, we recognize German Orientalism in *Ostforschung* as a fait accompli, but also *Drang nach Westen* in the Polish historical imagination as a latent stigma.

Some Polish postcommunist high school history textbooks are more explicit in claiming Poland's position in the West. The textbook *Człowiek i Historia* (2004) emphasizes that Poland has been a part of the West, and thus the history of the West is most relevant for Poles.[68] Another history textbook, coauthored by Wojciech Roszkowski, a representative historian of the "second circulation" under the communist regime in the 1980s, defined the nineteenth century as the history of the expansion of European civilization into the "Rest." He writes plainly that Eurocentrism is inevitable and justifiable to a certain extent.[69] With its "first in Europe, then elsewhere" structure, his narrative typifies Eurocentric diffusionism. The division of Poland and Russia in these history textbooks continues the Polish intellectual tradition of justifying Poland's Western aspirations by Orientalizing Russia and its Eastern neighbors. It is reminiscent of Japanese intellectuals' strategy of inventing their own Orient to escape from the European invention of the Orient discussed earlier.[70]

Polish socialists, like Polish nationalists, were also Orientalists, imbued with red Orientalism. Under the slogan "from sea to sea," Polish Socialist

Party (PPS) theoreticians argued that nonhistoric and backward nationalities on the borderlands, such as Lithuanians, Belarusians, and Ukrainians, should civilize themselves under the guidance of Polish high culture.[71] Red Orientalism was not peculiar only to the social patriotic wing of Polish socialism. Even Rosa Luxemburg, a most uncompromising proletarian internationalist in favor of collaboration with the Russian social democrats, was not hesitant to label Leninism as "Tartar Marxism."[72] Aleksander Wat, a brilliant Marxist literary critic in interwar Poland, remembered Soviet Russia as "Asia at its most Asian." He frequently described how he suffered from those Mongol-like Asiatic faces with sweaty feet in the Soviet Union.[73] Poles have developed a contemptuous attitude toward their more "Eastern," less "Western," and more "Slavic" neighbors. Polish Orientalism produced a central national myth that Catholic Poland has been a bulwark of Western Christendom, defending Europe against the infidel, against the barbarian and the Asian threat.[74] This century-long Polish Orientalism helps explain the straightforward Eurocentrism in postcommunist history textbooks as well as in historical discourse in civil society.

Under the scrutiny of Polish medievalists, however, Polish Orientalism reveals the illusory nature and outright fictionality of the East-West bifurcation. From Caesar's conquest of Gauls to the eighteenth century, the civilized South has located backwardness and barbarism in the North.[75] During the Enlightenment, the historical dichotomy of the civilized South and barbaric North axis shifted to the civilized West and backward East. As Europe's financial and cultural gravity moved from Italy—Florence, Rome, and Venice—to northwestern Europe—Amsterdam, London, and Paris—the Enlightenment "invented Eastern Europe as its complementary other half," even as it "cultivated and appropriated to itself the new notion of 'civilization,' an eighteenth-century neologism." Thus Eastern Europe became the West's "first model of underdevelopment," which helped define Western Europe by contrast. The invention of Eastern Europe was only "the intellectual project of demi-Orientalization." It was not coincidental that Eastern Europe was discovered "on the geographic frontier between Europe and Asia, on the philosophical frontier between civilization and barbarism, and on the academic frontier between ancient history and modern anthropology."[76]

Toward a De-cofiguration

Historians of Global Easts have resisted their classification as "Easts" by creating their own "Easts," in comparison to which they are superior "Wests." When considered as parts of the "East," their history was one of "lack"; when considered as their own "Wests," their histories could celebrate their national superiority relative to their own "Easts." Nations could have different positions in the "imaginative geography" of the global chain of national histories. Different ways to cast East and West—of cofiguring them—had ambiguous effects on the writing of history. In resisting their own classification as backward, as decadent, as atavisms in the course of history, however, they retained the East-West dichotomy, instead of critiquing and abandoning it.

The Japanese discourse intended to dislocate its past from Asia by inventing Japan's Orient of China and Korea and simultaneously positioning Japan in the West. By dislocating Japan from the East, Japanese exceptionalism rested on a new cofiguration of China and Korea as Japan's Orient and Japan as the East Asian Occident. The idea of Japan as an exceptional Asia presupposed a historical peculiarity that put Japan closer to the developmental narrative of European history. Attempting to discover Korean equivalents to European history, contemporary Korean historians have likewise sought to locate themselves in the putative West. The history of Korea could escape from the Sinocentric worldview dominating traditional historiography by riding on the coattails of the Japanese discourse of toyoshi and constructing its own national history based on the Eurocentric model. For all their efforts, neither Japanese nor Korean historians could find symmetrical equivalents to European history. Theirs was an impossible mission. The closer historians came to finding analogs to European history, the deeper their frustration became.

The Global East's desire for a stable location in the putative West has never been satisfied, nor can it be. So long as the historians of Global Easts are entangled in the Eurocentric model of history, they must depend on the cofiguration of East and West of the Orientalist discourse. This cofiguration requires them to recognize a gap between East and West within the universal historicist scheme. Historians may be able to locate their national histories in different positions within the "imaginative geography," but the gap between East and West can never be closed. In recognizing the impossibility of overcoming East/West binary, we see why we must deconstruct the global chain of national history that feeds on Eurocentrism. Without untying that chain, the national histories of the Global Easts will necessarily sustain their own Eurocentric nationalism or create another anti-Western Orientalism. Most important, the cofiguration of East and West needs to be refigured. The new cofiguration of the world's geohistory demands a more radical politics capable of deconstructing national histories and their global chain. An alternative narrative to national history needs to be found, not only in the local but in the global.

Notes

1. Stefan Berger, Mark Donovan, and Kevin Passmore, "Apologias for the Nation-State in Western Europe Since 1800," *Writing National Histories: Western Europe Since 1800*, ed. Stefan Berger et al. (London: Routledge, 1999), 3–14.
2. Benedict Anderson, *Imagined Communities: Reflections on the Origin and Spread of Nationalism* (London: Verson, 1983), 198.
3. Anderson, 205.
4. Berger, Donovan, and Passmore, "Apologias," 12.
5. Nishikawa Nagao, 국민이라는 괴물 [The monstrous nation], trans. Yoon Daesuk (Seoul: Somyeongchulpan, 2002), 56.
6. James M. Blaut, *The Colonizer's Model of the World: Geographical Diffusionism and Eurocentric History* (New York: Guilford Press, 1993), 5–6.
7. Dipesh Chakrabarty, *Provincializing Europe: Postcolonial Thought and Historical Difference* (Princeton, N.J.: Princeton University Press, 2000), 7.
8. Blaut, *The Colonizer's Model*, 1.
9. Naoki Sakai, *Translation and Subjectivity: On "Japan" and Cultural Nationalism* (Minneapolis: University of Minnesota Press, 1997), 50.
10. Larry Wolff, *Inventing Eastern Europe: The Map of Civilization on the Mind of the Enlightenment* (Stanford, Calif.: Stanford University Press, 1994), 7, 9; Jerzy Jedlicki, *Jakiej Cywilizaji Polacy Potrzebują* (Warsaw: Wydawnictwo CiS, 2002), 19, 39–41.
11. Maria Todorova, *Imagining the Balkans* (Oxford: Oxford University Press, 2009), 16.
12. Wollf, *Inventing Eastern Europe*, 18–21, 354–55; Todorova, *Imagining the Balkans*, 16.
13. Partha Chatterjee, *The Nation and Its Fragments: Colonial and Postcolonial Histories* (Princeton, N.J.: Princeton University Press, 1993), 30.
14. Gyan Prakash, "AHR Forum: Subaltern Studies as Postcolonial Criticism," *American Historical Review* 99 (1994): 1475.
15. Immanuel Wallerstein, *The End of World as We Know It: Social Science for the Twenty-First Century*, Korean trans. Baek Seunguk (Seoul: Changjakgwabipyuong, 2001), 248.

16. Andre Gunther Frank, *ReOrient: Global Economy in the Asian Age* (Berkeley: University of California Press, 1998), 2.

17. Lee Sungsi, 만들어진 고대 [The ancient invented], trans. Park Kyunghee (Seoul: Samin, 2001), 197–98.

18. Lee Sungsi, 199.

19. Tessa Morris-Suzuki, *Reinventing Japan: Time, Space, Nation* (Armonk, N.Y.: M. E. Sharpe, 1998), 23.

20. Lee Sungsi, 만들어진 고대, 199–203.

21. Takagi Hiroshi, "日本美術史の成立試論" [A sketch of the formation of the Japanese art history], *Nihonshikenkyu*, no. 400 (1995): 74.

22. Takagi Hiroshi, "일본미술사와 조선미술사의 성립" [Formation of Japanese history of art and Korean history of art], in 국사의 신화를 넘어서 [Beyond the myth of national history], ed. Jie-Hyun Lim and Sungsi Lee (Seoul: Humanist 2004), 169–70.

23. It is intriguing to witness that many Japanese national treasures related to Buddhism are imported goods. The imported national treasures of Shosōin Repository in Nara, often called the eastern end of the Silk Road, would not have been imaginable without the Silk Road trade.

24. Edward Said, *Orientalism* (New York: Vintage Books, 1979), 42.

25. Sōkichi Tsuda, "Shiratori hakushi shoden," cited in Stefan Tanaka, *Japan's Orient: Rendering Pasts Into History* (Berkeley: University of California Press, 1993), 26.

26. Lee Sungsi, "植民地文化政策の價値を通じて見た歴史認識" [Historical consciousness represented by colonial cultural policies], paper presented to Kyoto Forum of Public Philosophy, March 13, 2004.

27. Cemil Aydin, *The Politics of Anti-Westernism in Asia: Visions of World Order in Pan-Islamic and Pan-Asian Thought* (New York: Columbia University Press, 2007), 9.

28. Tanaka, *Japan's Orient*, 4.

29. Shiratori Kurakichi, quoted in Tanaka, *Japan's Orient*, 60.

30. Kang Sang-jung, 오리엔탈리즘을 넘어서 [Orientalism no kanatae], trans. Im Seongmo (Seoul: Isan, 1997), 94–95.

31. John K. Fairbank, Edwin O. Reischauer, and Albert M. Craig, *East Asia: Tradition and Transformation* (Boston: Houghton Mifflin, 1976), 358–91.

32. Teshale Tibebu, "On the Question of Feudalism, Absolutism and the Bourgeois Revolution," *Review* 13 (1990): 49–152.

33. See Shlomo Avineri, ed., *Karl Marx on Colonialism and Modernization* (Garden City, N.Y.: Doubleday, 1968). Isn't it wrong to ask that this collection be used to justify Israeli's occupation of Palestine from the Marxist perspective?

34. Victor Koschmann, introduction to English edition of *Total War and "Modernization,"* ed. Yasushi Yamanouchi et al. (Ithaca, N.Y.: Cornell University Press, 1998), xi–xii.

35. See Reinhard Zöllner, "Die Konstruktion 'Ostasiens:' die duetsche und japanische Rolle bei der Entdeckung eines imaginierten Raumes," in *Die Verräumlichung des Welt-Bildes*, ed. Sebastian Lentz and Ferjan Ormaling (Stuttgart: Franz Steiner, 2008).

36. Jan M. Piskorski, "After Occidentalism: The Third Europe Writes Its Own History," in *Historiographical Approaches to Medieval Colonization of East Central Europe*, ed. Jan M. Piskorski (Boulder: East European Monographs, 2002), 14–18.

37. Thaddeus Sunseri, "Exploiting the 'Urwald': German Postcolonial Forestry in Poland and Central Africa," *Past & Present*, no. 214 (2012): 307–8.

38. Kristin Kopp, *Germany's Wild East: Constructing Poland as Colonial Space* (Ann Arbor: University of Michigan Press, 2012).

39. "Hirtenbrief der polnischen Bischöfe an ihre deutschen Amtsbrüder vom 18. November 1965," in *German Polish Dialogue: Letters of the Polish and German Bishops and International Statements* (Bonn-Brussels-New York: Edition Atlantic Forum, 1966), 13–14.

40. B. Łagowski, "Ideologia Polska. Zachodnie aspiracje i wschodnie sklonnosci," in *Polska i Korea: Proces modernizacji w perspektywie historycznej*, ed. Jie-Hyun Lim and Michał Śliwa (Kraków: Wydawnictwo Naukowe WSP, 1997), 88–97.

41. David Furber, "Near as Far in the Colonies: The Nazi Occupation of Poland," *International History Review* 26, no. 3 (2004): 560–64; Martin Winstone, *The Dark Heart of Hitler's Europe: Nazi Rule in Poland Under the General Government* (London: I. B. Tauris, 2015), 15, 30.

42. Fyodor Dostoyevsky, *A Writer's Diary*, trans. Kenneth Lantz (Evanston, Ill: Northwestern University Press, 1993), 1374.

43. Do Myeon-Hoi, "한말 역사학의 근대성 재론" [Reconsidering the modernity in the historiography of the late nineteenth and early twentieth centuries], paper presented to the sixth Korean-Japanese workshop, East Asian History Forum for Criticism and Solidarity, Kyoto, May 14–17, 2004.

44. Andre Schmid, *Korea Between Empires 1895-1919* (New York: Columbia University Press, 2002), 11–12, 35–36, 56–59.

45. Schmid, 80.

46. Kim Byung Chul, 한국근대번역문학사연구 [A study of translations of modern literature in Korea] (Seoul: Eulyoo Munhwasa, 1975), 171–72.

47. Schmid, *Korea Between Empires*, 13.

48. See Norbert Elias, 매너의 역사:문명화 과정 [*Über den Prozess der Zivilisation*], trans. Yu Huisu (Seoul: Sinseowon, 1996), 33–75; Andrzej Walicki, *A History of Russian Thought: From the Enlightenment to Marxism* (Oxford: Clarendon Press, 1979), 93–106; Chatterjee, *The Nation and Its Fragments*, 3–13.

49. It is interesting to note that there is no considerable tension between individual and community or individualism and communalism in the sociology of Poland, where the organic concept of the nation has been dominant. See Joanna Kurczewska, "Nation in Polish Sociology," *Polish Sociological Bulletin* 15, no. 1-2 (1976): 62.

50. Ji Su-gŏl, "민족과 근대의 이중주 [Dual play of nation and modernity]," *Contemporary Criticism*, special issue on history report 1 (2002): 58–67.

51. Lee Ki-baek, "독자들에게" [To readers], 한국사시민강좌 [Korean history lecture for citizens] 20 (1997). See Lee Ki-baek, *A New History of Korea*, trans. Edward W. Wagner and Edward J. Shultz (Cambridge, Mass.: Harvard University Press, 1984).

52. For the cultural transfer between Japanese imperialist historians and Korean nationalist historians in the colonial period, see Park Hwanmoo, "제국 일본과 민족 한국의 역사학적 교차로" [Historiographical crossroads of imperial Japan and colonial Korea], paper presented at seminar of Korean Committee of the East Asian History Forum for Criticism and Solidarity, May 19, 2001.

53. Takagi, "일본미술사와 조선미술사의 성립," 180, 187.

54. Sylvia Walby, "Woman and Nation," in *Mapping the Nation*, ed. Gopal Balakrishnan and Benedict Anderson (London: Verso, 1996), 241.

55. See Shin Hyung-ki, "이효석과 식민지근대 [Yi Hyosŏk and colonial modernity]," in Lim and Lee, 국사의 신화를 넘어서, 329–54.

56. Prasenjit Duara, "Knowledge and Power in the Discourse of Modernity," *Journal of Asian Studies* 50 (1991): 68.

57. Karl Marx, preface to first edition of *Capital*, vol. 1, trans. Ben Fowkes, (Harmondsworth, UK: Penguin, 1990), 91.

58. See chapter 10.

59. Prakash, "AHR Forum," 1477. I have to confess that, in my twenties as a young Marxist history student, I planned to study Korean economic history to find the sprouts of capitalism after reading Marx, Maurice Dobb, Rodney Hilton, and especially the controversy over the transition from feudalism to capitalism. Although I no longer agree with this dominant Marxist historical narrative in Korea, I still vividly recall the persuading power of Marxist historicism.

60. Bryan S. Turner, *Orientalism, Postmodernism and Globalism* (London: Routledge, 1994), 140.

61. Avineri, ed., *Karl Marx on Colonialism and Modernization*, 125.

62. Jerzy Kłoczowski, "Wprowadzenie," in *Historia Europy Środkowo-Wschodniej* (Lublin: Instytut Europy Środkowo-Wschodniej, 2000), 1:10–12.

63. Robin Okey, "Central Europe / Eastern Europe: Behind the Definitions," *Past & Present*, no. 137 (November 1992): 137.

64. Kłoczowski, *Historia Europy Środkowo-Wschodniej*, 18; Janusz Żarnowski, "Europa Środkowo-Wschodnia jako peryferie 'prwadziwej Europy?'" *Przegląd Historyczny* 89, no. 4 (1998): 615–23.

65. Gennadii Korolov, "Dwie Europy Środkowe Oskara Haleckiego w Cieniu Imperializmów," *Kwartalnyk Historyczny* 124, no. 4 (2017): 677–78, 680.

66. Maciej Górny, "Użyteczność i granice. Europa Środkowo-Wschodnia jako narzędzie badawcze," *Kwartalnik Historyczny* 120, no. 4 (2013): 808.

67. Jedlicki, *Jakiej Cywilizaji Polacy Potrzebują*, 19.

68. Jerzy Kochanowski and Przemysław Matusik, *Człowiek i Historia: Czesc 4. Czasy Nowe i Najnowsze (XIX I XX wiek)* (Warsaw: WSiP, 2004), 12.

69. Anna Radziwiłł and Wojciech Roszkowski, *Historia dla Maturzysty. Wiek XIX* (Warsaw: Wydawnictwo Szkolne PWN, 2004), 7.

70. Stefan Tanaka, *Japan's Orient* (Berkeley: University of California Press, 1993).

71. J. Radziejowski, "Ukrainians and Poles, the Shaping of Reciprocal Images and Stereotypes," *Acta Poloniae Historica* 50 (1984): 117–27.

72. Jie-Hyun Lim, "Labour and the National Question in Poland," in *Nationalism, Labour and Ethnicity 1870-1939*, ed. Stefan Berger and Angel Smith (Manchester, UK: Manchester University Press, 1999).

73. Alexander Wat, *My Century: The Odyssey of a Polish Intellectual* (New York: Norton, 1990), 98, 108, 114, and passim.

74. Lucy Mably et al., " 'Other' Posts in 'Other' Places: Poland Through a Postcolonial Lens?," *Sociology* 50, no. 1 (2016): 66–67; "Polska myśl zachodnia XIX I XX wieku," 95, http://www.wbc.poznan.pl/Content/158969/6.%20Polska%20my%C5%9Bl%20 zachodnia%20XIX%20I%20XX%20wieku.pdf.

75. Jan Kieniewicz, "The Eastern Frontiers and the Civilisational Dimension of Europe," *Acta Poloniae Historica*, no. 107 (2013): 167–68.

76. Wolff, *Inventing Eastern Europe*, 4, 7, 9, 331.

6

World History as a Nationalist Rationale

How the National Appropriated the Transnational in East Asian Historiography

The Cofiguration of the Global and the National

The most common misunderstanding of nationalism is that it is national. Nationalism is one of the most peculiar *transnational* phenomena, for nationalist imagination can be nurtured only in transnational space. In his observation that "all history is tainted with the comparative history," Marc Bloch hinted at the transnationality of nationalist imagination. Comparative history throws into relief and essentializes the peculiarities of a national history. National history is also a product of worldwide cultural interactions and transnational discourses, which demand "an attempt at a globalized (not total) description" as Edward Said suggests.[1] A globalized description helps to position national histories sequentially in a linear developmental trajectory of historicism. In the sequence of national histories, at least as these came into being in academic history-writing during the nineteenth century, Western countries occupy the higher positions, to be followed and taken as models by backward Easterners. Thus, making national histories in East Asia was not conceivable without referring to a world history based on the dichotomy of "normative" Western history and a "deviated" Eastern variation.[2]

A history of cultural encounters between "East" and "West" reveals the ways in which people of Global Easts have been obliged to respond to the conceptual categories brought into play by "Western" modernity. Conscripted to modernity at large, willingly or unwillingly, "Easterners" rendered themselves the objects and agents of Western modernity, which was thought to become global over time. Confronting challenges of European modernity, historians of Global Easts have tried to prove their civilizational potential by finding European elements such as rationalism, science, freedom, equality, and industrialism in their national histories. Any national history lacking "Western" modernity would risk being branded as the history of "historyless people." Modern historiography in Japan and Korea was, in large part, a struggle for a recognition that would come only through proving their national potential for modernist development to skeptical Westerners. This struggle for recognition was more successful when written to be intelligible and appealing to Western readers, with East and West, Orient and Occident, cofigured and structured in a grammar familiar to European history—all giving rise to a consequential Eurocentrism in the East.[3] Writing national history in East Asia became a voluntary act of inscribing Eurocentrism on its own past.

World history, paradoxically, functioned as a nationalist rationale in East Asia. A popular Chinese history documentary series on CCTV, *The Rise of Great Powers* (*Daguo jueqi*), is a good indication. Renowned Chinese world historians contributed to the historical arc of the series, designed to justify the government's contemporary modernization project. The documentary deals with nine foreign countries in sequence: Portugal, Spain, the Netherlands, Great Britain, France, Germany, Japan, Russia, and the United States.[4] The tenth, hence the ultimate, country of the Great Powers in the linear historical sequence of global modernization is, of course, the People's Republic of China.[5] In this historicist schema, the "civilized" Westerners serve as models for "backward" Easterners. *The Rise of Great Powers* is evidence of the political complicity of Eurocentrism and Sinocentrism. National history in East Asia was inconceivable without reference to a world history based on the dichotomy of "normative-universal-developed-modern" Western history and its "deviated-particular-underdeveloped-premodern" Eastern variation. The cofiguration of norm and deviation, of West and East, and of the national and the global is crucial to understanding the historicist complicity of national history and world history.

The accommodation of national history, or even the promotion of nationalist agendas, through world history is hardly unique to East Asia.

The thesis of German Sonderweg debates originated in the same schematic cofiguration: the English history of a universal-normal-democratic path is posited as the measure of the German history of a particular-abnormal-fascist path.[6] "Western Civilization," designed as part of the core curriculum of many American universities, is another excellent example. The "Western Civilization" course was created during World War I to encourage the national integration of massive numbers of immigrants of diverse nationalities. The history of "Western Civilization" presented the United States as the culmination of a civilized "Western" tradition and imprinted the American national identity with a more "Western" than European identity.[7] This "patriotic world history" highlights and celebrates American political and ideological values, and its parochial understanding of humankind's history has a century-long tradition.[8]

Similar to Eurocentric world history, Asiacentric world history consolidated a nationalist rationale in East Asia. Discourses of pan-Asianism and the Greater East Asia Co-Prosperity Sphere before World War II and the postwar discourses of an "Asiatic value-system," "East Asian community," "East Asia as a project," and "East Asia as a methodology" can be listed in the catalog of Asian regionalism. From the beginning, the discourses of regionalist Asia have been loaded with nationalist repugnance, impulses, and aspirations. Most revealing in the trajectory of regional histories are the discursive complicity of the Eurocentric Orientalism of "Western Civilization" and the anti-Western Occidentalism of "Asian Civilization" in their promotion of civilization as a self-regulating entity. This realization reveals the urgent task of problematizing the complicity of national, regional (Oriental) and world (Western) history in abusing history for a nationalist rationale.[9] This chapter explores world history debates in conjunction with the national and regional history in East Asia, where world history functioned as a nationalist rationale.

From World History to National History, Not Vice Versa

World history came to Japan in the 1870s with the Meiji Ishin—the Meiji Regeneration.[10] The Japanese government took the initiative of introducing world history in the name of *Bankokushi*, meaning "the history of all countries of the world." The project stressed current world affairs rather than the study of the histories of others. It aimed to introduce Western things to Japan to speed the nation's adaptation to modern economic and cultural developments and its entry into civilization. Among the various "world history" and "universal history" books, the most popular one initially was *Bankokushi* (1876), a Japanese translation of Samuel G. Goodrich's *Universal History on the Basis of Geography* (1870). This book is a simple compilation of many histories, covering every region on Earth like a travel guidebook. Some of the other *Bankokushi* books carry more explicitly Eurocentric messages than Goodrich's book. For example, William Swinton's *Outlines of World History* views world history as the histories of the European people (Aryan races) who led the progress of civilization. The Swinton line of *Bankokushi* was called "civilization history," and its Eurocentric interpretation of world history became dominant in 1880s Japan.[11]

Thus world history textbooks preceded the national history textbooks *A Brief History of Japan* (日本史略, 1878) and *View of National History* (國史眼, 1888) in Meiji Japan. The cognitive sequence from the world to the nation was approved by Fukuzawa Yukichi, who, in championing modernity in Meiji Japan, famously said that "the knowledge of oneself develops in direct proportion to the knowledge of others: the more we know about them (the West), the more we care about our own destiny."[12] However, Japanese Enlightenment intellectuals were stuck: the more they learned about European history, the wider the gap grew between Japan and Europe. The more they tried to find equivalence with the history of the West, the more they suffered from a sense of inferiority. When historicism mapped vertical evolutionary time onto "imaginative geography," Japan discovered that it lagged behind the unilinear development scheme of world history. To escape this dilemma, Japanese modern historiography adopted its own Orientalist strategy of highlighting the Japanese differences from the rest of Asia. Japanese historians invented Japan's own "Orient"—of Asian neighbors—to make up for that lack. They put China and Chosŏn (a historical name for Korea between 1392 and 1897) in place of Japan (in Western imagination) and allowed Japan to join the West in the imaginative geography of the period.

Toyoshi (history of the Orient) was established as a Japanese version of Orientalism in a broad scheme of world history, while *kokushi* (Japanese national history) tries to capture European historical elements in Japan's past. By wielding discourses of toyoshi and kokushi simultaneously,

Japanese historians tried to free Japan from the image of it as the Orient invented by European Orientalists. The establishment of toyoshi happened in the wake of the Sino-Japanese War (1894–1895) and Russo-Japanese War (1904–1905) as its historical background; the two victories over Great Powers enhanced Japanese national pride. As a result, historical research and pedagogy were divided into three departments: national, Oriental, and Occidental.[13] This tripartite structure helped to elevate the strategic location of Japan in world history into the "West" by differentiating Japanese history from the Oriental history of China and Korea. That noble dream of de-Asianizing and Europeanizing Japan could best be realized through the trilateral discursive complicity of national (Japanese), regional (Asian), and world (Western) history. This tripartite structure of national history, regional/Oriental history, and world/Occidental history still dominates historical research and education in contemporary Japan and Korea. One cannot but see a paradox of nationalism that national history writing and the unique tripartite structure of historiography in postcolonial Korea are colonial legacies inherited from the Japanese Empire.

World history also thrived in late nineteenth-century Korea. An editorial in *Hwangseongsinmun* on June 28, 1907, notes, "One knows oneself through knowing others" (知彼知己), under the title "Necessity of Translating Foreign Books."[14] Using colloquial phrases, more than twenty articles and editorials from that time stress the necessity of knowing Western others as a way to achieve national wealth and strength. National crisis spurred Koreans' desire to know others. Their first world history textbook was *The Short History of the World,* published in 1896. In tandem with this, many other works of Western history were published in translation, including *The Outline of English History* (1896), *A Short History of Russia* (1898), *History of American Independence* (1899), *History of the Fall of Poland* (1899), *A History of Modern Egypt* (1905), *History of the Independence of Italy* (1907), and *World History of Colonialism* (1908). World history was promoted as a means of inspiring patriotism and justifying "civilization and enlightenment" (*munmyeong kaehwa*). In this regard, Korea can be seen as a predecessor to America in creating a "patriotic world history." The dual historical tasks of modernization and independence led Korean intellectuals to study world history, which would show them the path toward a strong and wealthy nation. As the term *nationalism* in English appeared only after the spread of the term *international* at the Great International

Exhibition in London in 1862,[15] national history was preceded by world history in East Asia.

The newly acquired knowledge of world history provoked comparisons between Korea and the Great Powers, between East and West. World history, with its Western character, signaled the deconstruction of the traditional Sinocentric world order and the repositioning of East Asia in the new international order. Korean Enlightenment intellectuals adopted Japanese Orientalist thinking in order to decenter and provincialize China. By shaking the Sinocentric world order, world history helped to promote the national sovereignty of Korea. Public history was much more active in decentering China than official history.[16] World history, at the same time, reinforced a Eurocentric definition of a historically inferior East by replacing the traditional Sinocentrism with Eurocentrism. The cofiguration of Korea and the West underscored Korea's potential for following and catching up to the West, but at the cost of presenting Korea as backward. Korea was frequently compared to Western countries of two or three centuries ago by a temporalization of space into a homogeneous and unified time of "History." Here we see the cognitive sequence from the world to the nation as present in Korean historical thought. The sequence of "first world history, then national history" seems to reflect the "first in Europe, then elsewhere" structure of global historicist time that accommodates the Eurocentric diffusionism of the hierarchical flow from Europe to the "Rest."[17] That explains why Korean national history based on the cofiguration of East and West gave rise to a consequential Eurocentrism.[18]

Overcoming Western History

Confronting the threat of Western imperialism, "East Asian" intellectuals intermittently heralded visions of a peaceful, united, and racially defined Asia. Pan-Asianism connected the political ideas of Asian unity with the racial physiology of yellow peoples. Theoretically, the yellow race included all Asian peoples, but practically it was equated with a narrowly conceived East Asia comprising only Korea, China, and Japan, which all shared Confucian culture. Leading Chinese intellectuals such as Liang Qichao and Sun Yatsen promoted peace and unity in a racially defined East in their speeches. Pan-Asianism translated the struggle for national survival within the frame of a racial struggle between "white people" and "yellow people." Pan-Asianism as an antithesis to European imperialist racism was supposed to assure the national independence and regional security through joint action in East Asia. The pan-Asianist ideal attracted many Korean intellectuals. Alongside *Ilchinhoe*, the group that was in collaboration with Japanese colonialism for the unity of the yellow race, Korean Enlightened intellectuals advocated the unity of Asian people on different grounds. Enlightened Reformists assumed pan-Asianism as an ideological weapon to guarantee national independence and regional security and peace. To the Korean Enlightenment activists, pan-Asianism meant an alliance of the three individually sovereign nations—China, Japan, and Korea. The treaty establishing a Japanese protectorate over Korea in 1905 was thus read as a betrayal of pan-Asianism.[19]

Upon the colonial conquest of Taiwan and annexation of Korea, pan-Asianism revealed its hidden agenda of Japanese regional hegemony, as it was meant to integrate multinational colonial subjects into the Japanese Empire. In the late 1930s Japan's revivified pan-Asianism urged a return to Asian solidarity for its fight against the European colonialists, which proved to be a stepping-stone toward the transnational ideal of helping to persuade colonial subjects more effectively into a total war system based on "voluntary mobilization." Hypocritically, the idea of a Greater East Asian Co-Prosperity Sphere echoed Western colonialisms for its colonial atrocities and brutal military action in the Asia-Pacific region. Pan-Asianism as Japan's official foreign policy rhetoric after the Manchurian Incident in 1931 was different from its beginning.[20] *Ilseontongjoron* (日鮮同祖論, common bloodline between Japanese and Koreans) in the first phase of pan-Asianism contended that Koreans and Japanese shared a common bloodline and ancestors. Arguing for ethnic-racial homogeneity between colonizers and colonized, Ilseontongjoron served to justify the Japanese integration of the Korean nation into the empire in stark contrast to the racist discourse of European colonialism. The Japanese-Korean blood lineage thesis was asserted as a sort of official historiography by professors such as Kume Kunitake in the national history department at Tokyo Imperial University.[21] Ironically, Ilseontongjoron, as the first version of transnational history in East Asia, was formulated by pioneers of the national history of Japan. Transnational history served Japanese nationalism recurrently and in a variety of contexts.

Ilseontongjoron met furious opposition from the aggressive national-ist wing of Japan, who believed in the cultural uniqueness of Japanese *Kokutai* (國體)—a complex of imperial family and nationality. They thought the family tree of the Japanese emperor should not be traced back to ancient Chosŏn. When Professor Kume was fired from Tokyo Imperial University in 1892, the Japanese minister of education explicitly criticized the pan-Asianist thesis that the Japanese and Koreans shared an ancestry.[22] At the turn of the twentieth century, pioneer historians of toyoshi, such as Kuroita Katsumi and Shiratori Kurakichi, began to distance themselves from Ilseontongjoron, too. They admitted the linguistic and ethnic affinity between the Japanese and Koreans but argued that nationality made a much greater difference than any cultural or ethnic characteristics did. The primordial concept of nation made it difficult for these toyoshi histo-rians to accept that the Japanese shared a common origin with Koreans. It was unthinkable for Japanese Orientalists to equate the Japanese with Koreans: Ilseontongjoron undermined the very basis of Japanese Oriental-ism. What divided Japanese scholars on Ilseontongjoron were the internal tensions of the Japanese nationalism, between the multiethnic national-ism of imperial integration and the ethnic nationalism of biocultural authenticity, which foreshadowed the strain between transnational and national historiographic variants.

Yet a common thread binding these two divergent currents was found in the historical discourse about the Japanese commandery, called *Imna*, supposedly established in Kaya (on the southern shore of the Korean pen-insula) around the fourth century CE. The Japanese interpretation of the inscription on Goguryeo King Gwanggaeto's monument led them to con-clude that the Yamato royal court had led its army across the sea to Chosŏn and established a military base on the southern coast of the Korean pen-insula.[23] This Japanese enclave in ancient Korea provided historical justi-fication not only for Ilseontongjoron but also for Japanese historical claims to Korean territory. The Japanese annexation of the Korean peninsula in 1910 revived the theory of a common origin for the Japanese and Koreans. Encouraged by physical anthropologists, Ilseontongjoron now had the form of scientific (or pseudo-scientific) discourse. Across more than four hundred articles, Japanese physical anthropologists surveyed the physi-cal characteristics of ancient and contemporary Koreans, collaborating with archeologists to study the remains of ancient Koreans and with physiologists to study contemporary Korean physiognomy. The theory of the common origin of the Japanese and Koreans backed up by physical anthropology was quickly connected with the ethnological thesis of ancient migration between the Korean peninsula and the Japanese archipelago. This thesis proposed that the authentic Japanese comprised mainly immigrants from the Korean peninsula.[24]

The scientific discourse of Ilseontongjoron became more influential immediately after the March First Movement for Korean independence in 1919. The thesis of the common origin of the Japanese and Koreans was used to assert that Korean national self-determination and independence were wrong, and that unification of peoples of common roots, a euphemistic expression for justifying Japanese colonial rule, was right. At the same time, the thesis of a common bloodline between the Japanese and Korean faced strong opposition by anthropologists—eugenicists opposed the assimilation policy. They saw the policy as promoting dangerous miscegenation between inferior Koreans and superior Japanese and emphasized the linear development of the Japanese nation from the Stone Age.[25] These scholars failed to dominate the historical discourse, however, because the Japanese Empire had to deploy the *kōminka* (皇民化, nationalization of colonial subjects) policy in order to mobilize colonial subjects to sustain the "total war" system. The *kōminka* movement was an extreme form of assimilation designed to transform colonial subjects into the "true Japanese," not only in action but also in spirit.[26] Ilseontongjoron provided the historical alibi for the forced nationalization of colonial masses by the Japanese Empire.

The historical discourse of the common origin of Koreans and the Japanese experienced a nationalist turn in postliberation Korean historiography. Korean nationalist historians rejected the Japanese *Imna* commandery, a historiographical byproduct of *Ilseontongjoron*, as an invention of Japanese colonialism. At the same time, they highlighted the entangled history of ancient Korea and Japan in their stress on a unidirectional cultural transfer from ancient Korea to Japan. They argued that the Korean writing system of *idu* and *hyangch'al* influenced Japanese *Man'yō-kana* as a system of transcribing Chinese characters. They also alleged that the highly developed fine arts in ancient Korea contributed to Japanese art, as proven by the superiority of Korean immigrant-made works such as the murals at the Hōryūji Temple and the portrait of Shōtoku Taishi.[27] The thesis of the high-culture diffusion from Korea to Japan in ancient history fit nicely with their nationalist argument. Kim Seok-hyung, a leading North Korean party historian, published the most extreme account of this one-way cultural transfer from Korea to Japan, arguing that emigrants from the three Korean kingdoms (Goguryeo, Baekje, Silla) had settled in western Japan and were cultural pioneers who contributed to the progress of Japanese history.[28] What one finds in his writings is not Marxism but "national communism."[29] Kim's argument upset a group of Japanese historians and provoked angry counterarguments. Inoue Mitsusada described in highly emotive terms of "attack and defense" a quasi-physical battle between himself and Kim. Indeed, Inoue attributed the heart attack he experienced to the tension caused by this controversy.[30]

The controversy took material form in arguments about how to interpret the inscription on King Gwanggaeto's monument. Although the two sides differed sharply in their reading of the texts, they shared the same platform of Ilseontongjoron. For both, the cultural and anthropological homogeneity of Koreans and Japanese was a given; the only issue was which ethnicity was dominant. The transnational history of Korea and Japan, initiated by the Japanese colonial discourse of the common origins of the Japanese and Koreans, became a battleground for hegemony over a shared heritage. World history tended to be supplanted by pan-Asianist regional history in colonial Korea and to a lesser extent in imperial Japan, but the grand narrative of pan-Asianist regional history was oversimplified and one-directional. Ordinary people, everyday practices, minor events, and historical ambiguities were all at odds with this grand narrative. The reciprocal relations between colonizers and colonized and between the colonies and the Japanese metropole were disregarded in place of an abstract pan-Asianism. Pan-Asianist regional history could not articulate that the empire (Japan) was made by its imperial projects.[31]

The structure of the history department at Keizo (Seoul) Imperial University, the only university in colonial Korea (opened on May 1, 1926), is a good indication of this problem. In his speech inaugurating the university, its president, Hattori Unokichi, emphasized the academy's duty to serve the state and announced a blueprint for making Keizo Imperial University a center for Oriental studies. Due to this Orient-centered research strategy, the history department offered three majors: national (Japanese) history, Chosŏn (Korean) history, and Oriental history. What distinguished

Keizo Imperial University's history department from those of other imperial universities in the Japanese archipelago was that Western history was
replaced by Korean history. Kaneko Kosuke had taught Western history at
the university since 1928, but there was no official Western history major.[32]
Of the eighty graduates from the history department between 1929 and
1941, eighteen students majored in Japanese history, thirty-four in Oriental
history, and twenty-eight in Korean history.[33] Seoul National University
(the postliberation successor to Keizo Imperial University) had no professor lecturing on European history until 1962, long after liberation.

The outbreak of World War II in the Pacific hastened the decline of world
history in East Asia. As the war against the West broke out, the Japanese
national "modernists against modernity" stopped looking to "Western
civilization" as a model for Japan's future. Under the strident slogan of
"overcoming modernity," the West became an object to be conquered by
Japanese national culture.[34] "Asian civilization," as represented by Japan,
was thought to deserve a much more serious investigation than Western
history. National history, under the slogan of pan-Asianism or "overcoming modernity," overwhelmed Western/world history. World history was
diagnosed as having been infected by the Western "disease," and Japanese
intellectuals who supported "overcoming modernity" lamented the way
that Western modernity had distorted the Japanese spirit. The Kyoto school
advocated an alternative world history based on a new "Asian" world order
through which European dominance of world history could be overcome.
This alternative world history would be one that emanated from the Japanese Empire. The intellectual project of "overcoming modernity" was seen
as the theoretical lever that would lift Asia into an active subject of world
history and make an alternative world history of "overcoming Western history." This Asiacentric new world history was much discussed but never
articulated, structured, or written.

Overcome by Western History

The Eurocentric nexus of national and world history has been reinforced
in post-1945 historiography in East Asia. World history as both scholarship
and pedagogy went through a sea change that was most visible in the postwar school curricula, influenced most directly by the American military

government. Korea was much more receptive to this change than Japan, because the new school curriculum was designed as a departure from the Japanese colonial legacy. World history was introduced in 1946 to the new school curriculum of postcolonial Korea. World history was integrated into social studies, along with geography, politics, economics, and ethics, in primary (grades 1–6) and middle school (grades 7–9). James Harvey Robinson's conception of the New History, aligned with the educational reform of American Progressivism, was the force behind this change. History as education stopped being "art for art's sake" and became a subject self-consciously intended for promoting democratic citizenship. History also remained a part of the social studies program in high school (grades 10–12).[35]

Within this new field of social studies, history courses in middle school retained the colonial legacy of the Japanese tripartite structure of "Oriental history," "Occidental history," and "national history." The division of world history and national history into two parts rather than three was introduced only in the high school curriculum. Notably, the terms *world civilization* and *Korean civilization* were used instead of "world history" and "Korean history." In the postcolonial turbulence immediately following liberation, Koreans did not produce their own world history textbooks. They translated and adopted a modified version of *World Civilization*, a text originally written for American GIs. In postwar Japan, despite the peculiar tripartite structure of professional historiography and education at the university level, middle and high school history education kept the division of "world history" and "Japanese history" in line with American military government after 1949. Education reforms in Japan took more time: the Supreme Command of Allied Powers (SCAP) issued an order on December 31, 1945, for a complete "blacking out" of textbooks in history, ethics, and geography.[36]

World history thus came back to postwar East Asia as an educational project, at the implicit behest of American military authorities. It became a required subject at the middle and high school levels in Japan, and part of the required high school curriculum in Korea, during the educational reforms that took place immediately after World War II. Although world history's status did shift periodically in Korea (as later curricular reforms meant it was sometimes optional and sometimes required), it consistently remained a required subject in Japan. In some world history textbooks from the late 1940s and early 1950s, Western history overwhelms Eastern history by a ratio of about three to one. Course periodizations were also based on European historiography: the progression of stages from ancient to medieval to modern to contemporary. Liberalism, democracy, bourgeois revolution, the industrial revolution, and nationalism were the most popular problematics in world history textbooks, which in turn reinforced the Eurocentric understanding of world history.

Research subjects echoed world history education. The rise of capitalism, the Renaissance and Reformation, the German Peasants' War, the English Revolution and gentry debates, the American Revolution and slavery, Enlightenment and the French Revolution, agrarian reforms in Prussia, and the Industrial Revolution were among the most popular topics for world historians. All those topics address the transition from feudalism to capitalism; in other words, the history of modernization in Europe. Eurocentric world history was promoted to accelerate the historical process of industrialization, political democracy, and modern nation-building.[37] Japanese historians relatively free from Cold War imposition could expand their research frontiers to Eastern Europe, Latin America, Middle East, and Africa in the 1970s, and leftist critical historiography has been relatively dominant in Japan. An amalgam of Marxism and modernization theory, represented by Ōtsuka Hisao's economic history, has been the main explanatory framework for the Japanese transition from the feudal to the modern on a world-historical scale.

Conversely, Korean historians, deprived of academic freedom under the anti-Communist dictatorship in the 1970s and 1980s, struggled to pursue "history from below." The postcolonial generation, born in the 1950s and attending university in the 1970s, were eyewitnesses of a typical process of primitive accumulation of capital under the South Korean developmental dictatorship. A sort of enclosure movement, not by force but by a market manipulation of keeping low prices for agrarian products, a massive migration of peasants to the city as a reserve army of labor, the misery of the working masses, the mobilization of worker-peasants to the project of modernizing the fatherland and social patriotism—all these phenomena of nineteenth-century European social history seemed to recur in twentieth-century South Korea. In these circumstances, it is not surprising to see the emergence of Korean *narodniks* and their concern for "history from below." By transposing the national epic from the field of high politics to that of everyday life, however, "history from below" contributed to the making of national history within Korea.[38]

Although Marxist historiography has been regarded as a potential alternative world history for its criticism of capitalist modernity, it is hardly free from Eurocentrism. Marxist historiography has never been free from the practice of cofiguring East and West hierarchically in historical thinking and writing. When Marx's *Das Kapital* was translated into Russian, the Russian bourgeoisie was second to none in welcoming it, because they saw an argument for the historical necessity of capitalist development in Russia.[39] Marxist historiography in twentieth-century East Asia was still the offspring of Eurocentric world history. The famous Marxist controversy over the Meiji Ishin of 1868 and subsequent capitalist development between the *Kōza-ha* (Lecture's faction) and the *Rono-ha* (Labor-Peasant faction) is a good example. *Rono-ha* Marxists insisted that the socialist revolution in Japan was imminent, given the universal crisis of world capitalism in the interwar period. In opposition to the *Rono-ha* group, the *Kōza-ha* Marxists emphasized Japanese backwardness and the peculiarities of military and semifeudal capitalism in Japan. *Kōza-ha*'s definition of Japanese capitalism closely resembles Lenin's description of the "Prussian path" of capitalist development.[40] Caught in the Marxist unilinear schema of the development of socioeconomic formations, both factions presumed that every country must experience a bourgeois revolution prior to the institution of the worker state.

Marxist historiography in post-1945 Japan was in continuity with the *Kōza-ha* tradition.[41] The dominant discourse in the historical evaluation of Japanese modernity was that Japanese militarism and colonial expansion could be attributed to the pathological factors of an immature civil society, its semifeudal backwardness and authoritarian political culture, both of which are inherent in its "premodern residues." Postwar Japan should be reformed to eliminate premodern irrationality and complete the democratic revolution. This diagnosis can be seen as the partial convergence of the SCAP's official view of the Pacific War and the *Kōza-ha* Marxist faction's interpretation of Japanese modernity.[42] Nishikawa Masao, a lifelong Marxist historian of Western history in postwar Japan, admitted that Orientalism in Japanese historiography was a concomitant of Karl Marx's and Max Weber's tremendous influence.[43] Democratic liberals participated in this interpretation mainly through the work of Ōtsuka Hisao, who bridged the gap between *Kōza-ha* Marxists and modernization theory. Despite the sharp ideological antagonism between Rostow and Marxists, Rostow's theory of the stages of historical growth was similar to the Marxian concept of unilinear history.[44] Developmental historicism explains why world history books in Japan, especially in the 1950s and 1960s, were full of tropes about the necessity of a "follow and catch up" strategy of countries in the periphery.[45]

Marxist historiography in colonial Korea was also marked by the Eurocentric vision of world capitalist development. The Eurocentric unilinear development model ended up defending the autogenous capitalist development of colonized Korea against the colonizer Japan's stagnancy theory. Marxist universal history and its consequential Eurocentrism was able to accommodate the nationalist rationale with its stress on the autogenous development of capitalism. The peculiar fusion of Marxist historicism and the Rostovian take-off model of economic growth was influential in postwar Korean historiography, too. Sometimes one person, such as Min Seok-Hong, first professor of Western history at Seoul National University, could endorse the stubborn Marxist interpretation of the French Revolution of 1798 and advocate Rostow's modernization theory at the same time.[46] The desire for modernity—in both of these ways—was a locomotive to drive the study and education of world/Western history. In this context, world history meant exclusively Western history, because the failed modernization in Asia could not be used as a model. World history was an exercise in identifying a reasonable model to spur postwar Korean development.

In less developed countries, socialism under the slogan of "the creative application of Marxism-Leninism" became a development strategy of rapid industrialization intended to catch up with and overtake advanced capitalism at the cost of the working masses. To many East Asian intellectuals suffering from the identity crisis between Westernization and national identity, socialism came as a two-birds-with-one-stone solution. Socialism was expected to solve the historical dilemma of anti-Western modernization because of its vision of anti-imperialist national liberation and rapid industrialization from above. The popularity of the dependency theory among Korean-left historians and social scientists in the late 1970s can be understood in the same vein. Dependency theorists based colonial history on the premise that at the heart of colonialism lay the one-way transfer of capital from the colony to the metropole and the additional transfer of surplus through the unequal exchange between the center and periphery. The hated Japanese colonial rule was seen as the prime cause of contemporary Korean economic backwardness, military dictatorship, an immature civil society, the division of two Koreas, and all sorts of pre-modern residues.

Dependency theory and its aftermath in historical research did not shatter the dichotomy of the normative West and the deviated East, nor of model modernization and deviated modernization. With its sharp criticism of the unequal exchange and unilateral surplus transfer between center and periphery, dependency theory and its historical arguments were more often than not based on an oversimplified opposition between East and West as well as essentialized regional differences represented by the concept of the "Third World." Thus it fails to pick up historical tensions inherent in any specific unit of either peripheries or centers. It tends to essentialize the homogeneity and heterogeneity of both nation-states and the region. In the final instance, dependency theory and its worldview came to serve world history as a nationalist rationale by justifying the accumulation of capital by the nation-state for rapid industrialization. Once again, both modernist and Marxist world history in postwar East Asia was overcome by Western history.

Beyond National History?

In 2005 the joint East Asian history textbook *A History to Open the Future* (*HOF*) was published simultaneously in Korea, Japan, and China.[47] A watershed in textbook cooperation, it was designed to counteract the nationalist polemics over history in East Asia. In the midst of the turbulent historical controversy ignited by the Japanese *New History Textbook*, *HOF* achieved a remarkable marketing success. In 2005 alone, roughly 120,000 copies of Chinese versions, about 70,000 Japanese copies and nearly 30,000 copies of the Korean version were sold. More than fifty historians, history teachers, and citizens of the three countries participated in this project, and thirteen conferences have been held consecutively in China, Japan, and Korea since 2002. *HOF* encouraged hope about the future topography of East Asian historiography, and it has led historical discourse in East Asia toward regional peace and historical reconciliation. The broad press coverage of that book, in Korea at least, disseminated this optimistic vision, and indeed *HOF* may deserve credit as the first transnational history book in postwar East Asia. Given the current East Asian "History War," this book is an impressive achievement.

Yet a scrupulous reading of *HOF* raises questions about its transnational character. In short, it is a transnational history based on the national history paradigm. First of all, many nationalist historians from the three countries took part in the project. On the Korean committee, nationalist (left) historians constituted the majority. The Japanese committee comprised mainly "postwar historiography" historians who expressed remorse for Japan's wartime past. In China, the main contributor was the Institute of Modern History of the Chinese Academy of Social Sciences (CASS). Whether nationalists, left-leaning democrats, or Marxists, a common positivist thread connects the contributors' different political approaches. They all claim to have sought "historical truth and lessons" through the textbook project. Perhaps the positivist stance narrowed the scope of the book, because trilateral agreement on the facts was a prerequisite, which explains why the book is rather simplistically focused on Japan's wartime aggression and invasion.

Second, as Narita Ryūichi has rightly pointed out, the book never questions that the nation-state is a collective subject. The editorial committee's proud declaration that *HOF* incorporates the viewpoints of women, minorities, and the oppressed is somewhat true. The goal of *HOF* to be "free from narrow-minded chauvinism" seems partially accomplished. One should pay attention to the intentional usage of "chauvinism" instead of "nationalism": the target of *HOF* was not "nationalism" per se, but perceived "bad nationalism," that is, narrow-minded chauvinism. The (Korean) editorial committee did not recognize that even "good nationalism" betrays the principle of standing for minorities. Insofar as the nation-state continues to be the subject of history, a transnational East Asia has no place for national minorities lacking their own nation-states. It should be noted, too, that *HOF* represents East Asia exclusively as the three countries of South Korea, Japan, and China. Taiwan, Vietnam, Mongolia, and even North Korea are excluded from scope of the *HOF* project.[48]

Third, *HOF* sacrificed issues of transnationality and translocality for its own national history paradigm. The global context of modernity is missing in the first chapter on the "opening of ports and modernization." *HOF* arranges China's, Japan's, and Korea's separate responses to the challenge of the Western Great Powers along parallel lines. It presupposes each fledgling nation-state as independent agents reacting against the Western impact. There is no description of how the geocultural East Asia came into being in the dialectical interplay between East Asia and the transatlantic Great Powers. Without Europe, Asia is not imaginable, and vice versa. The historical positivism intrinsic to *HOF* tends to regard "East Asia" as a positivist rather than as a constructed reality. This means that *HOF* has essentially bundled together the histories of three nation-states rather than achieving its stated goal of creating an entangled history of transnational East Asia.

Despite its problems, the strides *HOF* made toward creating a new kind of regional history of Asia become clearer if one looks at two reports of bilateral histories published about five years later. The merits of *HOF* become apparent in contrast to reports the Chinese-Japanese and the Japanese-Korean Joint History Research Committee, respectively, released in January and March 2010. Covering the bilateral relations of "China" and "Japan" from ancient to contemporary history in 549 pages, the Chinese-Japanese Joint Committee's final report contains a series of essays on the same topics written separately by both Japanese and Chinese scholars. The *Asahi shimbun* described this Sino-Japanese joint history effort as "an unprecedented undertaking," but despite this reserved optimism, the newspaper could not hide its disappointment with the wide gaps between Chinese and Japanese historians. Worse was the committee's decision to block public access to the part of the report on the history of the postwar era. Allegedly the Chinese justified the decision on the basis that the report could hurt the feelings of ordinary Chinese people who suffered under Japan's aggression during World War II. Without doubt, Chinese concerns about political turbulence, including the Tiananmen massacre, fueled the decision not to make the report public.

In principle, differences among East Asian historians are not necessarily a problem. Without invoking more skeptical approaches to history such as constructivism, dissenting voices and different opinions are inherent in historical research. The question is why historical interpretations diverge along national borders. Despite its stress on "objective understanding," "facing history squarely," "fact-based research," and its general positivistic stance, the report could not but be politicized by projecting the present nation-state into the past. While the Chinese *People's Daily* used positive metaphors such as "thaw," "the latest sign of warming ties between Beijing and Tokyo," and "a milestone for the authoritative version of history acceptable to both nations," these anodyne words cannot erase doubts about historiographical conflicts.[49] So long as national history is used as a lever to amplify national conflicts, and so long as a national lens dominates the perception of the past, no political blueprint comprising East Asia is possible. This, in part, explains why this joint history research project was initiated not by scholars but by politicians.

The Chinese-Japanese report was followed by a report numbering more than three thousand pages produced by the Japanese-Korean Joint History Research Committee, which was made public on March 23, 2010.[50] The Japanese-Korean report consists of four parts—ancient, medieval, modern/contemporary, and textbooks. The compartmentalization reflects the organizing principle of the Joint Committee, which divided participants into subcommittees based on historical periodization. Each subcommittee under the umbrella of the Japanese-Korean Joint History Research Committee was relatively autonomous, with its own principles and research agenda. A cursory look at the report reveals the persistence of national history and its attendant problems. In their joint preface, the chairpersons of the Korean and Japanese delegations express their belief that the committee's effort will be "a stepping stone to make a scholars' community for common prosperity in the future with mutual trust." However, prefaces individually authored by the two chairpersons each contain nuanced complaints about their counterpart. Despite the stated desire to improve ties between Japan and South Korea, this joint history project spiraled into disagreement, criticism, and heated exchanges, mainly over Japan's colonial rule of the Korean peninsula. Bitter disagreements can be found elsewhere, especially in the minutes of the modern/contemporary history and history textbook subcommittees. The polemical comments and countercomments in these two panels often led to radical doubts about the project itself, with members in both countries bluntly saying that they found little reason to continue the project. A Japanese participant on the textbook panel reported that "this Korean presentation proves the Japanese-Korean joint-history research was to no avail."

Perhaps the *Asahi shimbun*'s description that the committee turned into something of a "proxy war" is too gloomy and pessimistic. The situation was much less heated, for instance, in the ancient and medieval history subcommittees. For all the disagreements, discrepancy, discord, and even quarrels found there, they remain scholarly debates—nonantagonistic. Given the heated disagreements around ancient history—especially century-long contestation about the alleged Japanese *Imna* Commandery in the southern part of the Korean peninsula, the fact that the disagreements remained nonantagonistic can be considered a breakthrough. This tells us once again that what is in question is not a choice between agreement and disagreement. Total agreement is neither possible nor desirable. Different interpretations and dissenting voices, if reconcilable or, at least, symbiotic, give a productive tension to historical research and make historical dialogues dialectical. Erasing differences and homogenizing historical interpretation are problematic because they impose a single-minded history. The question is not whether the difference exists, but whether that difference is symbiotic or antagonistic. The prospect of bilateral or multilateral historical dialogues depends on whether disagreements remain symbiotic. Antagonistic dialogues about historical interpretations yield at best political compromises rather than frank discussion and fruitful disagreement about history.

Unfortunately, these two bilateral historical dialogues in East Asia are dotted with arguments more antagonistic than symbiotic. The ways that China, Japan, and Korea distinguish true and false in historical epistemology reflect their different ways of governing themselves and others. In this game of veracity, the problem of truth becomes the political problems of national history. As long as the national history paradigm is allowed to structure the conditions of possibility for historical truth, no stress on "objective understanding," "facing history squarely," "fact-based research," and a general positivistic stance can resolve the antagonistic disagreement implicit in national histories. What is required as "a stepping-stone to make a scholars' community for common prosperity in the future with mutual trust" is the change of episteme in historical thinking and reasoning. The goodwill to improve ties through historical reconciliation cannot be realized unless historical disputes, historiographical disagreements, and different opinions can be symbiotic and free from the egocentric national history paradigm. Historical dialogues in East Asia, represented by two joint national history research committees, should shift from international dialogues between national histories to transnational dialogues beyond national history.

Decentering World History

Since its introduction to Japan and Korea in the late nineteenth century, world history has fluctuated between Eurocentric world history and an Asiacentric world vision. This pendulum of world history pedagogy and scholarship can be located within the intellectual history of "overcoming modernity" and being "overcome by modernity." Eurocentric world history dominated the intellectual milieus that favored Western-oriented modernization during the Meiji Ishin, Enlightened Reformism, and the post–World War II era. While the focus was on Western rather than Asian history in this period, an Asiacentric world vision can be found in the various discourses of pan-Asianism in the late nineteenth century, through "overcoming modernity" in the colonial period, and into contemporary discussions of the East Asian community. However much these alternate versions of world history conflict, they are all complicit with visions of national history. Whatever the antagonisms between Eurocentric and Asiacentric world history, they provide alternate forms of the same nationalist agenda: a European "normative" path or an Asian "peculiar" path of modernization in the capitalist world system. Both versions of world history presuppose that capitalist development is inevitable on a worldwide scale.

As Sebastian Conrad argues, "The appeal to world history emphasized not a spatial but a temporal category."[51] Marxists and nationalists alike emphasize uniform historical time and a unilinear development of world history, leading to a Eurocentric diffusionism of a unilateral flow from Europe to the "Rest." This cofiguration of national history and world history gave rise to what I would call a consequential Eurocentrism in postwar Japan and Korea. Pluralizing world history demands deconstructing the historicist impetus to temporalize spaces along a unilinear historical time. We can pay attention to historical discourses to pluralize and decentralize world history in the twenty-first century: Andre G. Frank and Barry K. Gills's "five thousand years world system," Janet Abu-Lughod's arguments about the proto-capitalist systems in the thirteenth century, Patrick Manning's multipolar world system with a focus on West Africa, and David Ludden's focus on South Asia all come to mind. Many Korean historians, who introduced (and popularized) these recent trends in the world or global history, were not trained specifically in world history but began their academic careers as researchers of Western history.[52]

Historians of Asian history joined them by introducing the works of the California school, such as the writings of Kenneth Pomeranz and Bin Wong. Their contention about the dynamism of the Chinese versus the European economy as late as the eighteenth century provoked serious interest among many historians across different fields. If contemporary Chinese nationalist historians and intellectuals have appropriated these arguments for their purposes, some Korean nationalists read the California school as evidence of the wider superiority of Eastern civilization over the Western civilization; by working within a fundamentally Eurocentric East/West dichotomy, they confirmed their Occidentalist worldview. At the same time, scholars of history education have been concerned about the pedagogy of world history or global history. They have written about worldwide trends in global history and introduced contemporary debates on how to write world history. The urgent task of writing world history textbooks inclined them to stay abreast of the newest trends in world history.

The influence of those path-breaking studies in world history on Korean historiography is not yet clear. Korean historians are on the threshold of new world history, one that is neither Orientalist nor Occidentalist. From the perspective of the Korean academy, world history looks double-edged. Any critic of Eurocentrism risks Occidentalism as a reversed form of Orientalism, which serves to justify nationalist politics.[53] The Japanese historiography of world history has been remarkably productive. Most recently, a global economic history has produced impressive work. In a sense, the rise of the East Asian economy has been a driving force of the development of a new Asian economic history on the platform of global history. What distinguishes this new global economic history from pre-existing comparative economic histories is its focus on relationships, linkages, encounters, and various networks of merchants and migration. As a criticism of the Eurocentric world system, a globally linked network of cotton supply and its final demand has also been explored fruitfully, and a unique chain of the global linkage comprising Japan, China, British India, Burma, the Dutch East Indies, and Great Britain and other European countries has also been mapped.[54]

In line with the development of this new global economic history, Japanese world history textbooks, particularly since 1989, have begun to emphasize cultural interconnectedness and trade networks between different cultures. World history textbooks in Japanese high schools now come in two varieties: one written for "World History A," a course for students in the vocational system, and the other for "World History B," intended for those headed toward university. While shorter, the textbook for "World History A" has a more impressive structure and narrative, perhaps partly because it is not intended as part of a university entrance examination. What is most striking in both textbooks is that they eschew the conventional periodization of ancient–medieval–modern. Instead of a vertical chronological structure, they stress horizontal networks as the historical space of cultural interactions and transregional trade. Modernity stops being Eurocentric from this perspective. It is a global modernity that Europe, Africa, America, and Asia coproduced through interregional networks and interactions.[55] The substantial academic accumulation in global economic history in Japan made this world history textbook remarkable.

World history is on the verge of blossoming in Japan and Korea. This new world history or global history has been freed in the last two decades from the organizing bias of Eurocentric world history as a nationalist rationale to promote Westernization or modernization, although it may remain vulnerable to a particular kind of Asiacentric world history because of its regional accent. There arises a necessity of "worlding" instead of "regionalizing." "Worlding" history would bring local, national, and regional history into the world and bring the world into local, national, and regional history.[56] But "worlding" history should also be followed by decentering world history. This sequential combination may give us a clue to finding an exit from the vicious circle of Eurocentric and Asiacentric world history and reconstructing world history per se. A stress on the interaction and connectedness between West and East may presuppose that East and West are the geopositivistic reality. In the course of decentering world history, we can trace when and where the distinction between West and East was fixed. Genealogies of Global Easts come to light.

Notes

1. Edward Said, *Culture and Imperialism* (London: Vintage, 1994), 233.
2. Kenneth Pomeranz and Daniel A. Segal, "World History: Departures and Variations," in *A Companion to World History*, ed. Douglas Northlop (Chicester, UK: Wiley-Blackwell, 2012), 15–17.
3. See chapter 5.

4. Q. Edward Wang, " 'Rise of Great Powers' = Rise of China?," *Contemporary China* 19 (March 2010).

5. When I watched the series by the Education Broadcasting Station (EBS) of Korea, I was surprised to see that its historical narrative was so close to the historical narrative of global modernization under the right-wing military development dictatorship in South Korea.

6. See chapter 4.

7. Ross E. Dunn, "Rethinking Civilizations and History in the New Age of Globalization," in *Proceedings of the 34th International Symposium at the National Academy of Sciences, Korea*, October 12, 2007.

8. Jerry Bentley, "Myths, Wagers, and Some Moral Implications of World History," *Journal of World History* 16, no. 1 (2005).

9. In this context, "world history" has more often than not been identified with "Western history" as a hegemonic discourse in East Asia.

10. In place of Meiji Restoration, I will use the term *Meiji Regeneration* here for its emphasis on the national regeneration project, either restorative or revolutionary. See Mitani Hiroshi, 明治維新を考える [Reconsidering Meiji regeneration] (Tokyo: Yusisha, 2006), 2–3.

11. Shingo Minamizuka, "How to Overcome Euro-Centrism in the Western History in Japan: Some Lessons from '*Bankokushi*' in the Meiji Era," in *Proceedings of the Conference Commemorating the Fiftieth Anniversary of the Korean Society for Western History*, Seoul National University, July 5–6, 2007, 190–91.

12. Kazuhiko Kondo, "The Studies of Western History in Japan and the Understanding of Modernity" in *Proceedings of the Conference of Commemorating the Fiftieth Anniversary of the Korean Society for Western History*, 117.

13. Stefan Tanaka, *Japan's Orient: Rendering Past Into History* (Berkeley: University of California Press, 1993).

14. "外籍譯出의 必要" [Necessity of translating foreign books], *Hwangseongsinmun* June 28, 1907, https://www.nl.go.kr/newspaper/searchEla.do.

15. Timothy Mitchell, "The Stage of Modernity," in *Questions of Modernity*, ed. Timothy Mitchell (Minneapolis: University of Minnesota Press, 2000), 4.

16. Andre Schmid, *Korea Between Empires, 1895–1919* (New York: Columbia University Press, 2002), 32–36, 56–59, 80.

17. Dipesh Chakrabarthy, *Provincializing Europe: Postcolonial Thought and Historical Difference* (Princeton, N.J.: Princeton University Press, 2000), 7.

18. World history in China is a bit different. A register of Western history has been kept in China, but world history has been treated more often as a synonym for "foreign history." See Weiwei Zhang, "The World from China," in Northlop, *A Companion to World History*, 405.

19. Schmid, *Korea Between Empires*, 86–100.

20. Cemil Aydin, *The Politics of Anti-Westernism in Asia: Visions of World Order in Pan-Islamic and Pan-Asian Thought* (New York: Columbia University Press, 2007), 161, 189.

21. Mitsui Takashi, "일선동조론의 학문적 기반에 관한 시론" [A study on the origins and development of Ilseontongjoron in modern Japanese academism before and after Japanese annexation of Korea], *Hankukmunhwa* 33 (2004): 249–52.

22. Mitsui, 253–54.

23. Lee Sungsi, 만들어진 고대 [The ancient invented], trans. Park Kyunghee (Seoul: Samin, 2001), 41–45.

24. Pak Sunyoung, "일제 식민주의와 조선의 몸에 대한 인류학적 시선" [The anthropological gaze at the Korean bodies under Japanese colonialism], *Bikyomunhwa yŏngu* 12, no. 2 (2006): 57–92.

25. Pak, 65, 72, 73, and passim.

26. Wan-yao Chou, "The Kōminka Movement in Taiwan and Korea: Comparisons and Interpretations," in *The Japanese Wartime Empire 1931–1945*, ed. Peter Duus, Ramon H. Myers, and Mark R. Peattie, (Princeton, N.J.: Princeton University Press, 1996), 41ff.

27. Lee Ki-baek, *A New History of Korea*, trans. Edward W. Wagner and Edward J. Shultz (Cambridge, Mass.: Harvard University Press, 1984), 57, 64.

28. Quoted in Lee Sungsi, 만들어진 고대, 47.

29. For the nationalist historiography of the Marxist party in North Korea, see chap. 8.

30. Lee Sungsi, 만들어진 고대, 51.

31. Here I paraphrase Cooper and Stoler on imperial history. See Ann Laura Stoler and Frederick Cooper, "Between Metropole and Colony: Rethinking a Research Agenda," in *Tensions of Empire*, ed. Cooper and Stoler (Berkeley: University of California Press, 1997).

32. It is interesting that Takahashi Kohachiro, the renowned Marxist economic historian on postwar Japan and a commentator on the Marxist discussion of the transition from feudalism to capitalism, taught Western history at Keizo Imperial University in the colonial period.

33. Park Gwanghyun, "식민지조선에서 동양사학은 어떻게 형성되었나?" [How was East Asian history formulated in colonial Korea?], in *Yŏksahakui Segi*, ed. Do Myunhoi and Yoon Haedong (Seoul: Humanist, 2009), 217–34.

34. Harry Hartoonian, *Overcome by Modernity: History, Culture, and Community in Interwar Japan* (Princeton, N.J.: Princeton University Press, 2000).

35. Cha Hasoon, 서양사학의 수용과 발전 [Reception and development of Western history] (Seoul: Nanam, 1988), 138–52.

36. Yoshihiko Nozaki, *War Memory, Nationalism and Education in Postwar Japan, 1945–2007: The Japanese History Textbook Controversy and Ienaga Saburo's Court Challenge* (London: Routledge, 2008), 3.

37. Lim Jie-Hyun, "한국 서양사학의 반성과 전망-'시민계급적 관점'에서 '민중적 관점'까지-" [Critical reviews of Western historiography in Korea], *Yŏksabipyung* 8 (Spring 1990): 99–122.

38. Lim, 99–122. For the British model case, see Raphael Samuel, preface to *Patriotism: The Making and Unmaking of British National Identity*, vol. 1 (London: Verso, 1989), xi.

39. Albert Resis, "Das *Kapital* Comes to Russia," *Slavic Review* 29 (June 1970): 219–37.

40. See Sebastian Conrad, *The Quest for the Lost Nation,* trans. Alan Nothnagle (Berkeley: University of California Press, 2010).

41. For its view of world capitalism as a single unit of economic development, the Kansai school differed from the main current of Marxist historiography and contributed to study of global economic history and the East Asian trade network, with a critical tint of Eurocentric Marxist world history in Japan. However, the *Kōza-ha* tradition was unbeatable for its influence.

42. J. Victor Koschmann, introduction to English edition of *Total War and Modernization,* ed. Y. Yamanouchi, J. V. Koschmann, and R. Narita (Ithaca, N.Y.: Cornell University Press, 1998), xi–xii.

43. Masao Nishikawa, "A Specter Is Still haunting: The Specter of World History," *Radical History Review* 91 (Winter 2005): 114.

44. The subtitle of Rostow's book is "A Non-Communist Manifesto." Interestingly, Rostow praised Japan in comparison to China for reaching economic maturity sooner. See W. W. Rostow, *The Stages of Economic Growth: A Non-Communist Manifesto* (Cambridge: Cambridge University Press, 1960).

45. Yuji Geto, "일본의 세계사 교과서" [Japanese world history textbook], in 동아시아 역사 교과서는 어떻게 쓰여졌는가? [How have East Asian history texts been written?], ed. Nakamura Satoru (Seoul: Editor, 2006), 166.

46. Yook Youngsoo, "국가 근대화 기획으로서의 서양사" [Western history as a national modernization project], in *Yŏksahakui Segi* (Seoul: Humanist, 2009), 331–48.

47. China-Japan-Korea Common History Text Tri-National Committee, 미래를 여는 역사 [A history to open the future] (Seoul: Hangyŏrechulpan, 2005).

48. Narita Ryūichi, "동아시아의 가능성" [Possibility of East Asian history], *Changjakgwa Bipyŏng,* no. 131 (Spring 2006): 406.

49. "Report to Signal Thaw in China, Japan Relations," *People's Daily Online,* December 24, 2009, http://english.peopledaily.com.cn/90001/90776/90883/6850633.html.

50. One can find both Korean and Japanese versions of the full report at the Northeast Asia History Foundation website, http://www.historyfoundation.or.kr/?sidx =119&stype=1.

51. Sebastian Conrad, *The Quest for the Lost Nation,* trans. Alan Nothnagle (Berkeley: University of California Press, 2010), 171.

52. See Hankook Sŏyangsahakhoi, ed., 유럽중심주의 세계사를 넘어 [Beyond a Eurocentric world history] (Seoul: Purunyŏksa, 2009).

53. Xiaomei Chen, *Occidentalism* (Oxford: Oxford University Press, 1995).

54. Shigeru Akita, "World History and the Creation of a New Global History: Japanese Perspectives," in *Global History, Globally,* Harvard University, February 8–9, 2018.

55. Michio Shibata et al., 世界の歴史 [World history] (Tokyo: Yamakawashuppan, 2007).

56. Arif Dirlik, "Contemporary Perspectives on Modernity: Critical Discussion," lecture delivered to East Asian Academy, Sŏngkyunkwan University, 2007.

7

Nationalist Phenomenology in East Asian History Textbooks

On the Antagonistic Complicity of Nationalisms

Nationalist Complicity

In winter 1999 a Japanese neonationalist group published *The History of the Nation* as a pilot edition of their forthcoming revisionist history textbook. Their revisionist *New History Textbook* (*Atarashii rekishi kyōkasho*) was soon authorized as one of the texts approved for use in Japan's junior high schools. This authorization incited criticism and furious responses in Japan and abroad for its historical affirmation of Japanese colonialism, shameless nationalism, and intentional neglect of imperialist war atrocities of the Nanjing massacre, comfort women, forced labor, and other colonial atrocities. Amid tumultuous historical debates provoked by the publication of *New History Textbook* in 2001, *Sankei shinbun*, a conservative Japanese daily newspaper, published a striking series of articles analyzing the South Korean history textbook *National History*, produced under state monopoly, in the paper's general sequence analyzing Asian history textbooks.[1]

The *Sankei shinbun*'s editorial position aligned it with the *New History Textbook*'s take on Japan's colonization of Korea, and its articles on South Korean textbooks found a surprising affinity. Not only were the articles not hostile, *Sankei shinbun*'s Seoul correspondent even praised the Korean national history textbook for its firm grounding in ethnocentric history. In these articles on Asian history textbooks, the *Sankei* correspondent justified the *New History Textbook* by repeated reference to ethnocentric Korean national history textbooks. In comparing Korean and Japanese history textbooks, he identified a common master narrative, one in which "our nation" is the subject of history. Korean history textbooks thus confirmed his conviction that history textbooks should teach children of all nationalities "national pride" and "love for our own history."[2] The *Sankei* correspondent barely hid his jealousy of the Korean national history textbook's state monopoly status, with no competition from other history textbooks.

This ironic episode brings into relief the topography of warring national histories in East Asia. Leaving aside blatant falsehoods, visible distortions, intentional oblivion, obvious erasures, and forced silences, the national history textbook conflict in East Asia is not a question of "right or wrong" to be proven by objective facts but is precisely the inevitable collision of conflicting nationalisms. Historical facts in those textbooks may be said to be constructed by the nationalist episteme; that is, the reality of the past is composed by the present idea of the nation. I would call this a "nationalist phenomenology" because nationalism not only informs but ultimately determines the construction of historical narratives in East Asian history textbooks. Nationalist phenomenology also confirms the historical relativism of the nation. As stated in the *New History Textbook*, "History is different from nation to nation by nature, and there are as many histories as there are nation-states."[3] This nationalist pluralism conferred credibility on the *New History Textbook* through its history from a nation-centric perspective.

The new narrative tactic of the Japanese revisionists reveals a fundamental reorientation in the concept and use of historical constructivism. Historical constructivism in Japan was initially an efficient tool for opposing the conservatism of Japanese positivist historians, who had denied the grassroots history interpretations by pointing out the absence of official documents or authentic written evidence. The case of "comfort women" is a good example to show the tension between the positivistic denialism and constructivist criticism. Through the testimonies and witnesses of comfort women, constructivist historians challenged the monopoly on truth of official written documents that conveyed only official viewpoints and proved the existence of sexual slavery. The fashion for constructivist approaches to history, however, was soon co-opted by nationalist revisionists, who saluted historical relativism in producing openly nationalist textbooks: every nation constructs its peculiar national history, after all. This metamorphosis of historical constructivism to serve Japanese revisionist ends in turn strengthened the position of Korean nationalist historiography, which claimed to pit objective truth against Japanese falsification and distortion of historical facts. Korean nationalist historians used the Japanese nationalist revisionism to justify their own nationalist historiography. They argued against the broader constructivist criticism of their national history paradigm by dismissing historical constructivism as nothing but a way of benefiting Japanese nationalist revisionism.

If a twisted form of constructivism justified Japanese historical revisionism, Korean nationalist historiography has been nourished by historical positivism. The positivism became more dominant, especially in the official nationalist Korean historiography, in the wake of the textbook controversy. The constructivist approach of Japanese revisionism and the positivist approach of Korean historiography created two nationalist histories that rarely engaged in historical specificities and operated more like parallel polemics. The logical similarities in the sharp polemics explain how national histories in East Asia, and perhaps in many other regions besides, have formed a relationship of "antagonistic complicity" behind the scenes of open conflict.[4] The parallel nation-centered histories could never converge to a point where a reconciliation of historical interpretations might take place. Opposing parties could not move beyond national history toward a reconceptualization of their shared pasts as "entangled history," "transnational history," "border history," or "overlapping history." Instead, they impose the general public to choose between "our own national history" and "their own national history."

With escalating tensions over the past, societal demands on history education have increased. Some historians, who benefit most from these circumstances, seize the opportunity to advance their professional interests in Korea. They participate unhesitatingly in a disciplinary project to enculturate the masses into the nation-state, using history textbooks as a tool for "the nationalization of the masses." The crisis of history as a waning science thus ends, and a sudden boom in history as a prominent national project begins. The state-sponsored history foundations and committees, such as the Goguryeo (高句麗) Research Foundation, which was launched in 2004 and later changed into the Northeast Asian History Foundation (NAHK), are endowed with extensive financial resources to trumpet the glories of national history and contest what they regard as national dishonoring and defamation by neighboring countries. The Japan Foundation, Korea Foundation, and many other organizations have been under government control, sometimes strict and sometimes loose. While international and domestic organizers of the Association for Asian Studies in Asia conference were preparing the Kyoto conference in 2016, they met firm opposition from the Japan Foundation, the major conference sponsor, over the proposed theme of memory and responsibility in East Asia. In the end, organizers had to change the theme of the conference to the future of "hope" in the midst of tense memory wars among East Asian neighbors. The NAHK's website promotes a nationalist research agenda focused on topics such as the Korean historical sovereignty over disputed border history, including Dokdo and Goguryeo, the international campaign for the East Sea instead of the Sea of Japan, and the origin and birth of the Korean race—all under the rubric of "Correcting History."[5]

The recent "history wars" in East Asia show that this antagonistic complicity strengthens the discursive hegemony of national history transnationally over the region. National histories in East Asia have thus been deadlocked in a mutual siege. Under the nationalist tension as a transnational phenomenon in East Asia, any serious academic attempt to go beyond national history is typically denounced as antipatriotic, and any practitioner as a national traitor. The difficulty of overcoming national history is increasing because any breakthrough in the current stalemate over history textbooks must be attempted mutually and simultaneously by critical historians in the East Asian region. The antagonistic complicity of warring nationalisms stubbornly persists in the domain of history research and education, which makes it extremely difficult to overcome the national history in the region. Looking at the century-long history of competing nationalist accounts in this region, one finds numerous cultural exchanges between ostensible rivals and examples of antagonistic acculturation in which the hegemonic discourses of the colonizers have been appropriated by the colonized as the basis for anticolonial resistance and their nationalist projects.[6] This chapter accordingly tries to deconstruct the nationalist episteme of history textbooks in East Asia by unveiling the antagonistic complicity of warring national histories in South Korea and Japan.

Collective Subject: "We-the Nation"

The two-page preface to the state-monopolized middle school history textbook in South Korea in 2002 frequently uses "we," "we-the nation," and "our own history." The first sentence declares that "national history plays a role in making our national identity through exploring the substance of our national soul and lives." In the preface alone, "we" appears twelve times, "our own history" seven times, and "we-the nation" once.[7] That is twenty instances of words emphasizing that this history textbook is all about "Us"! "Our Korean nation" clearly is the most important historical actor in the narrative structure of the text. The textbook makes the implicit assumption that every society calls for some collective identity, and that national history should respond to that demand by creating national identities. In contradiction to this call for the creation of national identity, it presumes that national history is "the real," not a "perceived reality" created to fulfill such functions.

In its introduction, under the heading of the "universality and particularity of Korean history," the high school textbook stresses that Korea has a history of more than five thousand years and emphasizes the exceptional continuity of the homogenous nation as a peculiarity of Korean history. The national virtues are loyalty to the state, filial piety, and community-(*Gemeinschaft-*) oriented values.[8] This self-asserted particularity of Korean history fits well with Ernest Gellner's definition of nationalism as "a phenomenon of *Gesellschaft* (atomized society) using the idiom of *Gemeinschaft* (organic community)."[9] As long as "we-the nation" as a homogenous entity occupies the privileged position of historical agency, the organic unity of *Gemeinschaft* cannot disintegrate into the various fragmented interests of *Gesellschaft*. As long as "our nation" remains the collective subject of the narrative, it would be blasphemy to ask "whose imagined community" this nation is. That question implies the nation to be a *Gesellschaft*, thereby challenging the organic unity of the nation as *Gemeinschaft*.[10]

The *New History Textbook* in Japan similarly posits the nation as the collective subject of history. Compared to Korean history textbooks, however, it is more euphemistic. Instead of using "our nation" and "our history," it refers to "the Japanese" and "the history of Japan." The different way of registering the subject between the first-person collective of "our nation" and the third-person collective of "the Japanese" shows a similarity in a greater or less degree—homogenizing diverse historical actors into the national collective. While Korean history textbooks stick to the term *national history* (國史), an ideological term borrowed from the *kokushi* of Japanese colonialism, the *New History Textbook* keeps the term *Japanese history* (日本史) instead. The Japanese history textbook's narrative sounds more modest than the Korean one because it seems to be aloof from emotional attachment to the nation by avoiding the use of possessives such as "our nation" and "our history." Despite the difference in the accent, however, both textbooks deploy the same terminology of the primordialist concept of nation, presupposing ahistorical eternity of the nation from the immemorial past.

In contrast, the Chinese conception of nation is not primordialist, because it incorporates the traces of many national minorities into the integral history of a multiethnic/multinational state. The People's Republic of China, consisting of fifty-six ethnic groups, cannot sustain a primordialist vision of the nation-state. In the official Chinese history, the territorial border of the PRC determines the boundary of national history.[11] The national history legitimizes the national sovereignty of the PRC over disputed territories of the Diaoyu (Senkaku) Islands, Spratly Islands, Heilong-Ussuri river basin, and other contested regions by incorporating the transnational border zones of the hybrid culture and history within the today's borderline of the PRC. In contrast to the primordialist concept of a cultural nation emphasizing semipermanent attributes of nation such as language, ethnicity, culture, history, and tradition, the modernist view of the political nation stresses the people's will to live together by forming one nation-state. That explains why the primordialist national history tends to look back to prehistoric times for historical legitimacy much more eagerly than the modernist national history.[12] The ultimate question, however, is not whether national history assumes the primordialist or the modernist view of the nation. In making national histories, the multinational state and the "ethnically homogenous" state deploy different narratives, but their goals remain the same.

The preface of the *New History Textbook* states explicitly that, "in other words, Japanese history means the history of forefathers who share the same bloodline as you [student readers]."[13] This direct address to the reader indicates that the book considers the nation in terms of biological descent, something it shares with Korean history textbooks. The epilogue is explicit that it aims to restore national pride hurt by the defeat of World War II and to give the nation more self-respect.[14] While Korean history textbooks aimed at the nationalization of the masses in a newly independent nation-state, the Japanese book contributes to the renationalization of postwar Japanese in transition from a multinational empire to an ethnic state. The discourse of (re)nationalization of the masses in both history texts only ostensibly present the primordialist concept of the nation while incubating staunch racist and xenophobic components beneath the surface. The same mechanism of inclusion and exclusion works in the primordialist and the modernist ways of nationalizing the masses.

An Organic Geo-body: Embodiment of Borders

While the nation remains the collective subject in these history textbooks, homogeneity is consistently emphasized over heterogeneity. The primordialist concept reinforces national homogeneity by assuming national unity to be natural and beyond historical, while the modernist concept regards the nation as a product of modernity itself. The modernist concept openly accepts the existence of the political, social, economic, and cultural schisms in the premodern period in order to stress the national unity among legal equals in the modern nation-state. Ernest Renan's dictum that "a nation's existence is . . . a daily plebiscite" represents the modernist conception in a succinct way.[15] The modernist theory also argues that national unity and integration are not imaginable without the "people's sovereignty," realized only in the wake of the French Revolution of 1789. That is, modernist history historicizes the nation by situating it in the context of nation-state formation.

The primordialist view tends to neglect the various historical conflicts and schisms among rival political and social formations because it assumes the existence of the nation as an organic unity, uninterrupted since time immemorial. The eternal life of the nation is displayed on maps as well as in the narrative in history textbooks. As Tessa Morris-Suzuki has observed, a small map illustrating the gradual introduction of rice farming to Japan in the *New History Textbook* shows the flow of rice cultivation technology between three places, labeled "China" (Zhongguo), "Korea" (Chosŏn), and "Japan" (Nihon). The use of these comparatively recent names for modern polities encourages readers to understand the categories "China," "Korea," and "Japan" as natural and eternal by projecting their labels back onto the world of six thousand years ago. The map illustrates a pervasive and pro- foundly influential view that equates the history of East Asia with the history of centralized states and sees these large centralized states as permanent, persisting entities throughout historical time.[16]

The handful of historical Paleolithic and Neolithic sites shown on the first map of the Korean textbook are confined to the Korean peninsula. This map tends to reinforce indirectly a notion that national history may stretch back to the Paleolithic age.[17] While the South Korean history textbook never openly mentions that continuity in the text, the desire for the undisrupted continuity of the national history from the immemorial past to the pres- ent resides in this map. Maps of ancient history in Korean history textbooks are interesting in how they depict the *Drang nach Manchuria*—the drive toward Manchuria. Maps illustrating the development of the Three King- doms (Silla, Baekje, Goguryeo) in ancient Korea blur the national bound- ary of the Yalu and Tumen Rivers in the Paleolithic and Neolithic ages and stretch deep into Manchuria to include the kingdom of Goguryeo as one of three ancient kingdoms that give rise to modern Korea. Contemporary place names such as "Japan," "Yellow Sea," and "Eastern Sea (Sea of Japan)" are inscribed on these maps. In this anachronistic way, maps in both Japanese and Korean history textbooks instill a "geo-body" among their teenage readers.

The concept of the nation as a geo-body presumes a naturally and organ- ically integrated territorial unit that persists throughout time.[18] In this conception, a violation of the organic geo-body of a nation equals an ampu- tation of some part of the human body. By visually constructing the social, maps don't just represent the Earth but actually can emotionally move people and thus "do" things—map-fare—by provoking affective com- munities of sense. Maps as imaginary but visual emotives provide the performative structure and affective politics of geopolitical and geohistori- cal practices.[19] That explains how contemporary political claims to the Dokdo/Takeshima, Senkaku/Diaoyu Islands or the southern part of the Chishima/Kurile Archipelago in East Asia have been inflamed by the map-fare, evoking the grassroots nationalist imagination. In Japan and Korea, the geo-body has been especially compelling because their geog- raphies contributed to the image of a naturally self-contained homogenous entity. These claims resist examining the historical justifications for today's national borders because it would raise crucial, often dramatic questions concerning citizenship, identity, political loyalty, exclusion, inclusion, and the goals of the state.[20]

Borders can also be constructed in social practice and discourse, through narrative, and through a consciousness of common experience, history, and memory. All borders are historical. All borders are created by human beings. Though we might think of some borders as "natural," because they are defined by geographical features such as seas, deserts, mountains, or rivers, they are still historically constructed and contingent. History textbooks in East Asia are constantly propagating natural borders. Natural borders leave no room for the possibility that political allegiances may be regionalized within certain nation-states. Schools, media, novels, memorials, ceremonies, and other public spectacles also inscribe boundaries. The history textbook writes the nation. The geo-body continually embodies the nation emotionally, and map-fare reinforces national belonging by making nation the affective community of sense.

Essentialism: Nation as "the Real"

The dominant concept of nation in the Japanese and Korean history textbooks is the primordialist one, which treats national integration as a fait accompli even without the principle of people's sovereignty. In this view, the chemistry of the nation as an organic unity surpasses the national integration achieved through the artifice of politics. It pays scant attention to any other social collectives, such as peasants, plebeians, slaves, and citizens, not to mention individual subjects that might shatter national homogeneity. To establish and to preserve the homogeneity, unitary will, and common destiny of the nation, dissenting voices in the past have been neglected, suppressed, and silenced. Both the Japanese and Korean history textbooks deal with social conflicts, class struggles, and gender inequalities either minimally or not at all. In each book of three hundred pages, the number of pages focused on societal conflict can be counted almost on one hand. Whatever does not fit the linear development of the nation-state is pared off, since social conflict threatens national homogeneity.

What little consideration of historical conflict that exists primarily concerns the political struggles of ruling elites as they are instrumental to the linear narrative of nation-state development. Hegemonic struggles between the king and ruling elites, court and local elites, and civilian and military elites warrant study over other social conflicts. Very often these power struggles result in a change of dynasty, ruling elite group, or the political structure of the state—outcomes that lead to the current nation. Political struggles between competing small political entities were included only if formative of a centralized state corresponding roughly to today's national territory—the proto-nation-state. The sole criterion for including a specific historical struggle is whether it contributes to constructing the nation-state's linear development. Nation as the supreme "Real" is never shattered in this primordialist narrative of national history.

In contrast, the modernist narrative readily deals with social conflicts. The existence of social conflict or class struggle, especially in the premodern era, clarifies how the nation-state arose out of the integration of nominally equal citizens of a unified will. In the global process of modern nation-state building, the politics of successive levels of representation, whereby the interests of the many are refined into ever fewer bodies, is the key nation-building mechanism: "the people representing the multitude, the nation representing the people, and the state representing the nation." The nationalist politics of representation invokes an imagined equality among its citizens to facilitate integration.[21] However, the modernist and the primordialist views are more often entwined than separated. Even though modernist national thought developed through appropriating the republicanism of the French Revolution, very often it went hand in hand with primordialist concepts of the nation. Colonialism helped to define the identity of the colonizers by making native people the Other. In the history of colonialism, the modernist nation-state is shot through with primordialist racism. The oscillation of the Japanese colonialist discourse between multinational pan-Asianism and primordialist ethnic homogeneity is a good example.[22]

The primordialist view of East Asian history textbooks never overlooks "people's history." While it includes descriptions of manners, customs, and the everyday lives of ordinary people, especially in Korean history textbooks, the descriptions are quite different in their methodology and orientation from *Alltagsgeschichte* (everyday history) as "history from below." To draw a parallel with academic historiography, it is closer to G. M. Trevelyan's "antiquarian history" rather than Alf Lüdtke's *Alltagsgeschichte*. "People's history" in East Asian history textbooks involves a simplistic history of "what they ate, what they wore, and how they lived," deprived of any of the political meaning immanent in the history of everyday lives as critical historiography of everyday life. The accumulation of these miscellaneous and trivial aspects of "antiquarian history" is supposed to form the matrix of national culture. Very often it develops into a "monumental history" of national heroes dear to grassroots patriots. Like the British "people's history" as critiqued by Raphael Samuel, this uncritical "people's history" treats "the common people" as a collective subject, transposing the national epic from the field of high politics to that of everyday life.[23]

In this way, the nation is the underlying telos, regardless of whether the narrative focuses on the high politics of ruling elites or the everyday lives of ordinary people. The organic concept of nation precludes any schism, especially when dealing with national crises, such as wars and domestic instability. Particular attention is paid to the history of national struggles against foreign invaders and to the struggle for national sovereignty. This is especially pronounced in Korean history textbooks, which stress the role of the people who defended the nation's freedom and independence in the face of the thirteenth-century Mongol invasion and the Japanese invasion of 1592. In the case of the Mongol invasion, the narrative contrasts the patriotic resistance of the slaves who fought ferociously in the battle of Ch'ungju with the cowardly aristocratic officials who fled the battlefield. The description of the Korean-Japanese War of 1592–1598 (Imjin War), meanwhile, emphasizes the resistance of a coalition made up of the ruling elites, peasant farmers, and Buddhist monks.[24] These examples illustrate how easily nationalist discourse swallows up "people's history" or "history from below" in history textbooks. People appear in history textbooks only insofar as they serve the nation.

But there is no mention at all of the slaves who set fire to the royal palace before the Japanese army's conquest of Seoul (Hanyang) in 1592. The peasants' capitulation en masse to the Mongol Army is blacked out by an emphasis on the peasants' and even slaves' patriotic resistance during the Mongol invasion; the partisan leader's complaint that the peasants welcomed the Japanese Army and did not respond to his call for arms against the foreign invaders is also completely ignored in the description of the Imjin War. Although Korean history textbooks ostensibly cherish the values of historical positivism and factuality, those facts that are unfavorable to nationalist essentialism are omitted. Here as elsewhere, primordialism posits the nation as the "essence" of identity under all historical circumstances. The nation is the ontological essence beyond historical change, the true subject underlying the full range of historical phenomena. In history, however, the nation has become divided by class, estates, and gender lines. Nation has fragmented. National oppression is linked with other forms of oppression in a way too complicated and contradictory to essentialize the nation as the prime agent. Nevertheless, the nation as the essence of identity remains undiluted in history textbooks.

Heroic nationalism goes hand in hand with victimhood nationalism in history textbooks. Nationalist essentialism is reinforced by the self-perception of "hereditary victimhood" inherent in both Japanese and Korean history textbooks. This hereditary victimhood constructs an image of a people with a unitary will formed through shared suffering as an oppressed nation.[25] Japan's *New History Textbook* depicts the nation as a victim of atomic bombs, carpet bombing, and the Red Army's atrocities and stresses the need to regain national pride hurt by defeat in war, and to shake the nation free of a widespread guilty consciousness imposed by the Tokyo trials. Korean history textbooks, meanwhile, tend to categorize all Japanese people as collectively guilty of Japan's wartime aggression and atrocities, and all Koreans as the hereditary victims of Japanese colonialism.[26] They are both competing to position themselves as victims in history. Victimhood nationalism justifies nationalism, and in fact, by going backward in time, some victimizers transform themselves into victims, wholly oblivious to the irony. Regardless of whether one occupies the position of victim or victimizer, the nation as historical subject dominates both sets of textbooks. It feeds the essentialism of the nation and thus constitutes the backbone of national history.

Originism: We Were First, You After Me

Despite its insistence on the nation as an eternal entity, even the primordialist concept cannot avoid the question of the origins of the nation. In contrast to the modernist concept, which is satisfied with locating the origins of the (proto-) nation-state in relatively recent history, the primordialist concept traces the nation's origin back to the earliest possible moment in time, or even to immemorial time. Thus the originism of the primordialist concept tends to mean "the older, the better." The discourse of national origins, often assisted by historical anthropology, stresses ethnic homogeneity or even purity and cultivates a disinclination for ethnic mixing. The first edition of the *New History Textbook* describes "Jōmon pottery," produced 16,500 years ago, as the oldest pottery in the world.[27] While the second edition revises this claim to read "one of the oldest,"[28] this syndrome of claiming things to be "the oldest in the world" lingers on in a few other examples, such as the five-story wooden pagoda of Hōryū Temple. In fact, both editions put an emphasis on the historical investigation of origin in their introductions. The broad usage of words such as "Japanese" and "Japanese culture" in the ancient past makes it quite natural and plausible to seek the origins of the nation in the immemorial past—what I will call "originism."

This tenacious originism conceals a secret of national history as "a curious inversion of a conventional genealogy" by starting from the "originary present."[29] The originism of the primordialist concept of nation is much more stubborn than that of the modernist concept: the primordialist regards the nation as an ancient community. Insofar as it remains a patriotic duty for historians to discover the ancient history of the nation, the tenet of "the older, the better" takes on great importance. Once attached to originism, the reciprocal transcultural exchange is denied. Rather, culture is presupposed to flow from the developed to the underdeveloped—a cultural osmosis. In this way, originism conjures up the past glory of "our own national culture" and gives rise to "monumental history."

Korean history textbooks, which share the primordialist view with the *New History Textbook* in Japan, are second to none in their originism. They trace the world's first movable metal type to thirteenth-century Korea.[30] One of the key assertions in the *New History Textbook* against which Korean historians have argued is the sentence "Silla and Baekje paid tribute to Japan." Korean historians denounced this claim, because they believed the highly developed Korean culture of the time to have diffused to the islands of Japan. The Korean high school history textbook devotes two pages to cultural diffusion from the kingdoms of Baekje and Silla to the Japanese isles under the heading "Our Culture Went to Japan." This section enumerates cultural items that Japan received from Korea: Chinese literature,

Confucianism, Buddhist architecture, and sculptures (such as the medi-tating half-seated Maitreya figure of Horyū Temple), medicine, mural paintings, shipbuilding, music, and many more.[31] It reads like a Korean ver-sion of the famous historicist motto of "first in Europe, then elsewhere" coined by Dipesh Chakrabarty.

The *New History Textbook*, on the other hand, interprets this "cultural diffusion" as Baekje paying tribute to the Yamato kingdom, or as a result of Japanese intervention in the politics of the Korean peninsula. A few sen-tences in the Japanese textbook make it explicit that this culture origi-nated not in Korea but in China.[32] The textbook also stresses the contact between China and Japan, often skipping over Korea entirely. This narra-tive is in tune with the Okakura Tenshin's (1862–1913) thesis that the Japa-nese nation constructed its own art by appropriating the quintessence of Oriental art of China and India. Even though he could not deny the imported goods or artistic influence from China and India, he could glorify Japanese art by stressing its ability to develop the national culture by appropriat-ing the foreign culture. Thus Oriental art could be represented by neither China nor India, but only by Japanese art.[33] Each textbook emphasizes its nation's uniqueness, superiority, and eternalness by comparison with "inferior" countries. In this way, the two rival books strengthen their ori-gin stories through the primordialist concept of the nation.

The originist stance assumes national culture as "the Real." In this sense, "What is the essence of the national culture?" is a rhetorical question. Living culture—how people produce, consume, and interact on multiple levels in their everyday lives—is replaced by the fossilized essence of the so-called national culture. The particularity discourse helps to construct national culture by insisting on the peculiarity of the national experience. The narrative of national history cofigures the particular and the univer-sal in order to distill the peculiar essence of national culture. Where China occupied the position of the universal in premodern East Asia, today Europe offers the hegemonic mirror by which both Japanese and Korean national cultures judge their progress and see their future. The discourse of national culture in history textbooks essentializes not only their own national cultures but also the national cultures of Others, which in turn results in cultural reinforcement of national essentialism. Originism emphasizes ancestry while simultaneously assuming the perpetuity of nationality to be self-evident. The synchrony of the historical roots and ahistorical perpetuity in originism shows that it is a bid for immortality and an insistence that people be mindful of their ethnic origin.[34] Nation is immemorial and immortal.

Autochthonism: Lest Their History Step Into "Our Own Territory"

In the primordialist concept of nation, even prehistory can be an instrument of modern territorial claims. Contemporary political claims to disputed territory tend to derive from primordialist viewpoints and are likely to be linked to historical controversies. This explains why autochthonism prevails in East Asian and East European historiography, rather than historiography based on the modernist concept of nation. Autochthonism tends either to ignore "foreign" enclaves or to extend the reaches of "native" territory as far as possible. National archaeological research, meanwhile, reinforces this autochthonism. Very often nationalized archaeology is also linked with historical anthropology, which further contributes to the national mythos by distinguishing between "foreign blood" and "unmixed peoples."[35] Supported by "objective and scientific" archaeological excavations, autochthonism wears the material authenticity. In contrast to words, things do not lie.

In East Asia, autochthonism is most palpable in the controversy between Korean and Japanese historians over the alleged Japanese commandery, Imna, established in the southeastern part of the Korean peninsula around the fourth century CE. The *New History Textbook* states that the "Yamato royal court led its army cross the sea to Chosŏn and established a military base in Imna—on the southern coast of the Korean peninsula—in the late fourth century." The Yamato army, the text continues, helped Silla and Baekje to fight against the army of Goguryeo, and, in return for Japanese assistance, Silla and Baekje paid tribute to Yamato.[36] Leaving aside the question of factual accuracy, this controversy reveals the deep roots of nationalist politics. "Fact or fake," the Imna commandery originated in the discursive process of making China and Chosŏn/Korea Japan's "Orient." Japanese colonial historians constructed the account of the Japanese commandery of Imna to justify Japanese colonial rule over Korea in the twentieth century. Korean historians, wise to the political implications, have reacted vehemently to the Japanese claims of the Imna commandery, criticizing it as neocolonialist history. As a result, Imna exists only in Japanese history textbooks.

The controversy over the Imna commandery brings to mind the dispute between German *Ostforschung* (Eastern studies) and Polish *Studia Zachodnie* (Western studies). *Ostforschung* has interpreted the medieval German settlement in East Central Europe as Germany's right to "land and rule" and used it to justify the so-called civilizing mission of the *Kulturvölker* (cultural nations) over the barbarians.[37] The Polish response emphasized the cultural continuity and Slavic nature of the "Regained Land" (*ziemia odzyskana*)—Western lands of former East Prussian territory newly acquired after World War II.[38] Whereas German *Ostforschung* represents the view of German Orientalism vis-à-vis the Slavic East, Polish *Studia Zachodnie* is deeply imbued with *Drang nach Westen* (drive toward the West). The heuristic congruence between East Asian and Eastern European nationalist historiography originates in the autochthonism immanent in the national history paradigm.

Korean historians do not stop at denying the existence of an ancient Japanese enclave in "our own territory." Confronting the undeniable fact of "Han commanderies" in the north of the Korean peninsula, Korean history textbooks typically mention them in just one vague sentence.[39] Never using the word "commandery," the national history textbook in Korea merely mentions the fall of Old Chosŏn in 108 BCE, which is said to have extended into Manchuria as far as the lower reaches of the Liao River. Regardless of historical facts, Korean history textbooks do not acknowledge foreign enclaves on the Korean peninsula. The autochthonism undergirding these histories never makes room for understanding the "Han commanderies" as a historical moment at which a foreign culture was introduced to the Korean peninsula; rather, it finds in the commanderies a shameful proto-colonial relationship between Han-China and Chosŏn-Korea. Nationalist presentism overwhelms historical contextualism in this debate.

Autochthonism also dominated the controversy between Korean and Chinese historians over the historical sovereignty of Goguryeo.[40] The dispute broke out when Chinese historians began to insist that Goguryeo was part of the "local history" of the ancient Chinese state and attempted to incorporate it into Chinese national history. That view reflected a fundamental principle of Chinese national history, which defines the present territory of the People's Republic (as well as some currently disputed territories) and the fifty-six ethnic groups who inhabit it as China's historical space. This approach contrasts sharply with traditional Chinese perception of minorities as barbarians. The barbarian Others of traditional historiography have suddenly become "we-Chinese" in contemporary Chinese historiography, which integrates national minorities in border areas into the history of a unitary and centralized multinational state. Goguryeo's shift from the barbarian Other to China's "own history" is attributable to the magic of "national history." The retrospective genealogy inherent in the national history paradigm looks back on the premodern past with the multinational state of the PRC as the reference.

In Korean history textbooks, Goguryeo belongs to Korean history from the perspective of historical origin, not territorial integrity within the present borders. They trace the descent of the Goguryeo people to the Yemaek people of Buyeo, an ancient tribe in the northern part of Korean peninsula and Manchuria. Korean history textbooks emphasize that the Korean peninsula and Manchuria-Liaodong have been closely linked to each other in cultural and physical terms since the prehistoric era. Some ultranationalist Koreans, under the slogan of "reclamation of old territories," argue that Korean state sovereignty should include Manchuria. This desire for sovereignty manifests in a "drive toward Manchuria"—the Korean version of the Polish "drive toward the West." While China defines the present political border of the PRC as its historical domain, Korea tends to look back to prehistoric times for historical legitimacy in the ongoing historical disputes over Goguryeo between China and Korea.

Neither historiography makes room for the Khitan, Mohe, Jurchen, and other nomadic peoples who also established polities or states within these regions, such as Liao and Jin in present-day Manchuria. Their traces are suppressed, ignored, and erased in the service of the national narratives of China or Korea. At best, histories of these nationalities are marginalized in the teleologies of the national histories of the PRC or the Republic of Korea. In Chinese history textbooks, the states established by the Jurchen and other steppe peoples serve principally to bolster the grand narrative of "ethnic integration" and "national unification." The paradigm of national history thereby, assimilates plural "histories" into a single "History." National history cannot but be violent as well as shameless. The controversy over Goguryeo between Korean and Chinese historians shows that the autochthonism is not peculiar to the primordialist ethnic nation but is equally central in the modernist political nation.

Unpredictable Past

History textbooks in East Asia are hotbeds for cultivating nationalism or dense minefields for historians. The anachronisms inherent in projecting the modern nation-state onto the remote past do not appear to matter. By disseminating the idea that a modern nation-state is a natural entity with a destiny dating from the immemorial past, these anachronisms strengthen national legitimacy; indeed, in the presentist cause of serving the nation, such anachronisms are positively encouraged. The past seems unpredictable in the face of nationalist historians who pompously alter the past for the nation. In East Asia, it is difficult to predict the future more than the past, which is subject to a constant change according the political manipulation. Even "God" cannot alter the "Past." But historians can because the past comes to us as perceived reality. That is why identifying and analyzing cognitive frameworks is more important than questions of "right" or "wrong" regarding facts in the analysis of history textbooks. In other words, one should ask the phenomenological question before the positivist question.

Finally, it should be remembered that the ruling regime's speech rather than scholars' speech dominates history textbooks in East Asia, primarily due to government screening systems. The result of a regime-dominated narrative is a nationalist phenomenology, which sets the nationalist episteme as the cognitive norm by which historical facts are constructed. Viewed from the perspective of this nationalist phenomenology, the antagonistic complicity of national histories, long hidden behind a thick screen of vociferous disputes, controversies, and arguments over the past, is revealed. I would hope that the past is not entirely unpredictable thanks to critical history. Only through deconstructing the national history paradigm can a path be cleared for the development of a mature culture of understanding the past of East Asia as a transnational history. I never mean a return to naïve positivism; instead, it demands the deconstruction of the nationalist myth wearing the positivist costume. Perhaps the greatest myth in modern historiography has been the claim of nationalist historians to the "scientific status" of their knowledge.

Notes

1. Currently in Korea, history textbooks are no longer state monopolized but are still subject to screening by the Ministry of Education, as they are in Japan.
2. Kurota Katsuhiro, "教科書が教えている歴史19/20, 韓国11/12" [History as taught by textbooks 19/20, Korea 11/12], *Sankei shinbun*, June 25 and 26, 2001.
3. Preface to *A New History Textbook*, first ed., Korean translation by the Korean Committee for Correcting Distortions of Japanese History Textbook (Seoul, 2000), 7.
4. For the antagonistic complicity of conflicting nationalisms in Northeast Asia, see Lim Jie-Hyun, 적대적 공범자들 [Antagonistic accomplices] (Seoul: Sonamu, 2005); Lim Jie-Hyun, "朝鮮半島の民族主義と權力の言說" [Korean nationalism and the power discourse], trans. Itagaki Ryuta, *Gendaishiso* 28 (June 2000): 126–44.
5. "Correcting History," Northeast Asian History Foundation, accessed February 6, 2020, https://www.nahf.or.kr/eng/gnb02/snb01.do.
6. Indeed, the basic concepts that anticolonial movements have adopted were often the discursive products of imperialist cultures. See Ashis Nandy, *The Intimate Enemy: Loss and Recovery of Self Under Colonialism* (Delhi: Oxford University Press, 1983).
7. Kuksa p'yŏnch'an wiwonhoe·Kukjŏng tosŏ p'yŏnch'an wiwonhoe, 고등학교 국사 [National history textbook in high school] (Seoul: Kyohaksa, 2002), 2.
8. 고등학교 국사, 12.
9. Ernest Gellner, *Nationalism* (New York: New York University Press, 1997), 74.
10. Partha Chatterjee, "Whose Imagined Community?," in *Mapping the Nation*, ed. Gopal Balakrishnan and Benedict Anderson (London: Verso, 1996), 214–25.
11. See Kim Han-gyu, "History of 'a Single Ethnic Nation' and History of a 'Multi-Ethnic Nation'—Historical Descriptions and Understanding of South Korean and Chinese Textbooks," in *Struggle of Memory and History*, special edition of *Dangdae Bipyeong* (Seoul: Samin, 2002), 100–112.
12. Miroslav Hroch, epilogue to *Nationalism and Archeology in Europe*, ed. M. Diaz-Andreu and T. Champion (London: UCL Press, 1996), 295.
13. *A New History Textbook*, second ed., Korean translation by Korean Committee for Correcting Distortions of Japanese History Textbooks (Seoul: Asia Peace and History Education Network, 2005), 7 (limited edition, not for public distribution).
14. *A New History Textbook*, 227.
15. Ernest Renan, "Qu'est-ce qu'une nation? Conférence faite en Sorbonne, le 11 Mars 1882," in *Œuvres complètes de Ernest Renan*, vol. 1, ed. Henriette Psichari (Paris: Calmann-Lévy, 1947), 904.
16. Tessa Morris-Suzuki, "근대 일본의 국경 만들기 - 일본사 속의 변경과 국가.국민 이미지" [An integral part of our national territory: Frontiers and the image of nation in

Japanese history], in 근대의 국경, 역사의 변경 [Frontiers or borders?], ed. Lim Jie-Hyun (Seoul: Humanist, 2004), 198ff.

17. 중학교 국사 [National history textbook in middle school], 11. The official historiography in North Korea is not that different from the South Korean imagination of the ancient. Party historiography in North Korea asserts that Paleolithic inhabitants evolved into contemporary Koreans without any ethnic or cultural rupture. See chapter 8.

18. Thongchai Winichakul, *Siam-Mapped: A History of the Geo-Body of a Nation*, (Honolulu: University of Hawai'i Press, 1994). The geo-body of a nation is a "man-made territorial definition which creates effects by classifying, communicating, and enforcement on people, things, relationships."

19. William A. Callahan, *Sensible Politics: Visualizing International Relations* (Oxford: Oxford University Press, 2020), 148–49.

20. Malcom Anderson, *Frontiers: Territory and State Formation in the Modern World* (Cambridge, Mass.: Polity Press, 1996), 1.

21. Michael Hardt and Antonio Negri, *Empire* (Cambridge, Mass.: Harvard University Press, 2000), 93–113, 134.

22. See chapter 6.

23. Raphael Samuel, *Patriotism: The Making and Unmaking of British National Identity*, vol. 1 (London: Routledge, 1989), xi.

24. 중학교 국사, 111ff., 147–49; 고등학교 국사, 90ff.

25. For hereditary victimhood, see Zygmunt Bauman, "The Holocaust's Life as a Ghost," *Tikkun* 13, no. 4 (1998): 33–38; Bauman, "Afterword to the 2000 Edition," *Modernity and the Holocaust* (Ithaca, N.Y.: Cornell University Press, 2000), 236.

26. See *A New History Textbook*, first ed., 214ff; 중학교 국사, 254–62. The discrepancy some readers may observe between the 2000 publication date of this textbook and the controversy arising in 2001 is attributable to the fact that the version of the textbook cited here is an unofficial Korean translation of the original *Tsukuru-kai* draft submitted for inspection to Japan's Ministry of Education, not a translation of the published textbook. The unofficial translation was published in 2000; the *New History Textbook* was not published in Japan until 2001.

27. *A New History Textbook*, first ed., 24.

28. *A New History Textbook*, second ed., 18.

29. Benedict Anderson, *Imagined Communities* (London: Verso, 1991), 205.

30. 중학교 국사, 279.

31. 고등학교 국사, 267ff.

32. *A New History Textbook*, second ed., 33.

33. Takagi Hiroshi, "일본 미술사와 조선 미술사의 성립 [Formation of Japanese history of art and Korean history of art]," in 국사의 신화를 넘어서 [Beyond the myth of national history], ed. Lim Jie-Hyun and Lee Sungsi (Seoul: Humanist, 2004), 171–73.

34. Timothy Brennan, "The National Longing for Form," in *Nation and Narration*, ed. Homi K. Bhabha (London: RKP, 1990), 51

35. Hroch, epilogue to *Nationalism and Archeology in Europe*, 295.

36. *A New History Textbook*, first ed., 37–40.

37. Jan M. Piskorski, "After Occidentalism: The Third Europe Writes Its Own History," in *Historiographical Approaches to Medieval Colonisation of East Central Europe*, ed. Piskorski (New York: Columbia University Press, 2002), 7–23.

38. Włodzimierz Rączkowski, "Drang nach Westen? Polish Archaeology and National Identity," in Diaz-Andreu and Champion, *Nationalism and Archaeology in Europe*, 208–13.

39. 중학교 국사, 19

40. Jie-Hyun Lim, "Rescuing Koguryŏ from the Nation," in *Nationalism and History Textbooks in Asia and Europe*, ed. Academy of Korean Studies (Seoul: Editor, 2005), 66–83.

8

Nationalist Messages in Socialist Code

On the Party Historiography in People's Poland and North Korea

Alien Socialism Versus Ethno-nationalism

The fall of the communist regime in Eastern Europe in 1989 shed fresh light on the ideological topology of the twentieth century. Conventional wisdom holds that after the fall, nationalism replaced failed socialist utopias and triggered the eruption of many different old-fashioned patriotisms, revivalist messianisms, conservative nationalisms, and xenophobia. Historically speaking, communist regimes had long leaned on nationalist pillars for legitimacy. Even before the fall, nationalism had been a dominant and official part of government; state propaganda celebrated socialist patriotism and proletarian internationalism. As Adam Michnik writes, "Nationalism was the last word of Communism. A final attempt to find a social basis for dictatorship."[1] However, nationalism was neither the last word nor the final attempt of the communist regime. Nationalism hovered over Eastern Europe in the initial period of building the Stalinist regime there. For instance, the Polish Communist Party shared the political goal of an ethnically pure state with the fascist nationalism of the *Narodowa Demokracja* (National Democracy).

"Nomenklatura-apparatchik nationalism" as the official nationalism, supported by party leaders and cadres, was a widespread phenomenon in Eastern European communist regimes.[2] Especially since de-Stalinization in 1956, one can witness the nationalist turn under the banner of "our own road to socialism" in Eastern Europe by and large. While intertwined with the "Great Russian Patriotism" in the Soviet Union, Stalinism meant the proletarian internationalism under Russian hegemony in Eastern Europe. Thus de-Stalinization of 1956 signaled a shift from national nihilism to national communism, alongside a mild democratization, in the Eastern European communist regime. The Polish October in 1956 represents that shift.[3] A serious intraparty factional struggle broke out during the shift to national communism, which raised the Jewish question as a political instrument.[4] Anti-Semitism had been affiliated with nomenklatura-apparatchik nationalism in the Eastern European communist regime. Grassroots anti-Semitism among the communist rank-and-file can be traced back to the interwar period.[5]

Nomenklatura-apparatchik nationalism has been closely tied to the ethno-nationalization of communism, especially since the Polish October of 1956. Communist leaders in People's Poland often used the rhetorical and emotional leverage of nationalism to compensate for their lack of political legitimacy. Similarly, anticommunist leaders used national symbolism to mobilize people, tapping into the deeply entrenched grassroots ethno-nationalism sowed by party propaganda. An antiquated understanding of nation thus bound together opposing political camps in Poland. The socialist ideal of ethical and political unity of society unintentionally reinforced the primordialist concept of the nation; that is, the nation as an organic community and even a family. Fulfilling the dream of Polish nationalists, Polish communists made Poland an ethnically homogeneous nation-state after the war. The political ethics of the primordialist nation asserts that a nation should determine its own fate directly and unanimously.[6]

Nomenklatura-apparatchik nationalism was not the only form of nationalism adopting the primordialist concept of the nation. Political opposition to communism often took expression in popular nationalism. While nomenklatura-apparatchik nationalism supported national communism, popular nationalism considered communism to be an alien, foreign ideology forced on people by the Soviet Union. From their viewpoint, the communist regime attempted to "nationalize" and monopolize history and forcefully reprogrammed popular memory according to the needs of official nationalism. Both the communist government and the opposition believed that all individual and group interests should be subordinate to the nation. They both believed in realizing the "nation's will" and "collective identity." The moral code of national collectivity made the people subject to arbitrary political power under the guise of the "nation's will." The "Red Court" historiography of the existing socialist regime and the nationalist historiography of the anticommunist opposition in Poland shared a nationalist discourse. The historiography of the Polish United Workers' Party (PZPR) shows how they encoded nationalism in the socialist jargon. PZPR historiography constantly floundered between proletarian internationalism in form and official nationalism in content. The oxymoron of communist nationalism was its primary symptom.

North Korean Communist Party historiography represents the extreme version of the nomenklatura-apparatchik nationalism. Combined with its embrace of the primordialist nation based on *Jucheism*, party historiography in North Korea unabashedly displayed its naked nationalist biases. North Korea's official historiography of ancient history found echoes in the ultra-right-wing nationalist historiography of South Korea. The party historiography in the North and ultra-right-wing nationalist history in the South share the ultranationalist discourse and imaginary transcending the oppositional ideological constellation of the Cold War. What makes North Korean historiography worse is its personification of nationalism, with the Great Leader Kim Il-sŏng as the incarnation of the nation. For its emphasis on *Juche*, which literally means "subjectivity" that cherishes human beings' agency in making history and national "sovereignty" in international relationships, North Korean Party historiography embraced a grain of Marxist voluntarism. Combined with the extreme form of personal cult, however, the Marxist voluntarism became subject to the mythologized history of the Great Leader, especially in the twentieth-century history of the anticolonial resistance movement.

Despite all the radical historical discontinuities of the twentieth century, from interwar authoritarian nationalism, to nomenklatura-apparatchik nationalism, to postcommunist nationalism, nationalism never lost the "war of position" to either liberalism or socialism. Sometimes nationalism lost the "war of maneuver," but its hegemonic position was rarely questioned. In this chapter, I will examine the interplay of the official and vernacular nationalisms in People's Poland and North Korea, with a focus on historiography. A critical juxtaposition of the official party historiographies reveals that nationalism was foundational to both communist regimes. Nationalist communism made every effort to nationalize more than revolutionize the working masses. Anticommunist historiography in the oppositional popular nationalism was partly an offspring of nomenklatura-apparatchik nationalism.

People's Poland Between Proletarian Internationalism and Ethno-nationalism

The Congress of Polish Sciences in 1950 opened a new era in the PZPR's official historical interpretations. The congress rebuked interwar historiography as "an ideological endorsement of the mad and criminal policies of Polish fascism." The political shift of the official historiography in communist Poland was more radicalized in the first conference on historical methodology in Otwock (December 28, 1951–January 12, 1952), which marked the Marxist turn of Polish historiography. In his opening address, Tadeusz Manteuffel emphasized historical science's role in transforming the bourgeois nation into a socialist nation. Historians had to adopt Marxist methodology to serve that cause. While he accused the Second Republic of Polish imperialism, Manteuffel identified Ludwik Waryński's "Proletaryat," Rosa Luxemburg's "Social Democratic Party of the Kingdom of Poland and Lithuania (SDKPiL)," and "the Polish Communist Party (KPP)" as key successors of the legitimate revolutionary tradition in Poland.[7] This effort severed postwar Marxist historiography from the interwar period's nationalist historiography that accused the KPP of alienation from Polish society and nation, of alternatively being agents of the Soviets, the Jews, or the Freemasons.[8]

The Proletaryat, SDKPiL, and KPP were named the ideological heirs of proletarian internationalism, which emphasized the close collaboration between the Russian and Polish working classes for the Russian revolution. The Communist Party's omission of the Polish Socialist Party (PPS), the representative of the social patriotic tradition, was deliberate. In the following years, party historiography would deride the PPS for its anti-Bolshevism, reformism, revisionism, and petty-bourgeois nationalism. The PPS was even accused of spying on the labor and socialist movement for the propertied class. The USSR and the ruling Communist Party in

People's Poland regarded proletarian internationalism as an ideological weapon to counter anti-Russian sentiments among the Polish people. The official party historiography in People's Poland could not allow even for social patriotism, much less nationalist tradition. It was only after the de-Stalinization in October 1956 that the PPS-Lewica (left) was rehabilitated in the history of the socialist movement in Poland.

A schism was evident between the Red Court historiography and the grassroots memory, keeper of the private and collective memory of the Soviet-Polish War, the Molotov-Ribbentrop Pact, the deportation of Poles, and the Stalinist massacre of Polish Army officers in Katyń. To many Poles, "proletarian internationalism" implied nothing more than the curtailment of Poland's sovereignty within the Soviet bloc and erasure of the grassroots and vernacular memory of the Stalinist crime. Paradoxically, Stalinist historiography in People's Poland discreetly discouraged the study of SDKPiL leadership despite its staunch internationalism. Rosa Luxemburg's severe criticism of the Leninist theory of democratic centrism, national self-determination, and land reform policies countervailed the positive side of the SDKPiL's proletarian internationalism. Stalin's identification of Luxemburg as an enemy of Bolshevism in 1931 remained an unbreakable barrier.[9] Stalin eventually disbanded the party and purged most of the KPP leaders who lived in exile in the USSR. The leaderless party was then accused of Trotskyist deviations and finally dissolved by the Comintern in 1938.[10] The party line might have been right, but leaders were wrong.

However, Polish party historiography even in the Stalinist era was not free from nationalist influence. After World War II, Poland acquired the Western lands from defeated Germany. Polish archaeologists excavated western Poland to prove that the "Regained Land" (ziemia odzyskana) had been Polish since prehistoric times. Many traveling exhibitions on the "Regained Land" told of its Slavic origin story and its cultural continuity. The primary task of Polish archaeology immediately after the war was to prove the presence of Slavs between the Oder and the Bug since the second millennium BCE. This project diverted public attention away from the loss of eastern territory and stoked nationalist fervor against Germans as enemies of the Polish nation. Polish archaeology satisfied the PZPR's demand for Drang nach Westen (Drive toward the West).[11] Historical writings reinforced archaeological findings by emphasizing the destructive effects of the German interference in the Polish civilization of the "Regained Land."

The Red Court historiography in the Stalinist era straddled between internationalism and nationalism—international solidarity with the neighboring socialist nations and nationalist antipathy against the capitalist (West) Germany. Stalinist official historiography repeated the prewar KPP's denunciation of the PPS's social patriotism as the agency of the bourgeoisie contaminated by petty-bourgeois nationalism.[12] From the viewpoint of the vernacular memory constructed of anti-Russian sentiments, the Stalinist historiography of stubborn internationalism seemed to justify the anticommunist nationalists' blaming of the PZPR as "national traitors," "Russian spies," and "Jewish commies."[13] Amid de-Stalinization in the socialist ecumene, the Polish October in 1956 was a turning point in official party historiography. With the return of Władysław Gomułka, a proponent of the "Polish road to socialism," the political climate changed. Polish communists, thanks to Gomułka's resolute stand against Khrushchev's demands, unexpectedly found themselves leading the national liberation movement, or "progressive nationalism" (nacjonalizm postępowy).[14] In Antoni Czubiński's words, 1956 was a turning point in "nationalizing" communist Poland.[15]

The post-1956 historiography criticized Stalinist historiography for its exclusive emphasis on class struggle: if a singular focus on the nation results in bourgeois nationalism, a preoccupation with class leads to national nihilism.[16] No longer afraid of being charged with "rightist nationalist deviation," Polish historians openly condemned Stalinist historiography for its negativity about the nation's past. The reestablished balance between class and nation in historical writing made it possible to positively assess the interwar statehood and national uprisings of the nineteenth century. Rightist political camps such as the Peasant Party, National Democracy, and Christian Democracy were no longer taboo in the post-October historiography.[17] While these rightist currents were still subject to a harsh criticism, the enforced silence about them was gone. The lifting of the taboo against the nationalist current opened the doors to new historical research. The liberalization of historical studies was highlighted in a bold assertion that the SDKPiL and KPP as the politically legitimate predecessors of the PZPR have continually had difficulties in appealing to the working masses because of their failure to understand the national question in Poland.[18] Despite its reservations about nationalism, this movement directly challenged the official historiography that gave historical legitimacy exclusively to the internationalist SDKPiL and KPP.

Even before the Polish October, Stalinist historiography had come under critique, with the focus primarily on the Central Committee's Department of Party History (Wydział Historii Partii, WHP). In June 1956 party historians adopted a resolution, "On the Most Urgent Tasks of the Party in History." The WHP director, Tadeusz Daniszewski, had to make a public self-criticism that party historians had overlooked the necessity of extensive scholarly research and simplified complex problems. Moreover, the historical rehabilitation of the KPP at the Twentieth Congress of the Communist Party of the Soviet Union (CPSU) signaled the loosening of political control over modern and contemporary history writings.[19] Why Stalin dissolved the KPP remains unexplained. Still erased from the official record are KPP leaders' criticisms of Stalin and Zinoviev, criticisms that resonated with Rosa Luxemburg's critique of Lenin. The PPS for its social patriotism, not the KPP for its proletarian internationalism, drew the most attention from Polish historians encouraged by the limited democratization of the party after the Polish October.[20] The nationalism that erupted from the bottom up could not remain unbridled. It had to be brought into the ideological orbit of the party.

Dashing expectations that the Polish October of 1956 would bring about academic freedom, what freedom that was gained proved to be very marginal. The Stalinist historiography was replaced—with nothing plural but the Leninist one. Leninism remained inviolable, and the only allowable yardstick to measure and judge the socialist past. Within these strictures, the criticism of the Leninist ultracentralist party principle by the SDKPiL led by Rosa Luxemburg could not be brought to light. Instead, the PPS-left was now accepted as legitimate, in two ways. First, the PPS theoretician Julian Hochfeld defined the PPS-left as a tribune of "open Marxism," a characterization that meshed with the evolving self-conceptualization of the PZPR.[21] Second, the PPS-left was now seen as having properly grasped the dialectical interplay of social revolution and national liberation, proletarian internationalism and social patriotism. The second point fit well with the claims of Gomułka, who proclaimed a struggle against national nihilism and cosmopolitanism.[22] Moreover, the PPS-left's political and theoretical stance was resonant with Lenin's criticism of Rosa Luxemburg regarding the national question.

The Polish October changed the political climate in favor of PPS studies in social patriotism. Henryk Jabłoński, a founding member of the Marxist

Historians' Association, organized a seminar for graduate students and brought in specialists on the history of the PPS. In 1958 the Institute of Party History (Zakład Historii Partii, ZHP) held a historians' forum on PPS studies and subsequently published a collection of materials and documents on the PPS-left in 1961. The discussion on the pilot edition of the third volume of the History of Poland prepared by the History Institute of the Polish Academy of Sciences was a milestone in the interpretation of PPS history.[23] The discussion on the PPS-left organized by the ZHP on December 12, 1961, confirmed the new interpretation of the PPS. Seminar participants criticized the historical reductionism that automatically treated social patriotism and the slogan of independence as reformist deviation. This moment conferred a historical legitimacy on the PPS-left that combined the slogan of independence with socialist revolution.[24] Concerning party history, however, there was very little room for Polish Marxist historians to maneuver ideologically. The PPS-left's social patriotism was the upper limit that the party leadership could countenance. Political conditions could not yet allow the study of the PPS-right and its anti-Bolshevism that prioritized an independent Poland over proletarian internationalism.

Focusing on nationalism within the history of the socialist movement was possible only insofar as it celebrated the proletarian internationalism, or at least the Soviet Union's hegemony disguised in the garb of proletarian internationalism. By stressing the Bolshevik hegemony in the Comintern, international communist historiography reduced the SDKPiL and KPP to satellite organizations of the Bolshevik Party. Both Rosa Luxemburg's criticism of Leninist principles and the KPP's dissident role within the Comintern were ignored.[25] Polish historians faced the dire predicament of reconciling the surging patriotic tide with proletarian internationalism. They solved it through complacency by declaring that social patriotism could be combined with proletarian internationalism. They distinguished sharply between internationalism and cosmopolitanism—whereas the former could be reconciled with socialist patriotism, the latter implied national nihilism. The traditional Polish socialist dichotomy between "good patriotism" and "bad nationalism," made by Bolesław Limanowski, was the last exit from that dilemma.

Forced to compromise with the distorted proletarian internationalism enforced by the Soviet Union, the patriotic tide nonetheless kept rising in historians' circles throughout the 1960s. Zbigniew Załuski asserted that the Marxist historiography in postwar Poland had failed to produce a new socialist patriotism. He lamented that its denigration of the national past bred national nihilism among the postwar generation. The party's daily newspaper dismissed his argument as incompatible with communist ideology, but it could not hold back the rising nationalist tide.[26] Following Załuski's book, a similar concern about the grave consequences wrought by national nihilism and pessimism was voiced in the Ninth Congress of Polish Historians in Lublin in 1963. Thanks to the rising patriotic mood, Polish historians could comprehensively rehabilitate the nineteenth-century national uprisings led by the patriotic feudal nobility and gentry, who were mocked by peasant-serfs who suffered from the yoke of feudalism. The class-centric interpretation began to fade away.

In the official party historiography, the historical and ideological legitimacy of the SDKPiL and KPP's revolutionary internationalism remained intact. Proletarian internationalism, an ideological shield of the Soviet Union's hegemony in the Eastern bloc, was the sacred and inviolable guide for historical interpretations. Despite that, the PZPR deployed outright nationalist propaganda to mobilize popular support from the working masses indifferent to the socialist cause. Political posters featured the most popular slogans coined by the party propaganda machine: "Party with the nation, for the nation"; "unified will—well-being for our nation, for our fatherland"; "Party with the nation, the nation with party"; "Our labor is the greatest resource of the nation"; "Young ones, the future of our nation with the party"; "The defender and builder of the fatherland."[27] These posters beat the drum for nation, not class. The nationalist discourse had supplanted the socialist one in party propaganda. Party ideologues confronted a "mission impossible": how to simultaneously represent proletarian internationalism and official nationalism.

That dilemma deepened with the advent of General Moczar's faction in the PZPR's platform. Moczar's faction developed a nomenklatura-apparatchik nationalism that legitimized the old idea of the nation as the supreme moral cause, as Roman Dmowski, an ultranationalist in the interwar Poland, had preached. Alluding to the national communism purged of Soviet and Jewish contamination, the nationalist faction attacked both revisionists and Jewish members for the "rootless cosmopolitanism."[28] The anti-Zionist campaign, initiated by Communist Parties of the Soviet bloc immediately after the third Israeli-Arab War in 1967, signaled the nationalist turn. The grotesque anti-Semitic campaign led by Moczar's people was the joint product of hard-line communism and primitive nationalism. Patriotism provided cover, allowing them to disguise themselves as "good" patriots against the bad bourgeois nationalists.[29] The upsurge of the nationalist faction in party leadership made a deep impact on official party historiography. The controversy over so-called objective patriotism is a good indication of this.

The discussion organized by the editorial board of Z Pola Walki in 1970, under the title of "Internationalism-Patriotism-Nationalism in the History of the Polish Labor Movement," sparked controversy. In his speech, Stanisław Wroński declared that proletarian internationalism should be tuned to historical conditions. He asked how today's Marxists could reinterpret the purpose of contemporary internationalism. His suggestion found echoes in some participants' arguments that Marxist internationalism could be reconciled with social patriotism of workers and peasants, but not with the bourgeois nationalism. Based on this proposition, they paid attention, not to the traditional dichotomy between the irredentist PPS and the internationalist SDKPiL, but to the schism on the national question within the SDKPiL. They tried to identify the SDKPiL's patriotic faction as opposed to Rosa Luxemburgist national nihilism. Verification of the existence of this patriotic group within the SDKPiL would solve in one stroke the dilemma of reconciling patriotism with proletarian internationalism. Ultimately, they could not convince other participants of their thesis due to the lack of historical evidence.[30] When Aleksander Kochański published a new study on the SDKPiL in 1971, the controversy stepped into the second phase. In the conclusion, Kochański proposed a thesis of "objective patriotism." He meant that the SDKPiL objectively contributed to the independence of Poland despite its programmatic negation of the PPS's slogan of independence.[31]

Kochański's thesis was showered immediately with sharp criticism. His critics pointed out that Kochański had disregarded the patriotic current, represented by Julian Marchlewski and Cezaryna Wojnarowska, within the SDKPiL. Norbert Michta, who was the deputy director of the military Institute of History (WIH) and the central political committee of the Polish Army (GZP WP), was a key critic. He argued that Kochański overestimated the role of Rosa Luxemburg and disregarded the patriotic faction who opposed her. Michta insisted Luxemburg was just a theoretician and therefore played no vital role in party activities and management of the SDKPiL. In Michta's analysis, Julian Marchlewski and Cezaryna Wojnarowska, who were key members of patriotic internationalism, actually led the SDKPiL.[32] The dividing line between the so-called patriotic internationalists and the alleged "nonpatriotic cosmopolitans" within SDKPiL tracks with the ethnic divide between Polish members and Jewish members. As deputy director of the military institute of history and a core member of General Moczar's faction, Nobert Michta represented the anti-Zionist current of the partisan national communists. In that conspicuous way, anti-Semitism infiltrated official Communist Party historiography in the name of patriotic internationalism. This weird anti-Semitism provided an exit from the dilemma of reconciling the nomenklatura-apparatchik nationalism of the PZPR with the enforced internationalism by the Soviet Union.

Despite the striking political contrast to party historiography, the opposition's anticommunist historiography in the 1980s deployed the similar nationalist discourse. Historico-political journalism of a particularly anticommunist nature cast the Polish socialist past in the image of the devil. Compared to party historiography, the opposition did not need the disguise of proletarian internationalism and therefore could support nationalism outright. Communist organizations were portrayed in this literature as "active in favor of, and using the money of, a foreign power that aimed at destroying the independence of Poland," or "a sign of the activity of international Jewish agents attempting to constrain Poles."[33] Gomułka's infamous speech on "the fifth column" on June 19, 1967, after the end of the Six-Day War in the Middle East, denouncing Jewish communists as Zionists loyal to Israel rather than to Poland, resonated with the epithet "national traitors," favored by anticommunist nationalism.[34] After the Polish October of 1956, and especially after the anti-Zionism campaign, principles of Marxism survived only in the domain of rhetoric. As the party as a whole degenerated into nationalism, party historiography became a nationalist historiography in the communist code.

Nationalist language persisted from the interwar period's anticommunist nationalist historiography, through the anti-Zionist party historiography, to contemporary postcommunist nationalism. Common rhetorical moves of branding political opponents as agents of foreign powers, or the plot of anti-Polish international Jews, and Freemasonry bound these political opponents in the historical imagination. The Solidarity press always stressed that the nation is the highest end of society. Their propaganda paid more attention to the nation's rights than to human rights. While Solidarity's collectivist thinking stemmed from its socialist populism, the ultrarightist nationalism was a precursor or continuation of nomenklatura-apparatchik nationalism.[35] The ultrarightists and communists shared a primordialist concept of nation, which fused the party's integral nationalism and the opposition's anticommunist nationalism. Some ex-communist historians crossed the Rubicon to join the rightist camp after the fall. Opportunistic careerism and ideological affinity led them to join the nationalist camp without hesitation.

North Korea: Extreme Voluntarism and Racist Nationalism

Vulgar Marxist dogmatism held sway over the historical sciences in North Korea from 1945 to 1955. When the Korean peninsula was liberated from Japanese colonial rule in 1945, North Korea had no higher educational institutions. One local historical museum and several poor local libraries were all that North Korea had when it came to academic resources. After the Korean Civil War in 1950–1953 destroyed the remaining academic infrastructure, it was almost impossible for North Koreans to develop their own historiography for a decade after 1945. Though a few Marxist historians who studied in prewar Japan led the new historical research in this decade, it was just a first step to the Marxist understanding of Korean history. They tried to mechanically apply the Stalinist version of historical materialism to Korean history. Under the slogan of "Learn from the experience of the Soviet Union," the eyes of North Korean Marxist historians were fixed on Moscow. De-Stalinization marked another turning point in North Korea. At the end of 1955, Kim Il-sŏng gave a famous speech criticizing the "dogmatism" and "formalism" in party propaganda. Kim blamed party ideologues for their unpatriotic adoration of the history of the USSR and for their relative indifference to the Korean national heritage. He deployed the term "toadyism subject to Great Powers" (事大主義), which was reminiscent of the feudal Yi dynasty's dependence on imperial China. He stressed the creative application of Marxism-Leninism to Korean conditions on the principle of sovereignty and subjectivity.[36]

Politically, Kim's speech signaled the purge of the pro-Soviet faction within the Chosŏn Worker's Party (CWP). Ideologically, his speech endorsed the nationalist turn of Marxism in the name of the creative application of Marxism-Leninism. This speech was a milestone in its implicit declaration of the end of pro-Soviet dependency, an inevitable result of the "occupation communism" after the Second World War. Officially, Kim Il-sŏng never denied proletarian internationalism. Just as Polish Communists tried to reconcile patriotism with internationalism, he asserted that patriotism was inseparable from internationalism. The dialectics of proletarian internationalism and social patriotism remained just a political tautology: "a person who does not love her/his fatherland cannot be true to internationalism, and a person who is not true to internationalism cannot love her/his fatherland and her/his people. A good patriot is an internationalist, and a true internationalist is a patriot."[37] In the same address, Kim confessed that "I am a nationalist as much as a communist," reflecting the predominant stance many Korean Marxists had held under Japanese colonial rule. In this address, Kim Il-sŏng stressed *Juche*, whose literal meaning connotes inward subjectivity and outward sovereignty.

The nationalist turn of Marxism had a significant impact on historiography in North Korea, as shown in two volumes of *A General History of Korea* published in 1956–1958. The Central Committee's Institute of History of the Party, established at the end of 1956, focused on the history of the Korean communist movement instead of the history of the Bolsheviks. The symposium of party historians organized by the Central Committee in 1958 trumpeted the open criticism of the national nihilism in historical writings. In 1959 the Institute of History in the Chosŏn Academy of Sciences published the "Ten-Year Plan of the Development of Science." It identified four major areas of study for historical inquiry: (1) the peaceful reunification of the fatherland and the building of socialism, (2) the revolutionary and patriotic tradition of the Korean people, (3) historical regularities of the social development in Korea, and (4) traditional national culture.[38] These four focal points of historical research underscored the importance of national history of Korea within the framework of revolutionary Marxism and the historical materialism of social developments.

The nationalist turn of official historiography in North Korea looks similar to that of Polish party historiography after Polish October of 1956.

The de-Stalinization process in the communist bloc after 1956 explains the otherwise unlikely convergence of the two nationalist turns in the socialist Global East, given the different political course of de-Stalinization in People's Poland and North Korea. If the political amalgam of reformist communism and patriotism dominated the Polish October, antireformist Stalinism in conjunction with native communism drove the nationalist turn in North Korea. Equipped with the nationalist metaphors, Kim Il-sŏng could win the factional power struggle against the reformist wing. Under the aegis of national sovereignty, Kim defended himself against the reformists' charge that he was creating a Stalinist personal cult. Kim counterattacked the reformist demand for a de-Stalinization antipersonal cult in North Korea as pro-Russian, reformist, nonpatriotic dependentism or toadyism. His counterattack received broad support from the native partisan communists, because the reformist wing comprised mainly pro-Soviet and pro-Chinese factions. Kim and the partisan communist bloc cast reformism as a foreign ideology, imported from the Khrushchev's Russia, that did not fit Korea. With its emphasis on the Korean way of Marxism, *Juche* was the key concept that could block reformist demands and justify Kim's personal cult. The reformist wing was branded as nonpatriotic revisionists, alien conspirators, and dogmatists and eventually was purged.[39]

The nationalist turn in official historiography encouraged research and writing on Korea as a national history. Kim Il-sŏng instructed party historians to find the "eternality of our history," "shining heritage of the national culture," and "decent patriotic tradition." With the full support of the regime, national history writing in North Korea blossomed and bore fruit in the 1960s. Even conservative South Korean historians admit that the quality of the historical research in North Korea was higher than that of South Korean historiography until the late 1960s. The most remarkable achievement of North Korean historiography in the 1960s was that a view of the autonomous and endogenous historical development replaced the Japanese colonialist view of the stagnancy of Korean history. North Korean national history rejected the applicability of the theory of the Asiatic mode of production to Korea. Viewed from the postcolonial perspective, the Asiatic mode of production employed red Orientalism to contrast the stagnancy and backwardness of precolonial Korea against the modernizing force of the Japanese colonialism. North Korean Marxist historiography instead traced a history of the indigenous capitalist development in the feudal Chosŏn and tried to find evidence of endogenously emerging capitalism in premodern Korea. Like other national histories of the non-Western peripheries, *Juche*'s extreme nationalist vision of Korean history was not exempt from the Marxist Eurocentrism framing West European history within a universal mode-of-production narrative, that is, the unilinear development model of world history.

Politically, the consolidation of the extreme nationalism of *Juche* as a ruling ideology strengthened the nationalization of historiography in North Korea. The *Juche* ideology intimated two points concerning historical studies. First, it was explicitly Marxist voluntarism premised on the belief that "man is the master and determinant of everything" and that "man is the social being with self-autonomy, creativity, and consciousness." In North Korea, where neither the economic nor political institution of modernity existed, the people were the only available resource for the development strategy. Invoking the people's will was a typical way of mobilizing the popular masses in Third World countries.[40] The people's will, more than means of production, was a driving force of history. Second, *Juche* emphasized the spirit of sovereignty, independence, and the national struggle against foreign invaders. In order not to be squeezed by the Sino-Soviet conflict, the North Korean regime had to stand on its own; it found an ideological solution in Jucheism. In 1967 the CWP proclaimed Jucheism as the ideological pillar of the party, and in 1970 the CWP replaced Marxism-Leninism with the Jucheism as the official Weltanschauung.[41]

The consolidation of Jucheism was another turning point in North Korean historiography. The nationalist historiography made way for a chauvinism based on blood and race. The blind patriotic turn was most explicit in the change of the concept of nation. Throughout the 1960s North Korean academics adhered to Stalin's definition of the nation as a community of people formed on the basis of a common language, territory, economic life, and psychological makeup. The *Dictionary of Philosophy*, published in North Korea in 1970, modified Stalin's conception slightly by adding "the eternal history of Korea," which suggested that the Korean nation had existed from the immemorial past. The North Korean version of the *Dictionary of Political Science* in 1973 included "common bloodline" in defining the nation. A shared economic life came to be replaced by a common bloodline in the North Korean conception of the nation. The biological primordialist view of a nation trumped the Marxist modernist concept. North Korean historiography regarded the nation as a nonhistorical being, which pressured historians into fulfilling their patriotic duty by discovering or inventing its glorious history from eternity.

The primordialist concept of nation nurtured originism, autochthonism, and anachronism. Originism led to a belief: "the older, the better."[42] The North Korean text *A General History of Chosŏn* assumes that Paleolithic humans began to inhabit the Korean peninsula about 600,000 to 400,000 BCE, while the South Korean *A New History of Korea* reckons it as some 40,000 to 50,000 years ago. North Korean historiography asserts that Paleolithic inhabitants evolved into the contemporary Koreans without any ethnic and cultural rupture, while the South Korean national history questions whether the Korean people of today are directly descended from Paleolithic inhabitants.[43] The Red Court historiography in North Korea argues that physical anthropology proves the uninterrupted bloodline of the Korean people. The archaeological fake of the tomb of Dangun, the alleged first ruler of Old Chosŏn in the thirty-first century BCE, can be understood in the same context. Thanks to originism, North Korean historiography places the Bronze Age and the Iron Age each about ten centuries earlier than South Korean historiography does. North Korean historiography maintains that a feudal society established itself in the Korean peninsula around the first century CE, maybe for the first time in world history.

Autochthonism, with its rejection of the existence of "foreign" enclaves in national spaces, is most palpable in historical writings about the Old Chosŏn, which lasted from about 800 to 108 BCE. Han China established three commanderies within the former domain of Old Chosŏn in 108 BCE and the next year completed the formation of the so-called Four Commanderies of Han by creating Hyŏndo in the Ye territory. The settled opinion in South Korea is that, except for Hyŏndo, which spanned the middle reaches of the Yalu and the Tongjia River basin, the other three commanderies were on the Korean peninsula. North Koreans argue that Nangnang, the most important commandery, was located in Manchuria. Archaeological excavation shows, however, that Nangnang's location is the Daedong River basin at Pyŏngyang. Against the archaeological evidence, North Koreans refuse to recognize the foreign enclaves in the Korean peninsula. As a result, North Korean historiography shows that the territory of Old Chosŏn reached Manchuria, and its center moved from the Daedong River basin to the lower reaches of Liao River.[44]

If Polish archaeology satisfied the PZPR's demand of *Drang nach Westen*, North Korean historiography fulfilled the dream of *Drang nach*

Manchuria. Ultrarightist historiography in South Korea shares *Drang nach Manchuria* with the official *Juche* historiography in North Korea. The shared nationalist discourse eroded in this case the political rivalry between the ultraright in South and the communists in the North. A folk religion, worshiping Dangun—a legendary founder of Old Chosŏn in 2333 BCE, connected the politically opposing Koreas in history. In April 1995 the North Korean communist regime officially invited Dr. Ahn Hosang, a South Korean ultraright-wing nationalist historian, to the newly excavated fake tomb of Dangun in Pyŏngyang on Dangun's Accession Day.[45] It shows dramatically how the nationalist narrative can transcend the sharp political rivalry between the North and South. It is reminiscent of the nationalist affinity between the PZPR's nomenklatura-apparatchik nationalism and anticommunist popular nationalism in Poland.

Official historians in North Korea were keen to refute the alleged Japanese commandery in Kaya around the fifth century CE, which Japanese imperialist historians misused and abused. Japanese imperialist historians took the Imna commandery as a historical precedent to justify Japanese colonial rule in Korea. When party historians in North Korea read the world history book published by the Soviet Union's Academy of Sciences, they found that the USSR's world history described the alleged Japanese commandery in ancient Korea as a fact. North Korean historians suggested an alternative history claiming the existence of Korean colonies in ancient Japanese islands. They argued that three ancient Korean kingdoms and Kaya established in the Japanese isles their colonies, and that these colonies played a crucial role in state formation in ancient Japan. The North Koreans' alternative history to the Japanese commandery reflects their autochthonism that the foreign enclaves did not exist in the national boundary of contemporary Korean nation-states. If Japanese imperialist historians abused the Japanese commandery to justify Japanese colonial rule over Korea, North Korean official historians countered with Korean colonies in Japan. Nationalist presentism superseded historical contextualism.

Autochthonism also demands an emphasis on cultural autarky. The North Korean history textbook never recognizes the influx of Chinese iron culture and Scythe-Siberian bronze culture. Omitting these influences, the textbook implies that bronze and iron culture developed independently in Old Chosŏn. The broad criticism of Buddhism and Confucianism is related to the obsession with the cultural originality in national history writing in North Korea. The textbook claims that Buddhism, as "a foreign religion," exerted a harmful influence on the free development of the indigenous art and national culture, while Plebian Korean artists successfully defended popular and national art against the influx of this foreign religion.[46] The attachment to cultural originality promoted the "the oldest or for the first time in the world" syndrome. The textbook boasts of the world first metal printing type invented in 1234, during the Goryeo dynasty. Celadon ware is highly praised as the proud national heritage, even though it was the product of the Goryeo aristocracy's life of luxury.[47] Nation overrode class in North Korean historiography.

An anachronistic interpretation of history characterizes the primordialist view of the nation. It never hesitates to project the modern nation-state onto the ancient past. The emphasis on *Juche*, sovereignty, has made North Korean historiography preoccupied with the national struggle for sovereignty. It tells the long history of the national fight against foreign invaders from the third century BCE—that of Old Chosŏn people against the Yan invasion. The title "History of the Anti-invasion Struggle of the Korean Nation" in the era of Old Chosŏn presupposes the existence of the Korean nation and its national unity. The anachronism is most visible in its approach to the unification of three kingdoms in the Korean peninsula by Silla in alliance with the Tang dynasty (668 CE). North Korean historiography rebuked Silla for its dependency on Tang, a Chinese dynasty: "The ruling class of Silla, disregarding the fate of the country, brought in the foreign opponent for its class interest and went to civil war with the support of the foreign power. . . . It committed an irrevocable crime on the nation."[48] Without the nationalist anachronism, a historical interpretation might be that the unification of the three kingdoms by Silla was the first step in the formation of the Korean nationality in future.

This *Juche* narrative overvalues the history of the national struggle for sovereignty. In the North Korean *A General History of Korea*, the text concerning the national struggle for sovereignty represents 22 percent and 30 percent, respectively, of the sections devoted to the era of the Three Kingdoms (57–668 CE) and the Goryeo dynasty (918–1392). It reminds me of the Polish history textbook that sought to awake a patriotic sentiment by teaching the ancient Greeks' heroic struggle against the Persians. The only national struggle in world history comparable to the fight of the Polish nation against Nazi Germany was the struggle of the small nations of the ancient Greeks against their colossal neighbor, Persia.[49] North Korean historiography also alludes that Silla, with its dependency on Tang, is the historical equivalent of South Korea for its dependency on the United States, while Goguryeo is the ancient equivalent of North Korea, with its striving for sovereignty against foreign powers. While Silla developed in the southern part of the Korean peninsula, Goguryeo was located in its northern part of today's North Korea. The political implication of this historical allusion is that sovereign North Korea, as the heir of Goguryeo, has historical legitimacy over dependent South Korea, the successor of Silla. The primordialist view of the nation made this far-fetched anachronistic presentism possible. If originism, autochthonism, and anachronism are the offspring of the primordialist conception of the nation, far-fetched presentism is its constant.

Modern and contemporary historiography in North Korea shows how far the personification of nationalism can develop. The history of the national liberation movement is reduced to the biography of Kim Il-sŏng, his parents, grandparents, and family history. Kim is described as the brain of the social organism and the patriarch of the nation as a family with a common bloodline. The primordialist concept of the nation seeded the personification of nationalism by viewing the nation as an organic community and even as a family community. The personification of nationalism went hand in hand with the consolidation of *Juche*. This brief sketch of party historiography in North Korea shows how Marxist historiography degenerated into *Legitimationswissenschaft*, a political instrument of the nomenklatura. Party historiography contributed to the Red Court of communism much as the feudal dynasty historians served the feudal court.

The Oxymoron of National Communism

Czesław Miłosz wrote that the PZPR, the long-ruling Polish Communist Party, "descends directly from the fascist Right." Miłosz sharply criticized Konstanty Ildefons Gałczyński, a prominent spokesman for the party's socialist realism, for "penning a Polish Horst Wessel Lied."[50] Miłosz's apocalyptic prophecy was realized in North Korea much more than in People's Poland. A video blog by Matthew Heimbach, an American white nationalist who advocates dividing the United States into ethnically and culturally homogenous states, shows "a hall in North Korea, decorated with depictions of Adolf Hitler, where Kim Jŏng-un sits ready to give a rousing speech." The list of white supremacist leaders, who are attracted to North Korea's ideas of self-reliance and the "cleanest race," include David Duke, the former head of the Ku Klux Klan; Alexander Dugin, the Russian ideologue of white nationalism; German neo-Nazi leaders like Michael Koth; and more.[51] Some neo-Nazis admire the North Korean regime because they believe that North Korea exemplified ideas of race-based nationalism and a centrally planned economy advocated by Gregor Strasser.[52]

The alleged socialist regimes in People's Poland and North Korea manipulated popular memory through nationalist discourse. Their use of race-based ethno-nationalism cannot be covered with the term *social patriotism*. When unwrapped, the socialist Red Court historiography revealed its secret message of ultra-right-wing nationalism. Socialist metaphors were just alluring prints on the wrapping papers of nomenklatura-apparatchik nationalist historiography. When the state degenerated the concept of the left and the idea of socialism and thus, alienated itself from ordinary workers, the nomenklatura needed an alternative ruling ideology to mobilize the working masses. National communism, or nomenklatura-apparatchik nationalism based on the primordialist concept of nation, proved a viable ideological alternative when ordinary workers turned their backs against socialism. The historical experience of a long foreign occupation and colony proved fertile soil for nationalist manipulation. The ideology of emancipation succumbed to the realism of political power, the key to understanding the oxymoron of Red Court historiography—nationalism in socialist code.

Notes

1. Adam Michnik, "Nationalism," *Social Research* 58 (Winter 1991): 759.
2. David A. Dyker, "*Nomenklatura* Nationalism: The Key to an Understanding of the New East European Politics?," *Australian Journal of Politics and History* 41, no. 1 (April 1995): 55–69. I add "apparatchik" after nomenklatura because party leaders initiated official nationalism with the support of party cadres from below.
3. Marcin Zaremba, *Komunizm, legitymizacja, nacjonalizm: Nacjonalistyczna legitymizacja władzy komunistycznej w Polsce* (Warsaw: Trio, 2001), 30, 36.

4. Krystyna Kersten, *Polacy, Żydzi, Komunizm: Anatomia półprawd 1939-68* (Warsaw: Krytyka, 1992), 159; Zaremba, *Komunizm*, 23–34; Paweł Machcewicz, *Polski Rok 1956* (Warsaw: Mowią Wieki, 1993), 216–30.

5. Jie-Hyun Lim, "Labour and the National Question in Poland," in *Nationalism, Labour and Ethnicity 1870-1939*, ed. Stefan Berger and Angel Smith (Manchester, UK: Manchester University Press, 1999), 141–43.

6. Andrzej Walicki, *Trzy patriotyzmy* (Warsaw: Res Publica, 1991), 35–36.

7. Tadeusz Manteuffel, "Otwarcie konferencji," *Pierwsza Konferencja Metodologiczna Historyków Polskich*, vol. 1 (Warsaw: PWN, 1953), 15, 19.

8. The oppositional anticommunist nationalist historiography in the "second circulation" of the 1980s repeated this interpretation of anti-Semitic and anticommunist nationalism. R. Szczemietiew, *W obcym interesie: zarys historii KPP* (n.p., 1983); N. Naruszewicz (L. Moczulski), *Zarys historii PRL* (Warsaw, 1981), 10; *Czerwone palmy historii* (Warsaw, 1982); *XYZ: Judeopolonia* (Kraków, 1989). See also Michał Śliwa, "The Image of the Communist Movement in Contemporary Polish Historiography," in *Jahrbuch fuer historische Kommunismusforschung* (1994), 306–15.

9. Bronisław Radlak, "Stan Badań nad Diejami SDKPiL," *Z Pola Walki*, no. 1 (1969): 33.

10. Andrzej Korbonski, "The Polish Communist Party 1938–1942," *Slavic Review* 26, no. 3 (September 1967), 430–44; Robert Conquest, *The Great Terror: A Reassessment* (Oxford: Oxford University, 1990), 405–7.

11. Władysław Rączkowski, "*Drang nach Westen?* Polish Archeology and National Identity," in *Nationalism and Archeology in Europe*, ed. Margarita Diaz-Andreu and Timothy Champion (London: Westview Press, 1996), 208–13.

12. Andrzej Garlicki, J. Kasprzakowa, A. Tymienicka, and Anna Żarnowska, "Stan Badań nad Dziejami PPS," *Z Pola Walki* 20, no 4 (1962): 128–60.

13. Paweł Samuś, "Syndrom 'oblężonej twierdzy' w KPP," in *Między Wschodem a Zachodem: Studia Z Dziejów Polskiego Ruchu i Myśli Socjalistycznej*, ed. Andrzej F. Grabski and Paweł Samuś, (Łódź: Wydawnictwo Uniwersytetu Łódzkiego, 1995), 183–202.

14. Pawel Machcewicz, "Social Protest and Political Crisis in 1956," in *Stalinism in Poland, 1944-1956*, ed. A. Kemp Welch (London: Macmillan, 1999), 117; see also Zaremba, *Komunizm*.

15. Antoni Czubiński, *Dzieje najnowsze Polski* (Poznań: Wielkopolska Agancja Wydawnicza, 1992), 8.

16. Tadeusz Jędruszczak, "O kryteriach oceny dziejów Polski w okresie międzywojennym (1918–39)," *Kwartalnik historyczny* 65 (1958): 488.

17. Janusz Żarnowski, "Wege und Erfolge der polnischen Historiographie 1945-1975," *Zeitschrift fuer Geschichtswissenschaft* 25, no. 8 (1977): 963.

18. Radlak, "Stan Badań nad Diejami SDKPiL," 56–58; Jędruszczak, "O kyrteriach," 492.

19. Elizabeth Kridl Valkenier, "Sovietization and Liberalization in Polish Postwar Historiography," *Journal of Central European Affairs* 19 (July 1959): 164–65.

20. See Garlicki et al., "Stan Badań nad Dziejami PPS."

21. Hochfeld's speech on "open Marxism" in London was published initially in the foreign journals *Cahiers internationaux* and *International Affairs* in 1956. It was widely introduced to Poland when the selected works of Hochfeld were published after

the Solidarity movement in 1981. See Julian Hochfeld, *Marksizm, Socjologia, Socjalizm* (Warsaw: PWN, 1982).

22. Jie-Hyun Lim, "'The Good Old Cause' in the New Polish Left Historiography," *Science & Society* 61 (Winter 1997/98): 543.

23. "Dyskusja nad próbnym wydaniem części III tomu Historii Polski," *Kwartalnik historyczny* 68, no. 3 (1961).

24. "Rewizja założeń programowych przedrozłamowej PPS przez PPS-Lewicę (Dyskusja w Zakładzie Historii Partii)," *Z Pola Walki* 5, no.1 (1962).

25. Lim, "Good Old Cause," 543.

26. Elizabeth Kridl Valkenier, "The Rise and Decline of Official Marxist Historiography in Poland, 1945–1983," *Slavic Review* 44, no. 4 (1985): 665. It is intriguing that Załuski was a frequent guest speaker at the Union of Fighters for Freedom and Democracy (ZBoWid) in the mid-1960s, when the ZBoWid under Mieczysław Moczar accelerated the nationalist turn. See Joanna Wawrzyniak, *Veterans, Victims, and Memory: the Politics of the Second World War in Communist Poland* (Frankfurt am Main: Peter Lang, 2015), 194.

27. *Polski plakat polityczny* (Warsaw: KAW, 1980), posters 5, 8, 42, 59, 71.

28. Interestingly, the revived cosmopolitanism with the globalization in the twenty-first century labeled itself as "rooted cosmopolitanism."

29. Jerzy J. Wiatr, *Co nam zostało z tych lat* (Toruń: Wydawnictwo Adam Marszałek, 1995), 23.

30. "Internacjonalizm-patriotyzm-nacjonalizm w dziejach polskiego ruchu robotniczego," *Z Pola Walki* 13, no. 2 (1970): 117, 130–32, 135, and passim.

31. Aleksander Kochański, *SDKPiL 1907-1910* (Warsaw: Książka i Wiedza, 1971), 218–59.

32. Norbert Michta, "O rzetelną ocenę SDKPiL," *Z Pola Walki* 15, no. 3 (1973): 121–45; Michta, "Tak to właściwie było," *Z Pola Walki* 15, no. 4 (1973): 67–82; Michta, *Julian Marchlewski* (Warsaw: Książka i Wiedza, 1984).

33. Śliwa, "The Image of the Communist Movement," 312–13.

34. *Stenogram wystąpienia Władysława Gomułki na Kongresie Związków Zawodowych 19 czerwca 1967 r.*, cited in Dariusz Stola, *Kampania antysyjonistyczna w Polsce 1967-1968* (Warsaw: ISP PAN, 2000), 274. A memory plaque at Dworzec Gdański, a train station in the north of Warsaw, says, "Here they left behind more than they possessed." About fifteen thousand Jews were forced to leave Poland during the Anti-Zionist campaign between 1968 and 1971. For numbers, see Jerzy Eisler, "Jews, Antisemitism, Emigration," in *Polin-1968: Forty Years After*, vol. 21, ed. Leszek W. Głuchowski and Antony Polonsky (Oxford: Littman Library of Jewish Civilization, 2009), 42.

35. Michał Śliwa, "Idee polityczne opozycji antykomunistycznej w Polsce, 1976–1989," ms., 17.

36. Kim Il-sŏng, 김일성선집 [Selected works], vol. 4 (Pyŏngyang: Chŏsunrodongdangchulpansa, 1960), 325–31.

37. Kim Il-sŏng, 김일성선집, 4:338.

38. "8.15 해방이후 조선 역사학계가 걸은 길" [The path of North Korean historical studies after the liberation of August 15], *Ryuksagwahak*, no. 2 (1960): 10.

39. Sŏh Dongman, "1950년대 북한의 정치갈등과 이데올로기 상황" [Political conflicts and ideological situation in North Korea in the 1950s], 년대남북한의 선택과 굴절 (Seoul: Yoksabipyungsa 1998), 323–24.

40. See Jie-Hyun Lim, "Socjalizm, ale jaki. . . . ? Ideologia mobilizacji ludu w procesie modernizacji w Azji Wschodniej," *Dzieje Najnowsze*, 31, no. 1 (2000): 163–76.

41. "좌담: 북한에서는 우리 역사를 어떻게 보는가?" [Roundtable: How to view our history in North Korea?], *Yuksapipyung*, no. 5 (1988): 4–12.

42. See chapter 7.

43. See Yŏksa Yŏnguso, 조선통사 [A general history of Chosŏn] (Pyŏngyang: Gwahak·baigwasajŏn chulpansa, 1977); and with Lee Ki-baek, 한국사신론 [A new history of Korea] (Seoul: Ilchogak, 1984).

44. Lee Sunkŭn, "고조선의 성립과 사회성격" [The social formation of Old Chosŏn], in 북한의 한국사 인식, ed. Ahn Byungwoo and Do Jinsoon, vol. 1 (Seoul: Hangilsa 1990), 86–92.

45. "안호상씨 불법입국" [Ahn Hosang's illegal entry to North Korea], *Chosun ilbo*, April 12, 1995; "안호상 대종교대표 방북" [Ahn Hosang visits North Korea], *Hangyeoreshinmun*, April 13, 1995. Ahn received his doctoral degree in Germany in the 1930s and founded the national history committee in postliberation Korea.

46. Yŏksa Yŏnguso, 조선통사 [A general history of Chosŏn], 157.

47. Yŏksa Yŏnguso, 217–18.

48. Yŏksa Yŏnguso, 136.

49. Marc Ferro, *The Use and Abuse of History* (London: Routledge, 1984), 170.

50. When Gałczyński criticized Miłosz by writing "a poem for traitor" (Poemat dla zdrajcy), Miłosz thought Gałczyński's poem was the same as the Nazi propaganda literature glorifying the Nazi hero Horst Wessel. Czesław Miłosz, *New and Collected Poems* (New York: Ecco, 2001), 122–23.

51. Bradley Jardine and Casey Michel, "Alt-Reich: North Korea and the Far Right," *Diplomat*, July 6, 2017, https://thediplomat.com/2017/07/alt-reich-north-korea-and-the-far-right/; "White Supremacists and Neo-Nazis Are Forming Alliances with North Korea," *CBC.ca*, October 27, 2014, https://www.cbc.ca/radio/thecurrent/white-supremacists-and-neo-nazis-are-forming-alliances-with-north-korea-oct-27-2014-1.2814105.

52. "The German Neo-Nazi Fascination with North Korea," *NK News*, December 3, 2013, https://www.nknews.org/2013/12/the-german-neo-nazi-fascination-with-north-korea/.

PART III
MOBILIZING

9

Mapping Mass Dictatorship
Toward a Transnational History of
Twentieth-Century Dictatorship

Beyond the History of Martyrdom

The idea of "mass dictatorship" originated in my encounter with the politics of coming to terms with the past in South Korea and Poland. Amid radical democratic transformations sweeping through these two countries upon the end of the Cold War, I have lived a complicated history as a participatory observer wandering the transnational space between Korea and Poland. In the past two decades, these two post-totalitarian democracies have shared a history of martyrdom supported by twin pillars of memory: tragic victimhood and heroic resistance.[1] Any challenge to this memory in the post-totalitarian era would have been dismissed as "incorrect" in both countries. A history of martyrdom was made possible only by ironing crooked histories and memories into a neat history. Plural memories betray and rupture a linear history. As Vaclav Havel constantly stressed, no line clearly divides victimizers from victims. Rather, the determination runs through each individual. Not everyone was an accomplice, but everyone was in some measure coresponsible for what had been done.[2] Adam Michnik's stance, articulated by his slogan of "amnesty yes, amnesia no," alludes to the complexity of coming to terms with the past in post-totalitarian Poland.[3] The controversy over *lustracja*, the cleansing of former officials from the government, shows that coming to terms with the past of communist dictatorship is more complex than the popular history of martyrdom permits.

In South Korea, the memory war over Park Chung-hee's developmental dictatorship generated new problems concerning "what happened in and to the dictatorship." Widespread nostalgia for Park's era has embarrassed left-wing intellectuals including myself, who did not expect a surge of Park's popularity in the context of a democratized Korea. The Korean memory war and its version of the *lustracja* controversy center on "how to read this perplexing nostalgia." My essay "Reading the Code of Everyday Fascism" (1999) triggered a sharp polemic over the legacy of the developmental dictatorship. I asked how the fascist habitus and *mentalité* have been accommodated in the everyday life of many a Korean since the dictatorship era. Although the political regime of the dictatorship is long gone, a fascist habitus still reigns in everyday practices and influences people's way of thinking. The legacy of dictatorship haunts Korea's nascent political democracy. In a subsequent essay, "Fascists' War of Position and Dictatorship of Consent" (2000), I proposed a transnational history of dictatorship. By reflecting on the history of coming to terms with the past in postwar Germany, Italy, and Poland, I suggested that popular nostalgia for an era of dictatorship is not a Korean peculiarity. Koreans also do not have an exclusive claim on the attempts to reduce that nostalgia to a product of a certain political propaganda machine.[4] Many memories, however, are framed according to their precepts—conspiratorial propaganda theory alone cannot explain the circumstances under which popular memories become susceptible to propaganda.

Most intriguing in the transnational history of dictatorship is the contrast among the political constellations arrayed around coming to terms with the past. Anticommunist Korean right-wingers and Polish nomenklatura communists, leftist socialism-oriented South Korean dissidents and rightist anticommunist Polish dissidents counterintuitively converge. Korean right-wing conservatives and Polish communist conservatives have respectively misused and abused popular nostalgia to excuse the developmental dictatorship and communist regime. The peculiarities of these convergences go further: my essays on "everyday fascism" and "fascist's war of position" have met with fierce opposition from the Korean left-wing intellectual establishment, just as Havel's and Michnik's stance against the *lustracja* provoked angry responses from anti-Communist right-wingers in the Czech Republic and Poland.[5] In the transnational space, political rivals become bizarre mnemonic companions. Recognizing this freed me from the demonology, whether right- or left-wing, of the Cold War. These surprising convergences place into question the usefulness of totalitarian and Marxist paradigms, both saddled with a simplistic dualism that posits a few vicious perpetrators (the dictator and his cronies) and many innocent victims (the people). The Manichean presentism of the Cold War blinded both sides to the diverse forms of popular support for the dictatorships. A historicization freed from the Cold War demonology casts serious doubts on that moralist and cliché-ridden Cold War saga of the history of martyrdom. *Mass dictatorship* is a term coined in light of this transnational reflection possible in the post–Cold War era.

Mass Dictatorship in Postcolonial Perspectives

Mass dictatorship theory starts from a simple question: What is the difference between premodern despotism and modern dictatorship? My tentative answer is that despotism does not need massive support from below, but modern dictatorship presupposes that mass support. Mass dictatorship theory focuses on the attempted mobilization of the masses by dictatorships, and how these dictatorships frequently secured voluntary mass participation and support.[6] Once the masses made their appearance on the historical scene, no regime, whether democratic or dictatorial, could silence or disregard the voices of ordinary people. The sociopolitical engineering of the modern state system demanded the recruitment and mobilization of the masses for the nation-state project and indeed commanded their enthusiasm and voluntary participation. The experiences of the two world wars demonstrated the vital importance to the total war system of the voluntary mobilization and significant contribution of the masses. That helps explain why both democracies and dictatorships adopted a modern state system whose defining features included "universal suffrage-plebiscite as a popular endorsement," "compulsory education-nationalization of the masses," "universal conscription-national appellation," and "social welfare-social bribery." Mass dictatorship appropriates modern statecraft and egalitarian ideology. Its study needs to be situated in a broader transnational context of political modernity understood in terms of territoriality, sovereignty, and population. At this moment, "dictatorship from above" transforms itself into a "dictatorship from below."[7]

Mass dictatorship is far from being an inevitable product of an aberration from a standard path to modernity, or of the dominance of preindustrial, precapitalist, and prebourgeois authoritarian and feudal traditions that obstruct that path. Mass dictatorship argues against the *Sonderweg* thesis that sets Nazism and other manifestations of fascism apart from parliamentary democracies of the "West" on account of the German bourgeoisie's alleged lack of "emancipatory will" and "sense of citizenship."[8] The dichotomy of a particular-abnormal path in the "Rest"—quintessentially represented by Germany—and a universal-normal path in the "West" presupposes a hierarchy topped by the "West." In this dichotomy, the comparison of aberrant dictatorship and normative democracy strengthens a Western/European claim to exceptionalism, according to which democracy, equality, freedom, human rights, rationalism, science, and industrialism promulgated by the European Enlightenment are phenomena of the "West." Since the "West" has uniquely achieved the maturation of the historical conditions necessary for democracy and human rights, the normative presupposition inherent in the *Sonderweg* thesis implies Eurocentrism. In the "Rest," by contrast, these economic and political conditions remained un- or underdeveloped. This Eurocentrism alleges that fascism and the Holocaust can be reduced to manifestations of peculiarities of the premodern "Rest." This historical alibi exempts the modernist "West" from association with a barbarism defined *ab initio* as premodern.[9] Once we put the mass dictatorship on the map of the transnational history of modernity, the landscape of democracy and dictatorship looks different.[10]

Eurocentrism is reinforced by clichés of East and West, of Asia and Europe. But neither Europe nor Asia sprang into existence fully and immutably formed. Neither is geographically fixed. The strategic location of each is always in flux in historical discourse. Each is a relational concept that takes shape and gains coherence only when cofigured in relationship to the other in the discursive context of the "problem space."[11] The problem space of mass dictatorship enables us to see twentieth-century dictatorship not as the end-point of a particular path of the premodern, but as one of the normal paths of the modern; this conceptualization displaces East and West as usable categories. Interwar Germany, Italy, and Russia as the problem space of mass dictatorship is equivalent to a semiperiphery or to the East in the West. In short, those countries that experienced mass dictatorship were the East in imaginative geography.[12] Global Easts, as the problem space of mass dictatorship, question the hierarchical order of Asia–Europe and East–West. Shifting from the reified geography of the dichotomy of East and West to the problem space of the cofiguration of East and West makes it possible to see both mass dictatorship and mass democracy as twin products of global modernity.[13] The East–West divide does not make any substantial difference since each side belongs to the same problem space of modernity.

Through a transnational history of mass dictatorship, one can put the dictatorship of the East and democracy of the West together on the global horizon of modernity. Both democracy and dictatorship are located not in some preexisting spaces but in the problem space of becoming. Once conscripted to modernity's project, people were coercively obliged to render themselves as both objects and agents of modernity.[14] The historical singularity of dictatorship or democracy can be analyzed from global perspectives on the formation of the modern nation-state. Each nation-state is the result of negotiations among various conscripts of modernity. Viewed from a global perspective, traditionalism as the ideological proponent of mass dictatorship is not a product of the premodern but a variant of modernist discourse. Traditionalism is distinct from traditions as accumulated everyday practices for the very reason that it comes into being through the interaction between East and West.[15] More sophisticated discourses on "alternative modernity," "retroactive modernity," "modernism against the modernity," and "capitalism without capitalism" are familiar elements of the figurative language of mass dictatorship. They reflect a consciousness that "oscillated furiously between recognizing the peril of being overcome by modernity and the impossible imperative of overcoming it" in the latecomers' society.[16]

Zygmunt Bauman's warning that Holocaust-style genocide should be recognized as a logical outcome of the civilizing tendency to subordinate the use of violence to a rational calculus resonates through the transnational perspective. He is suspicious of any attempt to attribute the Nazi atrocities either to certain peculiar convolutions of German history or to the moral indifference and latent anti-Semitism of ordinary Germans.[17] To him, the German Sonderweg thesis seems to exonerate the modernity and "West" from the potentiality of the genocide. Understanding mass dictatorship happens at the point where transnational perspectives meet postcolonial perspectives.[18] To say that "the transnational meets the post-colonial" is not to imply a linear continuity between German colonialism in South-West Africa and the Holocaust. The Holocaust should not be reduced to another peculiarity of the German colonialism. Rather, the Holocaust should be seen in the context of the continuity of "Western" colonialism, as Hannah Arendt suggested when she articulated the concept of "administered mass killing" (*Verwaltungsmassenmord*) in respect to the British colonial experience.[19] In other words, the German colonialists' genocide in Namibia in 1904–1907 can be better explained from the trans-national perspectives of Euro-colonialism than by recourse to German peculiarities deriving from the circumstance of a latecomer's colonialism. More broadly, one cannot miss the history of primitive accumulation of capital, full of conquest, enslavement, robbery, murder, and all forms of violence in the making of the modern nation-state. The emergence of capitalism and democracy in the "Western" nation-state should be viewed as having taken place, in Marx's terms, "under circumstances of ruthless terrorism."[20]

The Nazi utopia of a racially purified German empire was a mimicry of Western colonialism, "turning imperialism on its head and treating Europeans as Africans."[21] Nazi Germans likely felt a kind of "white men's burden" inside Europe as they regarded Slavic people as "white negroes" and Slavic land as "Asia." Hitler did not stick to a reified geography. He stated that "the border between Europe and Asia is not the Urals, but the place where the settlements of Germanic type of people stop and pure Slavdom begins."[22] In Ian Kershaw's reinterpretation, Hitler thought that "the Slavs would provide the German equivalent of the conquered native populations of India and Africa in the British empire."[23] Among Germans in the occupied "East," it was not difficult to find a sense of cultural superiority similar to that of colonial missions. Indeed, "Western" colonialism provided an important historical precedent for the Nazis' genocidal thinking. A certain historical connection between colonial genocide and Nazi criminality is undeniable. Genocide of Native Americans on the frontier, British colonial genocide in India and Africa, the Stalinist political genocide of the people's enemy, and the Holocaust all belong to the same category of the "categorical murder" spurred by the essentialist tendency to categorize others based on race, ethnicity, class, and any other arbitrary boundaries.[24] From the viewpoint of "colonialism within," this colonial legacy was bequeathed to colonial subjects who were to be reborn as modern subjects of the independent nation-state in the postcolonial era. The postcolonial mass dictatorship, such as the developmental dictatorship in South Korea, provides a vivid example of the making of modern subjectivity.[25] The interaction of colonizers and the colonized is a key to understanding mass dictatorship in the postcolonial era.

The Interpenetration of Mass Dictatorship and Democracy

Postcolonial, and perhaps also poststructuralist, perspectives on the transnational history of mass dictatorship demand a reformulation of the question: What is the difference between mass dictatorship and democracy? The answer is not that simple. What if a majoritarian democracy in the modern nation-state persuades many to marginalize and categorize minorities as Others in terms of nation, class, gender, race, and ethnicity? What if the majority tyrannize minorities by the principle of majority rule? Is that democracy, or is it dictatorship?

Arguably, the cliché of dictatorship imposed by a willful minority on a confused majority would not withstand historical scrutiny. A history of modern colonies reveals that, for instance, settler democracies have been more murderous than authoritarian colonial governments. Michael Mann astutely notes that "regimes newly embarked upon democratization are more likely to commit murderous ethnic cleansings than are stable authoritarian regimes."[26] Much later, the Hutus' slogan "majoritarian democracy" in Rwanda expressed their conviction that "whoever rules in the name of the *majority people* is ontologically democratic." This reasoning opened the road to the massacre of Tutsis.[27] The characterization of American democracy as a "tyranny through masses" (Alexis Tocqueville) and the identification of "totalitarian democracy" among French Jacobins (J. L. Talmon) point toward the features of mass dictatorship in more telling ways than does Mao Zedong's declaration, "Dictatorship is a dictatorship by the masses."[28] As *People's Public Security* in the People's Republic of China explained in a classified document of 1965, "the entire Party and the masses all have to become involved, if dictatorship is to be exercised successfully."[29]

Socialist regimes used the metaphor of "people's democracy" in defining themselves as a variant of proletarian dictatorship.

If mass democracy means rule by the ordinary people, mass dictatorship presupposes the transformation of the chaotic crowd of ordinary people into a disciplined uniform mass, a collective characterized by its homogenous identity, unitary will, and a common goal. A disciplined uniformity and homogenous collectivity of the masses is imaginary. Insofar as the imaginary homogenous collectivity is shared among the masses, it remains active, because the perceived reality shapes the thoughts and practice of the many in their everyday lives. As an imaginary reality, the general will (or people's will, or nation's will) links mass democracy and mass dictatorship in their shared objective to nationalize masses. This analysis finds its most eccentric expression in Simon Tormey's statement that "liberal democracy is the most refined version of totalitarianism."[30] Synchronic comparisons aside, a diachronic comparison of pre- and postwar Japan shows that postwar democracy and the welfare state in Japan were continuous with the systematic social integration and consolidation that had marked the era of mass dictatorship.[31] The upshot is not that mass dictatorship is democratic, but that mass democracy is no more democratic than mass dictatorship.

The blurring of boundaries between dictatorship and democracy in a transnational history of mass dictatorship leads us to rethink domination, violence, coercion, and other means of repression. The superior efficiency of Britain's total war system by comparison with Germany's suggests that domination is most effective when people do not realize that they are being dominated.[32] Feeling dominated discourages and dampens the enthusiasm of otherwise supporters of a regime. The most virulent and penetrating forms of domination were found in those systems where the appearance of freedom and rationality were greatest. The slow but relentless buildup of pressure on the individual to conform is much more efficient and cost-effective than any means of terror. Any regime's favorite mode of ruling/subjection is the "internal coercion" produced by structuring thought and feeling.[33] The success of a mass dictatorship depends on its ability to enroll people in rituals of legitimacy and make them surrender their own identity and subjectivity in conformity with the model subject manufactured by the regime. A modern subject, whether in dictatorial or in democratic regimes, has been exposed to the "controlled and guided massification" in which a notionally inalienable right of individual freedom proves to be legitimately alienable after all.[34] It is not a coincidence that both Italian fascism and Stalinism very loudly proclaimed their intention to create the "new man," *homo fascistus* and *homo sovieticus*, respectively, through an anthropological revolution. Neither of these regimes reached perfection, but both had been driven by an unstinting effort to perform that revolution.[35]

Once launched, the anthropological revolution shifted from revolutionary mass movements to institutionalized mass politics. If the consent of high Stalinism was fed by the fever of the anthropological revolution, post-Stalinist regimes depended on shared guilt or public complicity for mass consent. As a dissident witness, Vaclav Havel adumbrated the peculiar mass psychology of public complicity or shared guilt in his thesis positing "post-totalitarianism" as a kind of compromised dictatorship.[36] In time, the large scale of public complicity was bound to create conformity, especially in and after the era of de-Stalinization. When the post-Stalinist regime abandoned the totalitarian anthropological revolutionary effort to create a "new man," it lost the ambition to dominate private lives and tolerated people's cynicism even as the official media continued to deplore the passivity and indifference of the people. Generally speaking, East Europeans in the post-1956 era adapted themselves to the system without much enthusiasm for the state project, and the regime was obliged to rest content with such passive consent. Compromised in their everyday lives, ordinary people fled into various depoliticized "niches" where "they could feel themselves." The result was a "niche society" (*Nischengesellschaft*).[37] The heritage of Marxist ideas was reduced to a handful of empty and decontextualized slogans, and people's passive consent to this fossilized Marxism was compensated by material rewards. According to Andrzej Walicki, the de-Stalinization of 1956 marked a turning point from totalitarianism to authoritarianism.[38]

A reengagement with Antonio Gramsci can complement this analysis since his conceptualization of hegemony helps us to problematize the self- or voluntary mobilization of the masses. Contrary to a common belief that his concept of hegemony is confined to an analysis of liberal democratic regimes, Gramsci explicitly wrote that fascism represents a war of position.[39] His intuition was that fascism was entrenched solidly at a grass-roots level. Gramsci's grave concern about fascist hegemony chimes with

Mussolini's keen interest in "general economic mobilization of citizens as means and agents of production, real conscription, a real civic and economic recruitment of all Italians." Under the scrutiny of the concept of hegemony, the organization of consent cannot be equated simply with the process of molding public opinion. Popular consent was not just imposed by state terror and all-pervasive propaganda. It was important to inspire self-motivation among the masses. That explains Mussolini's burning concern with building "a capillary network of associations with vast powers of social and cultural persuasion."[40] Japan's Moral Suasion Mobilization Campaign (1929–1930) was second to none in its pursuit of total social control through moral suasion (kyōka).[41] With its later development into the kōminka (imperial nationalization) campaign, Japanese imperialism undertook the ambitious task of nationalizing Koreans and Taiwanese colonial subjects, making them into Japanese citizens. The project of nationalizing masses in the developmental dictatorship in postcolonial Korea and Taiwan continues the Japanese imperial kōminka policy. Mass dictatorship is an experiment in plebiscitary democracy, which legitimizes the regime. Hegemony, in Gramscian terms, paves the way to the "dictatorship of consent."[42]

Mass dictatorship is not only a "hard" power utterly dominating the political sphere but also a "soft" power, retuning civil society to its own normative key. Fascist hegemony, entrenched in the grass roots, often attempts to penetrate the private sphere of individuals. As shown in its pursuit of anthropological revolution, it strives to maximize the hegemonic effect by infiltrating the praxis of everyday life to mold people's minds. Along with Gramsci's interpretation, Louis Althusser's concept of "appellation" and Michel Foucault's analysis of the modern subject as tailor-made can be very suggestive for an understanding of the fascist habitus and the internalization of coercion.[43] Like all other modern regimes, mass dictatorship struggles to legitimize its political application to multiple arrays of medical, legal, administrative, and juridical instruments. In a word, mass dictatorship is a form of democracy in a state of emergency. Mass dictatorship shares with other forms of the modern nation-state similar mechanisms for constructing a people of unitary will and action. First it alienates nonconforming insiders into Others, and then it hegemonically appropriates the rest of the population in the name of "the nation's will." Nazi slogans about Volksgemeinschaft and Volksgenosse are good examples that symbolize the organic integration that transcended class and political divisions achieved by alienating Others through anti-Semitism, anti-Bolshevism, and anti-Westernism outwardly, and by inventing a new ethnic unity of the Aryan race inwardly.[44]

State racism is an effective means of creating "biologized" internal or international enemies, against whom society must defend itself. Nazi culture as a contemporary allegory of intolerance, existential extremity, and radical evil was, in a sense, the tragic culmination of enlightened science and rationality.[45] Again, Michel Foucault's concept of a "bio-power" based on the triangular relationship between biopolitics, population, and race is evocative of that. If a disciplinary society constructs a capillary network of apparatuses to produce and regulate customs, habits, habitus, and practices, bio-power regulates social life from its interior. Power can achieve effective command over the entire life of the population at the birth of bio-power.[46] One cannot say whether mass dictatorship did perfect bio-power, but it seems to have harnessed the productive dimension of bio-power for the modern disciplinary state. Mass dictatorship never fulfilled the ambition of the anthropological revolution to create a new man, but it also never abandoned the modernist dream of the "society of control." The fascist aesthetics of the beautiful male body, as furnishing a bridge between the public and private sphere, may be one dimension of biopolitics in a mass dictatorship. The history of sexuality shows us that the mentalities and behaviors of the masses hinged on controlling passions and ideals of human beauty, love, friendship, and sexual habitus. Mass dictatorships, no less than mass democracies, deployed the biopolitics of sexuality.[47]

People's Sovereignty and Political Religion

Mass dictatorship as a working hypothesis pays due attention to the intellectual history of popular sovereignty. Carl Schmitt's advocacy of Nazism as "an anti-liberal, but not necessarily anti-democratic" regime represented the climax of the "new politics" based on the idea of popular sovereignty.[48] In other words, mass dictatorship is congruent with the change from liberalism to democracy, and then from a parliamentary democracy to "decisionist" or plebiscitary democracy. Popular sovereignty transformed populations from passive subjects into active citizens and thus paved the way for participatory dictatorship. Once the "general will" is hoaxed into becoming the will of the people or nation, the people or nation as the "constituent power" is not subject to a constitution. The nation now has the legislative power to make constitutions. By its own will, the nation can amend the constitution because it has the constituent power. The violation of the constitution by the constituent power might be illegal but constitutional.

This constitutional subversion reveals the secret of "sovereign dictatorship": its justification by the logical chain of representation with "the people representing the multitude, the nation representing the people, and the state representing the nation." In this way, the multitude is transformed into an ordered totality.[49] The sovereign dictatorship can enjoy unlimited constitutional legitimacy insofar as the people's will as the constituent power supports that dictatorship. In his address to the National Convention (1793), Barère could justify Jacobin dictatorship on the ground that the nation was exercising dictatorship over itself. By the same logic, "the might of the dictatorship of the masses knows no bounds" in Maoist China. Mao's public security police tried hard "to continue the all-round implementation of the long-term policy of relying on the masses in the exercise of dictatorship."[50] Seen in this light, George Mosse's eccentric assertion that Robespierre would have felt at home in the Nazi's mass rallies is not groundless at all.[51] The Nazi *Volksgemeinschaft* was not a bizarre premodern political concept but a meta-modern political order in which people regarded themselves as the real political sovereign. In Eugene Weber's expression, Nazism looked "much like the Jacobinism of our time."[52]

The idea of sovereign dictatorship also provides a clue to understanding the ironic affinity between rightist dictatorships/fascism and leftist dictatorships/Stalinism. The cliché that "the two extremes meet" explains nothing. Hardt and Negri's suggestion that "the abstract machine of national sovereignty is at the heart of both" seems more trenchant.[53] Even for the Left, the national community meant a working people's unity forged against the people's enemy. As seen in the nationalist discourse in People's Poland and North Korea, the socialist ideal of the ethical and political unity of society unintentionally reinforced the primordialist concept of the nation, that is, a way of seeing it as an organic community and even a family community.[54] As a response to the "West," the nationalist discourse of mass dictatorship inclined toward Occidentalism. What is most remarkable in this regard is the awkward convergence of fascism and socialism in an anti-Western modernization project. The dichotomy of the "bourgeois nation" and the "proletarian nation," shared by Italian fascists and post-war Third World Marxists of "dependency theory," implied a shift from the class struggle between bourgeoisie and proletariat to national struggle between wealthy nations and impoverished nations. Both fascism and Stalinism focused on a developmental strategy designed to overtake advanced capitalism at all costs, and both justified that strategy by invoking the nation's will.[55]

Once situated within a broader sociocultural history, popular sovereignty ideologically supports "the nationalization of the masses."[56] This kind of massification corresponds to "equalization" and "homogenization" in the realm of perceived reality.[57] The nationalized masses as a tailor-made totality, assisted by fascist spectacles, deny the liberal image of an autonomous modern subject. The proponents of that transformation asserted that the disenchanted modern subject should be tailored to the demands of the nation-state, which they again justified by referring to a nation's will. Ideology alone will not make people internalize norms and disciplines in everyday life. Popular sovereignty is too abstract to discipline people through bio-power. Beyond the conceptual level, what is needed for the emotional reproduction of a tailor-made subject is anthropo-cultural reenchantment. A political religion or civic religion can satisfy the demand for reenchantment. It confers a sacred status on earthly entities like the nation, state, class, history, revolution, and race, by turning them into absolute principles of collective identity. Intermingled with a code of ethical and social commandments, political religion binds the individual to the sacralized secular entity.[58] If many people embodied the message of fascist aesthetics, many of them were people reenchanted by nationalism, whose emotional appeal transforms politics into a political religion.

The nationalist narrative of a collective life flowing from the immemorial past into an infinite future could turn the mortal life of the individual into the eternal life of the collective and thus fill the vacuum caused by the extinction of the mythic along with the religious community.[59] Political religion became the inheritance of mass dictatorship and mass democracy—a legacy of the French Enlightenment. Theoretically, modern political messianism should be traced back to Rousseau, who insisted on the necessity of "civil religion" and national festivals that would infuse the people with a feeling of moral unity and absolute love of the fatherland in his advice to Poles. The American Revolution of 1776 and the French Revolution of 1789 provided nationalist affirmation of secular religion and an apocalyptic vision of national regeneration through politics. Political religion can be found in mass democracy no less than in a mass dictatorship. In George Bush's address on the day he announced victory in Iraq in 2003, American troops stopped being terrestrial combatants and became missionaries. They were no longer merely killing enemies: they were casting out demons in Iraq.[60] From a transnational history of mass dictatorship, Emilio Gentile's binary of "democratic civil religion" and "totalitarian political religion" seems to miss the point.[61] They are two sides of the same coin of sociopolitical engineering in the modern nation-state.

The emphasis in the conceptualization of mass dictatorship on the willing consent of the masses may suggest that scholars are failing to recognize the centrality of terror. The explication of consent and hegemonic effects in mass dictatorship never denies coercion, violence, terror, repression, and punishment. Instead, mass dictatorship questions the naïve dichotomy between coercion and consent by asking why a large part of the population ignores, endorses, agrees with, and even implements the violent oppression employed by dictatorial regimes like the Nazis. Terror is an indispensable means of creating consent, appealing not only to fear but also to a sense of relief among "national comrades." Terror was used highly selectively on "enemies of the people." Mass dictatorship deployed massive terror in a radicalized version of a strategy of negative integration, provoking violence against Others as a way of homogenizing a mass into "our national community." Terror and coercion created chaos and fear among outcasts, but they never directly endangered faithful insiders. The fear of being an outcast posed an even more significant threat than terror to the members of the community. Out of this fear, ordinary people readily became active perpetrators, tacit collaborators, or passive bystanders. This fear explains how even extreme terror could count on consent from below.[62] Coercion and consent are intimately interwoven integral parts of mass dictatorship. The mass dictatorship was indeed Janus-faced: Jekyll to insiders and Hyde to outcasts.

Despite its frequently overt patriarchal ideologies, mass dictatorship appealed to some feminists due to its imaginary equality among citizens.

To establish a productive and effective self-mobilization system, mass dictatorship regimes often appealed to a sense of sovereignty that regards women of the same ethnicity and nationality as "national comrades," in contrast to men of a different nationality, ethnicity, race, or class, who seem to be national or class enemies. The interplay between the construction of gender identities and the formation of identities of nation, class, and race shows that women in mass dictatorships were not passive victims. Women were often invited into the public sphere by mass dictatorships. Japanese feminist leaders' participation in the total war system and women's role as perpetrators in Nazi Germany show how the self-mobilization system could be complete only with women's enthusiastic response to the regime's call to participate in the public sphere. Women activists in the British Union of Fascists and female leaders of the New Village Movement (Saemaeul Undong) in South Korea's developmental dictatorship similarly answered the call.

Agency in Everyday Life

Mass dictatorship may look like a behemoth—a perfect, tightly-sutured political machine—that does not allow even a tiny space for dissent and resistance. Foucault's account of power and modernity, which the mass dictatorship refers to methodologically, is partially responsible for this impression. In its focus on the microphysics of power to show how power functions at the level of everyday life, Foucault's explanation tends to reduce the functioning of a whole society to a single, dominant type of procedure: the panoptical or the disciplinary. Practices disseminated through unofficial realms supported the panoptical procedures. While these minor practices remained "unprivileged by history," they formed tactical "antidisciplines" that undermined strategies of official power. Thanks to the silent and unacknowledged forms of resistance that "breaks through the grid of the established order and accepted disciplines," mass dictatorship ceases to be a perfect, tightly sutured machine.[63] Together, the Foucauldian genealogy of discipline and Certeau's antidisciplines make up the topography of mass dictatorship and mass democracy. The crooked lines of history from below, oscillating between optimism and pessimism, resistance and subjugation, and hegemony and counterhegemony, are in themselves causes for reflection on the coexistence of disciplines and antidisciplines.[64]

A question of terminology arises. In the "Western" intellectual tradition, the term *masses* is pregnant with the political implication that many ordinary people would be passive objects to be manipulated. But that political implication is only partially merited. As the American socialist magazine the *Masses* (1911–1917) suggests, masses were regarded by some liberal leftists as the true agents of societal transformation. In bourgeois and aristocratic circles, however, masses were the common herd, characterized by irrationality, disorderliness, and poverty. The bourgeois establishment's contempt, which found its classic expression in Gustave LeBon's writings, denotes fear of the chaotic masses' rebellion. Jose Ortega y Gasset straightforwardly confessed that fear of the situation where masses rule and decide. In the twentieth century, masses stopped being passive objects and began to be active agents to challenge for power.[65] The bourgeoisie's very fear of the masses, in fact, indicates the masses' power as agents. The words for "masses" in East Asian languages—*daejung* (Korean), *dazhong* (Chinese), *taishu* (Japan)—denote recognition of the agency of the masses, save for some exceptional usages. Often combined with "working," "masses" in the East Asian usage of the term "working masses" (勤勞大衆) implies historical actors. Considering the terms for "masses" connote agency in East Asian usage, the mass dictatorship should not be confused with the top-down manipulation of the mass.

Historical actors are back onstage in mass dictatorship discourses. Resting on the "empirical turn" in particular, or on an "investigative turn" more broadly, the concept of mass dictatorship calls attention to "the patchwork of practices and orientations which people co-produce and which they themselves live with and operate in."[66] Human agents are not politically predestined. Swinging between self-empowerment and self-mobilization, they undergo historical moments. Explanations need to be multilinear rather than unilinear, pluralist rather than dualist, ambiguous rather than absolute. The room for maneuver available to every single human agent is a niche from which mass dictatorship, and perhaps also mass democracy, can be deconstructed. Dualities of "coercion and consent" and "resistance and collaboration" can be deconstructed and pluralized. Every single agent—to say nothing of the masses—eludes compartmentalization and is constitutive of heterogeneous entities. Agency cannot be contained en masse within the tightly woven social and cultural matrix. Selfhood is inescapably a duality, comprising both object and subject in the interactions between the self and the world.[67]

The more the system of mobilization develops, the wider the range of nonconformist behavior among the mobilized people becomes. Resistance arises at the very moment when the regime appears to have secured total domination. For many people, participation in a self-mobilizing regime means subjection to the structure *and* an opportunity to appropriate the structure for their own purposes. Mobilized to participate in and to support mass dictatorship, people did not simply submit to top-down subjectification. Under the facade of voluntary participation and support, they actively mobilized and often appropriated the subjectification process for self-empowerment from below. The dialectics of "internalizing the external" and "externalizing the internal" characterizes every single human agent. What one finds among the masses in the mass dictatorship regime are contradictions and dissonance in people's practices or modes of conduct. In lieu of the term "self-mobilizing," Alf Lüdtke suggests the expression of "self-energizing." It captures these contradictory practices of subjection and appropriation in everyday lives.[68]

Self-contradictions in the modes of the everyday life of the masses cast doubt on the binaries of consent and coercion, desire and repression, and self-mobilization and forced mobilization. These are not irreconcilable opposites but aspects of the same process. The question is not of choosing "*either* control *or* consent producing longevity (of the mass dictatorship regime)." Instead, we need to consider "control *and* consent (or, perhaps better, compliance)—a combination providing ambivalent reactions to the regime."[69] This insight leads us to postulate that the experience of consent and coercion is itself multilayered, spanning internalized coercion, forced consent, passive conformity, consensus, self-mobilization, and forced participation. Subjection was not a one-way street. Many people pretended to be subservient to the regime, but very often the subservience was a way of harnessing the world for their benefit. The tasks awaiting historians of mass dictatorship, then, must include the deconstruction and pluralization of terms such as "consent," "coercion," "conformity," "adaptation," "resistance," "opposition," and "mobilization."[70] Similarly, "resistance" can be pluralized; *Resistenz* ("structural resistance," a term used to define the defense of identities and social practices threatened by a regime),

Widerstand ("organized resistance"—Resistance with a capital "R"), "ideologically driven resistance," "existentialist resistance," "resistance subject to hegemony," "obedience pregnant with resistance."[71]

Coming to terms with the past dictatorship demands a "thick description" of yesterday's consent and coercion and today's nostalgia *for* and *against* as a multilayered experience in everyday lives. Historical actors should pay for their agency when they cease to be passive objects.[72] Given its emphasis on agency, mass dictatorship does not exonerate ordinary people from historical responsibility and juridical culpability. The dictum "structure does not kill, but individuals do" points to the guilt of historical actors. The mass dictatorship hypothesis challenges the moralist dualism between a few bad perpetrators and many innocent victims. The dualism of a small number of victimizers and many victims displaces the historical responsibility of "ordinary" people by shifting culpability away from them. When Raul Hilberg asked, "Wouldn't you be happier if I had been able to show you that all perpetrators were crazy?," he supplied his own answer by implying that history brings no comfort.[73] Mass killers were everyday human beings—normal people.[74] The moral comfort that the image of extraordinary perpetrators brings to us results not only in self-exculpation but also in moral disarmament. As Bauman put it, "The most frightening news brought about the Holocaust and by what we learned of its perpetrators was not the likelihood that 'this' could be done to us, but the idea that we could do it."[75] In other words, "placed in comparable situations and similar social constituencies, you or I might also commit murderous ethnic cleansing."[76]

In light of this moral reflection, agents come to possess the reflexive dimension of the self. The reflexive self opens up the possibility for historical actors to stand outside the order of external determinations, though "in a manner limited by their inherence in that order."[77] Regarding mass dictatorship, these historical actors qua reflexive selves will frustrate the regime's ambition to nationalize the masses and change the uniform mass of a unitary will into the multitude "to communicate and act in common while remaining internally different" and to transform themselves from the tailor-made subjects of the identification politics to the autonomous individuals of innumerable differences. And finally, they will rupture and rip through the seemingly tightly sutured political machine, that is, mass dictatorship. Globally, fascism lost a war of maneuver, but it is still scoring victories in a war of position. When Umberto Eco warned about "fuzzy totalitarianism and endless fascism" and Felix Guattari cautioned against "recurrent fascism," they reminded us that the war of position against fascism is ongoing.[78] What makes fascism dangerous is "its molecular or micropolitical power" that proliferates itself. Freed from the Manichean moralism of a few bad victimizers and many innocent victims, the historicism of mass dictatorship turns itself into reflexive presentism.

Notes

1. Andrzej Paczkowski, "Czy historycy dokonali 'obrachunku' z PRL?," in *Ofiary czy Współwinni* (Warsaw: Volumen, 1997), 13–29; Cho Heeyeon, "박정희 시대의 강압과 동의-의 관계를 다시 생각한다" [Rethinking the oppression and consent in the era of Park Chung-hee], *Yŏksabipyung* 67 (Summer 2004): 135–90; Lim Jie-Hyun and Lee Sangrok, "'대중독재'와 '포스트 파시즘' -조희연 교수의 비판에 부쳐-" [Mass dictatorship and postfascims—a reply to Cho Heeyeon's critique], *Yŏksabipyung* 68 (Autumn 2004): 298–330.

2. Timothy Garton Ash, *History of the Present* (New York: Vintage Books, 1999), 264. The Polish word *współwinni* is better translated as "coresponsible" than as "accomplice" in this context.

3. Adam Michnik, "Rozmowa z Vaclavem Havelem," *Gazeta Wyborcza*, November 30, 1991.

4. Lim Jie-Hyun, "일상적 파시즘의 코드 읽기" [Reading the code of everyday fascism], *Contemporary Criticism* 8 (Fall 1999); "파시즘의 진지전과 '합의 독재'" [Fascists' war of position and dictatorship of consent], *Contemporary Criticism* 12 (Fall 2000).

5. For *lustracja* controversies in Poland and Korea, see Piotr Grzelak, *Wojna o lustrację* (Warsaw: Trio, 2005); appendix to 대중독재 II: 정치종교와 헤게모니 [Mass dictatorship II: Political religion and gegemony], ed. Lim Jie-Hyun and Kim Yong-Woo (Seoul: Chaiksesang, 2005), 401–596.

6. Francoism is often defined as *despotismo moderno* (modern despotism) because it constitutes an alliance of conservatives and the military without mass involvement. Modern despotism of this kind differs from mass dictatorship in that it does not rely on the mobilization of the masses or on intervention in their private lives. See Salvador Giner, "Political Economy, Legitimacy and the State in Southern Europe," in *Uneven Developments in Southern Europe*, ed. Ray Hudson and Jim Lewis (London: Methuen, 1985).

7. For the dictatorship of consent, see Konrad H. Jarausch, ed., *Dictatorship as Experience: Towards a Socio-Cultural History of the GDR* (New York: Berghahn Books, 1999); Robert Paxton, 파시즘: 열정과 광기의 정치 혁명 [*The Anatomy of Fascism*], trans. Son Myeonghui and Choe Huiyeong (Seoul: Gyoyangin, 2005), 307–8; Victoria de Grazia, *The Culture of Consent: Mass Organization of Leisure in Fascist Italy* (Cambridge:

Cambridge University Press, 1981), 3–5; Robert Gellately, *Backing Hitler: Consent and Coercion in Nazi Germany* (Oxford: Oxford University Press, 2001); Patrick Colm Hogan, *The Culture of Conformism: Understanding Social Consent* (Durham, N.C.: Duke University Press, 2001); Robert Mallett, "Consent or Dissent?," *Totalitarian Movements and Political Religions* 1, no. 2 (Autumn 2000).

8. See David Blackbourn and Geoff Eley, *The Peculiarities of German History* (Oxford: Oxford University Press, 1984); Ian Kershaw, *The Nazi Dictatorship: Problems and Perspectives of Interpretation* (London: Arnold, 2000), 20–23. From the mass dictatorship viewpoint, Jürgen Kocka's term "modern dictatorship," which he applies to the GDR, seems a kind of tautology. Mass dictatorship buys rather into the term *Fuersorgediktatur* (welfare dictatorship) to characterize the GDR's dictatorship. See Konrad Jarausch, "Beyond Uniformity," and Jürgen Kocka, "The GDR: A Special Kind of Modern Dictatorship," in Jarausch, *Dictatorship as Experience*, 3–26.

9. It should be noted that Germany had to refer to France as its own putative "West" because it was situated in the "East" from France's perspective. The cofiguration of French "civilization" and German "culture" in Norbert Elias's analysis shows this succinctly. See Nishikawa Nagao, 国境の越え方 [How to cross national borders] (Tokyo: Heibonsha, 2001), chap. 6.

10. Today's Trumpism and Brexit syndromes in Anglo-America indicate that populism is an integral part of "Western" democracy.

11. David Scott, *Conscripts of Modernity: The Tragedy of Colonial Enlightenment* (Durham, N.C.: Duke University Press, 2004), 4.

12. For "East" and "West" as the imaginative geography and the schema of cofiguration of East and West, see Edward Said, *Orientalism* (New York: Vintage Books, 1979), 49–72; Naoki Sakai, *Translation and Subjectivity* (Minneapolis: University of Minnesota Press, 1997), 40–71.

13. Daniel Schoenpflug's attempt to comprehend François Furet's and Ernst Nolte's comparative history of totalitarian movements within the framework of *histoire croisée* is suggestive, but its limits are clear. To say nothing of "linear causality" and "potential oversimplifications" in Nolte's thesis on "Bolshevik's challenge and Nazi's response," Furet seemed to stop at the point of making the analogy between French Jacobins of 1793 and Russian Bolsheviks of 1917. Despite Furet and Nolte's alleged contribution to the *histoire croisée* of totalitarian movements, its scale of comparison remains confined to Europe. See Daniel Schoenpflug, "Histoires Croisées: François Furet, Ernst Nolte and a Comparative History of Totalitarian Movements," *European History Quarterly* 37, no. 2 (2007): 265–90.

14. Scott, *Conscripts of Modernity*, 4–9.

15. Dominic Sachsenmaier, "Searching for Alternatives to Western Modernity—Cross-Cultural Approaches in the Aftermath of the Great War," ms.

16. Harry Harootunian, *Overcome by Modernity: History, Culture, and Community in Interwar Japan* (Princeton, N.J.: Princeton University Press, 2000), x.

17. Zygmunt Bauman, *Modernity and the Holocaust* (Ithaca, N.Y.: Cornell University Press, 2000), xi–xii, 28, 152, and passim.

18. For the continuities between colonial genocide and the Holocaust, see Jürgen Zimmerer, "Die Geburt des Ostlandes aus dem Geiste des Kolonialismus: Die nationalsozialistische Eroberungs- und Beherrschungspolitik in (post-)kolonialer Perspektive," *Sozial Geschichte* 19, no. 1 (2004); Benjamin Madley, "From Africa to Auschwitz: How German South West Africa Incubated Ideas and Methods Adopted and Developed by the Nazis in Eastern Europe," *European History Quarterly* 35, no. 3 (2005); Sven Lindquist, *Exterminate All the Brutes* (New York: New Press, 1996); Enzo Traverso, *The Origins of Nazi Violence* (New York: New Press, 2003).

19. Robert Gerwarth and Stephan Malinowski, "Der Holocaust als 'kolonialer Genozid?' Europaeische Kolonialgewalt und nationalsozialistischer Vernichtungskrieg," *Geschichte und Gesellschaft* 33 (2007): 445.

20. Karl Marx, *Capital*, vol. 1, trans. Ben Fowkes (London: Penguin Books, 1990), 895.

21. Mark Mazower, *Dark Continent: Europe's Twentieth Century* (New York: Vintage Books, 1998), xiii.

22. "Aufzeichnungen des persönlichen Referenten Rosenbergs Dr Koeppen über Hitlers Tischgespräche 1941," fol. 28 (September 23, 1941); Ian Kershaw, *Hitler, 1936–45: Nemesis* (New York: Norton, 2001), 400.

23. Kershaw, *Hitler, 1936–45*, 405.

24. Bauman, *Modernity and the Holocaust*, 227–28.

25. Hwang Byung-Joo, "박정희체제의 지배담론과 대중의 국민화" [The discourse of domination and nationalization of the masses in the Park Chung-Hee regime], in 대중독재 I: 강제와 동의 사이에서 [Mass dictatorship I: Between coercion and consent), ed. Lim Jie-Hyun and Kim Yong-Woo (Seoul: Chaiksesang, 2004), 475–515.

26. Michael Mann, *The Dark Side of Democracy* (Cambridge: Cambridge University Press, 2005), 4.

27. Mann, 70–110, 430–34.

28. Richard Shorten, "Francois Furet and Totalitarianism: A Recent Intervention in the Misuse of a Notion," *Totalitarian Movements and Political Religions* 3, no. 1 (Summer 2002), 11; Jacob L. Talmon, *Origins of Totalitarian Democracy* (New York: Norton, 1970).

29. 人民公安 [People's public security], no. 15 (1965): 4–6, quoted in Michael Schoenhals, "Sex in Big-Character Posters from China's Cultural Revolution: Gendering the Class Enemy," in *Gender Politics and Mass Dictatorship: Global Perspectives*, ed. Jie-Hyun Lim and Karen Petrone (Basingstoke, UK: Palgrave Macmillan, 2011), 237–38.

30. Simon Tormey, *Making Sense of Tyranny: Interpretations of Totalitarianism* (Manchester, UK: Manchester University Press, 1995), 115.

31. Toshio Nagano, "일본의 총력전체제" [Japanese total war system], in Lim and Kim, 대중독재I, 517–32; Yasushi Yamanouchi, J. Victor Koschmann, and Ryūichi Narita, eds., *Total War and Modernization* (Ithaca, N.Y.: Cornell University East Asia Program, 1998).

32. See Stefan Berger, "독일과 영국의 총력전체제" [Total war system in Germany and Britain], in Lim and Kim, 대중독재 I, 149–74.

33. Hogan, *The Culture of Conformism*, 58.

34. Georgi Schischkoff, *Die gesteuerte Vermassung* (Meisenheim: Anton Hain, 1964), 120–21.

35. Leszek Kołakowski, "Totalitarianism and the Virtue of the Lie," in *1984 Revisited: Totalitarianism in Our Century*, ed. Irving Howe (New York: Harper Collins, 1983), 133.

36. Vaclav Havel, "The Power of the Powerless," in *The Power of the Powerless: Citizens Against the State in Central-Eastern Europe*, ed. John Keane (London: Hutchinson, 1985).

37. Grzegorz Miernik, ed., *Polacy Wobec PRL: Strategie przystosowawcze* (Kielce: Kieleckie Towarzystwo Naukowe, 2003), 7; Harald Dehne, "소비하거나 몰락하거나" [Satisfying consumption as a social policy present from the leadership? Sisyphus between securing central planning and people's desire], in 대중독재 III: 일상의 욕망과 미망 [Mass dictatorship III: Between desire and delusion], ed. Lim Jie-Hyun and Kim Yong-Woo (Seoul: Chaeksesang, 2007), 304–5.

38. Andrzej Walicki, *Polskie zmagania z wolnością* (Kraków: Universitas, 2000), 102–9.

39. Antonio Gramsci, *Selections from the Prison Notebooks*, ed. and trans. Q. Hoare and Geoffrey N. Smith (New York: International, 1971), 120.

40. de Grazia, *The Culture of Consent*, 12, 21–22, and passim.

41. Sheldon Garon, *Molding Japanese Minds: The State in Everyday Life* (Princeton, N.J.: Princeton University Press, 1997).

42. The term *consensus dictatorship* is found in Martin Sabrow, "Dictatorship as Discourse: Cultural Perspectives on SED Legitimacy," in *Dictatorship as Experience: Towards a Socio-Cultural History of the GDR*, ed. Konrad H. Jarausch (New York: Berghahn Books, 1999), 208. Translating the term into English is tricky since the German word *Konsens* implies both "consent" and "consensus."

43. Žižek's suggestion for reading Havel with Althusser may be altered to the suggestion that one might read Havel with Althusser, Foucault, and Gramsci in the context of mass dictatorship studies. See Slavoj Žižek, *Did Somebody Say Totalitarianism?* (London: Verso, 2001), 90.

44. See Michael Wildt, "나치의 민족공동체-새로운 정치질서" [The national socialist *Volksgemeinschaft*—a new political order], in Lim and Kim, 대중독재 I. For its appeal to ordinary people, see Wildt, *Volksgemeinschaft als Selbstermaechtigung: Gewalt gegen Juden in der deutschen Provinz 1919 bis 1939* (Hamburg: Hamburger Edition, 2007).

45. Paul Betts, "The New Fascination with Fascism: The Case of Nazi Modernism," *Journal of Contemporary History* 37 (October 2002): 544.

46. Michel Foucault, *The History of Sexuality*, vol. 1, trans. Robert Hurley (New York: Vintage, 1978), 135–45; Michel Foucault, "The Politics of Health in the Eighteenth Century," in *Power/Knowledge*, ed. Colin Gordon (New York: Pantheon, 1980), 166–82.

47. George L. Mosse, *The Fascist Revolution* (New York: Howard Fertig, 1999), 48; Mosse, *Nationalism and Sexuality* (Madison: University of Wisconsin Press, 1985), 21–22.

48. Carl Schmitt, "Der Gegensatz von Parlamentarismus und moderner Massendemokratie," in 정치신학 外 [*Political Theology and Other Writings*], trans. Kim Hyo Jeon (Seoul: Bupmunsa, 1988), 102.

49. Michael Hardt and Antonio Negri, *Empire* (Cambridge, Mass.: Harvard University Press, 2000), 87, 134. Hardt and Negri's sharp criticism of the "sovereign machine" and Schmitt's ardent advocacy of "sovereign dictatorship" stand on the same historical ground of the formation of the modern sovereign state.

50. Schoenhals, "Sex in Big-Character Posters," 238.

51. Mosse, *The Fascist Revolution*, 76.

52. Weber, *Varieties of Fascism*, 139.

53. Hardt and Negri, *Empire*, 112.

54. See chapter 8.

55. Jie-Hyun Lim, "Befreiung oder Modernisierung? Sozialismus als ein Weg der anti-westlichen Moderniseirung in unterentwickelten Laendern," *Beitraege zur Geschichte der Arbeiter-bewegung* 43, no. 2 (2001): 5–23; Jie-Hyun Lim, "Socjalizm, ale jaki . . .? Ideologia mobilizacji ludu w procesie modernizacji w Azji Wschodniej," *Dzieje Najnowsze* 31, 1 (2000), 163–76.

56. George L. Mosse, *The Nationalization of the Masses* (New York: Howard Fertig, 1975).

57. Salvador Giner, *Mass Society* (New York: Academic Press, 1976), 127.

58. Emilio Gentile, "The Sacralisation of Politics: Definitions, Interpretations and Reflections on the Question of Secular Religion and Totalitarianism," *Totalitarian Movements and Political Religions* 1 (Summer 2000).

59. Benedict Anderson, *Imagined Communities* (London: Verso, 1991), 9–19.

60. George Monbiot, "America Is a Religion," *Guardian*, July 29, 2003.

61. Emilio Gentile, "Sacralisation of Politics," 24–25.

62. See Konrad H. Jarausch, ed., *Dictatorship as Experience*; Robert Gellately, *Backing Hitler: Consent and Coercion in Nazi Germany* (Oxford: Oxford University Press, 2001); Robert Mallet, "Consent or Dissent?," *Totalitarian Movements and Political Religions* 1 (Autumn 2000).

63. Michel de Certeau, *Heterologies: Discoures on the Other*, trans. Brian Massumi (Minneapolis: Minnesota University Press, 1986), 188, 189, 197.

64. Peter Lambert, "아래로부터의 역사-나치즘과 제3제국" [History from below, Nazism and Third Reich: Paradigm shift and problems], in Lim and Kim, 대중독재 III, 41–70.

65. Jose Ortega y Gasset, *La rebellión de las masas*, trans. Young-Jo Hwangbo (Seoul: Yoksabipyŏngsa, 2005).

66. Alf Lüdtke, "꾸불꾸불가기" [Practicing and meandering], in Lim and Kim, 대중독재 III, 13–37.

67. Jerrold Seigel, "Problematizing the Self," in *Beyond the Cultural Turn: New Directions in the Study of Society and Culture*, ed. Victoria E. Bonnell and Lynn Hunt (Berkeley: University of California Press, 1999), 287.

68. Alf Lüdtke, "Attraction and Power of (Self-)Energizing: National Socialism in Germany, 1933–1945," paper delivered at 123rd Annual Meeting of AHA, New York, January 4, 2008.

69. Paul Corner, "Self-Mobilisation in Mass Dictatorships-the Italian Example," paper delivered at 123rd Annual Meeting of AHA, New York, January 4, 2008.

70. Jie-Hyun Lim, "Conference Report: Coercion and Consent: A Comparative Study of 'Mass Dictatorship,'" *Contemporary European History* 13, no. 2 (2004).

71. The academic achievement of *Alltagsgeschichte* is very suggestive in this context. See Alf Lüdtke, ed., *The History of Everyday Life*, trans. William Templer (Princeton, N.J.: Princeton University Press, 1995); Detlev J. K. Peukert, *Inside Nazi Germany*, trans. Richard Deveson (New Haven, Conn.: Yale University Press, 1987).

72. This task will prove more than complex than usual because it will involve crossing the line between perceived reality and objective reality.

73. Raul Hilberg, "Significance of the Holocaust," in *The Holocaust: Ideology, Bureaucracy, and Genocide*, ed. Henry Friedlander and Sybil Milton (Millwood, N.Y.: Kraus International, 1980), 101.

74. Most recently, war criminals in the former Yugoslavia confirmed this once again. See Slavenka Drakulić, *They Would Never Hurt a Fly: War Criminals on Trial in the Hague* (London: Abacus, 2004).

75. Bauman, *Modernity and the Holocaust*, 152.

76. Mann, *The Dark Side*, 9.

77. Seigel, "Problematizing the Self," 289.

78. Felix Guattari, *Molecular Revolution* (Harmondsworth, UK: Penguin, 1984), 229.

10

Nationalizing the Bolshevik Revolution Transnationally

In Search of Non-Western Modernization
Among "Proletarian" Nations

Socialist Governmentality and Collective Subjectivity

In late 1979 the state-owned media in the "Cooperative Republic of Guyana" announced that mass games supervised by members of a socialist country of the Global East would soon be performed in the capital. The mass games would be a part of the festival to commemorate the tenth anniversary of the republic's founding. On February 23, 1980, five thousand Guyanese spectators gathered at the National Park auditorium and watched spectacular multimedia performances with faultless choreography performed by three thousand students, artists, dancers, and musicians. Behind these performers, another thousand students created a gigantic mosaic by holding up cards. George Simon, an Amerindian muralist, led a group of Guyanese artists in directing the entire spectacle. Behind the scenes, seven artists from the Democratic People's Republic of Korea (North Korea), led by art director Kim Il-nam, oversaw the entire enterprise. The president of Guyana, Linden F. S. Burnham, had invited North Korean experts to transplant collectivism and teach the Guyanese how to stage the North Korean style of mass games.[1] The North Korean performers taught the Guyanese multimedia performance in the collectivist spirit. The spectacle required the mandatory participation of children enrolled in primary and secondary schools in order to initiate the next generation of

Guyanese in the mores of socialism and collectivism: it was used as a cultural and educational tool to promote a new socialist consciousness among the masses.[2]

The spectacle in Georgetown, performed by the Guyanese mass under North Korean supervision, was an example of socialist globalization in 1970s and 1980s. Guyana, under Burnham's leadership, had gained a reputation for its outspoken support for radical causes everywhere, from the Palestinian struggle to Basque separatism, and had become one of the most vocal supporters of the North Korean regime in the world. A certain ideological affinity existed between the North Korean *Juche* ideology and the concept of cooperative socialism in Guyana. Both countries, after a long period of colonial rule, wanted economic independence, and this desire was manifested in the nationalization of all foreign-owned enterprises and the espousal of autarky as a state principle. In both North Korea and Guyana, a multitude of ambitious educational and cultural reforms were inaugurated with the intent to create a New Man and a New Woman. This anthropological revolution aimed at making a total state by energizing Guyanese and Korean subjectivity and expunging the traces of colonial and capitalist vice from individual psychology. The North Korean and the Guyanese political states were trying to revitalize the earlier Soviet project of creating the *Homo sovieticus* with voluntary commitment to the revolution.

In this chapter I will discuss how the impact of the Bolshevik Revolution of 1917 reverberated far beyond the geopolitical parameters of the Cold War world and those set by Cold War historiography. In the Cold War era, postcolonial states were seeking to institute variations of the earlier Soviet attempts to create a collective society based on the radically transformed individual—but with one important difference. While the Soviet Union was firmly committed to the principle of fighting colonialism worldwide in its rhetoric, in practice it was an imperial power that was based at its core on a Russian ethnos. Postcolonial states in Asia, Africa, the Caribbean, and Latin America inherited the Soviet commitment to socialist subjectivity and collectivism but interpreted it through the lens of radical anticolonialism. A sense of historical backwardness, national humiliation, and wounded national pride that I have described elsewhere as "victimhood nationalism" created a hybrid political ideology that appropriated socialist forms of authoritarianism and rapid modernization.[3] Socialism as a hybrid of labor mobilization, national liberation, and rapid modernization was pervasive in parts of the postcolonial world, although historians have paid it little attention.

Mass spectacles, a product of supposedly free men and women united by a common ideal who voluntarily subordinate themselves to the communal good, were used to inspire and mobilize millions. Mass games became a worldwide phenomenon during the interwar period, when, in the capitals of Nazi Germany and the Communist Soviet Union, men and women marched in menacing shows of strength, unity, and patriotism. Today the cult of mass games has died worldwide, and the only country where they are performed on a regular basis is North Korea. Mass games are a choreographed socialist spectacle consisting of over 100,000 participants in a hypersynchronized display of gymnastics, dance, acrobatics, and dramatic performances, accompanied by music and other audiovisual effects. A deeply politicized commentary guides viewers in their consumption of the cultural event.[4] The North Korean mass games must be situated within global history and the history of both postcolonial and socialist statecraft.

By fostering healthy and strong physiques and a high degree of organization, discipline, and collectivism, the mass games were originally a modernizing practice that was used to forge a revolutionary New Man, *Homo sovieticus*. Schoolchildren, conscious that a single slip in their action might spoil their mass-gymnastic performance, made every effort to subordinate all their thoughts and actions to the collective project they were engaged in, impervious to the pain their bodies were experiencing. Mass games were designed to create a modern subject through bodily discipline and exposure to "controlled and guided massification."[5] Indeed, participation in mass games is more efficient than organized sports in promoting a high degree of "emotional entrainment," "bodily synchronization," "people's consciousness of togetherness," and "charismatic mobilization" on the basis of mutual attention between the leader and masses.[6] To make people surrender their individual identities for the sake of a collective subjectivity desired by the regime constitutes a distinct art of government that has its roots in the early Soviet Union.[7]

Socialist Guyana was eager to import the mass games from North Korea to facilitate the sociopolitical engineering of its own population. Compared to the violence of capitalist Hong Kong's kung fu movies popular at that time among Guyanese youths, mass games were considered to be a clean and healthy pedagogy designed to teach the virtues of punctuality and discipline through bodily synchronization of the group. Indeed, the North Korean model appealed to many African and Caribbean socialist regimes that were building socialism in the conditions of deep material poverty that European colonial powers had wrought through much of Africa, Asia, and Latin America.[8] Comrade Leader Burnham regarded North Korea as a model for constructing Third World socialism in Guyana. Financial support from the North Korean regime played an important role in disseminating *Juche* ideology among national communist circles in the non-Western world. With its emphasis on autarky, national unity, and a collective subjectivity, *Juche* ideology attracted the nationalist elites of many postcolonial countries who were struggling with the imperialist legacies of economic backwardness and national disintegration.

The conjuncture of North Korean *Juche* ideology and Guyanese cooperative socialism as late as 1979 shows how Soviet models continued to be influential in the twentieth century and played a profound role in shaping the self-contradictory nature of socialist postcolonial states in the developing world. While leaders in the wider arc of the Global East and South implemented the Soviet model of forced modernization and industrialization, they jettisoned socialist principles of workers' autonomy and freedom for the sake of the national interest. Elites in postcolonial nation-states used a series of techniques to mobilize the masses, including the subjugation of the self to the collective and the biopolitical control of populations. Citizens were mobilized in a national and anti-Western political project of modernization that many in the developing world perceived to be the essence of Stalinism. As in Guyana, postcolonial states sought to achieve a disciplined and united collective that they believed to have been the core achievement of Stalinism. There were few attempts to re-create the revolutionary and often spontaneous mass movements that characterized the Russian revolutions of 1917. The Marxist concept of a class struggle between the propertied strata of society and the workers was reinterpreted as a geopolitical struggle between bourgeois and proletarian nations on the global stage. The anger of impoverished masses in many postcolonial states was directed away from their own elites and toward their former colonial masters, the Western powers.

This chapter traces the process through which Bolshevik ideas regarding proletariat revolution and class war were repurposed in the struggle of postcolonial and proletarian nations against their former, European oppressors. By analyzing the transnational interactions of socialism, nationalism, colonialism, and fascism, I demonstrate the ways in which the vocabulary of the Soviet Union was appropriated by popular nationalists in the decolonized world and used for national projects of non-Western and Soviet-style forced modernization.

Non-Western Modernization and Marxist Voluntarism

The Bolshevik Revolution in Russia seemed to have occurred at the periphery rather than at the center of global industrialization. It was a revolution that did not adhere to Karl Marx's formulations in *Das Kapital*. Indeed, Bolsheviks seemed to have gone against Marx's theory by carrying out a socialist revolution in supposedly backward Russia, where capitalism and industrialization were in their infancy.[9] In *Imperialism, the Highest Stage of Capitalism* (1917), Vladimir Lenin expanded on Marx's view that imperialism was central to the success of European capitalism, and with that theoretical groundwork, the Bolsheviks became the foremost advocates of decolonization and national liberation in the European empires. Immediately after the revolution, Lenin announced that the Soviet regime would annul all the unequal treaties implemented by tsarist Russia and affecting oppressed nations on its periphery. This unprecedented declaration from a former imperial power stimulated a great interest in Bolshevism among revolutionary nationalists in the Middle East, Africa, and Asia. In his "Draft Theses on National and Colonial Questions for the Second Congress of the Communist International," published in June 1920, Lenin insisted on support for bourgeois-democratic liberation movements and nationalist movements in states where "feudal or patriarchal and patriarchal-peasant relations" predominated.[10] He urged workers of the colonized nations to participate in national-liberation movements and argued that attacks on European capitalism worldwide would help bring about proletarian revolutions in the heart of Europe itself.

In the fifth session of the national and colonial debates that were held in Moscow on July 28, 1920, Park Chin-soon, the first Korean socialist representative to the 2nd Congress of the Comintern, reinforced Lenin's draft theses by stressing that Russia was the "link between the whole proletarian West and the revolutionary East." According to Park, "the whole task of the Communist International in the colonial question consists in correcting the mistakes made by the leaders of the 2nd International. The history of the ignominious collapse of the 2nd International has shown that the western European proletariat cannot win the fight against its bourgeoisie as long as the bourgeoisie has a source of strength in the colonies."[11] The Baku Congress of the Peoples of the East, held in September 1920, marked a commitment by the Comintern to support revolutionary nationalist movements in the colonized East. On September 7, 1920, the organization's head, Grigory Zinoviev, concluded the seventh session of the Baku Congress with the slogan, "Workers of all lands (countries) and oppressed peoples of the whole world, unite!" words that were uttered to tumultuous applause.[12]

At the 1st Congress of the Toilers of the Far East, held in 1922, the Korean delegation occupied 52 out of 144 seats. Many a Korean delegate remembered their meeting with Lenin and Zinoviev, leaders who stressed the importance of nationalism rather than socialism in colonial Korea.[13] Kim Kyu-sik, who had represented Korea as the chief delegate at Versailles and had participated in the 1st Congress of the Toilers of the Far East, expressed anger against the United States for betraying the nationalist causes of the oppressed nations. He raised his hope for Korean independence with the assistance of the Bolshevik government. Yi Sang-jae, a typical Korean social patriot, claimed that "nationalism is the offspring of socialism, and socialism is the main current of nationalism."[14] A police report submitted to the Japanese governor of the Korean peninsula pointed out that "the Korean Communist Party sees communism as a means to achieve national independence. . . . Communism remains just a mask to disguise their real aim of independence under it."[15] Later in North Korea, Kim Il-sŏng used this amalgam of nationalism and socialism. He confessed that "I am a nationalist as much as a communist," by which he banally reconciled patriotism with internationalism.[16] The enthusiasm for the Russian Revolution among revolutionary nationalists of the East cannot, however, be reduced to the aspirations for freedom and national self-determination. Considering that Russia was viewed as a developing or a peripheral capitalist society, the Bolshevik Revolution provided a successful model of noncapitalist modernization that appeared on the surface to be distinctly anti-Western.[17] Revolutionary nationalists found themselves in an insoluble dilemma: they believed that they inevitably would have to follow the West in order to overcome the West. There seemed to be no alternative but to transform and modernize their premodern and traditional societies by importing the essential elements of capitalism and social modernity in order to fight against colonial rule. Nationalists also worried that they would lose their cherished cultural identity in the process of modernization. Nationalists from the East suffered perennially from the tension of adopting Westernization wholesale while retaining their national culture and purity.

After the events of 1917, revolutionary Asian nationalists were offered the unprecedented opportunity of skipping or bypassing capitalism altogether in their path to modernity. They derived this approach from ideas born of the Bolshevik Revolution. The idea of bypassing the capitalist stage of development and proceeding through peasant communes directly to the stage of socialism had already been formulated within the Marxist intellectual tradition. When Russian agrarian socialists of the second half of the nineteenth century proposed this variation on the revolutionary road, Marx did not deny this option in his draft letters to Vera Zasulich.[18] Russian Populists in the late nineteenth century had connected the future of socialism with the traditional collectivism of the peasant commune, and they regarded socialism as a way of achieving "anti-Western modernization." Lenin claimed that the October Revolution presented colonies and semicolonies with the historical precedent of transitioning to socialism and bypassing the capitalist stage. In fact, "Lenin never broke from the theoretical and political traditions of Russian Populism, but completed Georgi Plekhanov's project by assimilating Marxism to the very different theoretical framework of Populism."[19] The Russian Populists' idea of bypassing capitalism as a model of development owed its second birth to Leninism. After the October Revolution, due to the depredations of World War I and the ongoing civil war, the Bolsheviks found themselves in a very poor country that lacked the material base for constructing socialism. Rapid industrialization soon became the top priority, something that both Leon Trotsky and, later, Joseph Stalin urged.

As Eric Hobsbawm said, "Bolshevism turned itself into an ideology for the rapid economic development for countries in which the conditions of capitalist development did not exist."[20] By showing the possibility of a noncapitalist path toward modernization in underdeveloped countries, the Bolshevik Revolution solved the historical dilemma of former colonies that were looking for an alternative to Western models of development. Indian reformist thinker Swami Vivekananda's observation that socialism was "neither traditionalism nor westernization" prevailed among the millions of colonized people in Asia. Revolutionary nationalists of the East perceived socialism to be a non-Western and even anti-Western ideology, despite its indubitably Western origin. It was not difficult for them to find, rediscover, or even invent the collectivist tradition in their respective national heritages and then proclaim that it represented the seeds of the imagined socialist future. According to Stuart Schram and Hélène Carrère d'Encausse, "It was Lenin who first opened the door wide to the implantation of Marxism in Asia."[21]

In Asia, revolutionary nationalists tried to discover socialism in religious scriptures, monuments of social thought, and oral traditions of past national cultures. Very often, native thinkers from ancient and medieval times were declared to have been the forerunners of scientific socialism. Premodern cultural and religious traditions were grafted onto socialist ideology, producing in the process an archaic and local image of socialism. Socialism was perceived as anti-Western Westernization as well as a form of native and premodern modernization. For instance, Mao Zedong believed that he was a savior of China in the tradition of bandit heroes of Liangshan marsh, featured in the great classical novel of Chinese literature, *Water Margin*. In Mao's favorite novel, the bandit heroes fought for justice and order in an unjust and chaotic world. In an interview with the American journalist Agnes Smedley in 1937, Mao said that "the Communists . . . are most passionately concerned with the fate of a Chinese nation, and moreover with its fate throughout all eternity."[22] The Chinese revolution was the victory of peasant nationalism and traditional values and represented the ascendance of the communist-peasant alliance over the Westernized elites represented by the Guomindang.

The process of nationalizing the Bolshevik Revolution began even before 1917. The patriotism of the Polish Socialist Party and social-imperialist leanings of the Social Democratic Party of Germany are also precursors to the nationalizing of socialism. It was Israel Alexander Helphand (1867–1924), alias Alexander Parvus, who theorized what a national socialism would look like. In Istanbul, he invented a cluster of significant intellectual convergences between the ideas of leftist revolutionaries and the conception of an authoritarian revolution held by rightist Young Turks.

Revolutionaries from the left and the right agreed on the primacy of anti-imperialism and desired a strong state based on a designated class or a specific ethnoreligious group. Many political groups conceived of eth-noreligious war, national struggle, and expropriation as forms of class struggle. Through the revolutionary concept of an exclusively Turkish-Muslim "national economy" (*millî iktisad*), Parvus provided an intellectual foundation for the appropriation of socialist concepts by the right-wing Young Turks. He regarded the Turkish Muslim peasantry as the "people" and the core of the "nation" (*millet*). While stressing the destructive role of European imperialism in generating the economic dependence of the Otto-mans on global financial systems, Parvus provided anti-imperialistic eco-nomic ideas derived from the arsenal of Marxism. He helped transform the Young Turks' political and economic agenda by conceptualizing a national economy.[23]

Stalin accelerated the process of nationalizing Bolshevism. In spelling out the connection between the First Five-Year Plan and the strategic con-cerns of the Soviet regime, he proclaimed that his main goal was to catch up with and overtake the economies of the advanced countries. Stalin's political strategy was backed by Evgenii Preobrazhensky's theory of prim-itive socialist accumulation, which had been developed earlier in the 1920s. During the First Five-Year Plan, Stalin extracted resources for the rapid development of the industrial sector by collectivizing peasant lands. Dur-ing the same period, he also concentrated vast powers in the hands of the Soviet state.[24] However, socialist modernization and the rapid industrial-ization of the Soviet Union came at the cost of the welfare of the workers and peasants in the USSR. Living standards fell dramatically as the pro-duction of food and consumer goods was ruthlessly subordinated to the drive to develop heavy industry. Stalin redefined Marxism as the coercive rule of the party over the state, and of the state over civil society. The goal of achieving socialism for the many was replaced by a quest to achieve eco-nomic and military parity with the core states of the capitalist world economy. Coercive rule plus state-sponsored industrialization became the new heart of the Stalinist reinterpretation of Marxism.[25]

The Bolshevik socialist economy was based on the militarization of labor, a concept borrowed from the German experience of the total war system during World War I. Karl Kautsky observed that the Soviet state had achieved success only in those spheres where military methods could be applied.[26] Julius Martov described the Soviet Union as a flourishing "trench army's quasi-socialism based on the general simplification of the whole of life."[27] Without the voluntary participation and self-mobilization of the working masses, socialist modernization soon began to rely heavily on military methods. A system of mass mobilization directed from above replaced the voluntary will of the people from below. The success of Stalinist modernization depended on the Soviet state's ability to recruit workers for economic development and military strength. Stakhanovites, the exemplary products of a triumphant Stalinism in the 1930s, worked tirelessly under Stalin's slogan that "there are no fortresses that the Bolsheviks cannot storm." Stakhanovite workers, who apparently willingly endured the deterioration of living standards coupled with increasing norms of productivity, were represented as the Promethean heroes of Soviet mythology. The Soviet media promoted them as exemplary models in order to encourage ordinary Soviet people to increase their work tempo and productivity.

The remarkable economic growth rate in the Soviet Union under the Five-Year Plans greatly impressed the new leaders of recently decolonized nations. Many of them persuaded themselves that, in the uncertain military conditions of the Cold War, their primary goal should be nation building and rapid economic modernization. Time was of the essence, and leaders such as Jawaharlal Nehru believed that capitalist developmental models derived from the West would take too long to implement and take even longer to start bearing fruit. Nehru wondered: "Should we follow the British, French, or American way? Do we really have as much time as 100 to 150 years to achieve our goal? This is absolutely unacceptable. In such an event we shall simply perish." Julius Nyerere, the leader of Tanzanian agrarian socialism, coined the slogan, "We must run while they walk." Mao Zedong and Kim Il-sŏng were also ardent advocates of rapid industrialization. The slogan of Mao's Great Leap Forward campaign launched in 1958 was "Let us overtake Britain and catch up with the United States in fifteen years." In the same year, Kim Il-sŏng stressed that "we can achieve in the period of two Five-Year Plans what other socialist countries achieved in the period of three Five-Year Plans." In the postcolonial setting, non-Western socialism shifted its ideological focus from gaining national liberation to the creation of a Soviet-style socialist economy. Many believed that state-managed industrialization would become the vehicle for the rapid development of countries that had been destroyed by centuries of colonial exploitation.[28]

In the developing world, Soviet socialism was perceived to be a non-Western or even an anti-Western form of modernization. As a philosophical system, unadulterated Marxism was unacceptable because of its insistence on a purely materialist understanding of history. Socialism had to be oriented away from its emphasis on dialectical materialism and economism and given a specific national content that was aligned with the spiritual and cultural heritage of Asian peoples.[29] The antimaterialist impetus to nationalize the Bolshevik Revolution in the East provided the philosophical justification for a reinterpretation of Marxism. Mao's political adaptation of Marxism culminated in the Great Leap Forward campaign in the years 1958–1960, as he claimed that the political mobilization of the masses was far more important than building the material resources of socialism. Mao thought that China could overcome its material scarcity by exalting the power of human will in small-scale people's communes. Mao's "military romanticism" reinforced the voluntarist tendency embedded within Marxism and took it to the very extreme. Mao's subjective interpretation of Marxism stemmed from Lenin's own creative adaptation of Marxism for the conditions of relatively backward Russia. While Lenin believed that the transformation of the political realm was possible through willpower, Mao extended this Nietzschean ideology to the realm of nature. A sense of revolutionary romanticism led Mao to the fatal illusion that his party could lay the foundations of communism in China within a very short time, even though the country lacked the necessary material conditions.[30]

Of all the nationalist leaders, Kim Il-sǒng was the most ardent advocate of a highly idiosyncratic interpretation of Marxism. He had to build socialism in a country that the United States Air Force completely flattened by military bombardment during the Korean Civil War (1950–1953). The only resource that Kim had at his disposal to power socialist reconstruction was the Korean population. Kim shared some theoretical points in common with Mao Zedong. If Mao had stressed that people are the motive force of world history, Kim defined *Juche* ideology as the idea signifying that "the popular masses are the master and driving force of the revolution and construction."[31] In Kim's view, mass mobilization was the philosophical basis for North Korean socialist development strategy, and this belief was made manifest in his four main slogans: independence of thought, political sovereignty, economic self-reliance, and military self-defense. Along with Mao, Kim argued that human willpower was the primary moving force in his country, and this could also be used fruitfully in the realm of development. According to him, it is not merely economic resources but a widespread revolutionary fervor that makes a society productive and highly developed.[32] Burmese Buddhist socialists also adopted the view that national and economic development could be powered by the application of human agency and will. With its abstract understanding of humanism, socialism of Global Easts, in its many variants, deviated sharply from Marx's dictum in his *Theses on Feuerbach* (1845) that "human essence is the ensemble of social relations."[33]

Marxist voluntarism in its extreme form was an ideological tool to persuade people to voluntarily participate in the state project. The reality, however, was more forced mobilization than persuaded mobilization. When authoritarian leaders in the socialist regions of Global Easts found widespread enthusiasm for socialist causes lacking, they forced the masses to participate in their development projects. The managed participation of millions of people in massive state-sponsored projects could typically be maintained only by the application of coercive and military methods. Military metaphors—references to shock tactics, cavalry charges, and partisan warfare—were constantly used in constructing the discourses of socialism in Global Easts and marked another overt borrowing from the Soviet model. Despite initial victories in the short term, the militarized form of mass mobilization for extensive economic development soon exhausted the labor force. The promise of a future socialist utopia without the accompaniment of tangible material rewards could not be used indefinitely to mobilize citizens. Socialist leaders then turned to nationalism as a way to strengthen their socialist doctrines. They invoked traditions of communalism and moral codes of reciprocity and obligations that had little affinity with modern socialism: in a surprising twist, Marxist militants readily took up Confucian political moralism.[34] They replaced the slogans of "equality and fraternity" among citizens with those that advocated popular loyalty and obedience to one's parents, the state, and the Great Leader. If the right-wing developmental dictatorship in South Korea defined itself as a Korean way of democracy, then Kim Il-sŏng's regime in North Korea played up its distinctive form of socialism.

Desire for Bourgeois Nation Status Among Proletarian Nations

Yi Sun-tak (1897–1950) was a leading Marxist economist in colonial Korea. During the 1920s he studied economics at Kyoto Imperial University in Japan under Kawakami Hajime, a well-known Marxist economist who translated *Das Kapital* into Japanese (*Shihonron*). After returning home, Yi Sun-tak taught economics at Yonhi College in Seoul (now Yonsei University). Until he was arrested for his leading role in the Red Professors' Group and fired in 1938, he had engaged wholeheartedly in popularizing Marxism among colonized Koreans. Among more than sixty articles that Yi Sun-tak published in various journals and newspapers, the most impressive was his account of his travels around the world, with visits to seventeen countries in Asia, the Middle East, Africa, Europe, and North America from April 24, 1933, to January 20, 1934. While traveling, Yi sent regular contributions to a Korean daily newspaper, *Chosun ilbo*.

Later in 1934, Yi published his travelogue as a book titled *A Recent Travel Around the World*. It was a comprehensive report on the contemporary world that depicted the geography, history, ethnography, customs, religion, art, politics, economy, and society in different regions and countries. As a colonial intellectual, Yi expressed his deep compassion for independence movements in China, India, Egypt, Poland, Ireland, and African countries that were struggling under the yoke of European colonialism. Yi's empathy with the national liberation movements of the colonized peoples coexisted with his bias against the savage "natives" who were the subjects of these movements. He reprimanded the unpatriotic Chinese who were willing to sell out their country for money and admonished the Indians to stop their internal class struggles and religious conflicts, which had been exacerbated by the British policies of divide and rule. Upon disembarking at the port of Aden, Yemen, Yi criticized the colonization of the African continent by European powers. Given Africa's immense contributions to world civilization, Yi found the situation in Africa to be particularly tragic.[35]

Yi's distress over Africa's predicament was parallel to his deep regret for the backwardness of colonial Korea. According to him, Korea was also partially to blame as it "did not open [its] eyes to the foreign market . . ., did not think of great national leadership to overcome the poisonous political partisanship."[36] Despite Yi's denunciation of colonialism, he could not conceal his envy of the colonial powers and the greatness of imperialist civilizations. A deep regret that "we, the Koreans, should have been the West" was paired with a poorly disguised envy of the West. A combination of denunciation and mimicry of Western civilization, a desire for and fear of the colonial powers, and an oscillation between self-empowerment and self-Orientalism ran as a subtext through Yi's travelogue. An ambivalent response to European colonialism was not peculiar to Yi, and, as postcolonial studies have shown, both right- and left-wing intellectuals living under colonial rule manifested these contradictory emotional reactions to both the perceived and the imaginary West. Yi's intellectual journey between an envious denunciation of the West and a morbid self-laceration can also be found in most of the travelogues written by Korean intellectuals between 1945 and 1966.[37]

The most intriguing aspect of Yi's travelogue is his idiosyncratic view of interwar Europe and the explicit empathy he exhibited for Fascist Italy. Except for a couple of reservations about the personality cult of Mussolini and political oppression, Yi did not conceal his admiration for Italian fascism. Yi's direct encounter with the Italian Fascist reality betrayed his earlier expectations of encountering gangs of beggars, pickpockets, and thieves on the streets of Italy. Yi could be rid of his past prejudices against fascism "because the army and police of Mussolini repressed wrongdoings completely, thus social justice and public righteousness are greatly improved now compared to the era of parliamentary democracy." He also recorded his cheerful conversation with a young Italian about Mussolini near the Garibaldi monument. When Yi asked him "if Mussolini could be a second Garibaldi," he answered: "Mussolini is better than Garibaldi."[38]

Yi visited the exhibition installed on Via Nazionale in Rome several times to commemorate the tenth anniversary of Fascist rule. In a humorous manner, Yi explained that since frequent visitors to the exhibition received a substantial discount on their train tickets, it was important for him to visit more than once. The propaganda exhibition of Fascist achievements made a deep impression on him. Yi was also very impressed by the Fascist impact on the Italian economy: the balanced budget, the recovery of credit through successful negotiations to reduce foreign debts, the dramatic reduction of unemployment, and the relative strength of the agrarian sector. He admired the well-built infrastructure, the steady growth of the population, and the well-thought-out migration policies of the Italian state. Yi noted that all this successful restructuring of the economy had converted Italy into a member of the "Gold Bloc," which stood firmly against the alliance representing Western Europe and the United States.[39]

Surprisingly, Yi's experiences with Italian fascism did not lead this leftist colonial intellectual to develop any critical thoughts about fascism, perhaps because Italy's colonial ambitions had yet to become apparent. Yi seems to have been uninterested in the Italian Fascists' desire for a second Roman Empire, nor did he critically evaluate the harm that such policies could do to a colonized Africa. Any leftist value judgment of Fascist exploitation of labor at home, or imperial tendencies abroad, remained suspended in Yi's glowing account of Mussolini's Italy. The successful building of a self-sustaining economy by the Fascist regime was an admirable fact, and one can discern in his writing Yi's hope that such a plan could be successfully implemented in Korea as well. For Yi, a colonial Marxist, a shift from Korean dependency to economic and national greatness seemed to be the most desirable goal, and it seemed to matter little if this process of autarkic development was carried out, whether a Fascist or a communist regime. Yi argued that the independence and self-regeneration of the colonies, under the auspices of either ideological system, would represent a blow against the colonial expansion of advanced capitalist countries. When he returned home after traveling around the world, Yi visited the headquarters of *Chosun Joongang ilbo*, a newspaper that had provided financial support for his travels. The paper published an article about Yi's visit to the newspaper's editorial office under the title "He Saw the Hope for the Korean Nation in the Future." During this visit, Yi stated that "what has impressed me the most in my travels is the transformation in Italy."[40]

Yi had discovered a development model for colonial Korea in Fascist Italy. It is not difficult to see the strong desire for power and modernity in Yi Sun-tak's account of Italy. But his desire cannot be reduced to a simple longing for Western modernity. Yi's praise for Italian fascism was in stark contrast to his sharp criticism of London. He saw London as a dirty cosmopolitan city tainted by the presence of beggars, the unemployed, and pollution. Despite its past glory, the British Empire seemed to be in decline.[41] Yi projected his desire for power and greatness onto Fascist Italy rather than the British Empire. Fascist Italy's remarkable advance "from a proletarian nation to a bourgeois nation" made him believe that such a transformation was also possible in Korea. The traditional Marxist view of class struggle was repurposed as a national struggle in the terms of Fascist ideology, and some colonial Marxists began to regard socialism as a means to achieve national liberation and enter a phase of rapid modernization as the Soviet Union did. Polish irredentist socialists, who invented the concept of "social patriotism" in the late nineteenth century, might have been the predecessors of those colonial Marxists in Asia.[42]

Yi Sun-tak was not the only colonial Marxist who discovered a model for national independence and the speedy modernization of a poor and underdeveloped colony in both socialist and fascist states. Subhas Chandra Bose, a well-known Indian Marxist-nationalist and founder of the Indian National Army, also traveled to the Soviet Union, Fascist Italy, Nazi Germany, and imperial Japan in search of a military alliance against the British Empire during the Second World War. He founded the Free Indian Centre in Berlin while broadcasting on the German-sponsored Azad Hind Radio to his fellow Indians. Bose succeeded in creating the Indian Legion, composed of some 4,500 British-Indian prisoners of war in North Africa. Disappointed that Hitler only intended to use his Indian Legion for purposes of propaganda, Bose left Germany in February 1943 onboard the German submarine U-180 and then transferred to the Japanese submarine I-29 in the sea between the Cape of Good Hope and Madagascar, which transported him to Japan. In Japan he was part of the Fascist-sponsored ideological movement the Greater East Asian Co-Prosperity Sphere. For Bose, who had been alienated by the Nazi regime's policies of extreme racism, the Japanese idea of pan-Asianism seemed much more attractive. Bose felt vindicated when the Japanese imperial regime helped him establish the Provisional Government of Azad Hind (Free India) and the Indian National Army, which fought together with Japanese forces against the British Army in the Asian theater of the Second World War.

Bose's Provisional Indian Government was recognized by eight Axis states—Nazi Germany, Hirohito's Japan, Fascist Italy, the Independent State of Croatia, the Wang Jingwei regime in Nanjing, and the provisional governments of Burma, Manchukuo, and Japanese-controlled Philippines—as well as the Soviet Union. Did Bose use international *Realpolitik* to exploit the enemy of his enemy, and was his alliance with the Axis during the war simply a pragmatic decision? The case of Yi Sun-tak, who had no political reason at all for advocating an alliance with Fascist Italy, which was the friend of the enemy imperial Japan, gives us some clues about how to interpret Bose's Marxist pan-Asianism.[43] Bose's address delivered at Tokyo

University in November 1944 is more revealing than his wartime travel to the Axis powers. He argued that "you cannot have a so-called democratic system if that system has to put through economic reforms on a socialist basis. . . . We have come to the conclusion that with a democratic system, we cannot solve the problems of Free India. Therefore, modern progressive thought in India is in favor of a State that is authoritarian in character."[44]

It is interesting that Bose called himself a socialist and believed that socialism in India owed its origin to Swami Vivekananda, the ascetic who defined socialism as "neither traditionalism nor westernization." Bose also admired the socialist authoritarianism of Kemal Atatürk's Turkey. When the Indonesian left-nationalist dictator Sukarno outraged Western diplomats by praising Hitler in a public address, he represented the ambiguity of the national-socialist thought that dominated the Beijing-Pyŏngyang-Hanoi-Phnom Penh-Jakarta Axis. Indeed, in his speeches, Sukarno had little hesitation in lining up Hitler, Sun Yat-sen, Kemal Atatürk, Mahatma Gandhi, and Ho Chi Minh as a pantheon of respectable nationalists, rather than detailing their ideological differences.[45] This intellectual trajectory through socialist and fascist authoritarianism, underpinned by an emphasis on economic development, turned Marxist ideology upside down. Instead of advocating for the emancipation of labor, colonial Marxists mobilized labor for reasons of national greatness. The common thread stitching together Asian colonial Marxists such as Yi Sun-tak, Subhas Chandra Bose, Sukarno, and other leaders was their collective belief in a nationalized version of socialism: one that promised a rapid, non-Western version of modernization.

As a colonial Marxist economist, Yi advocated a national united front of Marxists and nationalists and called for the establishment of class collaboration between the national bourgeoisie and the proletariat. The Communist International had advocated this policy from its very inception in 1919, as Lenin believed that successful colonial wars of independence in Asia and Africa would hasten the proletarian revolution in Europe. The emphasis on national unity originated in Yi's peculiar analysis of the transnational class structure in the Japanese Empire. Yi categorized all Korean colonial subjects as the total proletariat. In his view, the Japanese nation represented the ruling class of capitalists and landlords, while the exploited class of workers and tenant peasants epitomized the Korean nation. Thus he expected that the revolution in colonial Korea would be performed not by the Korean proletariat against the Korean bourgeoisie, but by the total proletariat of the Korean nation against the total bourgeoisie of the Japanese nation. Yi Sun-tak characterized the forthcoming revolution of colonial Korea as a national political revolution in which he recast the Marxist class struggle between the bourgeoisie and the proletariat into a national struggle between the Japanese people and the Korean people.

Strangely enough, the dichotomy between a bourgeois nation and a proletarian nation appears also in Italian Fascist discourse. As early as 1910, Enrico Corradini declared that "Italy is, materially and morally, a proletarian nation . . . whose living conditions are subject to the way of life of other nations." To compete with the bourgeois nations, Italy demanded "a means of national discipline" and "a pact of family solidarity between all classes of the Italian nation" in the moral domain, and "an economic society" to produce wealth and civilization in the material domain. Only through the production of a material and moral civilization would Italy acquire the "strength and the right to expand in the world." Insofar as "the conception of a wealthy people in a powerful nation is one imposed by the nature of modern civilization," the nationalist principle remained important for Italian Fascists.[46] Mussolini's radical syndicalism also partook in Corradini's nationalist view that Italy was a proletarian nation, disadvantaged in the competition with rich and plutocratic nations, which then justified Mussolini's subsequent commitment to modernization and industrialization.[47] Ramiro Ledesman Ramos, a Spanish Fascist who regarded Spain as an agrarian dependent nation, also shared this dichotomous worldview with Italian Fascists.[48]

In its opposition to advanced bourgeois nations, the ideological facade of fascism also looks like a variant of antimodern ideology. Historical observers of Fascist phenomena have been perplexed by the fact that these modernizing states often expressed antimodern ideas. According to Henry Turner, Jr., Italian Fascists' positive attitude toward the products of modern industry should not necessarily be equated with an approval of modernization in principle. Italian Fascists implemented many modernizing policies only as the means to achieve antimodernist ends.[49] Turner's interesting argument about fascism can be summed up in an oxymoronic phrase: antimodern modernization. If it is precisely the modern that conjures up prehistory, then traditionalism is nothing more than a variant of modernist nostalgia. Fascist discourse represented not just a simple desire to recover an ancient glory that had been either lost or denied but also an ideological combination of modernization and industrialization along with the recovery of a sense of primordial nationalism.[50]

Using Yi Sun-tak's arguments that the Italian nation was the total proletariat that should struggle against the total bourgeoisie of the bourgeois nations, I have found little proof to indicate that Yi knew about the Fascist dichotomy between the bourgeois nation and the proletarian nation. It might be a pure coincidence that Yi's idea of "total proletariat" and "total bourgeoisie" coevolved with the Fascist dichotomy of the bourgeois nation and the proletarian nation. But the coevolution of these ideas, even if by chance, can be placed within a certain context. The strategic location of colonial Korea and Fascist Italy in the discourse of global modernity is revealing about the coexistence of ideas regarding the total proletariat and the proletarian nation. A colonial Korean Marxist's encounter with Italian fascism was a strange variation of the trope of East-West encounters. The strategic positions of Italy and Germany in the interwar world system as that of semiperipheries, peripheries in the center, or even as the East in the West, dictated their self-understanding as the underdog in world systems. When Yi encountered fascism in Italy, it just so happened that one member of the East sympathized with another East located within Europe itself.[51]

The encounter between a colonial Korean Marxist and Italian fascism challenges the intellectual dichotomy of right-wing fascism and left-wing socialism. From the viewpoint of the transnational formation of modernity, the convergence of fascism and socialism as radical anti-Western modernization projects was not that improbable. The Italian futurist Filippo Marinetti, who became an inadvertent progenitor of Fascist art, was deeply respected by Russian Futurists, who in turn supported the Bolshevik Revolution. Left-wing Fascists such as Berto Ricci, and Ugo Spirito were also pleased when the Soviet Union began to incline toward fascism in the 1930s. Left-wing Fascists in Italy could see the shift of emphasis from revolutionary internationalism to nationalist strength and development in the Soviet Union.[52] Mussolini himself made it explicit that he would prefer "Italy as a Soviet republic" to "Italy as a British colony."[53] If the discursive position of Fascist Italy was that of the East in the West, Russia at the turn of the twentieth century was regarded as a developing or a peripheral capitalist society, if even that. When Asia or Europe stopped being solely geopolitical concepts, fascism and socialism could appear on the same horizon, and even on the spectrum of anti-Western modernization projects.[54] Colonial Korean Marxists, who occupied high administrative positions in postcolonial North Korea, traveled to the USSR as members of official government delegations. While they wrote unremarkable travelogues about their visits, almost all of them were deeply impressed by a Soviet modernity that was represented by automobile factories, high-rise buildings, trolley buses, double-decker buses, subway trains of high velocity, luxuriously decorated metro stations, a department store full of consumer goods, low illiteracy rates, the mechanization of agriculture, well-organized cultural events, decent cultural infrastructure, and the civilized modern life in Moscow and other cities in the postwar USSR.[55] In their estimation, Moscow, the socialist capital, was much more modern and more civilized than the imperial metropolis of Tokyo, and the socialist modernization project was more successful and efficient than the capitalist-imperialist modernization project. These travelogues are in sharp contrast with Western ones, such as Eric Hobsbawm's, in which he recorded his deep disappointment with the poverty and backwardness prevalent in the USSR.

Anti-Western Modernization and Global Easts

Andrzej Walicki remembered his lecture trip to Japan in 1977: "In Japan, where I lectured on Russian Populism and related topics at different universities, I was usually taken as a Marxist sympathizing with the Populists' idea of 'non-capitalist modernization'—a position which my audiences saw as very respectable and politically attractive."[56] A strong sympathy and desire for noncapitalist modernization was prevalent among Japanese left-wing intellectuals even in 1977, when Japan was contending with the Western Great Powers for supremacy in the world economy. While Japan was a founding member of the "Group of Six" in 1973 along with the United States, West Germany, Great Britain, Italy, and France, Japanese Marxists in 1977 were still considering the possibility of bypassing capitalism and achieving noncapitalist modernization. Despite the rise of Japan as one of the global capitalist economic powers, many Japanese posited the country as the colonized against the colonizing West. They adopted a postcolonial rather than the postimperial position that they actually inhabited. Contrary to the historical existence of the huge Japanese Empire in Asia during World War II, some Japanese Marxists saw themselves as victims of Western imperialism. Hayashi Husao, a former Marxist, labeled the history of modern Japan as the Hundred Years War against the West, and World War II as just one episode in the century-long epic struggle between Japan as the proletariat nation, on the one hand, and the West as the bourgeois nation, on the other.[57] This explains the continuing popularity of the ideas of noncapitalist and anti-Western modernization among left-wing intellectuals in Japan, even though it is one of the most developed capitalist countries in the world today.

Once they entered the stage of global modernity, the antimodernist self-image of Fascists was confirmed by either explicit or implicit references to the modernist Other, the West. Once the Fascist discourse of antimodernist ends is placed in the context of cultural transfer and interaction with modernity, then one can read the anti-Western modernization project as a transnational agenda of the weak states against the strong, or the reaction of postcolonial nations to the former colonial masters. In the nineteenth century, German intellectuals advocated their national culture against Anglo-French notions of civilization. The Russian Slavophile assertion that inner truth based on religion, culture, and moral convictions is much more important than external truth expressed by law and the state was very similar to the Indian nationalist discourse of the superiority of the spiritual domain over the material domain. Most of them thought that socialism was no other than the *Gemeinschaft* capitalism of the East overcoming the Western *Gesellschaft* capitalism.[58] Therefore the desire for anti-Western and socialist modernization overrode a genuine commitment to the classless society of socialism in much of the postcolonial world in the twentieth century. The nationalist appropriation and repurposing of socialist modernization in the postcolonial states of the Global East and South offers us a new way to think about the impact of the October Revolution.

Notes

1. See Moe Taylor, " 'Only a Disciplined People Can Build a Nation': North Korean Mass Games and Third Worldism in Guyana, 1980–1992," *Asia-Pacific Journal: Japan Focus* 13, issue 4, no. 2 (January 2015), https://apjjf.org/2015/13/4/Moe-Taylor/4258.html; Vicki Sung-yeon Kwon, "The Guyanese Mass Games: Historical Background and

Contemporary Meaning," ms.; "Mass and Individual: The Archive of the Guyanese Mass Games," exhibition curated by Wonseok Koh and Vicki Kwon, Arko Art Center, Seoul, October 21–November 27, 2017.

2. Kim Jŏng-il's remark that "the mass games are important in training children to be fully developed communists" illustrates the state's purpose in conducting mass games and explains the similar political reasons for the Guyanese comrade leader's keen interest in the adoption of such games. Kim Jŏng-il, *On Furthering Mass Games Gymnastics: Talk to Mass Gymnastics Producers, April 11, 1987* (Pyŏngyang: Foreign Languages Publishing House, 2006), 1.

3. See chapter 1.

4. "North Korea 2012 Mass Games," compazine, January 27, 2013, video, 1:29:38, https://youtu.be/67T9-43hb5I.

5. Georgi Schischkoff, *Die gesteuerte Vermassung: ein sozial-philosophischer Beitrag zur Zeitkritik* (Meisenheim: Anton Hain, 1964), 120–21.

6. For the mutual attention between the leader and masses, see Daniel Leese, "Rituals, Emotions, and Mobilization: The Leader Cult and Party Politics," in *The Palgrave Handbook of Mass Dictatorship*, ed. Paul Corner and Jie-Hyun Lim (London: Palgrave Macmillan, 2016), 221, 223.

7. It is not a coincidence that both Italian fascism and Stalinism loudly proclaimed their intention to create the New Man, *Homo fascistus* and *Homo sovieticus*, respectively, though neither regime could accomplish the goal despite their unstinting efforts. See chapter 9 and Karen Petrone, *Life Has Become More Joyous Comrades: Celebrations in the Time of Stalin* (Bloomington: Indiana University Press, 2000).

8. Cuban revolutionaries regarded North Korea as a model of Third World socialism. During his visit to North Korea in 1960, Che Guevara was deeply impressed by the postwar reconstruction and the quality of North Korea's industrial output, even though it had been almost destroyed by American bombardment during the Korean War. See Benjamin R. Young, "Revolutionary Solidarity: Castro's Cozy Relationship with North Korea," *NK News*, November 28, 2016, https://www.nknews.org/2016/11/revolutionary-solidarity-castros-cozy-relationship-with-north-korea/.

9. The Russian bourgeoisie, more than any other class, welcomed *Das Kapital* as a scientific certificate to promote capitalism in Russia. See Albert Resis, "*Das Kapital* Comes to Russia," *Slavic Review* 29, no. 2 (1970): 219–37.

10. See V. I. Lenin, "Draft Theses on National and Colonial Questions for the Second Congress of the Communist International," June 5, 1920, trans. Julius Katzer, Marxists Internet Archive, www.marxists.org/archive/lenin/works/1920/jun/05.htm.

11. See "Minutes of the 2nd Congress of the Communist International: Fifth Session," July 28, 1920, Marxists Internet Archive, www.marxists.org/history/international/comintern/2nd-congress/ch05.htm.

12. See "Baku Congress of the Peoples of the East: Seventh Session," September 7, 1920, Marxists Internet Archive, www.marxists.org/history/international/comintern/baku/ch07.htm#council.

13. Kim Joonyŏp and Kim Changsoon, eds., 한국공산주의 운동사 [History of the communist movement in Korea], vol. 1 (Seoul: Aseamoonje yŏnguso, 1967), 391, 396.

14. Dae-sook Suh, *The Korean Communist Movement 1918–1948* (Princeton, N.J.: Princeton University Press, 1967), 35–40.

15. Suh Joong-suk, 한국근현대 민족문제 연구 [A study of national questions in modern Korea] (Seoul: Yŏksabipyŏngsa, 1989), 23.

16. Kim Il-sŏng, 김일성선집 [Selected works], vol. 4 (Pyŏngyang: Chŏsunrodongdang-chulpansa, 1960), 325–31, 338.

17. Teodor Shanin, introduction to *Late Marx and the Russian Road: Marx and the "Peripheries of Capitalism,"* ed. Teodor Shanin (London: Verso, 1983), x.

18. See Haruki Wada, "Marx and Revolutionary Russia," in Shanin, *Late Marx and the Russian Road*, 40–76.

19. Simon Clarke, "Was Lenin a Marxist? The Populist Roots of Marxism-Leninism," *Historical Materialism* 3, no. 1 (1998): 3.

20. Eric J. Hobsbawm, "Out of the Ashes," in *After the Fall: The Failure of Communism and the Future of Socialism*, ed. Robin Blackburn (London: Verso, 1991), 318.

21. Stuart R. Schram and Hélène Carrère d'Encausse, introduction to *Marxism and Asia* (London: Allen Lane, 1969), 4.

22. Stuart Schram, *Mao Tse-Tung* (Harmondsworth, UK: Penguin, 1966), 43–44, 201.

23. Hans-Lukas Kieser, "World War and World Revolution: Alexander Helphand-Parvus in Germany and Turkey," *Kritika: Explorations in Russian and Eurasian History* 12, no. 2 (2011): 387, 400; M. Asim Karaömerlioglu, "Helphand-Parvus and His Impact on Turkish Intellectual Life," *Middle Eastern Studies* 40, no. 6 (2004): 151–53.

24. James R. Miller, "A Note on Primitive Accumulation in Marx and Preobrazhensky," *Soviet Studies* 30, no. 2 (1978): 384–93; Richard C. K. Burdekin, "Preobrazhensky's Theory of Primitive Socialist Accumulation," *Journal of Contemporary Asia* 19, no. 3 (1989): 297–307.

25. Giovanni Arrighi, "Marxist Century, American Century," in Blackburn, *After the Fall*, 155–56.

26. Karl Kautsky, *Bolshevism at a Deadlock*, trans. B. Pritchard (New York: Routledge, 2014), 81.

27. Cited in Jane Burbank, *Intelligentsia and Revolution: Russian Views of Bolshevism, 1917–1922* (New York: Oxford University Press, 1986), 19.

28. See Jie-Hyun Lim, "Befreiung oder Modernisierung? Sozialismus als ein Weg der anti-westlichen Modernisierung in unterentwickelten Ländern," *Beiträge zur Geschichte der Arbeiterbewegung* 43, no. 2 (2001): 5–23.

29. Rostislav A. Ulyanovsky, *National Liberation: Essays on Theory and Practice*, trans. David Fidlon and Yuri Shirokov (Moscow: Progress, 1978), 271–72.

30. Stuart Schram, "The Military Deviation of Mao Tse-tung," *Problems of Communism* 13, no. 1 (1964): 49–56.

31. Yi Jong Sŏk, 현대북한의 이해 [How to understand North Korea] (Seoul: Yŏksabipyŏngsa, 1995), 95.

32. Yi Jong Sŏk, 151.

33. Ulyanovsky, *National Liberation*, 277–79.

34. Gérard Chaliand, *Revolution in the Third World*, trans. Diana Johnstone, rev. ed. (New York: Viking Adult, 1989), 91, 145, 180.

35. Yi Sun-tak, 최근세계일주기 [My journey around the world] (1934; Seoul: Hakminsa, 1997), 15, 40, 43, 54, 76–77, and passim.

36. Yi Sun-tak, 41.

37. Jang Sejin, 슬픈 아시아 [Grieving Asia] (Seoul: Purŭn Yŏksa, 2012), 63, 81, 224, 240, and passim.

38. Yi Sun-tak, 최근세계일주기, 125, 116.

39. Yi Sun-tak, 116, 128–30.

40. *Chosun Joongang ilbo*, January 25, 1934, 2.

41. Yi Sun-tak, 최근세계일주기, 193–205.

42. For Polish socialist irredentists, see Jie-Hyun Lim, "Labour and the National Question in Poland," in *Nationalism, Labour, and Ethnicity, 1870-1939*, ed. Stefan Berger and Angel Smith (Manchester, UK: Manchester University Press, 1999), 13–32.

43. Recent studies of "Afro-Orientalism" and "Black Pacific Narrative" analyzing Afro-American radicals, including W. E. B. Du Bois, who were attracted to pan-Asianism as a way of transpacific antiracism, are suggestive. See Reginald Kearney, "The Pro-Japanese Utterances of W. E. B. Dubois," *Contributions in Black Studies* 13/14 (1995/1996): 201–17; Nahum Dimitri Chandler, "A Persistent Parallax: On the Writings of W. E. B. Du Bois on Japan and China, 1936–1937," *New Centennial Review*, 12, no. 1 (2012): 291–316; Seok-Won Lee, "The Paradox of Radical Liberation: W. E. B. Du Bois and Pan-Asianism in Wartime Japan, 1931–1945," *Inter-Asia Cultural Studies* 16, no. 4 (2015): 513–30.

44. Subhas Chandra Bose, "The Fundamental Problems of India," in *The Essential Writings of Netaji Subhas Chandra Bose*, ed. Sisir K. Bose and Sugata Bose (Delhi: Oxford University Press, 1997), 319–20; Sugata Bose, *His Majesty's Opponent: Subhas Chandra Bose and India's Struggle Against Empire* (Cambridge, Mass.: Belknap Press of Harvard University, 1992).

45. Benedict Anderson, *Spectres of Comparisons: Nationalism, Southeastern Asia, and the World* (London: Verso, 1998), 1–2.

46. Enrico Corradini, "The Principles of Nationalism" and "Nationalism and the Syndicates," in *Italian Fascisms: From Pareto to Gentile*, ed. Adrian Lyttleton (London: Harper and Row, 1973), 146–47, 159, 163.

47. A. James Gregor, "A Modernizing Dictatorship," in *International Fascism: Theories, Causes, and the New Consensus*, ed. Roger Griffin (London: Arnold, 1998), 130–32.

48. Juan J. Linz, "Political Space and Fascism as a Late-comer," in *Fascism: Critical Concepts in Political Science*, vol. 2, ed. Roger Griffin (London: Routledge, 2004), 152.

49. Henry A. Turner, Jr., "Fascism and Modernization," *World Politics* 24, no. 2 (1972): 547–64.

50. George L. Mosse, *The Fascist Revolution: Towards a General Theory of Fascism* (New York: H. Fertig, 1999), 28.

51. See chapters 4 and 5.

52. Stanley G. Payne, "Fascism and Communism," *Totalitarian Movements and Political Religions* 1, no. 3 (2000): 3, 5.

53. John Lukacs, "The Universality of National Socialism (The Mistaken Category of Fascism)," *Totalitarian Movements and Political Religions* 3, no. 3 (2002): 113.

54. See Shanin, introduction to *Late Marx*, x.

55. Yi Taejun, 소련기행 [A journey to the Soviet Union] (Pyŏngyang: Baikyangdang, 1947), 65, 69, 83, 100, 105, and passim; Baik Namwoon, 쏘련인상 [Impressive Soviet Union] (1950; Seoul: Sŏnin, 2005), 48, 65, 99–100, and passim.

56. Andrzej Walicki, *The Controversy Over Capitalism: Studies in the Social Philosophy of the Russian Populists* (Notre Dame, Ind.: University of Notre Dame Press, 1989), x.

57. Hayashi Husao, 大東亞戰爭肯定論 [Legitimizing the Great East Asia War] (Tokyo: Chuobunko, 2014).

58. See Norbert Elias, 매너의 역사: 문명화 과정 [*Über den Prozess der Zivilisation*], trans. Yu Huisu (Seoul: Sinsŏwon, 1995), 33–75; Andrzej Walicki, *A History of Russian Thought* (Oxford: Oxford University Press, 1979), 93–106; Partha Chatterjee, *The Nation and Its Fragments* (Princeton, N.J.: Princeton University Press, 1993), 3–13; and Harry Harootunian, *Overcome by Modernity* (Princeton, N.J.: Princeton University Press, 2000), xxx.

Epilogue

Blurring Dichotomy of Global Easts and Wests in the Age of Neopopulism

Do we love our nations enough to protect their sovereignty and to take ownership of their futures?

—Donald Trump, United Nations General Assembly, 2017

Shoot them [undocumented Latino immigrants]!

—Trump supporter, 2019

A report on populism, published by the Tony Blair Institute for Global Change, supports the hermeneutical potentiality of the mass dictatorship today. That report shows that the number of populists in power has remarkably increased worldwide fivefold, from four to twenty, between 1990 and 2018. Its euphemistic verdict that "populists are increasingly gaining power in systemically important countries" indicates the populist appeal to Global "Wests."[1] With its apogee in the white nationalism and open racism in Trump's America, followed by British prime minister Boris Johnson's no-deal Brexit and migration crisis in Europe, contemporary neopopulisms enjoy popularity in liberal democratic countries. Populism appears most prominently in the political landscapes of the United States and Britain. In the Americas, populism in the United States overshadows Latin American populism. In Europe, West

European populism competes with the populist regime of Poland and Hungary in Eastern Europe. France, Belgium, Netherlands, the Scandinavian countries, Italy, Austria, Spain, and Germany have all been drawn into the vortex of populist politics.

The unexpected rise of neopopulism in the Global West challenges the conventional dichotomy between the democratic "West" and dictatorial "East." For instance, antimigrant and anti-Muslim themes can be found in exclusionary nationalist discourse in many places, including Europe, India, Myanmar, and the United States.[2] The exclusionary nationalism is no longer the historical peculiarity of the Global East. The Global West of the twenty-first century shares and even leads that trend. The imaginative boundary between the dictatorial East and the democratic West is indeed being blurred. This story echoes Marx's claim that classic capitalism and democracy in the "West" emerged "under circumstances of ruthless terrorism."[3] Europeans achieved their dominance in global capitalism through murderous conquest, violent oppression, and imperialist expansion, so "war capitalism" and "industrial capitalism" have been continually interacting with each other for centuries.[4]

Mass dictatorship, an oxymoron, may provide a conceptual tool to understand the neopopulist tide in the democratic West. My use of the term is a deliberate attempt to understand the ubiquitous interplay of dictatorship and democracy across the globe. From the viewpoint of mass dictatorship, populism and liberal democracy are often married, so their mutual flourishing in contemporary Anglo-American politics is not unexpected. Contrary to common belief, the major twentieth-century dictatorships involved not merely threats of violence from above, but also social consent that merged people's acquiescence into active support. Mass dictatorship is where "internal coercion" produces consent by structuring thought and feeling.[5] As inherent in modern democracy as in mass dictatorship, "internal coercion" exerts a hegemonic effect of concealing oppression from the oppressors and the oppressed. Simon Tormey's remark that liberal democracy is the most refined form of totalitarianism carries a grain of truth, however exaggerated.[6] The ultimate effectiveness of any state initiative, be it dictatorial or democratic, would depend on the working of "a capillary network of associations with vast powers of social and cultural persuasion."[7] It demands a sort of ideological fetishism more than rational conformity deriving from people's self-interest.

If socialism or liberalism is a "thick ideology" with well-articulated tenets, populism is a "thin ideology." Populism comprises roughly two major facets: the idea of a pure people against a corrupt elite and the belief that politics should express the will of the people.[8] Populists claim that foreigners harm the common good of the "real" people, and that nothing can obstruct the collective sovereign will of the native people. The basic tenets of the insider-outsider division and the people's sovereignty run through all populist propaganda in the global political landscape. The Nazi ideal of "people's community" (*Volksgemeinschaft*) was pregnant with the imagination of a new politics in which native "Aryan" people regarded themselves as sovereign. Eugene Weber's statement that Nazism is a sort of "Jacobinism of our time"[9] is resonant with Carl Schmitt's apologetic justification of Nazism as "anti-liberal but not necessarily anti-democratic." More classically, in his address to the French National Convention (1793), Bertrand Barère tried to justify Jacobin dictatorship on the ground that the nation was exercising dictatorship over itself. And infamously, socialist regimes defined themselves as a "people's democracy"—a proletarian dictatorship. This vision of popular sovereignty conceptually supports the contemporary cultural populism that divides the native insiders of the nation-state from the immigrant outsiders, refugees, ethnic and religious minorities, and cosmopolitan elites.

As the most common form of populism today, cultural populism asks us to interrogate the cliché that a willful cohort of perpetrators forcefully imposed dictatorship on a confused majority. What if majoritarian democracy in the modern nation-state is based on the categorization of minorities as Others by the native majority? What if the majority tyrannizes minorities? Is that democracy or a dictatorship? In answering this set of questions, the common understanding that "whoever rules in the name of the 'majority' is ontologically democratic" becomes shaken. A "tyranny through masses" was a different naming of American democracy. Similarly, French Jacobins were identified as the "totalitarian democracy." History of democracies is stained with blood and violence, too. The history of modern colonies reveals that settler democracies have been more murderous than authoritarian colonial governments. "Regimes newly embarked upon democratization," Michael Mann has noted, "are more likely to commit murderous ethnic cleansings than are stable authoritarian regimes."[10] The political and ethical complacency in coming to terms with the fascist past of the 1930s—the naïve dichotomy of the political typology of democracy and dictatorship—facilitated the rise of neopopulism today.

More than an oxymoron, "mass dictatorship" represents a shift of focus from the classical idea of the coercive "dictatorship from above" to "dictatorship from below," in which one of the principal objectives of the regime is the self-mobilization of the people themselves. The efforts at popular conscription to the cause explain why some mass dictatorship regimes tried to arrive at a "dictatorship of consent" through the rhetoric of decisionist democracy.[11] The use of the term *welfare dictatorship* (*Fürsorgediktatur*) in describing the GDR, with its emphasis on consensus building, is a good example.[12] The distance between the "welfare dictatorship" of East Germany and the Scandinavian right-wing populists' "welfare chauvinism," which demands that welfare services be restricted to white natives, has been narrowed in the process of consensus building. In the trajectory of global modernity, democracy and dictatorship are not separated in some predetermined West and East: they are together in the problem space of constant evolution and becoming. For neither East nor West is a geopositivist concept; the "strategic location" of East and West in historical discourses is always in flux. What matters is not any national peculiarity but the strategic position of each historical unit in our imaginary geography. The global chain of East/West confrontations with ever-shifting positions knows no end. Many recent studies of mass dictatorship reflect these new global perspectives, arguing that the flux of East and West problematizes the dichotomy of a dictatorial East and a democratic West.[13]

The advent of neoliberalism, with its emphasis on the individual, appears to have reduced the role of the state. The state, however, while reducing its role in organizing the economy and providing social welfare, has reemerged strongly as the guarantor of individual security. The continual states of emergency in which we now live, marked by terrorism and international instability, justify and permit the concession to government of many nondemocratic powers—Patriot Acts, legislation suspending habeas corpus, and the like. Without needing to be paranoid about the intrusive powers of information technology, it is never wise to forget that the modern state knows much, much more about any individual citizen than did the Gestapo, the Stasi, or the NKVD. The modern state would appear to be moving in an increasingly authoritarian direction. Seen in this light, the distance and antagonism we generally assume to exist between mass dictatorship and modern democracy seem less than typically thought. The fundamental problem of social control implicit in the "democratic age" of mass society remains. With the changing nature of the public, the means of achieving that social control have become much more sophisticated, especially with the changing instruments available to government and to those who support the government. This is not to say that we still live in an age of mass dictatorship. It is simply that many of the questions and problems posed by the phenomenon of mass dictatorships continue to have great relevance in the contemporary world.

The medical emergency that the COVID-19 pandemic brought to the world is another touchstone of mass dictatorship. In the face of the high fatality rates from the disease, the ontological security issue for individuals was so overwhelming as to bury the issues of biopolitics and high-tech surveillance. Giorgio Agamben's grave concern about biopolitics has even been ridiculed.[14] The efficiency of South Korea in controlling COVID-19 was one of the focal points for this debate. The South Korean government tightened the grip of existing controls on the population with consent from below. The efficiency of the overly protective, patronizing state in South Korea has been subject to polemical debates around the balance between individual freedom and collective security. To what extent may the authority execute the coercive power entrusted to it for the purpose of public safety? In the case of COVID-19, where is the dividing line between medical welfare and medical fascism? What is the difference between the political emergency and medical emergency? *Per contra*: How can we evaluate the principle of rationality that would prioritize "the saved" over "the drowned" based on the calculation of probability? In the absence of effective "policing," the warring Emergency Room in almost every hospital becomes a history lab for "Leviathan 3.0" as the rationality of survival contradicts the morality of humanity in a state of emergency. On the other hand, the excessive "policing" to avoid that situation may produce a hygienic dictatorship. With massive support from below, it may constitute a grotesque behemoth worse than the mass dictatorship in the twentieth century. The state emergency was renewed as a medical emergency, when people's bare lives are threatened by the pandemic.

A global rise of nationalism is also a by-product of the nation-state's response to the pandemic.[15] With the rise of biases against some groups associated with the pandemic, migration policies have become more repressive and hate crimes have increased significantly among the member states of the Organization for Security and Co-operation in Europe. Among the grotesque images of the world that COVID-19 has connected, a Jewish-Chinese COVID-19 conspiracy theory stands out. A neo-Nazi "dark web" in the United States proclaims that COVID-19 is a Jewish-Chinese conspiracy, a theory that has prevailed among white supremacists and nationalists on social media since the outbreak of the pandemic. This far-right conspiracy theory represents an ideological pandemic sweeping the anti-Semitic dark web. Anti-Semitic images of Jews as poisoners and deliberate carriers of the disease are history-ridden, dating back to the Middle Ages. What is new is the idea of Coronavirus as a global plan engineered by the Chinese and Jews together.[16] Age-old anti-Semitism is thus conspicuously combined with a twenty-first-century version of the "Yellow Peril" bound to the fear of the rise of China as a global power. What is intriguing is how the white supremacist media crafted and proliferated their self-image as victims. According to white supremacists, American whites are victims of discrimination. David Duke's National Association for the Advancement of White People (NAAWP), as counterpoint to the National Association for the Advancement of Colored People (NAACP), diagnosed that the NAACP promotes racial discrimination by seeking discriminatory policies against white people in employment, promotions, scholarships, and college and union admittance. In Olga Khazan's wording in the *Atlantic*, "Victimhood, it seemed, is how the groups assured themselves they weren't being racist—the excuse being that, hey, they're suffering too."[17]

The nostalgia among Americans for a lost global hegemony, which produced Donald Trump's slogan "Make America Great Again" (MAGA), stands behind the imaginary threats and the self-victimhood among white supremacists. The fear of the Coronavirus and the Trump White House's incompetence in coping with the pandemic have twisted postcolonial melancholia in the United States into a global anti-Semitism and Yellow Peril. It is not at all surprising to witness the country's gradual erosion of liberal democracy and drift toward mass dictatorship. Matthew Abelman's painting of Hitler wearing a baseball cap with the MAGA slogan on it was removed from a bar in Portland, Oregon, but it touched a sort of historical reality.[18] Similarly, the *hikikomori* (reclusive withdrawal) nationalism as a postcolonial melancholia was connected to the *netto uyoku* (internet right-wingers) in today's Japan. The Japanese government openly wishes to return to the containment policies of the Cold War years under the Pax Americana in East Asia, while resurrecting the glorious image of the Japanese Empire that perished at the end of the Second World War.[19] *Hikikomori* is the peculiar form of the Japanese ultranationalism, but it shares a "postcolonial melancholia" with the global West. Brexit cannot be separated from the UK's own "postcolonial melancholia"—nostalgia and mourning for the lost empire and refusal to accept the reality of multicultural Europe that colonialism produced in the here and now.[20] One might add that the war framing of COVID-19, as in Australian prime minister Scott Morrison's interview, has fanned the male and white nostalgia for militarization, associated with sacrifice and leadership.[21]

As the increasing hate crimes against racial and national minorities imply, the reclusive nationalism combined with the imperial melancholy in the Global West may persist for the time being. While many short-term emergency measures will become a new normal, totalitarian surveillance will likely win the civic empowerment—not to mention China, where a range of mobile apps warn citizens about their proximity to infected patients, as well as the Israel Security Agency, which was authorized to deploy surveillance technology previously reserved for battling terrorists to track coronavirus patients. A dramatic transition from extrinsic to intrinsic surveillance can be found over the globe.[22] With its matrix-like vision of our future, the reinforced "Screen New Deal" might realize Mussolini's lifelong dream of the "total state." Naomi Klein warns that the "Pandemic Shock Doctrine" might bring a dystopian future "in which our very move, our every word, our every relationship is trackable, traceable, and data-mineable."[23] The medical fascism combined with the highly developed surveillance capitalism confronting the COVID-19 pandemic evidences again this book's argument that the geohistorical fixity of the Global West and East is delusive. In the state of medical emergency, it is hard to categorically differentiate between East and West. Intrinsic surveillance is practiced globally, again blurring the boundary. Once the global divide between East and West is disturbed, the Global East as the constitutive outside will no longer exist in the unilinear developmental scheme of history. Nevertheless, the ubiquitous delusive dichotomy between the Global East and Global West may persist in our historical imagination to regulate our everyday practices.

Notes

1. Jordan Kyle and Limor Gultschin, "Populists in Power Around the World," Tony Blair Institute for Global Change, November 7, 2018, https://institute.global /insight/renewing-centre/populists-power-around-world.

2. Florian Bieber, "Global Nationalism in Times of the COVID-19 Pandemic," *Nationalities Papers* (2020): 4, doi:10.1017/nps.2020.35.

3. Karl Marx, *Capital*, vol. 1 (Harmondsworth, UK: Penguin, 1990), 895.

4. For the concept of "war capitalism," see Sven Beckert, *Empire of Cotton: A Global History* (New York: Knopf, 2014).

5. Patrick Colm Hogan, *The Culture of Conformism: Understanding Social Consent* (Durham, N.C.: Duke University Press, 2001), 9, 58.

6. Simon Tormey, *Making Sense of Tyranny: Interpretations of Totalitarianism* (Manchester, UK: Manchester University Press, 1995), 115.

7. Victoria de Grazia, *The Culture of Consent: Mass Organization of Leisure in Fascist Italy* (Cambridge: Cambridge University Press, 1981), 22.

8. Cas Mudde, "The Populist Zeitgeist," *Government and Opposition* 39, no. 4 (2004): 542–63.

9. Eugene Weber, *Varieties of Fascism* (Princeton, N.J.: Van Nostrand, 1964), 139.

10. Michael Mann, *The Dark Side of Democracy* (Cambridge: Cambridge University Press, 2005), 4, 70–110.

11. Martin Sabrow, "Dictatorship as Discourse: Cultural Perspectives on SED Legitimacy," in *Dictatorship as Experience: Towards a Socio-Cultural History of the GDR*, ed. Konrad H. Jarausch (New York: Berghahn Books, 1999), 208.

12. Konrad Jarausch, "Beyond Uniformity: The Challenge of Historicizing the GDR," in Jarausch, *Dictatorship as Experience*, 6.

13. See Jie-Hyun Lim and Karen Petrone, eds., *Gender Politics and Mass Dictatorship* (Basingstoke, UK: Palgrave Macmillan, 2010); Michael Schoenhals and Karin Sarsenov, eds., *Imagining Mass Dictatorship* (Basingstoke, UK: Palgrave Macmillan, 2013); Michael Kim and Michael Schoenhals, eds., *Mass Dictatorship and Modernity* (Basingstoke, UK: Palgrave Macmillan, 2013); Jie-Hyun Lim, Barbara Walker, and Peter Lambert, eds., *Mass Dictatorship and Memory as Ever-present Past* (Basingstoke, UK: Palgrave Macmillan, 2014); Alf Lütke, ed., *Everyday Life in Mass Dictatorship* (London: Palgrave Macmillan, 2016); Paul Corner and Jie-Hyun Lim, eds. *Palgrave Handbook of Mass Dictatorship* (London: Palgrave Macmillan, 2016).

14. Panagiotis Sotiris, "Against Agamben: Is a Democratic Biopolitics Possible?," *Critical Legal Thinking*, March 14, 2020, https://criticallegalthinking.com/2020/03/14 /against-agamben-is-a-democratic-biopolitics-possible/.

15. Gideon Rachman, "Nationalism Is a Side Effect of the Coronavirus," *Financial Times*, March 23, 2020, https://www.ft.com/content/644fd920-6cea-11ea-9bca -bf503995cd6f.

16. Flora Cassen, "Jews Control Chinese Labs That Created Coronavirus: White Supremacists' Dangerous New Conspiracy Theory," *Haaretz*, May 3, 2020, https://www

.haaretz.com/us-news/.premium-the-jews-control-the-chinese-labs-that
-created-coronavirus-1.8809635.

17. Olga Khazan, "How White Supremacists Use Victimhood to Recruit," *Atlantic*,
August 15, 2017, https://www.theatlantic.com/science/archive/2017/08/the-worlds
-worst-support-group/536850/.

18. Mattie John Bamman, "Trump Hat Hitler Painting Removed from Portland Bar,"
Eater, Portland, August 8, 2016, https://pdx.eater.com/2016/8/8/12403410/portland
-bar-removes-hitler-trump-hat-artwork.

19. Naoki Sakai, "The End of Pax Americana and the Nationalism of 'Hikikomori': 酒井
直樹," CGSI, December 15, 2016, https://www.youtube.com/watch?v=eNfMAo_v9d8.

20. Paul Gilroy, *Postcolonial Melancholia* (New York: Columbia University Press, 2005);
Eve Rosenhaft, "Europe's Melancholias: Diasporas in Contention and the Unravelings
of the Postwar Settlement," in *Mnemonic Solidarity-Global Interventions*, ed. Jie-Hyun
Lim and Eve Rosenhaft (Basingstoke, UK: Palgrave Macmillan, 2020).

21. Amy Haddad, "Metaphorical Militarisation: Covid-19 and the Language of
War," *Strategist*, May 13, 2020, https://www.aspistrategist.org.au/metaphorical
-militarisation-covid-19-and-the-language-of-war/.

22. Yuval Noah Harari, "The World After Coronavirus," *Financial Times*, March 20, 2020,
https://www.ft.com/content/19d90308-6858-11ea-a3c9-1fe6fedcca75.

23. Daniel Møller Ølgaard, "Reflections on Naomi Klein's Pandemic Shock Doctrine,"
E-International Relations, September 15, 2020, https://www.e-ir.info/2020/09/15
/reflections-on-naomi-kleins-pandemic-shock-doctrine/.

Index

Aborigines, transnational memory and, 60–61. *See also* Cooper, William

absolutization, political, 117. *See also* instrumentalization; relativization

Abu-Lughod, Janet, 199

accomplices: anticolonial nationalism as, 116; complicity and, 65–67, 79–81; of dictatorship, 13, 251

Adenauer, Konrad, 47, 132

African Americans: anti-Semitism compared to racism and, 101; on Genocide Convention, 84; Japanese solidarity with, 102; postcolonialism and Jewish connection with, 101–3; slavery and, 59, 93, 116; South African apartheid activism of, 103. *See also* Du Bois, W. E. B.

Agamben, Giorgio, 94, 304

agency: mass dictatorship and everyday life, 265–69; postcolonial criticism and, 81–82; reflexive self and, 268; self-energizing, 267

Allied bombings: compared to Nazi bombing of Guernica, 48, 72–73; of

Dresden, 49, 74; German victims of, 72–74; Wieluń and, 72–73

Althusser, Louis, 260

American path, Prussian path compared to, 135, 144–45

anachronism, in history textbooks, 222, 243–44

Anatomy of Nazism, The, 36

Anderson, Benedict, 63

anticolonialism. *See* postcolonialism

anti-communist propaganda, 4; and *Żydokomuna*, 38, 98

Anti-Defamation League (ADL), 36

antinuclear pacifism, 45, 107–8

antiquarian history, 215

anti-Semitism, 12; anti-communism and, 38; COVID-19 pandemic conspiracy theories and, 305; Jedwabne massacre and, 27, 38–41; Kolbe and, 109–10; nationalization of memory and, 66; in Poland, 38–39, 66–67, 234–37; racism compared to, 101; victimhood nationalism and, 38. *See also* Holocaust

anti-Western modernization, 143–44,
263, 279–85, 294–95
appropriation: of Holocaust, Zionist, 83;
nationalist, 26, 75, 94, 108, 115–16; of
socialism by Young Turks, 282–83
Arendt, Hannah, 26, 42, 256
Armenian Americans: Korean comfort
women statue supported by, 110–12;
NCRR collaboration with, 112. *See also*
Glendale
Armenian genocide, 110–11, 126n97
art history: of Japan, 155–56; of Korea,
167–68
Asahi Journal, 62
Asahi shimbun, 109
Asiacentric world history, 181, 189, 199
Asia-Pacific War, 43, 45. *See also* Fifteen
Years' War; Great East Asia War;
Pacific War
atomic bomb: Hiroshima and, 45, 74–75,
104–8; Japan as victim of, 43–44,
69–71; Nagasaki and, 104–5, 108–9
Auschwitz-Birkenau: Frankfurt Trial, 37,
76; Hiroshima historical comparisons
to, 74–75, 104–8; Japanese visitors to,
103–4; Nagasaki connection to, 108–9.
See also Holocaust
Austrians, as victims, 46–47
autochthonism, history textbooks and,
219–22, 241–43. See also *Imna
Commandery*; "Regained Land"
Axis powers, as self-proclaimed victims,
68–69

Barère, Bertrand, 302
Bauman, Zygmunt, 15, 81, 100, 116,
255–56, 268
Begin, Menachem, 38
Belgium, 65
Ben Gurion, David, 35, 38
Berger, Stefan, 10
bio-power, 261
Bishop, Isabella Bird, 159

Blackburn, David, 18, 133
Black Germans, Nazism and, 103
Bloch, Marc, 179
Błoński, Jan, 40–41, 99
Bolshevism, 19; Asian nationalists and,
280–82; class struggle and, 278–79;
global impact of, 276; Marxist
voluntarism and, 284–86;
militarization of labor in, 283–84;
national socialism origins and,
282–83; Nazism as response to, 117
Bonn, Hans, 74
borders of nation-state, history books
on, 213
Bose, Subhas Chandra, 290–91
bourgeois nations versus proletarian
nations, 287–94
Brexit, 306
Brief History of Japan, A, 154, 182
Browning, Christopher, 80
Brown Orientalism, 73
Bücher, Karl, 159
Buddhism, North Korean criticism of,
242–43
Burnham, Linden F. S., 275–76

California school, 200
Canaan Commonwealth, 35
capitalist development: comprador,
140–41; Eurocapitalism compared to
world capitalism, 145–46; in India,
137; Japan and, 294–95; *Kōza-ha*
faction and, 192; Marxist historicism
on Eurocapitalism and, 133–35;
Marxist historicism on Korea's, 5–8,
135, 138, 142; passive revolution of,
135–36; *Rono-ha* faction and, 192; in
Russia, 141. *See also* Eurocapitalism;
Prussian path
capitalo-centrism, 8, 138–39
Carson, Ben, 96
Carter, Jimmy, 3–4
Césaire, Aimé, 100–101

Chakrabarty, Dipesh, 6, 132, 152

Chang, Iris, 34, 71, 77

chauvinism, welfare, 303. *See also* dictatorship, welfare

Chechen refugees, in Poland, 99

Chetnik, 103, 115

China: COVID-19 pandemic conspiracy theories and, 305; East Asian history books in, 194–98; Goguryeo sovereignty in historical textbooks of, 220–22; Great Leap Forward in, 284–85; Korea Orientalizing, 164–65; Maoism in, 77, 136, 262, 284–85; nationalism and history textbooks in, 210; pan-Asianism and, 184–85; Sino-Japanese War and, 158, 163, 183; Taiping Rebellion and, 136–37; totalitarian surveillance in, 306

Chinese Academy of Social Sciences (CASS), 195

Chinese-Japanese Joint History Research Committee, 196–97

Choi, Sook Nyul, 33–34

Chosŏn, 54n16

Chosŏn Joongang ilbo, 289

Churchill, Winston, 46–47

class struggle: Bolshevism and, 278–79; Communist International on collaboration in, 291–92; fascism and, 289–90; Marxism and, 278; Stalinism and, 231

coercion, mass dictatorship and, 264, 266, 301

cofiguration, 18, 132, 151, 154, 156, 163–64, 170, 173, 179–81, 184, 192, 199, 255. *See also* "East"; "West"

Cold War, 2; demonology, 11–15, 74, 253; resettlement and expulsion in, 73–74; thaw of, 92–93

collaboration/complicity, 41, 48, 62, 72, 79, 81, 92; genocidal, postcolonial criticism and, 80–81; German POWs and Soviet collaboration, 65–67

collective guilt, 26–27, 32, 52, 99; postcolonial criticism and, 79–80

collective innocence, 26

collective memory: antinuclear pacifism and, 45; of fascism, 50–51; global memory culture and, 26; global memory space and, 15–17; of Holocaust, 37–38; in postcommunist Poland, 99; sacralization of, 78; as untransferable, 28

collective subjectivity, socialism and, 275–79

colonial amnesia, in Japan, 63

colonial genocide, in Namibia, 79–80, 256

colonial guilt, postcolonial criticism and, 79–80

colonialism: of England in India, 137, 139, 143; Holocaust compared to, 94–95; of Japan in Korea, 33–34, 63, 142–43, 159–60, 193–94; Lenin on decolonization, 279; mass dictatorship and, 14; modernist view of nation-state in, 214; modernization and, 136–40; Nazism and, 100, 256; Polish history and, 97–98; Polish internal, 98–99; Sonderweg thesis and, 139–44; subaltern empire and, 98, 139; Yi Sun-tak on, 287–88

colonial modernity: Eurocapitalism and, 138–39; "history from below" and, 139; in Korea, 138; Marxist historicism and, 132–33, 136–39

comfort women, Korean, 68; Armenian Americans supporting statue of, 110–12; global awareness of, 112–13; Holocaust survivors and, 110; Japanese Americans protesting statue of, 111–12; transnational memory and, 59–60; Women's International War Crimes Tribunal on Japan's Military Sexual Slavery and, 113

"coming to terms with the past," 18, 27, 41, 79, 251–52, 268

Comintern (Communist International), 130, 230, 233, 279–80, 291–92

Commission on Wartime Relocation and Internment of Civilians, 112

communism: national, 188, 226–29, 238, 244–45; North Korean nationalism and, 228, 238; in Poland, 11; *Żydokomuna* and anti-communism, 38, 98

comparative history, 6, 145, 179, 270n13

complicity: of antagonistic nationalisms, 15, 18, 29, 38, 45, 50–51, 159, 198, 205–8, 222; genocidal, postcolonial criticism and, 80–81; German POWs and Soviet collaboration, 65–67

comprador capitalism, 140–41

comrade abuse trials, in Germany, 65–66

Confino, Alon, 95

Conrad, Sebastian, 199

consent: dictatorship of, 81, 303; mass dictatorship and, 266, 303

consequential Eurocentrism, 6, 138, 142, 180, 184, 193, 199

constructivism, revisionist history textbooks and, 206–7

Cooper, William, 60–61, 84

Corradini, Enrico, 292

cosmopolitanism, 66, 232–34

cosmopolitanization of Holocaust, 84, 93–96, 115–16

cosmopolitan memory, Hiroshima-Auschwitz Peace March and, 106–8

COVID-19 pandemic, 304–6

"crimes against humanity," 66, 73, 76, 83, 94, 113. *See also* colonial genocide, in Namibia; comfort women, Korean; Holocaust

Critical Global Studies Institute (CGSI), 16–17

critical memory: of dictatorship, 81–82; global emergence of, 77; testimonies in, 77–78

critical relativization, postcolonialism and, 21, 38, 93, 114–18

Croce, Benedetto, 50–51

cultural populism, 302–3

Czech Republic, 49–50

Czubiński, Antoni, 231

Dahrendorf, Ralf, 129

Daniszewski, Tadeusz, 232

Das Kapital (Marx), 5, 6, 134

decisionist democracy, mass dictatorship and, 2–3, 303

decontextualization: of history, 71–73; in victimhood nationalism, 29, 32–33, 50–51. *See also* overcontextualization

decosmopolitanization of German identity, 120n18

democracy: antithesis of, 2–3; dictatorship and, 2–3, 254–55; domination and, 258–59; mass, 258, 263–66; mass dictatorship and, 257–61, 303–4; totalitarian, 257–58

demonology, Cold War, 11–15, 74, 253

denationalization of memory, genocidal complicity and, 81. *See also* deterritorialization of memory

denialism, 16, 34, 61, 206

dependency (theory), 137, 139–41, 144, 194, 238, 243–44, 263; on Japanese colonialism in Korea, 193–94, 289

Der Bund der Vertriebenen (BdV), 49, 75

Der Untergang, 47–48

despotism, mass dictatorship and, 253, 269n6

deterritorialization of memory, 16, 84, 115

developmental dictatorship, in Korea, 1–5, 252

diaspora communities, victimhood nationalism and, 54n20

dictatorship: accomplices of, 13, 251; antithesis of, 2–3; conceptual history

of, 2; of consent, 81, 303; critical
memory of, 81–82; democracy and,
2–3, 254–55; developmental, 1–5, 252;
modern, 270n8; in state of emergency,
2; transnational memory and, 252;
welfare, 81, 270n8, 303. *See also specific
types*
Discours sur le colonialisme (Césaire),
100–101
Dobb, Maurice, 6, 134
domination, mass dictatorship,
democracy and, 258–59
Dostoyevsky, Fyodor, 9
Dower, John, 44
Drang nach Manchuria, 164, 212, 242
Drang nach Westen, 170–71, 220, 230,
241
Dresden, Allied bombing of, 49, 74
Dreyfus Affair, 66
Droysen, Johann Gustav, 162
Du Bois, W. E. B., 84, 101–2
Duke, David, 61, 245, 305. *See also* Ku Klux
Klan
Dziennik Polski, 106

"East": Global Easts arising from
displacement of, 4, 6, 10–12; as
imaginative geography, 9, 173–74,
254–55; Orientalism and, 131–32;
Poland as "West" and, 8–10
East Asia, 9, 11, 15, 18, 27, 160, 199;
memory and, 30–32, 38, 45, 68, 79, 95,
111–12; national history and, 180–81,
184–85, 189–90, 207; in Sonderweg
thesis, 6, 18, 130–32, 137, 139–44
East Asian History Forum for Criticism
and Solidarity, 15
East Asian history textbooks, 194–98,
206–8, 212–15, 222
Eastern Europe, 9–11, 21n19; memory
and, 27, 42, 49, 66, 76, 79, 82–83, 92,
95–96, 102, 115–16, 118; in Sonderweg
thesis, 10, 18, 130–32, 141

Eco, Umberto, 269
Eichmann trial, 37, 42–43, 77–78
Eley, Geoff, 18, 133
Elias, Norbert, 131, 270n9
Emancipatory, 143. *See also* technological
modernity
Endō Shūsaku, 109
Engels, Friedrich, 130, 136–37, 139–40
England: Brexit and, 306; India and
colonialism of, 137, 139, 143
entangled history, 16–18, 109, 145, 196,
207
entangled memory, 16–18, 26, 32, 61,
92–93
Estonia, 82
ethno-nationalism, in Poland, 227–28,
231, 234–37, 245, 247n34
Eurocapitalism: colonial modernity and,
138–39; Marxist historicism and,
133–35, 152, 192; world capitalism
compared to, 145–46
Eurocentrism: capitalo-centrism and, 8,
138–39; consequential, 199;
diffusionism and, 146, 153, 162, 171,
184, 199; historicism and, 5–8, 10, 18,
132–38, 144–45, 152–54, 157, 164, 168,
179, 182, 193; Holocaust and, 100;
Marxism and, 6–7; mass dictatorship
and, 254; national history and,
152–54; Prussian path and, 133; red
Orientalism and, 7–8, 169; Sonderweg
thesis and, 131–32; tunnel history
and, 151–52; world history and, 181,
199
Europa Środkowo-Wschodnia, 170–71
everyday fascism, 81, 252
exculpatory memory: sacralization of
memory and, 78–79; of victimhood
nationalism, 52–53, 71; of victimizers
in Holocaust, 42–43; war against, 77
expulsion: in Cold War, 73–74; *hikiage*
and, 16, 30–34, 41, 45, 70–71;
Vertreibung, 16, 30, 73

fascism: class struggle and, 289–90;
collective memory of, 50–51; COVID-19
pandemic and, 304; developmental
strategy of, 263; everyday, 81, 252;
hegemony and, 259–60; India and,
290–91; in Italy, 50–51, 259–60,
288–90, 292–93; in Japan, 142, 161;
Korea and Italy, 289–90, 293; Korean
developmental dictatorship and, 252;
in Poland, 229; as premodern, 131–32,
254; Soviet Union and, 293–94; in
Spain, 292; Yi Sun-tak on, 288–89.
See also mass dictatorship; Nazism
feminism, mass dictatorship and, 264–65
Fenollosa, Ernest, 156
feudalism, Japanese, 160–61
Fifteen Years' War, 46, 77
Fischer, Fritz, 76
"follow and catch-up," Marxism and, 7,
144, 168, 193
forced labor: Japanese empire, 16, 45, 111,
205; Third Reich, 16, 49, 75
forced modernization, Soviet Union and,
278–79
Forverts, 101–2
Foucault, Michel, 261, 265
France: genocidal complicity and, 81;
nationalization of memory of
Holocaust in, 64–65
Francoism, 269n6
Frank, Andre G., 199
Frank, Anne, 75, 108
Frankfurt Auschwitz trials, 37
Frankowski, Jan, 74
Free Indian Centre, 290
Friedrich, Jörg, 48, 72–73
Fujiwara Tei, 30
Fukuta Tokujo, 159
Fukuzawa Yukichi, 182
Furet, François, 270n13

Garvey, Marcus, 102
Gellner, Ernest, 209

gender: nationalization of memory and
discrimination of, 68; victimhood
nationalism and, 25
General Security of Military Information
Agreement (GSOMIA), 111
Gentile, Emilio, 264
geo-body, nation-state as, 212–13
German Orientalism, 161–63, 171.
See also Ostforschung
Germany: Allied bombing victims in,
72–74; Austrians as victims in, 46–47;
Black Germans and Nazism in, 103;
colonial genocide in Namibia and,
79–80, 256; comrade abuse trials in,
65–66; decosmopolitanization of
German identity, 120n18; "Documents
of Expulsion" and, 49; Hiroshima-
Auschwitz Peace March and, 74–75,
106–8; "Hitler's first victims" and,
46–47; "Hitler's last victims" and,
47–48; nationalization of memory of
Holocaust in, 65–68; Ostforschung in, 9,
131, 161–63, 171, 220; POWs from, in
Soviet Union, 65–67, 73; Prussians and
Nazism in, 47; refugees from, in
Poland and Czech Republic, 49–50;
reparation plan for Jews in, 65;
Vertreibung expulsion and, 16, 30, 73;
victimhood nationalism in, 46–49, 75;
Wilhelm Gustloff tragedy and, 48.
See also Nazism; Sonderweg thesis
Gills, Barry K., 199
Gilroy, Paul, 103
Glemp, Józef, 41
Glendale, 110–12
Global Easts: anti-Western
modernization and, 294–95; de-
configuration and, 173–74; "East" and
"West" displacement leading to,
10–11; modernity and, 179–80;
national history and, 153–54; problem
space of, 11
global history. See world history

globalization: national history and, 179; transnational memory and, 16–17

global memory culture: collective memory shaped by, 26; decontextualizing history and, 71–73; denial discourses and, 61; victimhood nationalism and, 25–29

global memory formation: Cold War thaw and, 92–93; cosmopolitanization of Holocaust and, 93–96, 116; nationalization of memory and, 96–97; postcolonialism and, 116; vulgarization and, 95–96

global memory space: collective memory shaped in, 15–17; Holocaust and, 60–61, 80–81, 94–95, 105; Korean victimhood nationalism in, 114; victim recognition battles in, 25–26

Gluck, Carol, 62, 113

Goguryeo, historical sovereignty, 220–22

Goldhagen, Daniel, 76

Gomułka, Władysław, 4, 66, 231–32, 236

Goodrich, Samuel G., 182

Grabowski, Jan, 117

Gramsci, Antonio, 20n8, 259–60

Grass, Günther, 48–49, 72

Great East Asia Co-Prosperity Zone, 44, 185

Great East Asia War, terminology of, 44–45

Great Leap Forward, China, 284–85

Gross, Jan, 15, 39, 41–42, 76, 90n66, 97

Guattari, Felix, 269

Guernica bombing, 48, 72–73

Guesde, Jules, 66

Guyana, 275–78

Hadler, Frank, 21n19

Halecki, Oskar, 170

Haraguchi Kikuya, 69–70

Harap, Louis, 102

Harris, Nigel, 137

Havel, Vaclav, 251

Heimbach, Matthew, 244–45

Helphand, Alexander (alias Parvus), 282–83

hereditary victimhood, 15, 26; Holocaust and, 37–42; nationalist essentialism and, 216; *So Far from the Bamboo Grove* and, 30–34

Herero-Nama wars, 79–80, 256

heroism: Holocaust and, 35–37; resistance and, 251

hikiage-monogatari literature, in Japan, 30–34, 41

hikiage repatriation, 16, 30–34, 41, 45, 70–71

Hilberg, Raul, 77, 268

Hilsenrath, Edgar, 84

Hirano Yumie, 74–75, 104

Hiroshima: antinuclear pacifism and, 45, 107–8; atom bomb survivor stories in, 104; Auschwitz-Birkenau historical comparisons to, 74–75, 104–8

Hiroshima-Auschwitz Peace March, 74–75, 106–8

Hiroshima Peace Memorial Park, 45–46, 104

Hirschbiegel, Oliver, 47–48

Histoire de l'art du Japon, 155

historical responsibility, as answerability to the perished, 51–53

historicism. *See* Marxist historicism

Historikerstreit: complicity/collaboration and, 79; global, 75–82; in Korea, 82; on mass dictatorship, 81–82; multidirectional memory and, 85; in Poland, 15, 76, 99; sacralization of memory and, 78–79; shame and, 81; transnational memory and, 76

"history from below": colonial modernity and, 139; in history textbooks, 215; Korean national history and, 191–92

history of everyday life, 215; in history textbooks, 214–15

history of martyrdom, mass dictatorship and, 251–53

history textbooks: anachronism in, 222, 243–44; autochthonism and, 219–22, 241–43; East Asia conflicts over, 15; East Asian, 194–98; everyday history in, 214–15; Goguryeo polemics in, 220–22; "history from below" in, 215; in Korea compared to Japan, 206; modernist view of nation in, 214; modernity of nation-state in, 211; Mongol invasion of Korea in, 215; national culture in, 218–19; nationalism and, 207–11; nationalist essentialism in, 213–16; nation-state as geo-body in, 212–13; nation-state borders in, 213; originism in, 216–19, 241; primordialist view of nation in, 213–16, 241–43; regime-dominated narrative in, 222–23; revisionist, in Japan, 205–7; revisionist, in Korea, 207–8; societal conflict in, 213–14; unpredictable past in, 222–23; victimhood nationalism and, 216; "we-the nation" in Korean, 209–11; on world history, in Japan, 182–83, 190–91, 200–201; on world history, in Korea, 183–84, 190, 200

History to Open the Future, A (HOF), 194–96

Hobsbawm, Eric, 281

Hochfeld, Julian, 232

Holocaust: Austrians as victims in, 46–47; collective memory of, 37–38; colonialism compared to, 94–95; cosmopolitanization of, 84, 93–96, 115–16; denial, 61, 96–97; Eurocentrism and, 100; exculpatory memory of victimizers in, 42–43; global memory space and, 60–61, 80–81, 94–95, 105; hereditary victimhood and, 37–42; heroism and, 35–37; "Hitler's first victims" and, 46–47; "Hitler's last victims" and, 47–48; indigenization, 117; Japan as atom bomb victims compared to Jews in, 69–71; Korean comfort women and survivors of, 110; as memory template, 94–95; multidirectional memory and, 84–85; nationalist appropriation of, 26, 75, 94, 108, 115–16; nationalization of memory and, 64–68; Polish postcolonial views on, 99–101; Polish victimhood nationalism and, 93–94; postcolonial criticism on, 79–80, 99–101, 256; Prague Declaration on, 82–83; reparation plan for Jews following, 65; Stockholm Declaration on, 75–76; in transnational memory, 18, 60–62; uniqueness of, 80, 83, 94; victimhood nationalism and, 33, 37–41; vulgarization of, 95–96; Warsaw Ghetto Uprising and, 40; *Wilhelm Gustloff* tragedy and, 48; Zionist appropriation of, 83. *See also* Auschwitz-Birkenau

Holocaust Remembrance Day, in Israel, 37

Homo Sacer (Agamben), 94

homosexuality, Nazism criminalizing, 68

Honda Katsuichi, 77

human rights: Carter's diplomacy of, 3–4; Pacific War violations of, 45

Ilseontongjoron (Japanese-Korean blood lineage thesis), 185–89

imaginative geography, "East" and "West" as, 9, 173–74, 254–55

Im Krebsgang (Grass), 48–49, 72

Imna Commandery, 186–87, 198, 219–20, 242

India: capitalist development in, 137; English colonialism in, 137, 139, 143; fascism and, 290–91; Indian Legion, 290; Marxism in Korea compared to, 6–7; socialism in, 291

Indonesia, 63–64

Inoue Mitsusada, 188
instrumentalization, 7, 95, 108–9
Instytut Pamięci Narodowej (IPN), 39
internal coercion, 301
internal colonialism, Poland and, 98–99
International Criminal Tribunal for
    Rwanda (ICTR), 113
International Criminal Tribunal for the
    former Yugoslavia (ICTY), 113
internationalism, 228–29, 233–36, 238
International Woman's Day, 59
Iran, Holocaust denial and, 61
Irredentism, 12, 98
Israel: hereditary victimhood and, 37–42;
    Holocaust heroism and, 35–37;
    Holocaust Remembrance Day in, 37;
    Holocaust vulgarization in, 95;
    Six-Day War and, 37; Zionism and, 83,
    234–37, 247n34
Italy: fascist economy in, 288–89; fascist
    hegemony in, 259–60; Korea and
    fascism in, 289–90, 293; modernity
    and fascism in, 292–93; as proletarian
    nation, 292–93; victimhood
    nationalism in post-Fascist, 50–51
Itō Hirobumi, 155
Iwakura Domomi, 155

Jabłoński, Henryk, 232–33
Jacobins, French, 257, 270n13, 302
James, C. L. R., 102
Japan: African American solidarity with,
    102; antinuclear pacifism and, 45,
    107–8; art history of, 155–56; as atom
    bomb victim, 43–44, 69–71;
    Auschwitz-Birkenau tours, 103–4;
    capitalist development and, 294–95;
    colonial amnesia in, 63; colonialism
    of, in Korea, 33–34, 63, 142–43, 159–60,
    193–94; East Asian history books in,
    194–98; fascism in, 142, 161; feudalism
    in, 160–61; Fifteen Years' War and, 77;
    Anne Frank in, 75, 108; hikiage and, 16,
    30–34, 41, 45, 70–71; hikiage-monogatari
    literature in, 30–34, 41; Hiroshima, 45,
    74–75, 104–8; Hiroshima-Auschwitz
    Peace March and, 74–75, 106–8;
    Hiroshima Peace Memorial Park in,
    45–46; history textbooks in Korea
    compared to, 206; Holocaust
    compared to atom bomb victimhood
    in, 69–71; Ilseontongjoron and,
    185–89; Korean-Japanese War,
    1592–1598, 215; Kōza-ha and, 192;
    Manchukuo legacies of colonial guilt
    in, 79; Marxism in, Sonderweg thesis
    origins and, 129–30, 161; Marxist
    historicism in, 192–94; Meiji Ishin in,
    160–61, 181–82; Moral Suasion
    Mobilization Campaign in, 260;
    Nagasaki, 104–5, 108–9; national
    history of, 154–62; nationalism and
    history textbooks in, 209–11;
    nationalization of memory in, 62–64;
    nation-state as geo-body in history
    textbooks of, 212–13; North Korea
    refuting history of, 242; originism in
    history textbooks of, 217; Pacific War
    terminology and, 44–45; pan-
    Asianism and, 165, 184–85;
    "postcolonial melancholia" in, 306;
    POWs from, in Soviet Union, 70–71;
    red Orientalism and, 161; revisionist
    history textbooks in, 205–7; Rono-ha
    and, 192; Russo-Japanese War and,
    158, 163, 183; Sino-Japanese War and,
    158, 163, 183; toyoshi and national
    history of, 158–59, 182–83; victimhood
    nationalism in, 43–46, 75, 105; world
    history textbooks in, 182–83, 190–91,
    200–201
Japanese-Korean Joint History Research
    Committee, 196–98
Japanese Orientalism, 158–62
Jedwabne massacre, 27, 38–41, 76
Jewish Life, 102

Jews: anti-Semitism compared to racism and, 101; Australian Aborigines supporting, 60–61; COVID-19 pandemic conspiracy theories and, 305; German reparation plan and, 65; hereditary victimhood and, 37–42; Holocaust, heroism and, 35–37; Japanese atomic bomb victims compared to Holocaust and, 69–71; Jedwabne massacre and, 27, 38–41; Korean historical parallelism with, 34–35; nationalization of memory of Holocaust and, 64–68; Polish ethno-nationalism and, 234–37, 247n34; postcolonialism and African Americans connecting with, 101–3; South African apartheid activism of, 103; Warsaw Ghetto Uprising and, 40. *See also* anti-Semitism; Holocaust; Zionism

Juche, in North Korea, 66, 240, 243–44, 278

Judeo-communism (*Żydokomuna*), 38, 98

Jun Hye Yeon Monica, 111

justificatory memory, victimhood nationalism and, 71

Kaczyński, Jarosław, 117

Katyń, 74, 82, 106, 230

Kautsky, Karl, 283–84

Keizo Imperial University, Korea, 188–89

Kershaw, Ian, 256

Kibbutz, 35

Kim Il-sŏng, 4, 66, 228, 237–39, 244, 280, 284–86

Kim Jŏng-il, 296n2

Kim Jŏng-un, 245

Kim Kyu-sik, 280

Kim Seok-hyung, 188

Klein, Naomi, 306

Kłoczowski, Jerzy, 170

Kochański, Aleksander, 235

Kocka, Jürgen, 129, 145, 270n8

Kołakowski, Leszek, 76

Kolbe, Maksymilian (Saint), 108–10

kōminka (皇民化, imperial nationalization), 187, 260

kŏnkookcha (tea of state-building), 35

Korea: art history of, 167–68; Civil War in, 237, 285; colonial modernity in, 138; Communist International and, 279–80; condensed modernization in, 4–5; COVID-19 pandemic and, 304; dependency theory on Japanese colonialism in, 193–94; developmental dictatorship in, 1–5, 252; East Asian history books in, 194–98; Goguryeo sovereignty in historical textbooks of, 220–22; *hikiage* repatriation and, 16, 30–34, 41, 45, 70–71; *Historikerstreit* on mass dictatorship in, 82; "history from below" and national history in, 191–92; history textbooks in Japan compared to, 206; Ilseontongjoron and, 185–89; Italian fascism and, 289–90, 293; Japanese colonialism in, 33–34, 63, 142–43, 159–60; Jews and historical parallelism with, 34–35; Keizo Imperial University in, 188–89; March First Movement in, 187; Marxism in India compared to, 6–7; Marxist historicism in, 168–70, 193; Marxist historicism on capitalist development in, 5–8, 135, 138, 142; Mongol invasion of, 215; national history origins in, 163–72; nationalism and history textbooks in, 209–11; nation-state as geo-body in history textbooks of, 212–13; nation-state origins in, 165–66; originism in history textbooks of, 217–18; pan-Asianism and, 165, 184–85; Social Darwinism and, 165; *So Far from the Bamboo Grove* in, 30–34; Sonderweg thesis and, 141–43; victimhood nationalism of, in global memory space, 114; "we-the nation" in history textbooks of, 209–11; world history textbooks in, 183–84, 190, 200. *See also* comfort women, Korean; North Korea

Korean American Civic Empowerment (KACE), 59–60

Korean-Japanese War (1592–1598), 215

Korean Orientalism, 164–65

Koth, Michael, 245

Kōza-ha (Japanese Marxism), 6, 129, 192–93, 204n41

KPP (Polish Communist Party), 229–34

Krygier, Martin, 61

Ku Klux Klan (KKK), 61

Kula, Witold, 25, 40, 130

Kume Kunitake, 155, 185–86

Kundera, Milan, 170

Kurihara Sadako, 106

Kuroita Katsumi, 157, 186

Kyunghyang, 54n16

labor, militarization of, in Bolshevism, 283–84

labor emancipation, 276–77, 291

Laub, Dori, 78

LeBon, Gustave, 266

Lee Ki-baek, 166, 241

Lemkin, Raphael, 84, 95

Lenin, Vladimir, 135, 140–41, 279–80

Leninism, 232–33. *See also* Bolshevism

Levy, Daniel, 96

Lewkovitz, Alain, 108

Liang Qichao, 184

Lipski, Jan József, 109–10

Ludden, David, 199

Lüdtke, Alf, 215, 267

lustracja, 14, 252

Luxemburg, Rosa, 11–12, 137, 141, 172, 230

"Make America Great Again" (MAGA), 305

Mały Dziennik (Kolbe), 109–10

Manchukuo, 79, 290

Mann, Michael, 257, 302

Manning, Patrick, 199

Manteuffel, Tadeusz, 229

Mao Zedong, 257, 262, 282, 284–85; Maoism and, 77, 136

March First Movement, 187

Marchlewski, Julian, 235–36

Marinetti, Filippo, 293

Martov, Julius, 284

martyrdom, mass dictatorship and, 251–53

Marx, Karl, 5, 6, 134, 136–37, 140, 169, 286

Marxism: on capitalist development, 133–34; capitalo-centrism and, 8; class struggle and, 278; Eurocentrism and, 6–7; "follow and catch-up" and, 7, 144, 168, 193; in India compared to Korea, 6–7; in Japan, Sonderweg thesis origins and, 129–30, 161; modernization and, 169, 191, 193; Polish, "really existing socialism" and, 12–13; Stalinism and, 283; Third World, 144. *See also* Sonderweg thesis

Marxist historicism: on capitalist development, 134; colonial modernity and, 132–33, 136–39; Eurocapitalism and, 133–35, 152, 192; guiding principle of, 168; in Japan, 192–94; in Korea, 168–70, 193; on Korea's capitalist development, 5–8, 135, 138, 142; Marx and Engels shaping, 136–37; North Korea and, 237; passive revolution of capitalist development and, 135–36; Sonderweg thesis and, 133–39; Third World Marxism and, 144; universalism compared to particularism in, 6, 142–43

Marxist voluntarism, 228, 240, 284–86

mass democracy, 258, 263–66

mass dictatorship, 3; agency in everyday life and, 265–69; alienating Others in, 260–61; bio-power and, 261; coercion and, 264, 266, 301; colonialism and, 14; concept of, 13–14, 251; consent and,

mass dictatorship (*continued*)
266, 303; democracy and, 257–61,
303–4; despotism and, 253, 269n6;
domination and, 258–59; "East" and
"West" as imaginative geography
and, 254–55; Eurocentrism and, 254;
feminism and, 264–65; *Historikerstreit*
on, 81–82; history of martyrdom and,
251–53; mobilizing and, 14–15, 19;
modernity and, 255; neopopulism and
potential of, 300–303; Occidentalism
and, 262–63; political religion and,
263–65; popular sovereignty and,
261–65; in postcolonial perspectives,
253–57; reflexive self and, 268;
resistance and, 265–66; state racism
and, 261; terror and, 264;
traditionalism and, 255;
transnational memory and, 19; as
transnational social formation, 14;
uniformity of, 258. *See also* fascism;
Nazism; Stalinism

masses, terminology of, 266

mass games, socialism and, 277–78, 296n2

McDonald, Gabrielle Kirk, 113

Meiji Ishin (Restoration/Regeneration),
160–61, 181–82, 202n10

Meir, Golda, 38

memory: critical, 77–78;
decontextualizing history and, 71–73;
denationalization of, genocidal
complicity and, 81;
deterritorialization of, 16, 84, 115;
entangled, 16–18, 26, 32, 61, 92–93;
global memory culture shaping
collective, 26; Holocaust as template
of, 94–95; multidirectional, 84–85;
politically correct, 76–77;
sacralization of, 28, 78–79. *See also*
collective memory; global memory
culture; global memory formation;
global memory space; nationalization
of memory; transnational memory

memory studies, 16–17

Michelet, Jules, 151–52

Michnik, Adam, 41, 52, 226, 251

Michta, Norbert, 235–36

Mikołajczyk, Stanisław, 66–67

militarization of labor, in Bolshevism,
283–84

Miłosz, Czesław, 244

"Miracle" (*kiseki*, Endō), 109

Mitchell, Timothy, 134

mnemonic nationalism, triple
victimhood and, 114–18

mobilization: Kim Il-sŏng on mass,
285–86; Marxist voluntarism and,
284–86; mass dictatorship and, 14–15,
19; resistance, mass dictatorship and,
265–68; self-energizing, 267; self-
mobilization, 259–60, 265–67, 284–86

modern dictatorship, 270n8

modernist view of nation, in history
textbooks, 214

modernity: colonial, 132–33, 136–39;
emancipatory, 143; Global Easts and,
179–80; Italy fascism and, 292–93; mass
dictatorship and, 255; of nation-state
in history textbooks, 211; overcoming/
overcome by, 199; socialism and, 144;
technological, 143–44

modernization: anti-Western, 143–44,
263, 279–85, 294–95; colonialism and,
136–40; Korean condensed, 4–5;
Marxism and, 169, 191, 193; Prussian
path and, 132–33; Soviet Union and
forced, 278–79

Moeller, Robert, 49

Molotov-Ribbentrop Pact, 83, 230

Mongol invasion, of Korea, 215

monumental history, 215

moral remembrance, 26

Moral Suasion Mobilization Campaign,
Japan, 260

Morrison, Scott, 306

Morris-Suzuki, Tessa, 211

Moscow Tripartite Conference (1943), 46

Mosse, George, 262

Mrożek, Sławomir, 151

multidirectional memory, 84–85

Museum of Occupations, Estonia, 82

Mussert, Anton, 64

Nagai Takashi, 69, 104–5, 108

Nagasaki: Auschwitz-Birkenau connection to, 108–9; Kolbe and, 108–9; survivor stories in, 104–5

Najarian, Ara, 110

Naka Michiyo, 158

Nakatani Takeshi, 103–4

Namibia, colonial genocide in, 79–80, 256

Nanjing massacre, 61, 70–71, 77, 93, 107, 205; Incident, 77. See also Chang, Iris; Honda Katsuichi

National Association for the Advancement of Colored People (NAACP), 305

National Association for the Advancement of White People (NAAWP), 305

national communism, 188, 226–29, 238, 244–45

National Democracy (Narodowa Demokracja), 226, 231

national history: Eurocentrism and, 152–54; Global Easts and, 153–54; globalization and, 179; "history from below" and Korean, 191–92; imaginative geography and, 173–74; of Japan, 154–62; Korean origins of, 163–72; nation-state legitimized by, 151–52; in North Korea, 239–41; pan-Asianism as, 189; toyoshi and Japanese, 158–59, 182–83; world history to, 180–84

nationalism: anticolonial, as accomplice, 116; appropriation and, 26, 75, 94, 108, 115–16; Bolshevism and Asian, 280–82; after communism in Eastern Europe,

226–29; cosmopolitanization of Holocaust and, 115; COVID-19 pandemic and, 304–5; East Asian history books and, 194–98; ethno-nationalism, in Poland, 227–28, 231, 234–37, 245, 247n34; hikikomori nationalism in Japan, 305–6; history textbooks and, 207–11; Ilseontongjoron and, 185–89; of Kim Il-sŏng, 66; nomenklatura-apparatchik, 226–29, 245; North Korean communism and, 228, 238; PZPR propaganda and, 234; PZPR using socialist jargon for, 228; regime-dominated narrative in history textbooks and, 222–23; Sukarno on, 63–64; as transnational phenomena, 179; triple victimhood and mnemonic, 114–18; world history and, 180. See also victimhood nationalism

nationalist essentialism, 213–16

nationalist phenomenology, 15, 18, 205–23

nationalization of memory: anti-Semitism and, 66; discrimination of gender and, 68; global memory formation and, 96–97; Holocaust denial and, 96–97; of Holocaust in Belgium, 65; of Holocaust in France, 64–65; of Holocaust in Germany, 65–68; in Japan, 62–64; in Poland, 66–67

national language, 163–64

national liberation, 137, 140–41, 244, 287, 290

national socialism, 282–83

nation-state: borders of, history books on, 213; as geo-body, 212–13; Korean origins of, 165–66; modernist view of, 214; modernity of, 211; originism of, 216–19, 241; primordialist view of, 213–16, 241–43

Nazism: alienating Others in, 260–61; Australian Aborigines denouncing, 60–61; Black Germans and, 103; Brown Orientalism and, 73; colonialism and, 100, 256; COVID-19 pandemic conspiracy theories and, 305; "Hitler's first victims" and, 46–47; "Hitler's last victims" and, 47–48; homosexuality criminalized by, 68; Jedwabne massacre and, 27, 38–41; North Korea and, 245; popular sovereignty and, 261; populism and, 302; Prussians and, 47; as response to Bolshevism, 117; South African apartheid and, 103; sovereign dictatorship and, 2; Stalinism compared to, 38, 82; state racism and, 261; "Strength Through Joy" campaign and, 72; *Wilhelm Gustloff* tragedy and, 48. *See also* Holocaust

Nehru, Jawaharlal, 284

Neighbors (Gross), 15, 41–42, 76

neoliberalism, 303–4

neopopulism, 300–303

Netanyahu, Benjamin, 95

New History (Robinson), 190

New History of Korea, A (Lee Ki-baek), 166, 241

New History Textbook, 205–6, 209–11, 216–19

New Negro movement, 102

Nikkei for Civil Rights & Redress (NCRR), 112

Nishikawa Masao, 192

NL (National Liberation), 7

Noda Masaaki, 72, 81

Nolte, Ernst, 38, 116–17, 270n13

nomenklatura-apparatchik nationalism, 226–29, 245

Non-Aligned Movement, 63

Northeast Asian History Foundation (NAHK), 208

North Korea: anachronism, 243–44; autochthonism, 241–43; Buddhism, 242–43; Civil War and, 237, 285; communism and nationalism in, 228, 238; de-Stalinization in, 239; Guyana performance by artists from, 275–76; Japanese history refuted by, 242; *Juche* in, 66, 240, 243–44, 278; Marxist historicism and, 237; mass games and, 275–78, 296n2; national history in, 239–41; Nazism and, 245; originism, 241; primordialist view of nation, 241–43; proletarian internationalism and, 238; "Ten-Year Plan of the Development of Science" in, 238; white supremacy and, 245

Nuremburg and Vietnam (Taylor, T.), 77

Nuremburg tribunal, 77

Occidentalism, 160–61, 181, 200; mass dictatorship and, 262–63; Orientalism interplay with, 160–61; Polish, 170–71; toyoshi and, 159

October Revolution, 281

Oe Kenzaburo, 107

Okakura Tenshin, 156, 218

Oriental history, 11, 158–59, 182–83, 189

Orientalism: Brown, 73; constraints of, 156; demi-Orientalism, 153–63, 172; "East"/"West" and, 131–32; German, 161–63, 171; Japanese, 158–62; Japanese national history and, 156–57; Korean, 164–65; Occidentalism interplay with, 161; *Ostforschung* compared to Japanese, 161–62; Polish, 172; red, 7–8, 142, 161, 169; Russia and, 73; SCAP and, 70; self-Orientalism, 132, 163, 288; of "West" proximity, 153

originism, 216–19, 241

Oshagan, Ara, 111

Ostforschung (Eastern/Polish studies), 9, 131, 161–63, 171, 220

Ōtsūka Hisao, 135, 191–92
Otwock, 229
overcontextualization, in victimhood nationalism, 29, 33, 50–51
oxymoron, 3, 228, 244–45, 292, 301, 303

Pacific War, 44–45, 74, 107, 192
Paik Namwoon, 138, 142
pan-Asianism, 165, 184–85, 189
Papon, Maurice, 81
Parents for an Accurate Asian History Education (PAAHE), 31–32
Park Chin-soon, 279–80
Park Chung-hee: Canaan Commonwealth visited by, 35; developmental dictatorship of, 1–5, 252; memorial project for, 13–14; state of emergency declared by, 2
particularism: Sonderweg thesis and, 129–31, 142–43, 146n2; universalism compared to, 6, 142–43
Parvus, Alexander (Alexander Helphand), 282–83
passive revolution, of capitalist development, 135–36
"patriotic" world history, 181
PD (People's Democracy), 7
peculiarity/particularity, Sonderweg thesis and, 129–31, 142–43, 146n2
people's history, 215
Pianist (Szpielman), 56n54
Poland: Allied bombing victims in, 72–73; anti-Semitism in, 38–39, 66–67, 234–37; anti-Zionism in, 234–37, 247n34; Chechen refugees in, 99; collective memory in postcommunist, 99; colonialism and history of, 97–98; communism in, 11; as "East" and "West," 8–10; ethno-nationalism in, 227–28, 231, 234–37, 245, 247n34; Europa Środkowo-Wschodnia and, 170–71; fascism in, 229; German refugees in, 49–50;

Hiroshima-Auschwitz Peace March and, 74–75, 106–8; internal colonialism and, 98–99; Islamic refugees in, 97–98; Jedwabne massacre and, 27, 38–41; Leninism replacing Stalinism in, 232; Marxism in, "really existing socialism" and, 12–13; nationalism propaganda in, 234; nationalization of memory in, 66–67; People's Poland (Communist Poland), 4, 11, 13, 15, 18, 27, 66, 100, 230, 239, 244–45, 262; postcolonial view of Holocaust in, 99–101; postcommunist, 4–5; poverty in, 20n17; proletarian internationalism in, 228–29, 233–36; "Regained Land" and, 220, 230; socialism in, 9–12, 171–72; Sonderweg thesis in, 141; *Studia Zachodnie* in, 9, 131–32, 220; victimhood nationalism in, 27, 38–42, 93–94; Warsaw Ghetto Uprising and, 40, 102; WHP in, 232; ZHP in, 233. *See also* Holocaust
Polish Communist Party (KPP), 229–34
Polish Occidentalism, 170–71
Polish October, 1956, 227, 231–33, 236
Polish Orientalism, 172
Polish Socialist Party (PPS), 11; Leninism and, 232–33; PZPR accusations against, 229–30; red Orientalism and, 171–72
Polish United Workers' Party (PZPR), 12, 74, 95; on Hiroshima-Auschwitz Peace March, 106; nationalism in socialist jargon of, 228; nationalist propaganda of, 234; PPS accusations of, 229–30
Polish Workers' Party (PPR), 41, 66
political religion: mass dictatorship and, 263–65; victimhood nationalism and, 105
"Poor Poles look at the ghetto" (Błoński), 40–41, 99. *See also* secular religion
popular sovereignty, 261–65

populism, 300–303

positivist historiography, 166, 207

postcolonialism: African Americans and Jewish connections and, 101–3; agency and responsibility and, 81–82; critical relativization and, 114–18; genocidal complicity and, 80–81; global memory formation and, 116; guilt and, 79–80; on Holocaust, 79–80, 99–101, 256; mass dictatorship in perspectives of, 253–57; Polish views on Holocaust and, 99–101; Sonderweg thesis and, 131–32, 145–46

"postcolonial melancholia," 306

postmodernism, 8, 116

POWs. *See* prisoners of war

PPS. *See* Polish Socialist Party

Prague Declaration on European Conscience and Communism (2008), 82–83

Prakash, Gyan, 143

Preobrazhensky, Evgenii, 283

primitive socialist accumulation, 283

primordialist view of nation, 213–16, 241–43

prisoners of war (POWs): from Germany in Soviet Union, 65–67, 73; from Japan in Soviet Union, 70–71; sexual exploitation of, 68; victimhood nationalism and, 43

proletarian internationalism: North Korea and, 238; Poland and, 228–29, 233–36

Prussian path: American path compared to, 135, 144–45; comprador capitalism and, 140–41; Eurocentrism and, 133; Lenin on, 135, 140–41; modernization and, 132–33; Sonderweg thesis and, 130, 132, 135

Prussians, Nazism and, 47

Putin, Vladimir, 98

PZPR. *See* Polish United Workers' Party

racism: anti-Semitism compared to, 101; South African apartheid and, 103; state, 261; white victimhood and, 305

radical juxtaposition, 18, 93, 116–18

Rafu shimpo, 112

Ramos, Ramiro Ledesman, 292

Ranke, Leopold von, 157, 166

Rape of Nanking, The (Chang), 34, 77

"really existing socialism," Polish Marxism and, 12–13

Recent Travel Around the World, A (Yi Sun-tak), 287

red Orientalism: colonial Sonderweg and, 142; Eurocentrism and, 7–8, 169; Japan and, 161; PPS and, 171–72

reflexive self, mass dictatorship and, 268

"Regained Land," 220, 230

relativization, 83; critical, 21, 38, 93, 114–18

Renan, Ernest, 26

renationalization of global memory, 96, 120n18, 211. *See also* reterritorialization

reparation plan, for Jews, 65

resettlement (Umsiedlung) in Cold War, 73–74. See also *Vertreibung* expulsion

resistance: heroic, 251; mass dictatorship and, 265–68; structural, 267

responsibility: answerability and historical, 51–53; collective guilt and historical, 52; political relativization of, 117; postcolonial criticism and, 81–82

reterritorialization, 96, 115, 118

revisionist history textbooks: constructivism and, 206–7; in Japan, 205–7; in Korea, 207–8; positivist historiography and, 207

Richthofen, Wolfram Freiherr von, 73

Riess, Ludwig, 157

Rise of Great Powers, The, 180

Robinson, James Harvey, 190

Roma, discrimination against, 67–68.
   See also Sinti
Rono-ha, Japanese Marxism, 192
Rosenfeld, Netty, 64
Rosenhaft, Eve, 17, 103
Roszkowski, Wojciech, 171
Rothberg, Michael, 84
Russell, Bertrand, 77
Russia: capitalist development in, 141;
   Orientalism and, 73. *See also*
   Bolshevism; Soviet Union
Russo-Japanese War, 158, 163, 183
Rwanda, 16, 80, 113, 257
Ryūichi, Narita, 195

sacralization of memory, 28, 78–79
Sadeh, Yitzhak, 36
Said, Edward, 9, 179
Sakai Naoki, 8–9, 62, 153
Salomon, Dieter, 113–14
SALT (Strategic Arms Limitation Talks), 2
Samuel, Raphael, 215
Sankei shinbun, 205–6
Sartre, Jean-Paul, 77
Satō Kyōtsū, 106
SCAP (Supreme Command of the Allied
   Powers), 44–45, 70
Schmitt, Carl, 2, 261, 302
SDKPiL (Social Democracy of the Kingdom
   of Poland and Lithuania), 11, 229–36
secular religion, 264. *See also* political
   religion
Sekino Tadashi, 167
self-energizing, 267
self-mobilization, 259–60, 265–67, 284–86
self-Orientalism, 132, 163, 288
Serbia, 96, 108, 115. *See also* Chetnik
Seventy Years Declaration, 2012, 83
sexual violence, 112–14
Shaltiel, David, 35
Sherwin, Byron K., 39
Shiratori Kurakichi, 158–59
Simon, George, 275

Sinanyan, Zareh, 110, 112
singularity, Sonderweg thesis and, 131,
   145–46
Sino-Japanese War, 158, 163, 183
Sinti, discrimination against, 67–68
Six-Day War, 1967, 37
slavery: African Americans and, 59, 93,
   116; sexual, 113–14
Slavic national movements, 136
Slawson, John, 36
Smedley, Agnes, 282
Smith, Angel, 10
Social-Christian Association, Poland
   (ChSS), 74
Social Darwinism, 165
socialism: Asian nationalists turning to,
   280–82; collective subjectivity and,
   275–79; in India, 291; Marxist
   voluntarism and, 284–86; mass games
   and, 277–78, 296n2; modernity and,
   144; national, 282–83; in Poland, 9–12,
   171–72; PZPR using nationalism in
   jargon of, 228; as thick ideology, 302;
   victimhood nationalism and, 276–77;
   Young Turks and, 282–83. *See also*
   Bolshevism
social patriotism, 245
So Far from the Bamboo Grove (Watkins),
   30–34
Sonderweg thesis, 6, 10; colonial, 139–44;
   dependency and, 140–41; "East" and
   "West" in, 131; Eurocentrism and,
   131–32; Japanese Marxism and origins
   of, 129–30, 161; Korea and, 141–43;
   Marxist historicism and, 133–39; from
   national to transnational, 144–46;
   peculiarity/particularity and, 129–31,
   142–43, 146n2; in Poland, 141;
   postcolonialism and, 131–32, 145–46;
   Prussian path and, 130, 132, 135;
   singularity and, 131, 145–46;
   underlying assumption of, 129; Whig
   historiography and, 133–34

Sono Ayako, 109

South African apartheid, 103

South Korea. *See* Korea

sovereign dictatorship: Nazism and, 2; popular sovereignty and, 261–65; representation and legitimacy of, 262. *See also* decisionist democracy

Soviet Union: Europa Środkowo-Wschodnia and, 170–71; fall of, 92–93; fascism and, 293–94; Five-Year Plans and growth of, 283–84; forced modernization and, 278–79; German POWs in, 65–67, 73; Japanese POWs in, 70–71; Soviet-Polish War, 230. *See also* Bolshevism; Russia

Spain, fascism in, 292

Stakhanovites, 284

Stalinism: class struggle and, 231; developmental strategy of, 263; domination and, 259; Leninism replacing, 232; Marxism and, 283; Nazism compared to, 38, 82; North Korea and de-Stalinization, 239; Polish October and, 232; Polish proletarian internationalism and, 230–31; primitive socialist accumulation and, 283

Stalinist crimes, 83, 92–93, 96, 230

state racism, 261

Stefanek, Stanisław, 41

Steinbach, Erika, 49, 75

Steinlauf, Michael, 40

Stockholm Declaration, 75–76

Stone, Lawrence, 5

Strategic Arms Limitation Talks (SALT), 2

"Strength Through Joy" campaign, 72

Studia Zachodnie (Western/German studies), 9, 131–32, 220

subaltern empire, 98, 139

subjectivity: collective, socialism and, 275–79; *Juche* and, 66, 240, 243–44, 278

Sukarno, 63–64, 291

Sun Yatsen, 184

Sweezy, Paul, 6, 134

Świda-Ziemba, Hanna, 41

Sznaider, Natan, 96

Szpielman, Władysław, 56n54

Taiping Rebellion, 136–37

Takahashi Kōhachirō, 6, 135. See also *Kōza-ha*

Taketani Etsuko, 102

Taylor, A. J. P., 133

Taylor, Telford, 77

technological modernity, 143–44

terror, mass dictatorship and, 264

testimonies, in critical memory, 77–78

Theses on Feuerbach (Marx), 286

Third World Marxism, 144

Toadyism, 237, 239

Tormey, Simon, 258

totalitarianism: democracy and, 257–58; fuzzy, 269; post-totalitarianism, 259; surveillance and, 306

toyoshi, Japanese national history and, 158–59, 182–83

traditionalism, mass dictatorship and, 255

transnational memory: Australian Aborigines and, 60–61; dictatorship and, 252; globalization and, 16–17; *Historikerstreit* and, 76; history textbooks, nationalism and, 15; Holocaust in, 18, 60–62; Korean comfort women commemoration and, 59–60; mass dictatorship and, 19; victimhood nationalism and politics of, 17–18, 28–29. *See also* victimhood nationalism

Treitschke, Heinrich von, 162

Trevelyan, G. M., 215

triple victimhood, mnemonic nationalism and, 114–18

Trotsky(-ist), 137, 230, 281

Trump, Donald, 300, 305

Tsuda Sōkichi, 157

Turner, Alf, 60

Turner, Henry, Jr., 292

Ulbricht, Walter, 73–74

Union of Fighters for Freedom and Democracy (ZBoWid), 247n26

Universal History on the Basis of Geography (Goodrich), 182

universalism, particularism compared to, 6, 142–43

Vajda, Mihály, 170

Vertreibung expulsion, 16, 30, 73

victimhood nationalism: anti-Semitism and, 38; collective guilt and, 26–27; concept of, 15–16, 27; diaspora communities and, 54n20; exculpatory memory of, 52–53, 71; gender and, 25; in Germany, 46–49, 75; global memory culture and, 25–29; history textbooks and, 216; Holocaust and, 33, 37–41; in Japan, 43–46, 75, 105; justificatory memory and, 71; Korean, in global memory space, 114; moral remembrance and, 26; opposing forces in, 38; overcontextualization and decontextualization in, 29, 51; in Poland, 27, 38–42, 93–94; political religion and, 105; in post-Fascist Italy, 50–51; POWs and, 43; sacralization of memory and, 28; socialism and, 276–77; transnational memory politics and, 17–18, 28–29. *See also* hereditary victimhood

victims: of Allied bombings in Germany, 72–74, 93; Austrians as, 46–47; Axis powers as self-proclaimed, 68–69; German refugees in Poland and Czech Republic as, 49–50; global memory space recognition battles for, 25–26; "Hitler's first victims," 46–47; "Hitler's last victims," 47–48; Japan as atom bomb, 43–44, 69–71; of Nazi

bombings in Poland, 72–73; victimizers compared to, 42–43; white victimhood, 305

Vietnam and Vietnamese, 99, 106–7, 195; My Lai, 61, 71; War, 71, 77, 93, 113

View of National History, 154–55, 182

Viseur-Sellers, Patricia, 113

voluntarism, Marxist, 228, 240, 284–86

vulgarization, global memory formation and, 95–96

Wałęsa, Lech, 1, 8

Walicki, Andrzej, 259, 294

Wannsee Conference (1942), 83

Warren, Bill, 137

Warsaw Ghetto Uprising, 37, 40, 96, 102

Warschawski, Michel, 37

Wasersztajn, Szmuel, 78, 90n66

Wat, Aleksander, 172

Watanabe Shōichi, 75

Watkins, Yoko Kawashima, 30–34, 48

Weber, Eugene, 262

Weidauer, Walter, 74

Weinberg, Werner, 35

Weizsäcker, Richard von, 152

welfare chauvinism, 303

welfare dictatorship, 81, 270n8, 303

Weltzel, Hans, 17

"West": Global Easts arising from displacement of, 10–11; as imaginative geography, 9, 173–74, 254–55; neopopulism and, 300–303; Orientalism and, 131–32; Orientalism by proximity to, 153; Poland as "East" and, 8–10; in Sonderweg thesis, 131

"Western Civilization," history of, 181

Western history: overcome by, 189–94; overcoming, 184–89

Western History Review, 21n19

Whig historiography, 133–34

white supremacy: African American and Japanese solidarity against, 102;

white supremacy (*continued*)
Holocaust denial and, 61; North Korea and, 245
white victimhood, 305
Wieluń, 72–73
Wilhelm Gustloff tragedy, 48
Wilsey, David, 105
Wojnarowska, Cezaryna, 235–36
Wolff, Larry, 130
Women's International War Crimes Tribunal on Japan's Military Sexual Slavery, 113
world capitalism, Eurocapitalism compared to, 145–46
world history: Asiacentric, 181, 189, 199; decentering, 199–201; Eurocentric, 181, 199; global historians, 199; Japanese textbooks on, 182–83, 190–91, 200–201; Keizo Imperial University teaching, 188–89; Korean textbooks on, 183–84, 190, 200; to national history, 180–84; nationalism and, 180; "patriotic," 181; post-war school curricula on, 189–90; tripartite structure of, 190
World War II. *See* Holocaust; Nazism; Pacific War

Wroński, Stanisław, 235
Wydział Historii Partii (WHP), 232
Wyrzykowska, Antonina, 41

Yamahata Yosuke, 46
Yanagi Muneyoshi, 167–68
Yang Chil-sung, 64
Year of Impossible Goodbyes (Choi), 33–34
"Yellow Peril," 305
Yeom Tae-young, 113–14
Yi Sun-tak, 287–90, 293
Yonehara Mari, 71–72
Young Turks, 282–83
Yugoslavia, 16, 106, 108, 113

Zakład Historii Partii (ZHP), 233
Załuski, Zbigniew, 234
Zasulich, Vera, 281
Zinoviev, Grigory, 280
Zionism: Holocaust appropriation and, 83; Polish anti-Zionism, 234–37, 247n34
Z Pola Walki, 235
Zwigenberg, Ron, 106
Żydokomuna (Judeo-communism), 38, 98